THE
LATHAM
DIARIES

THE
LATHAM
DIARIES

MARK LATHAM

MELBOURNE
UNIVERSITY
PRESS

MELBOURNE UNIVERSITY PRESS
An imprint of Melbourne University Publishing Ltd
187 Grattan Street, Carlton, Victoria 3053, Australia
mup-info@unimelb.edu.au
www.mup.com.au

First published 2005
Text © Mark Latham 2005
Design and typography © Melbourne University Publishing Ltd 2005
Cover and text design by Phil Campbell
Typeset in 10/13 Utopia by J&M Typesetting
Printed in Australia by Griffin Press, Netley, SA

National Library of Australia Cataloguing-in-Publication entry

Latham, Mark, 1961– .
The Latham diaries.

Bibliography.
Includes index.
ISBN 0 522 85215 7.

1. Latham, Mark, 1961– —Diaries. 2. Australian Labor
Party. 3. Politicians—Australia—Diaries. 4. Australia
—Politics and government—1990– . I. Title.

324.29407092

Contents

Author's Note

One of the challenges in publishing a political diary is to make it as reader-friendly as possible. Because my *Diaries* were not originally written for publication, the entries assumed a familiarity with the people, politics and issues of the day. Annotations have been provided to assist readers with any shorthand I may have used and to provide background information. The career details of politicians are provided as at the time of the diary entry. As their political roles and titles change, the information is updated in subsequent annotations.

My thanks to the staff of Melbourne University Publishing for their assistance in the preparation of this book. The head of MUP, Louise Adler, had great faith in this project and readily accepted the risks in publishing material of this kind. I hope future historians and students of Australian politics will be grateful for her courage in deciding that university publishing houses can legitimately publish accounts of the lively debates and controversies of the nation. Polemical books have a fine tradition in university life, and I thank Louise for keeping this tradition alive.

I also wish to thank my literary agent, Mary Cunnane, for her commitment to this project. Without her guidance and encouragement, I may not have seen it through to publication. She has provided valuable advice at all times, helping me manage this task without neglecting my responsibilities at home.

Inevitably, there are some errors of omission and judgement in a political diary. If I could, and with the benefit of hindsight, I would have expressed myself differently or made different political points. But to do so would sacrifice the immediacy and authenticity of this record. I trust that readers will understand the circumstances in which mistakes and misjudgements have been made. Most of the diary entries were made during busy periods of work and travel, not the most conducive conditions for writing a book. For the political diarist, however, there is no alternative. All errors and omissions are mine.

Acronyms & Abbreviations

2PP	two-party-preferred
ABA	Australian Broadcasting Authority
ABC	Australian Broadcasting Corporation
ACOSS	Australian Council of Social Services
ACT	Australian Capital Territory
ACTU	Australian Council of Trade Unions
AFL	Australian Football League
AFR	*Australian Financial Review*; also referred to as *Fin Review*
AHA	Australian Hotels Association
ALP	Australian Labor Party
AMA	Australian Medical Association
AMWU	Australian Manufacturing Workers' Union
APEC	Asia-Pacific Economic Cooperation
ASIO	Australian Secret Intelligence Organisation
AWA	Australian Workplace Agreement
AWU	Australian Workers' Union
BCA	Business Council of Australia
CAD	current account deficit
CAN	Community Action Network
CFMEU	Construction, Forestry, Mining and Energy Union
CIA	Central Intelligence Agency
COAG	Council of Australian Governments
CPA	Commonwealth Parliamentary Association
CPO	Commonwealth Parliamentary Offices
CSHA	Commonwealth–State Housing Agreement
CV	curriculum vitae
Dem.	Democrat (Party)
DLP	Democratic Labor Party
EMTR	effective marginal tax rates
FEC	Federal Electorate Council (ALP)
FIP	Families in Partnership
FPLP	Federal Parliamentary Labor Party
FTA	Free Trade Agreement
GDP	gross domestic product
GG	Governor-General
govt	government
GST	goods and services tax
HECS	Higher Education Contribution Scheme
IOC	International Olympic Committee
IR	industrial relations
Lib.	Liberal Party

MAD	mutually assured destruction
min.	minister
MLC	Member of the Legislative Council
MOB	Manager of Opposition Business
MP	Member of Parliament
MPI	Matter of Public Importance
MUA	Maritime Union of Australia
Nat. Exec.	National Executive (of the Labor Party)
NCC	National Civic Council
NESB	non-English speaking background
NP	National Party
NSW	New South Wales
NT	Northern Territory
Parl.	Parliament
PAYE	pay as you earn
PBS	Pharmaceutical Benefits Scheme
PM	Prime Minister
PRC	Priorities Review Committee
Pres.	President
PWC	PriceWaterhouseCoopers
Qld	Queensland
RAAF	Royal Australian Air Force
RBA	Reserve Bank of Australia
REDO	Regional Economic Development Organisation
RSL	Returned Services League
SA	South Australia
SCG	Sydney Cricket Ground
SDA	Shop Distributive and Allied Employees' Association
Sen.	Senator
SES	socioeconomic status
SMH	*Sydney Morning Herald*
STD	Subscriber Trunk Dialling
TA	travel allowance
TAFE	Technical and Further Education
Tas.	Tasmania
TCF	textile, clothing and footwear
TPV	Temporary Protection Visa
Treas.	Treasurer
UAP	United Australia Party
UN	United Nations
UNESCO	United Nations Educational Scientific and Cultural Organization
Vic.	Victoria
WA	Western Australia
WMD	Weapons of Mass Destruction

Introduction

Diaries are rare in Australian politics, too rare. In understanding political events, the Australian public depends heavily on journalists, people who can never go behind the scenes and provide a first-hand account of the political process. By its nature, their work is derivative, relying on other sources of information and second- and third-hand interpretations. This has weakened the reliability of the public record. The electorate has had little exposure to the other side of public life, to what happens behind the newspaper headlines, behind the political spin and manipulation of the daily news cycle.

This book aims to overcome this deficiency. It is a fly-on-the-wall record of my eleven years in the Australian Parliament, including my fourteen months as Leader of the Australian Labor Party (ALP). It offers a first-hand perspective on the state of our democracy, a contemporaneous record of events inside a major parliamentary party. A diary can go places that the media or historians can never see, and it does so with a striking immediacy, free from revisionism and party political censorship.

Last year, I used to call my community forums 'democracy in the raw'. These diaries are very much politics in the raw. Most people who write books after they leave Parliament offer sanitised versions of events to the public. They are still part of the system, one compromised foot on the gravy train, hoping for appointments and other forms of largesse. It is not in their interests to be frank about the nature of the political system.

I have no interest in the gravy train, in placating the Labor movement as a trade-off for future political patronage. Nor have I been intimidated by the threat of repercussions if I speak my mind and publish my observations as a Labor MP. I kept this diary as an uncut commentary on the culture of Australian politics, especially Labor politics, and I offer it to the reader in that form. It is a very raw document, a record of events as I saw them, unaffected by the niceties and party posturing of the day.

When I first went to Canberra, I noticed that Senator Stephen Loosley took notes and kept a diary at Caucus meetings. I decided to adopt a similar practice, to record significant policy debates, humorous episodes and landmarks in my parliamentary career. It was never a daily diary but, rather, an attempt to capture important events and conversations, items that would one day assist in the writing of Labor history.

I never announced publicly that I was keeping an occasional diary. Some of my parliamentary colleagues knew about it, but by and large, I saw it as a personal project—my safe haven away from the public spotlight in which I could record my thoughts and observations. So I kept my head down, literally, and maintained a regular pattern of entries.

Sometimes there would be a flurry of writing, such as after the 2004 election campaign, when it was important to diarise my efforts and thoughts about a major political event. I had more time available to me than earlier in the year, so I took advantage of it. These entries evolved into a detailed account of the post-election fallout within the ALP and the events leading to my resignation from Parliament in January 2005.

This was an opportunity to write at length about Labor politics and Australian society, and the result is rather like a series of essays. I thought it was important to reflect extensively on my experiences as Leader of the Opposition and diarise my conclusions. I regard this as the most significant part of the book, as it outlines the intractable problems facing the ALP and social democracy in this country.

On other occasions, the diary would run dry, such as in mid-1994 when I was preoccupied with testicular cancer. I was fighting for my life rather than writing about it. Generally, however, I was able to produce a steady flow of material throughout my time in Parliament. I wanted to chronicle my personal experience in politics, rather than repeat things that were being dealt with extensively on the public record. So, for instance, the diaries do not comment on September 11 because there was nothing I could usefully add to the blanket coverage provided by the US media conglomerates.

My style was to take down notes as things happened and write up the diary in full later, usually within a week. For the publication of this book, I transcribed these hand-written entries into the computer. Some entries have since been modified to protect the privacy and reputation of certain individuals. Otherwise, the original entries have been preserved.

I believe it was wise to maintain an occasional diary rather than a daily record. Given the time pressures of political life, daily diaries tend to provide only a basic sketch of events, with little scope for reflection and analysis. They can be quite tedious, as the author is obliged to record something every day, even when the days are mind-numbingly boring. Politicians always say that their work is interesting and relevant, but often this is a façade that hides what they really think about their schedules and the grindstone of public engagements.

Occasional diaries overcome this problem, instead allowing the author to chronicle the most important events and analyse them in greater depth. This is what authors such as Frank Moorhouse have called a 'discontinuous narrative', writing that lacks the flow of a daily record but compensates with its intensity and a sense of colour and movement. I experienced a fair bit of colour and movement during my time in Parliament and I hope it is captured in these pages.

When I left politics, I started to think about the *Diaries'* future use and readership. I decided to publish it this year for two important reasons. First, after the 2004 election, many Labor MPs and Party officials offered their views and analyses of the conduct of our campaign in background briefings to the media. This practice continued even after I had retired from Parliament. It would be extraordinary, having maintained this record and diarised so many events over eleven years, if I did not contribute to the historical record. I grew up with a love of Labor history, enchanted by the big characters and mystique of the movement. It is time to add my chapter to the story.

Second, for many years I have been a strong critic of the Australian media, objecting to the shallowness and inaccuracy of their reporting. In many cases, it is not actually reporting but a series of personal agendas and prejudices dressed up as journalism. The *Diaries* offer a countervailing view of events, and a critique of the media's role in public life. I believe that dissenting voices are important in a democracy, and the *Diaries* are a chance for mine to be heard.

In practice, journalists only ever see a small fraction of what happens in politics. Often they believe they have captured 'inside' information and stories when politicians give them off-the-record briefings. Yet when MPs are not willing to put their names to material, it is a sure sign that they are manipulating the media for their own advantage. Invariably, the public receives a jaundiced account of events. It is a measure of how badly the system has deteriorated that many journalists now report more off-the-record material than on-the-record. A political diary closes the gap between the public's knowledge and the private reality of Australian politics.

The *Diaries* focus primarily on the internal workings of Federal Labor, and show a political machine in action. During my time in Parliament, I wrote books and articles to outline my views on national policy issues and debates. I used Parliament itself to review and criticise the performance of the Liberal and National Parties and their fellow travellers in the media.

The *Diaries* gave me an outlet to record the things I couldn't say publicly about Labor Party politics then. They dealt with my hopes and frustrations, sometimes through the prism of personalities, but always with an eye on the big policy debates and revitalisation of social democracy in this country.

The entries cover the six phases of my parliamentary career:

- my work as a newly elected backbencher in the Keating Government, as our electoral prospects faded away, culminating in Labor's heavy defeat in March 1996
- my disappointment and despair as one of Kim Beazley's Shadow Ministers (1996–98), which resulted in my decision to go to the backbench after the 1998 election
- the freedom and frustrations of the Opposition backbench (1998–2001), a period in which I wrote and argued extensively for a new policy direction for Labor
- my return to the frontbench under Simon Crean's leadership (2001–03), during which I tried to re-establish my position inside Caucus and defend Crean against the worst elements of machine politics
- my election to the Labor leadership in December 2003 and the long, gruelling ten-month campaign leading up to the October 2004 Federal election
- the events after our election defeat, the upheaval inside the Labor Party and my resignation from Parliament.

My aim is not to rewrite my place in Australian political history. That is not possible. I never became a minister in a Labor Government. Under my leadership, the ALP lost seats at the 2004 Federal election. This disappointed many of my supporters, dashing their expectations of what I could achieve in public life. I failed in my mission to advance the cause of Labor, to make Australia a social democracy. By the conventional performance measures of Australian politics, my parliamentary career was unsuccessful.

Rather, the *Diaries* tell my story, as it happened. Readers will find within these pages incidents that reflect poorly on other people. They will also find things that reflect poorly on me, decisions and events that I regret.

This is not unusual in party politics. It's a rollercoaster ride, with cycles of success and failure, circumstances that are never ideal, careers that are always imperfect.

In my case, however, the peaks and troughs seemed to be more extreme, especially during my time as Leader. In early 2004, I was able to give the True Believers hope, and even the expectation of an election victory against the odds. By year's end, things had turned to seed. Some terrible things happened in the aftermath of our election loss last year, incidents that broke my faith in the cause of Labor.

This was not the first period, however, in which I was disenchanted with the ALP. It is a recurring theme in the *Diaries*, something that gathered force over time, reaching its nadir at the end of 2004. When I again fell ill with pancreatitis, I could see no reason to remain in Labor politics. My decision to leave was based on observations and conclusions that have built up over many years.

I no longer regard Labor as a viable force for social justice in this country. Its massive cultural and structural problems are insoluble. While the Labor machine is still capable of winning elections, it will not deliver on its original purpose for a fair society. I do not say these things lightly— they are based on my personal experiences and deep reflection about the Party's future. In many respects, the *Diaries* chart my journey to disillusionment with the ALP.

Machine Politics

Bismarck once declared there are two things the public should never see: the making of sausages and the making of laws. I have breached the second half of his decree. I know many politicians sit in Parliament House thinking to themselves, if only the electorate knew what really goes on here. I used to be one of them. That's why I kept a diary, so that when the time was right, I could offer the public a peek inside.

The view provided by the *Diaries* is frightening. It reveals a poisonous and opportunistic Labor culture in which the politics of personal destruction is commonplace. I am not overstating the bleakness of my experience. Politically, it was a Dickensian environment. As Jennie George wrote to me after my resignation, 'Politics is a brutal business. I thought the union movement was tough, but this was no comparison to the internal dysfunctional culture of the ALP'.[1]

---

1 Jennie George is the Member for Throsby
and a former President of the ACTU; I received
this letter on 27 January 2005

'Brutal' and 'dysfunctional' are apt descriptions of the way in which the Labor Caucus operates. Political methods of this kind, however, should be antipathetic to a social democratic organisation, a so-called party of compassion. But they have become a way of life inside the ALP. It gives me no joy to say these things and I can assure readers that they were even less enjoyable to experience.

I always expected our political opponents to play it hard, and from time to time, I gave as good as I got. I'm not proud of that but I saw it as a way of surviving the fight against the Tories. What I never anticipated, and still do not accept, is the way in which some Labor MPs saved their dirtiest and most personal attacks for those inside the Party. On any given day, dozens of Labor politicians would be on the phone gossiping, plotting and spreading rumours about their so-called colleagues. Nothing was off-limits. Personal and private matters were seen as fair game, and were often used to hound the vulnerable into submission.

My experience with the Labor politics of smear and personal destruction was sickening. In June 2000 it had tragic consequences when my friend, Greg Wilton, the Member for Isaacs, killed himself. I believe that Greg's opponents inside the Party set out to denigrate and pressure him, a barbaric act of abuse. This type of politics shatters the code of honour and respect on which a working-class organisation should be based. It affected Greg in the worst possible way, but the Labor Caucus quickly forgot the lessons of his death. The practice still continues; indeed, it is systemic to the way in which the ALP operates.

In part, it is a function of the frustrations of Opposition. Many Labor MPs find they have little constructive work with which to occupy their day, so gossiping with colleagues and big-noting themselves with journalists have become a way of life. I do not blame the individuals as much as the culture in which they find themselves. Each of them would have come into Parliament bright and optimistic about the process, but the insular nature of the workplace and its relentless negativity have worn them down.

The other powerful influence on the ALP has been the rise of machine politics. Since the 1980s, its key organisational unit has been the faction. This is what defines machine politics: the marginalisation of the Party's members and the creation of a political oligarchy under the control of a handful of powerbrokers. All other aspects of the Party's organisation—its administrative officers, policy committees and conferences, affiliated trade unions and local branches—have been absorbed into the factional system.

This is the irony of a so-called labour-based party. Inside the ALP, the trade unions do not operate as a voice for workers' interests and representation. They function as part of the factional system, providing numbers, resources and patronage for the dominant grouping in each State. This is how half a dozen union secretaries can sit around the table with the State Party officers and map out the preselection of parliamentary candidates for a decade or so. It's a classic oligarchy, using the tools of patronage and reward for loyalty, and punishment of non-compliance, to control the Party.

This culture of concentrated power has had an appalling impact on the Party's values and ethics. Dissidents and independent thinkers are systematically attacked and marginalised by factional bosses. What the powerbrokers cannot control they will destroy. And they are not very discerning about how this might be achieved. It has given rise to a culture that Graham Richardson popularised as 'whatever it takes'.[2] Or, in more recent times, a technique described as 'shock and awe'.

Undoubtedly, my *Diaries* will be subject to the same treatment. Machine politics demands compliance, and those who step outside the system and voice their experiences and concerns are relentlessly targeted. In this book, I challenge the methods and legitimacy of the modern Labor Party, and as such, my character and motivations will be attacked at every opportunity, publicly and through private whispering campaigns.

I accept this as the price of telling my story. I believe it would be wrong to remain silent about a political culture that is fundamentally broken. I believe it would be wrong and cowardly not to talk about Labor's problems for fear of retribution. Ultimately, machine politics survives through a code of silence. All those who adhere to the code are culpable: the Labor activists who know how bad the problem is but choose to hold their tongues, as much as the machine men who perpetuate the Party's culture.

The current ALP leaders will say that they are not interested in the past, only the future. That's because there are many things they want to keep from public view, incidents they want to leave behind, to be forgotten and neglected by history. Sadly, Labor's problems have become endemic, a regular part of the way in which the Party functions. They are a signpost to Labor's future prospects, as much as its past failings.

Machine politics has not only produced a crisis of methodology within the ALP; it has also led to a crisis of belief. The factional system of command and control has gutted the effectiveness of grassroots participation in the Party. Most local branches are rorted and empty. Labor conferences and

---

2 Graham Richardson, *Whatever It Takes*, Bantam Books, Sydney, 1994. Richardson was a minister in the Hawke and Keating governments and a leading Right-wing powerbroker

policy committees are tightly stage-managed, devoid of creativity and genuine debate. Party membership and activism are in inexorable decline.

The Party's defining purpose now revolves around power and patronage, the fuel that sustains its factions but that ultimately drains the True Believers of conviction and belief. It has become a conservative institution run by conservative people, the worst elements of machine politics. The problem of social democratic reform in Australia has become insoluble.

These are not necessarily new observations. Commentators and critics of the ALP have been saying something similar since the 1990s. What the *Diaries* offer, however, is a first-hand view of the impact of machine politics on the parliamentary party. They also raise an obvious question: how did someone like me ever become Leader of the Federal Labor Party?

For many years, especially after I went to the backbench in 1998, my relationship with the factions was ambivalent. In 2000, for instance, I almost lost my Labor preselection for Werriwa. I walked a fine line between my public role as a policy activist and my membership of the New South Wales Right faction, placating their interests when I needed to, especially if it meant keeping my job. I saw it as one of those awkward but necessary compromises that are required to stay alive in politics. I now feel ashamed of many of the decisions I made during this period.

In the December 2003 leadership ballot against Kim Beazley, I was opposed by almost every union and factional powerbroker in the Party, but still managed to win narrowly. I had several factors working in my favour, including the support of Caucus members personally loyal to Simon Crean, who were devastated by the destruction of his leadership by the Beazley machine men. Beazley had been weakened by his reputation as a two-time election loser and a weak Leader between 1996 and 2001. I also won the support of a small but significant group of Caucus members opposed to the major factions.

This unique coalition allowed me to achieve an upset victory against the will of the machine men. Realistically, it was an aberration. Once I lost the 2004 election, the powerbrokers quickly settled the score and marked me for the political scrapheap. Under Beazley, they have quickly reasserted their control of the Caucus numbers, determined to guard against further aberrations.

The *Diaries* show that in political interests and style, I was never of the modern Labor culture. This is why I was often described as a maverick MP. My devotion to the Party was to a political cause, not an organisational machine.

When I joined the ALP in the late 1970s, it was still possible to conceive of it as a democratic organisation in which grassroots effort could make a difference. I remember making lengthy policy submissions to the National Conference from the Werriwa Federal Electorate Council in the early 1980s, with some expectation they might influence and shape the debate. Such was my romantic attachment to the cause of Labor, inspired by the reforms of the Whitlam Government and a belief that working-class politics could change the country.

Today, such a notion is absurd. The prospect of local Party units influencing the national policy debate is inconceivable. Party members do not even try, knowing it to be a waste of time and effort.

Just as I was progressing through the ALP's ranks, the factions started to dominate the Party and narrow its base. The romantic cause of Labor ran into reality. Nonetheless, I never stopped making policy submissions: preparing papers, writing books and articles, making provocative speeches, trying to push the envelope of reform. I was living off a memory, my idealised notion of how the Party was supposed to function.

My primary influences, however, remained community-based: my memories of Green Valley, where I grew up in south-west Sydney; the introduction of open government reforms as Mayor of Liverpool Council; a commitment to local welfare reform and social entrepreneurship; and an ambitious electronic democracy trial in my seat of Werriwa. Even as Labor Leader, I tried to bypass the conventional forums of national politics by holding regular community forums and advocating another bold program of open government.

Throughout my time in politics, I believed in a smaller scale of social governance: community-building, localised service delivery and new forms of public participation. I regarded this as the big challenge for Left-of-Centre politics, to overcome the impersonal nature of bureaucracies and the market economy, to help people reconnect with society, to get them more involved in political and community life. In my eyes, it didn't make sense for the Left to condemn McDonald's but to support Centrelink—both were large-scale organisations that treated people as clients, not citizens.

I concluded that the true cause of Labor involved the dispersal of power and influence. We needed to break down the entrenched hierarchies that sustained the social elites and insiders, and to enable disenfranchised people in the suburbs and regions—the outsiders—to do more for themselves. I was against the concentration of power, whether in the public or private sectors.

Looking back, I am struck by how consistently anti-establishment I was. Issues and policies came and went, as they do in public life, but that first driving force, my motivation for joining the ALP in the late 1970s, remained intact. I wanted to transfer power and influence from those who had it to those who didn't, and was always aggressive in pushing the urgency of this task.

If there was an element of tragedy in my political career it was the incompatibility of this belief with the way in which, throughout the same period, the ALP became a tightly controlled machine party. I was inside an entrenched political hierarchy trying to break down the other hierarchies of power in society. No wonder they thought I was a loner.

The media certainly didn't welcome this approach: public participation bypasses their power and role in public life. They want to put the questions to the politicians, not hand over the microphone to citizens at community meetings. Labor's machine politicians also saw it as threatening. If the general public got actively involved in politics, what would be next? Rank-and-file members of the Labor Party having a real say?

These issues are not new to political science. Fifty years ago, Robert Michels pointed out in *Political Parties* that prominent Left-wing movements inevitably fall under the influence of paid officials and apparatchiks, men more committed to the bureaucratic control and administration of the party than the radical transformation of society.[3] The party machine offers its own rewards, in the form of careerism and enhanced social status. Over time, these benefits become an end in themselves. Idealism and ideology are superseded by the internal contest and maintenance of power— an intractable problem.

My experience inside the ALP replicates the Michels model. As the *Diaries* show, I thought about these issues for nearly a decade but was never able to find a feasible solution. Others might have more success in the future, but my conclusions then, as now, are overwhelmingly pessimistic. My efforts and enthusiasm for Labor politics have been exhausted.

As the Party's parliamentary Leader, I considered two possibilities for organisational reform but did not regard either option as viable. The first was to end our formal association with the trade union movement, the core of the factional system, but this would have split the ALP in two. This option is only feasible if social democrats in Australia are willing to start from scratch with a new party and political purpose. I am not convinced that the trauma of this exercise would be worthwhile, especially given the severe divisions and electoral damage it would cause. Certainly, it was not something I felt comfortable implementing as Leader.

The second option was to democratise the Party's structure, bypassing the State-based machines and transferring power to the rank-and-file

---

3 Robert Michels, *Political Parties*, Free Press, New York, 1959

membership. This reform relies on the development of a mass political organisation, the first in Australia's history. Given that most people have no desire to attend party meetings and devote their time to organised politics, it is difficult to envisage how these changes could succeed. My experience in 2004 convinced me that pursuing the democratisation of Labor was a futile task, even if the Party were willing to try.

I still regard my community forums as beneficial, in that they gave the public a chance to raise issues and interact with one of their political leaders. But realistically, engagement was limited to certain kinds of people—political and community activists. Self-evidently, the large number of Australians who have grown disillusioned with the political process did not attend. My efforts to engage and empower the outsiders in Australian politics were unsuccessful.

Oscar Wilde once said he didn't think that socialism would work because it would take up too many evenings. That is how Australians see political participation these days, especially in outer metropolitan areas, where the time pressures of working, commuting and raising a family are severe. They think that voting every three years is too big a burden, let alone belonging to a political party. The prospects of a mass social democratic party emerging in Australia are slim indeed.

In every other crisis in its history, the ALP has been able to draw strength from its past. We have all heard and used the bravado of Labor being a resilient beast and so forth. But this is merely a rhetorical device: it doesn't actually change things or guarantee success for the future. Today, romanticism of this kind is a long way removed from the depth and seriousness of Labor's structural problems. Fond memories of Curtin and Chifley are not going to resolve the crisis.

More importantly, those who currently hold power are not going to relinquish their machine control of the Party; it would be contrary to their values and beliefs, everything they have been conditioned to believe in and fight for in politics. Not all problems in public life can be solved and, I regret to say, this is one of them. The concentration of factional power has become a permanent feature of Labor's culture and political purpose.

The Sick Society

It would be a mistake, however, to position these issues solely within the realm of politics. Problems of apathy and disengagement are not restricted to our democracy; they are a defining feature of modern society. If families and communities are falling apart, if people feel alienated and empty in their relationships with others, if the bonds of social trust and support are weak, it is hardly surprising that our political parties are dominated by oligarchies.

Without a strong base of social capital, it is relatively easy for a small group of people to control and manipulate the political system—they simply fill the gap left by the paucity of public participation and community activism. History tells us this is how hierarchies of power are established and sustained. The weakness of our democracy is a function of the sickness of our society.

Traditionally, Left-of-Centre parties have tried to achieve their goals for social justice by tackling various forms of economic disadvantage. Today, however, the biggest problems in society, the things that cause hardship and distress for people, tend to be relationship-based—social issues, not economic. The paradox is stunning: we live in a nation with record levels of financial growth and prosperity, yet also with record levels of discontent and public angst. The evidence is all around us, in:

- the extraordinary loss of peace of mind in society, evident in record rates of stress, depression and mental illness
- the breakdown in basic relationships of family and community, generating new problems of loneliness and isolation in Australia. The traditional voluntary and mutual associations of community life have all but disappeared, replaced by home fortresses and gated housing estates
- the appalling incidence of crimes against family and loved ones: sexual assault, domestic violence and the sickness of child abuse
- the spillover of these problems onto the next generation of young Australians, in the form of street crime, drug and alcohol abuse and youth suicide.

A striking aspect of this phenomenon has been the way in which it has affected all parts of society, regardless of their economic standing. Poor communities, after several generations of long-term unemployment and financial disadvantage in Australia, now face the further challenge of social disintegration, a loss of self-esteem and solidarity. Thirty years ago, these communities were financially poor but socially rich. Today they face poverty on both fronts.

While the middle class in Australia has experienced the assets and wealth of an unprecedented economic boom, its social balance sheet has moved in the opposite direction. The treadmill of work and the endless accumulation of material goods have not necessarily made people happier. In many cases, they have denied them the time and pleasures of family life, replacing strong and loving social relationships with feelings of stress and alienation.

This is the savage trade-off of middle-class life: generating financial wealth but at a significant cost to social capital. Thus social exclusion needs to be understood as more than just financial poverty; it also involves the poverty of society, the exclusion of many affluent Australians from strong and trusting personal relationships.

These changes represent a huge shift in the structure of society. The market economy has expanded, while community life has been downsized. Today, when Australians see a social problem, they are more likely to pursue a market-based answer than a community solution. This has led to the commercialisation of public services and the grotesque expansion of market forces into social relationships.

Community-based sport, for instance, has been replaced by the coldness of commercial ownership and professionalism. So, too, the institution of marriage has been subject to the economic discipline of pre-nuptial agreements. People are contracting out to the private sector the maintenance and care of their home: their gardening, cooking and pet care. Matters that were once determined by mutual agreement and cooperation between people are now treated as routine financial transactions. The highly visible hand of the market reaches into most parts of life.

While market forces can achieve certain goals, such as increased economic incentive and growth, they are not a good way of running society. They treat people as rule followers, rather than rule makers. Everything is given a commercial value, and the value of life's intangibles, such as personal feelings, morality and cooperation, is downgraded. The importance of civil society is lost, the opportunities we need as citizens to freely determine our obligations and trust in each other.

Unlike other forms of capital, social capital is a learned habit. It exists in the experiences and relationships between people. If people cannot exercise their trust in each other, they are likely to lose it. This appears to be the unhappy state of Western society in the first decade of the twenty-first century. The relationship between international markets and local communities has become imbalanced. For too many citizens, global capital has become a substitute for social capital.[4]

4 For a more extensive outline of the theory and practice of social capital, see Ian Winter (ed.), *Social Capital and Public Policy in Australia*, Australian Institute of Family Studies, Melbourne, 2000

Unfortunately, Australia has been at the forefront of these changes. Two centuries ago, we started out as a convict society, held together by the common bonds of mateship. There was, literally, honour among thieves. Within their social and mateship groups, Australians developed the habit of treating other people as equals, irrespective of their economic status. The economic revolution of the 1980s and 1990s, however, has reshaped these values forever. Consumerism and economic competition have moved to the centre of our national ethos and identity.

Instead of chopping down tall poppies, our popular culture and media outlets now direct their angst towards the disadvantaged: a belief that the unemployed, newly arrived migrants, indigenous Australians and public housing tenants are undeserving of government support. Envy in Australia, perversely enough, now travels down the social ladder, not upwards, a phenomenon I've dubbed 'downward envy'.

Australia's egalitarian traditions have been supplanted by the bitter whingeing of talkback radio and commercial television. Far from treating other people as equals, the mass media have become a mechanism for prying into their lives and denigrating them. As a nation, questions of status and self-esteem are now determined by the accumulation of material goods, not the maintenance of mateship.

As a parliamentarian, I made speeches and wrote books about the decline of social capital in Australia. As Labor Leader, I tried to put this issue at the centre of our national agenda, with new policies for community development and public participation. Ultimately, however, people voted on economic issues, and many of the social issues I raised, such as childhood literacy and obesity, were derided in the media as trivial. I failed in my attempt to make the quality of our society a mainstream political concern. Perhaps I was a poor advocate for these issues or the wrong person to be raising them; there are elements of truth in both propositions. But I believe that other considerations that extend well beyond the party politics of 2004 are also important.

In my experience with and study of the new middle class, people have particular ways of dealing with social capital. While they would like to find a solution to a range of problems in their community, their faith in our system of governance is so weak that they have no expectation that this is possible. It is inconceivable to them that various forms of political and civic action might make a difference. They become resigned, therefore, to a weak set of social relationships.

In these circumstances, people tend to withdraw further from civil society and pursue other forms of personal recognition and self-esteem. The politics of 'me', the individual, replaces the politics of 'we', the community.

People try to escape relationship-based problems by turning inwards, pursuing temporary and artificial forms of personal gratification.

In this respect, advanced capitalism has provided two powerful forms of escapism for the middle class. The first is the emergence of a consumer society. All the messages in our public culture push people towards materialism: commercial advertising, the glorification of wealth, keeping up with the Joneses. The middle-class response to an unhappy life is further consumption, the temporary escapism of material goods.

Such is the treadmill effect in modern society: long working hours, less time for social relationships, short-term comfort from consumerism, and the need to work harder to finance this habit, which results in a further decline in social capital. Like most treadmills, people don't know how to get off. They feel the artificial excitement of acquiring something new, but when the feeling wears off, the problem has not gone away. In most cases, the sense of alienation from society has worsened.

The so-called sea-change phenomenon is a sign that some people are trying to put social relations at the forefront of their lives. But realistically, this is a privilege that applies only to a small proportion of society. Most Australians remain locked in the gulag of consumerism. And so the apparent paradox grows: the more middle Australia consumes and breaks retail records, the more problems people seem to encounter in other parts of their lives.

The second form of escapism is through the media. As people struggle with their relationships in society, they often peer into other people's lives, seeking solace in someone else's reality. This has generated a cult of celebrity that now dominates much of our public culture, through commercial television, talkback radio, tabloid newspapers and the Internet. People's thirst for celebrity seems insatiable: witness the power and popularity of reality television. Anyone can have his or her fifteen minutes of fame, while everyone else watches.

The media houses feed this habit because it sustains their profits. They try to legitimise it through 'the public's right to know'. In practice, they could not survive financially without fostering society's voyeurism. This is what gives the media their mass: everyone knowing what other people are doing, even if it has nothing to do with them.

This obsession has given people a peculiar standard of social worth: to be important, to have a high level of self-esteem, you need to be on television, to be recognised in public. When civil society was strong, there was no such thing as a celebrity. People were recognised for their contribution to community life, not their face on television screens.

Media escapism of this kind exacerbates the social capital problem. Like materialism, it is a temporary and artificial process. Past experience tells us that people are more likely to forge relationships of trust and co-operation through personal contact and community involvement. Yet a high proportion of the things we respond to in our daily lives are impersonal: media images we shall never feel or experience first-hand. This has weakened the natural bonds and interaction of society. Research in the United States, for instance, has shown a close correlation between increased television consumption and the post-war decline in social capital.[5]

Escapism is the new religion of middle Australia. This is the sorry state of advanced capitalism: the ruling culture encourages people to reach for four-wheel drives, double-storey homes, reality television and gossip magazines to find meaning and satisfaction in their lives. All of which offer false hope. Marx was wrong in predicting the alienation of labour from the economy as the catalyst of social discontent. It is the alienation of the individual from community life that is the cause of so many social problems.

As a Member of Parliament, one of my mistakes was to promote the importance of aspirational politics. I wanted working people to enjoy a better standard of living, but had assumed that as they climbed the economic ladder, they would still care about the community in which they lived, and take heed of the interests of others, especially the poor and disadvantaged. This was my misjudgement of modern society. Instead, as people have moved into middle-class affluence, they have left their old, working-class neighbourhoods behind and embraced the new values of consumerism.

Social capital in Australia is so weak and shallow that it does not extend across neighbourhood boundaries. I used to talk about the suburb where I grew up, and people thought I was strange for doing so. We have become a society obsessed with the places to which the economic caravan can take us, not the places it has left behind. Economic mobility has had a damaging impact on the habits of compassion and cooperation. As a society we are poorly equipped to meet the challenges of globalisation: building strong communities that are prepared to reach out and trust in strangers—people, values and information from across the globe.

The crisis in social capital is also a crisis for social democracy. If people do not practise mutual trust and cooperation in their lives, they are not likely to support the redistributive functions of government. If they have no interest or experience in helping their neighbours, why would

5 Robert Putnam, 'The Strange Disappearance of Civic America', *Policy*, Autumn 1996, pp. 3–15

they want the public sector to help people they have never met? Indeed, the dominant electoral mood is a desire to take resources away from other people and communities, as evidenced by the rise of downward envy in Australia.

I have agonised over these issues and tried to find ways of making the social democratic project sustainable. After a decade of research and analysis, my conclusions are bleak. The task of social reformers is extraordinarily difficult, if not impossible. Not only must they rebuild the trust and cohesiveness of civil society, they also need to motivate people about the value and possibilities of organised politics. If and when these formidable tasks are completed, they then need to win majority public support for a sweeping program of social justice.

The pillars of conservatism in our society have a much easier task: supporting the status quo and scaring people about the uncertainties of political change. They have no interest in generating public enthusiasm in politics and the reform process. This is what binds the ruling class together: the shared interests of the conservative parties, the commercial media and other parts of the business establishment in preserving the existing social order and the concentration of power in their hands.

Indeed, if the media were to promote solutions to society's problems, they would have very few stories left to report. A happy society full of good news does not sell newspapers or secure ratings. So, too, the media have a commercial interest in the denigration of politics, presenting it as just another form of conflict and scandal in society to feed the public's voyeurism. Like all big businesses, their interests lie in preserving the status quo and the ruling institutions and culture that sustain their profitability.

Is today's Labor Party, built around its own hierarchy of conservatism and machine politics, going to challenge and overcome this system? Not that I can see. Even if it were hungry to take on the ruling elite rather than be part of it, I doubt that the Party would embrace the appropriate reform program of grassroots policies to rebuild social cooperation and mutuality. Labor politicians come into Parliament to take control, to pull the levers of public administration. They support a top-down process of governance, based on an expectation that politicians and political machines can direct and control social outcomes. They are not familiar or comfortable with the methodology of social capital.

Community-building sits outside the conventional methods of party politics. Whereas public policy relies on a sense of order and predictability, the work of civil society is spontaneous and disorderly. Whereas governments try to have a direct and tangible impact on their citizens, the creation of mutual trust relies on processes that are diffuse and intangible.

There is no point in passing a Social Capital Bill and expecting it to make people community-minded.

Trust occurs as a by-product of the relationship between people. It is not like a well-ordered machine, whereby policy-makers can pull the levers and mandate a particular result. The best they can hope for is to influence the social environment in which trust is created. They need to see themselves as facilitators of social capital, rather than controllers of social outcomes.[6]

This is best achieved by transferring influence and resources to communities, devolving as many decisions and public services as possible. Real power comes from giving power away. But this is not how the parliamentary system works, especially a machine political party. Powerbrokers try to capture and control the authority of government, not give it away. They believe in the centralisation of power, not its dispersal. The square peg of Labor politics does not fit into the round hole of social capital.

Work and Family

For the first ten years of my parliamentary career, the *Diaries* were almost exclusively about politics; personal matters were raised only in passing. This changed when I became Labor Leader. In such a high-profile position, it seemed that everything I did was public information. I found the loss of privacy debilitating. The *Diaries*, therefore, became an outlet for grappling with the impact of politics on my private life.

As a politician, I spent a lot of time talking about policies to help people strike the right balance between work and family. In practice, I needed some myself. This was an unbearable part of the job. Even during the honeymoon period, my first months as Opposition Leader, I was worried about the way in which politics was overwhelming my family life, constantly colonising my private time. Throughout 2004, the *Diaries* record these emotional battles, and my determination not to neglect my family.

They also deal with the shocking level of media intrusion into our lives. Even today, I still shake my head in amazement at some of the things

6 This point is well made by James Scott, *Seeing Like a State*, Yale University Press, New Haven, Conn., 1998. He writes of how 'the utopian, immanent and continually frustrated goal of the modern state is to reduce the chaotic, disorderly, constantly changing social reality beneath it to something more closely resembling the administrative grid of its observations' (p. 82)

that happened. Undoubtedly, this is the worst aspect of public life: the assumption by the media and the general public that they own you, that everything you do is for public consumption. For a young family, in particular, this was untenable. You don't know how valuable your privacy is until you lose it.

Some political leaders seem to revel in the non-stop attention and busy schedule that these positions provide. I disliked this part of the job— what seemed like an endless series of short and superficial encounters with people. The real love and commitment in my life are in my home, yet all the Labor leadership ever did was take me away from it.

Worst of all, the job made me a stranger to my children. This caused me enormous guilt about something I regarded as the primary responsibility in my life: being a good father. I never spent enough time with my own dad, who passed away when I was a young man. Yet there I was, racing around the country, squandering the father–son relationship a second time. It felt like an act of folly. Fatherhood had been an unexpected gift in my life, the greatest personal bond and connection I have experienced. I must have asked myself a thousand times why I was wasting it.

Politics, with its constant travel and irregular hours, was also bad for my health. Since my retirement, there has not been a single moment when I have wanted to return. It may have been a high-profile and highly paid job, but it was a horrible way of life. Leaving politics behind has been liberating for myself and my family. I have no doubt it was the right decision. This book is my exit statement from all forms of politics.

The media correctly point out that I have disappeared from their lives. But I have reappeared in my children's lives, doing exactly what I said I was going to when I retired from politics. I'm no longer a tourist in my own home. I'm a resident, a busy home-dad and husband. This has been my own sea-change: looking after my sons, nurturing their interests, trying to protect them from the sick society. Some people told me I would get bored and restless. But, really, what can be more interesting than watching your own flesh and blood grow and develop? I love it.

My wife Janine works in the law and I am proud to support her career as much as possible. We have finally found the right balance between our work and family commitments, free from the obligations and restrictions of politics. It is also good to be free from the hypocrisy of political rhetoric—in particular, MPs moralising about the importance of family values while pursuing careers that take them away from their families on a semipermanent basis.

On 9 December 2004, my last day in the House of Representatives, as the Parliament wound down for the year and the party leaders issued their felicitations, Peter Costello said, 'We all indulge ourselves in politics, but it is our families that bear a lot of the brunt ... It is particularly hard, I think, on the mothers, who essentially become single mothers'. He is absolutely correct. It is indulgent and unfair to turn the people we love into single mothers. I could not do it any longer.

I have found that time with family helps to broaden one's perspective and interests in life. This is because it is built on the foundations of social trust and mutual support. It gives people the peace of mind and security from which they can grow as individuals. It is a very intimate form of social capital. By contrast, politics, with its culture of distrust and mutual hostility, is more likely to narrow down the individual. This breeds insecurity, encouraging people to run with the herd in order to find comfort and acceptance within the system. It makes them timid and inward-looking.

Most of the messages and influences in public life are conservative, pushing people into a culture of conformity—the acceptable way of thinking and expressing oneself. The conservative power-blocs of modern politics—the party machines, commercial media and business establishment—try to foster this one-dimensional approach. They prefer their politicians to be cautious, predictable and easily brought under control.

Multi-dimensional characters who are vibrant and progressive in their beliefs are seen as threatening to the status quo. They may do something radical, disturb the existing order of things and vested interests. Have no doubt: the elites who have accumulated power and privilege in our society will always fight hard to maintain it.

By and large, they have been highly successful. Over time, our national political culture has become more conservative and uniform. Just look along the benches of the Australian Parliament: it has lost its larrikins, its Australian originals. In their place sit the bland white-bread politicians, the true Tories of the parliamentary system. I battled against this tendency inside the Labor Party, determined to maintain a bold approach to public policy. I believed in adventurism as a way of public life. I believed that a party of reform needed to be proactive and progressive in its work.

The conservatives in the system said that this made me complex and contradictory. Anything more than one dimension was too much for them, too challenging and dangerous to their interests. Better that, I say, than reducing human nature to its most basic form: the narrowness of conservatism. A good life comes from broadening one's character and interests.

For me, the most valuable part of these diaries is towards the end. Naturally, one day, I want my children to appreciate these work and family considerations. I hope they will understand how their old man tried to be true to himself and the reason he got involved in Labor politics in the first place. And why, at the end of it all, he was more than happy to walk away, safe in the knowledge that there is indeed a better life than public life—the life I share with them and their mother.

And the last word on my time in politics? I am happy to leave it to my Liberal opponents. One of the nice rituals of Australian politics is that, after you retire, the other side starts telling the truth about you. In February I received the following note from a senior minister in the Howard Government:

> Whilst there will always be some things you and I will disagree on, I admire the contribution that you have made to public life. At Liverpool Council you changed the Old Guard and put in place a dynamic infrastructure. In Federal Parliament you took risks that gave you opportunities to change the nation from Opposition. I admire that.
>
> Now is a time for you and your family. I genuinely wish you a good life ahead. Enjoy the time you have with family. In a number of ways you have made Australia better.

Mark Latham
May 2005

1994

After Labor unexpectedly won the March 1993 Federal election, the Member for Werriwa, John Kerin, was dropped from the Ministry and began preparing for his departure from Parliament. Werriwa was a safe Labor seat, previously held by Gough Whitlam (1952–78), for whom I had worked between 1982 and 1987. Part of the electorate covered the southern section of the Liverpool local government area in south-west Sydney, where I had been the Mayor since September 1991 and an Alderman since 1987.

For many years I had hoped to enter Federal politics, so with word of Kerin's looming retirement, I started organising the numbers in the local ALP branches (NSW has a rank-and-file preselection system; Labor candidates are determined by the votes of local branch members). When Kerin formally announced his retirement in December 1993, I was elected unopposed in the preselection process.

The Prime Minister, Paul Keating, called the by-election to coincide with the quiet Christmas/January holiday period, denying the Opposition an opportunity to attract high-profile media coverage. This was the first test of the Government's popularity since its controversial August Budget (when it broke several election promises). It was also the first electoral test for the Liberal Leader, John Hewson, since his election loss with the 'Fightback!' package, which included the GST.

It was an incredibly hot January, with many parts of Sydney ravaged by bushfires, so community interest in the by-election campaign was subdued. On polling day, 29 January, I won with 50.1 per cent of the primary vote, 59.5

per cent two-party-preferred—a swing against the Government of 6.3 per cent, just above the national by-election average. At the age of 32, I had been elected to the House of Representatives for the great Labor constituency of Werriwa, a dream come true. I was a young man in a hurry.

I was also a young man with a health problem. Towards the end of 1993, I began to feel a strange tingling in and around my groin. In June 1994, somewhat by chance, I watched a segment on ABC television's 7.30 Report about testicular cancer, the most prevalent cancer for men in their twenties and thirties. I recognised the symptoms, saw my GP and, a week later, had a cancerous (left) testicle removed in Camden Hospital. The ABC had saved my life. I was also able to joke that the operation confirmed me, in factional terms, as a lifetime Right-winger.

My experience with cancer changed my outlook on life. I saw stress as a contributing factor: my busy time in local government and the extreme workload in holding down positions as Mayor of Liverpool and Member for Werriwa. I resigned from Council and commenced an intensive program of radiotherapy across the stomach region at Westmead Hospital near Parramatta. This explains the break in my diary between May and October 1994.

Fortunately I made a good recovery, but the experience had a profound impact on me. It softened my attitude to life, made me less career-driven and more carefree. It also made me highly aware of the way in which work-related stress could damage my health. For many years, I had regular cancer check-ups and was always worried about any other aches and twinges; I don't think the experience of having cancer ever really leaves you. It certainly shaped my attitude to work, health and longevity.

During the rest of the year, my diary entries were relatively brief and rudimentary. I was just starting this project, and in any case, as a newly arrived backbencher, I didn't have any significant access to the decision-making processes of the Keating Government. There was not a great deal of behind-the-scenes information to record. In subsequent years, as I moved through Labor's ranks and gained close access to its senior figures, my entries became more substantial.

Sunday, 30 January

The day after the Werriwa by-election. Paul Keating calls me at home with congratulations. He laments the lack of crusaders in the Government,

Paul Keating ALP member, Blaxland 1969–96; Treas. in Hawke govt 1983–91; PM 1991–96 people who campaign with passion and commitment. He sounds a bit downcast, like the glory days might be behind us. But then he peps up and is quite positive about the by-election result. He says he got into Parliament too early, at 26, but the train only pulls in once every twenty years in safe Labor seats. No doubt about that, you have to jump on board.

There were times when I thought I would never make it into Federal Parliament, particularly after the Liverpool preselection fight in 1989. At one point, I would have been happy enough to forget about politics and get a regular job. But it was worth batting on. Not that many Australians get to serve in the national Parliament—it's quite an honour.

The polling in our campaign showed a lot of negativity about the Government's broken promises in last year's Budget. The Opposition is not credible, however, under Hewson's leadership. He's the best thing we have going for us. But Keating is right to worry about the Government having to ask for sixteen years at the next election. It's a big ask.

Thursday, 24 March

Graham Richardson's private secretary Marion assures me he was all set to swap places with Bob Carr—Carr for the Senate, Richo for the NSW Labor leadership. Something changed Richardson's mind the weekend before his resignation from Parliament. A nice little mystery, as everyone smiles and gives Richo a happy send-off.

Wednesday, 4 May

Steve Loosley tells a Peter Knott classic from their delegation to Bougainville. Knott was keen to make contact with the independence movement, so he threw 500 of his business cards out of the helicopter over the jungle, hoping that the locals might pick them up. A new cargo cult god has been created in Bougainville.

Liverpool preselection fight After the State Labor member George Paciullo resigned from Parl. in early 1989, Paul Lynch, Casey Conway and I contested a close and bitterly fought preselection to become the ALP candidate for the Liverpool by-election. I was declared the winner of the ballot by two votes over Lynch, but Lynch's Left-wing faction protested the result, accusing the NSW branch office of rorting the ballot. The ALP National Executive intervened and installed Peter Anderson, a minister in the Wran and Unsworth govts who had lost his seat of Penrith at the 1988 NSW general election, as the ALP candidate
John Hewson Lib. member, Wentworth 1987–95; Opposition Leader 1990–94
Graham Richardson Gen. Sec., NSW ALP 1976–83; NSW ALP Sen. 1983–94; min. in Hawke and Keating govts; leader of NSW Right
Bob Carr ALP member, Maroubra in the NSW Parl. 1983– ; min. in Wran and Unsworth govts; NSW ALP Leader 1988– ; NSW Premier 1995– . I worked for Bob Carr 1988–89, 1990–91
Steve Loosley Gen. Sec., NSW ALP 1983–90; NSW ALP Sen. 1990–95
Peter Knott ALP member, Gilmore 1993–96

Later in the day, Keating delivered the Working Nation statement—a big, bold plan to overcome supply-side problems in the labour market. By providing the long-term unemployed with customised assistance and training, the Government hopes to close the skills gap and make all job-seekers job ready. It's a crackerjack of a policy.

It also dragged all the major journalists into Canberra, who then kicked on to the pub in Manuka. Ran into an old mate of mine (now working as a researcher in ABC current affairs) who said that his boss (a prominent TV presenter) was keen for everyone to piss on back at his place in Kingston. Sounded great until we jumped into the boss man's van and he started driving the wrong way down Canberra Avenue, blind as a bat. What a madman, a real nut. In a rare display of good sense, I jumped out and caught a cab home.

I'm told the party ended with one of the ABC journalists collapsed in the middle of the floor, her knickers dangling around her ankles. What a great woman. That, I am told, is the cream of Australia's current affairs media. Next week their high-tone ABC program will be doing stories on the evils of drink-driving, with the piss-pot presenter sitting sanctimoniously in the chair. It's a crack-up.

Thursday, 5 May

Laurie Brereton tells me how he might jump on a bulldozer and rip up the third runway at Mascot, which is giving the Government a fair bit of strife in Sydney. It's hard to know whether Laurie is joking or not. Interesting to think about his relationship with Keating. In his last speech to the Senate, Richardson recalled how Keating used to say that he found Brereton on a surfboard in the eastern suburbs of Sydney and he could put him back there any time he wanted. Mates all right, but one is more equal than the other.

Still, they strike me as a pair of Labor classics. Keating, in particular, loves all the old sayings in politics. He recalled to Caucus how Clyde Cameron used to say that you have made it in Parliament when you don't know half the faces. Something to aim for one day.

Working Nation Keating govt policy for employment expansion and improving workforce skills
Laurie Brereton Long-serving ALP member of NSW Parl.; min. in Wran and Unsworth govts; ALP member, Kingsford-Smith 1990–2004; Industrial Relations and Transport Min. 1993–96; nicknamed 'Danger Man' or 'Danger'

Mascot A controversial decision by the Keating govt to build a third runway to expand the capacity of Kingsford-Smith Airport at Mascot. This decision caused a backlash against the govt in inner Sydney.
Clyde Cameron ALP member, Hindmarsh 1949–80; min. in Whitlam govt 1972–75

Tuesday, 31 May

Keating tells Caucus how there are peppering punches and body punches in politics. A pretty good analogy. Later that day, over a beer, Clyde Holding describes how he worked on Jim Cairns's election campaign during the Split—punch-ups at street-corner meetings with the Groupers, a real blood-and-guts battle for the soul of Labor. He reckons that Cairns joined the Masons (as did most of the Victorian Left).

The Left faction lost Holding when the Labor-controlled Collingwood Council approved a factory next to a parish school in his electorate that would have blocked out all the sunlight in the playground. The ALP Councillors told him not to worry, as the kids were only Catholics. No wonder he joined the Right.

Tuesday, 11 October

Keating explains to Caucus how inflationary expectations and interest rates are still too high, an overhang from the long period of stagflation in the 1970s and 1980s. He claims that 'these markets always correct themselves in the end', pointing to lower inflation and interest rates in the future. He's far more optimistic about the effectiveness of market forces than the average Caucus member. We'll see if he's right about inflation and monetary policy.

Wednesday, 19 October

At a meeting of the Banking, Finance and Public Administration House Committee, Bernie Fraser predicts that sustained low inflation in Australia will break inflationary expectations in two to three years' time. He and Keating are very upbeat about the future direction of interest rates and the economy.

Clyde Holding ALP member, Richmond 1962–77; Vic. Opposition Leader 1967–77; Fed. member, Melbourne Ports 1977–98; min. in Hawke govt 1983–90
Jim Cairns ALP member, Yarra 1955–69; ALP member, Lalor 1969–77; min. in Whitlam govt 1972–75; Dep. PM and Fed. Treas. 1974–75

the Split An attempt by Right-wing Catholic forces to take over trade unions and the ALP in the early 1950s, which led to the Party splitting in 1955. The Catholic forces (known as industrial groups, or 'groupers') left the ALP and formed the DLP
Bernie Fraser RBA Governor 1989–96

Tuesday, 22 November

Simon Crean phones to advise that he has allocated 500 extra university places to Queensland and not many to the rest of the country. This follows a Caucus Committee campaign to increase higher education funding, but with a fair distribution of student places to under-resourced regions around the country (including Western Sydney). I'm pissed off that the Party has put a crude electoral pitch to Queensland ahead of regional equity principles and good public policy.

Crean tells me that Stephen Smith is prepared to sacrifice the interests of his State (WA) and that Wayne Swan from Queensland couldn't care less about equity principles. These two characters are real nuisances around Caucus—the rise of machine men within Federal Labor. Both fancy themselves as the new Richo, but it's impossible to take them seriously. They always look shrill and out of their depth, especially in Parliament. On this issue, Crean is a big disappointment. He's definitely not a public policy person, more a fixer. You live and learn in this business.

Wednesday, 30 November

Ten months in Caucus now, and the place is not really living up to expectations. The Government seems to be lacking passion and principles. Something has gone wrong. Something is missing in our political identikit. The real test will come when we go into Opposition. Keating strikes me as too busy and too removed to nurture the entire Government, especially the new backbenchers. Too much of the corridor talk is about political fixes. Yet for good government, the only things that need fixing are people's problems. While the issues are much bigger at a Federal level, the pace of decision-making is also much slower.

Monday, 5 December

Keating hosts Christmas drinks for the Caucus and gets heavily into nostalgia, very entertaining stuff. He tells the story of how Keith Johnson, Senator Poyser and other Caucus members would sit around the dinner table in the old Parliament House, circa 1970, talking up the need for

Simon Crean ACTU Pres. 1985–90; ALP member, Hotham 1990– ; min. in Hawke and Keating govts; Employment, Education & Training Min. 1993–96
Stephen Smith ALP member, Perth 1993– ; former State Sec. WA ALP

Wayne Swan ALP member, Lilley 1993–96; 1998– ; former State Sec. Qld ALP
Keith Johnson ALP member, Burke 1969–80
Senator Poyser Vic. ALP Sen. 1966–75

central economic planning. The young Keating sat there listening, thinking to himself, 'These old guys couldn't fill in their TA forms, let alone plan an economy'.

Keating reckons he was never able to centrally plan five ALP branches in his electorate in Bankstown, let alone complex industries. He describes industry protection as a mug's game: 'We were the bunnies defending the tariff walls but come election time the industrialists supported the other mob'.

He also speaks about the isolation and loneliness of the new Parliament House: 'Wandering around this big building wondering if you are part of anything. In Government you don't have to bore each other at dinner, unlike the Opposition that has nothing else to do. You can pick the company of those you like and avoid the ones you don't like. We can all get on with things in our nice, sullen way'.

Talks of how, against the odds, Bill Hayden put together a decent team in the late 1970s: 'Walshie, who hated anyone who had ever owned a farm; Dawks, with all the passion and fire; Gareth [Evans] who gave us the FOI Bill and ever since then we have been trying to give it back to him; Hurford, always pontificating about the tax system and Ralph [Willis] giving us lectures about the IR system. And then there was me, a gentle NSW Right-wing operator from the western suburbs of Sydney'.

Bill Hayden ALP member, Oxley 1961–88; ALP Opposition Leader 1977–83; Foreign Affairs Min. in Hawke govt 1983–88 ; GG 1989–96
Peter Walsh WA ALP Sen. 1974–93; min. in Hawke govt; Finance Min. 1984–90
John Dawkins ALP member, Tangney 1974–75; ALP member, Fremantle 1977–94; min. in Hawke and Keating govts, incl. Treas. 1991–93

Gareth Evans Vic. ALP Sen. 1978–96; min. in Hawke and Keating govts, incl. Foreign Affairs Min. 1988–96
Chris Hurford ALP member, Adelaide 1969–87; min. in Hawke govt
Ralph Willis ALP member, Gellibrand 1972–98; min. in Hawke and Keating govts, incl. Treas. 1991 and 1993–96

1995

The last full year of the Keating Government. It started badly for Labor, with the loss of the Canberra by-election on 25 March, with a punishing 16 per cent swing. From that point on, it was clear to many in the Labor Caucus that the Government would struggle to win the next election. The Government was unable to gain control of the political agenda and capitalise on the advantages of incumbency. After twelve years in office, there was a strong 'time for a change' sentiment in the electorate.

Caucus spent most of the year waiting for a miracle to arrive, as it had in 1993. If anything, this air of unreality made things worse. Nobody decisively tackled the Government's electoral problems—it was all left in the hands of Paul Keating. A few Ministers saw the writing on the wall. In June, the Deputy PM, Brian Howe, announced that he would not be contesting the next election and was replaced by Kim Beazley.

On the other side of politics, John Howard returned to the Liberal leadership on 30 January, replacing Alexander Downer. Howard adopted a small-target strategy of holding back his policies and keeping the pressure on the Government. I was sufficiently worried by our electoral prospects to run a strong re-election campaign for Werriwa, treating it like a marginal seat. Politics was changing in Western Sydney and I resolved not to be caught short.

I was also determined to develop my prowess as a parliamentarian. After the personal trauma of 1994, I settled into a smoother pattern of parliamentary life: speaking on Bills that matched my policy interests, distributing policy papers to colleagues, contributing to Caucus and parliamentary committees, and pushing for a continuation of the reform traditions of the Hawke/Keating Government. I had made the transition from local government and felt increasingly comfortable as a policy advocate at the national level.

Wednesday, 8 February

Keating hosts a Caucus BBQ at the Lodge. He is very frank in his remarks, maybe half-tanked at the time: 'I've been here too long, that's the truth of it; 26 years is a long time'. For a moment or two, I thought he was going to pull the pin and resign as PM. Not a bad time to do it, in fact. Twenty-six years is a long time indeed. He's won an unwinnable election for us and become a Labor legend. Why not go out on top? But Paul hates the Tories too much to ever leave them alone. It's the obsession of a lifetime.

The Liberals have gone back to John Howard as Leader, giving them greater weight and intent in the House. Downer was such a joke—we needed to get an election out of him. But Keating is a full-term man, as he keeps telling the Caucus. The BBQ is a beauty, one of those magnificent balmy nights in Canberra.

Tuesday, 28 March

After Ros Kelly's resignation from Parliament, we cop a hiding in the Canberra by-election. Keating tells Caucus: 'I know some people don't like my style, which has always been, if you've got a problem, make a decision; if you've had a rebuff, put on a blue. But it's got me this far okay'. He's right, of course. If you won't fight for yourself in politics, the public knows that you will never fight for them when it counts.

Keating seems sensitive to criticism of his parliamentary style, saying that in the House of Representatives, 'You either run over them or they run over you'. His style is not the problem. Rather, the government is seen by the electorate as failing to deliver on the bread-and-butter issues—living standards, basic services, supporting the majority instead of minority interest groups.

Gary Punch tells me that 'The really worrying thing about the by-election result is that Tuggeranong looks just like the middle suburbs of

---

John Howard Lib. member, Bennelong 1974– ; Opposition Leader 1985–89, 1995–96; PM 1996– **Alexander Downer** Liberal member, Mayo 1984– ; Opposition Leader 1994–95

Ros Kelly ALP member, Canberra 1980–95; min. in Hawke and Keating govts **Gary Punch** ALP member, Barton 1983–96; min. in Hawke and Keating govts

Campbelltown'. I drive out there later in the day and see exactly what he means. Quite frightening for Labor seats on the urban fringe.

Following my by-election, the margin in Werriwa is down to 9.5 per cent. The glory days of 15 per cent margins are gone for good. Time to start a grassroots campaign back home. The wave is coming up the beach. It's time to scramble further up the sand.

Ros Kelly's departure is a reminder of how temporary public life can be. After I won my by-election at the start of last year, I drove down to Canberra for the Caucus meeting on the Monday. That night there was a BBQ for the National Right at Kelly's home in Red Hill. She was holding court with the younger MPs, boasting of how much money she had shoehorned into their electorates under the sports grants program. She was so confident that the political controversy about the program would fade away over the New Year. A few months later she was sitting next to me on the backbench. And now she has gone for good and Howard has won her seat. It's enough to make you choke on your snags.

Friday, 21 April

Following the Canberra by-election disaster, a backbench consultative committee has been formed to talk through the politics of the forthcoming Budget. Our big meeting is with Keating, Treasurer Willis and Finance Minister Beazley.

Keating really believes in his capacity to fine-tune the economy, all that 'hands on the levers' stuff. He's a politician who thinks that government runs the economy, more than the investment decisions of the private sector. This type of rhetoric has lifted public expectations for Labor's management of the economy. The political weight is on, with our last Budget before the next election.

Keating laments the failure of business to take up the opportunities that flow from microeconomic reform. The recession may have killed capital accumulation, but competitiveness has improved by 40 per cent. But if this is true, why has the CAD reached 6 per cent of GDP, just as it did in 1983? This handbrake on growth still applies twelve years later.

Nonetheless, Keating seems optimistic about our political prospects. Reckons the next election is just like 1987 against Howard: the ALP has its

Sports grants program A program of grants to local electorates administered by Ros Kelly as the Arts, Sports, the Environment, Tourism & Territories Min. before the 1993 election. After the election she was accused of favouring ALP electorates, the so-called 'Sports Rorts' scandal. She was forced to resign in March 1994
Kim Beazley ALP member, Swan 1980–96; min. in Hawke and Keating govts

back to the wall, 'But the government will win support by governing'. Hard to believe, however, that the answers, economic or political, were at this meeting.

Friday, 28 April

Keating is a great Labor Leader, but behind the scenes he doesn't strike me as an overly generous person. This is the big difference between Gough Whitlam and the two current leaders of the NSW Right, Keating and Bob Carr: generosity of spirit. Whitlam is the genuine Labor item, incredibly generous to his staff and supporters. For him, compassion is not just a political slogan, it is a way of life.

Carr, however, couldn't give a shit about anyone bar himself. He's always struck me as the kid from the schoolyard who was so gawky that he got pounded with rocks every day. The rest of his life has been a solo mission to prove the rock-throwers wrong, that someone out there (anyone will do) might like him. From what I can see, it hasn't worked so far.

Keating has had an amazing progression in public life: stacking branches in Bankstown, to running the NSW ALP, to running the Australian economy, to running APEC and the Asia-Pacific. Unlike many Labor people, he believes in his ability to run things. He wants to nurture the Party and engage in continuous reform, but twelve years into government, perhaps he has become too big. His point of view and personal authority are so dominant within the Government that lively debate and original thinking have dried up. The average Labor MP now asks 'what would Paul think' before doing anything.

Our missed economic opportunity was to use the unexpected election win in 1993 to address the national savings issue. The 1993 Budget response to the Fitzgerald Report was a non-event. Yet the paucity of savings and high current account deficit are a permanent brake on economic growth.

As Bernie Fraser wrote in the 1994 *Reserve Bank Annual Report*, 'If demand runs ahead of capacity, it will spill over into imports and widen the Current Account Deficit (CAD). This is what happened in 1989–90 when the deficit reached 6 per cent of GDP. On this occasion the CAD is not expected to increase to the very high levels reached during the late 1980s'.

Gough Whitlam ALP member, Werriwa 1952–78; Fed. ALP Leader 1967–77; PM 1972–75

Fitzgerald Report A report on Australia's national savings problem by Vince Fitzgerald, head of Allen Consulting Group, delivered to the Keating govt in 1993

But now it has. Poor demand management is hurting our political prospects. We are going into the next election with weaker growth, rising inflation and a CAD problem, all off a 1995–96 Budget that is likely to have tax increases and spending cuts and privatisation. And time is running out for Paul to do anything about it.

Monday, 8 May

At Caucus, Keating recalls Arthur Calwell's advice: 'The secret to politics is to be at the first Caucus meeting after each election'. Survival is important, but so, too, are achievements. Is this an achievement-based Government any more, or just a political show trying to wangle one more election win out of the system?

The Cabinet ministers and factional bosses within the Government foster conformity, as it serves their own interests. No one can challenge their power without some original argument or angle. We need greater freedom for backbenchers to keep their minds alert and alive. They need to be a bit more detached from the decision-making processes of government.

Talking of conformity, what about the NSW Right? The reality is a long way removed from its public reputation. It strikes me as a strange mob without strike power, ambling together for a social chat every second sitting week. I can't find a policy agenda at any of its meetings.

Wednesday, 10 May

I attend the launch of Graeme Campbell's book by Peter Walsh in one of the committee rooms at Parliament House. It is a sad occasion, with no real purpose, just a small puzzled audience trying to work out why Campbell bothers with his isolationist ideas. His views reflect his own isolated geography within the nation. Knocking around the back blocks of WA would convince anyone that the rest of the world is against us.

I see no evidence that internationalism is inconsistent with equity. What is wrong with a world of free trade and investment, a world where people exchange products, ideas and information on a regular basis? Campbell is the last remnant of White Australia inside the Federal ALP. And

---

Arthur Calwell ALP member, Melbourne 1940–72; min. in Curtin and Chifley govts; Opposition Leader 1960–67
Graeme Campbell ALP member, Kalgoorlie 1980–Nov. 1995, after which he became an independent member

White Australia Policy Australia's racially discriminatory immigration policy from 1901 until its abolition by the Whitlam govt in 1973

why is Walsh here? His own book rails against stunting, yet Campbell is the biggest stuntman in the place.

Tuesday, 6 June

The Super League controversy has broken out and Steve Martin organises a meeting in his office to sort out a Labor position with Michael Lee. Footy fans Paul Elliott, Gary Punch, Michael Forshaw, Arch Bevis and I also attend. Basically, Lee is as weak as water.

The anti-siphon laws were supposed to provide an assurance of free-to-air rugby league, but Lee reckons they are vulnerable to court challenge, putting the blame on their author, Graham Richardson. Lee's goal is to 'Keep the number of communications laws to a minimum—the Government loses a minister for every piece of communications legislation in the Senate'.

He is too weak to take on the big media players, saying that, 'In the lead-up to an election, we would be mad to touch either Murdoch or Packer'. So Murdoch can screw over the great working-class game of rugby league and there is nothing a Labor Government will do to stop it. Lee is afraid to put a foot forward for fear of putting a foot wrong. Throughout the meeting he looks like a rabbit in the headlights.

Wednesday, 7 June

Keating provides Caucus with his model for the Republic. He reckons it will serve as a long-term policy for Federal Labor, even in Opposition. I doubt it. Instinctively, I am a direct-election Republican. This is the best way of carrying the popular vote, plus it fits the Republican ethos of power and sovereignty resting with the people.

Under the Keating model, why should I be the only voter in Werriwa to have a say in determining the President of the Republic? Mind you, Caucus

Super League controversy A break-away rugby league competition from the Australian Rugby League organised and funded by News Ltd. This became a public controversy in early 1995
Steve Martin ALP member, Macarthur 1984–93; ALP member, Cunningham 1993–2002; House of Representatives Speaker 1993–96
Michael Lee ALP member, Dobell 1984–2001; min. in Keating govt, incl. Communications & the Arts Min. 1994–96

Paul Elliott ALP member, Parramatta 1990–96
Michael Forshaw NSW ALP Sen. 1994–
Arch Bevis ALP member, Brisbane 1990–
Rupert Murdoch Head of the News Ltd media company
Kerry Packer Head of the Australian Consolidated Press media company
Republic Keating put forward a model under which the Fed. Cabinet and members of Fed. Parliament would determine the Pres.

is in no mood to challenge anything that Paul wants or says. For instance, Silvia Smith and Mary Crawford sit through his report to Caucus repeating his phrases, like a scene from *The Life of Brian*. But maybe he's not the messiah, just a naughty little boy.

Sunday, 18 June

I have emerged within Caucus as the strongest supporter of the Hilmer competition policy. In the eyes of some, I look like a fanatic. But my reasoning is simple: competition works better than monopoly, and why shouldn't working-class people get the benefit of lower prices? Let's clean out the rent-seekers and special interest groups who hang off the Labor movement like leeches.

Daryl Quinlivan, an adviser to the Assistant Treasurer, George Gear, tells me that Keating was never too keen on National Competition Policy (NCP). He said it was hard to sell politically and would lock in the government to a wide range of policy decisions. The stuff was written into his speeches anyway and 'went through despite the politics'. Apparently, Ralph Willis was also uneasy, saying that the NCP could have threatened the Accord Mark VIII. That's one thing the unions hate with a passion: competition.

Tuesday, 20 June

Brian Howe resigns as Deputy PM. Beazley and Crean are mentioned around the corridors as likely replacements. Carmen Lawrence is being touted in the media, but she won't run. Crean's support within the Right faction is limited to Harry Woods, Mary Easson and Con Sciacca. He had the support of the Left but blinked, leaving Beazley the only nominee.

With plenty of cameras outside the Caucus room, Carmen Lawrence is escorted along the corridor by two of her staff to give the impression that she is not alone. How do people think of these things, pay such amazing

---

Silvia Smith ALP member, Bass 1993–96
Mary Crawford ALP member, Forde 1987–96
Hilmer competition policy A report delivered to the Keating govt by Prof. Fred Hilmer in June 1995 applying competition principles to the public sector—Fed, State and local govts
George Gear ALP member, Tangney 1983–84; ALP member, Canning 1984–96
Accord Mark VIII The Prices & Incomes Accord was an agreement between the Hawke and Keating govts and the ACTU about economic policy in Australia

Brian Howe ALP member, Batman 1977–96, min. in Hawke and Keating govts, Dep. PM 1991–95
Carmen Lawrence WA Premier 1990–93; ALP member, Fremantle 1994– ; Human Services & Health Min. 1994–96
Harry Woods ALP member, Page 1990–96
Mary Easson ALP member, Lowe 1993–96
Con Sciacca ALP member, Bowman 1987–96; 1998–2004

attention to media image and detail? There's a lot more image-making and media consciousness in this place than I ever expected.

Wednesday, 28 June

Michael Lee provides a briefing on the new 15 per cent cross-media rules. The Left has agreed to the new rules, reflecting a convergence of interest across the Party to stop Packer. Lee is a fixer, not a reformer. As silly as it sounds, he sees a link between pay TV profitability and the Minister's image—that is, if the media barons are doing well with pay TV, they are more likely to lay off him. Michael's whole mission in life is to avoid controversy, and so far he's doing a fine job. Many people in Canberra see that as a virtue—Michael is a good political manager and communicator, but I am afraid it's not my go.

Thursday, 29 June

Gareth Evans gives me a Whitlam quote I had not heard before. Gough reckons, 'Paul [Keating] always preferred older men'. It's true when you think about it: Lang, Connor and Suharto. Maybe a product of getting into politics at such a young age, or losing your father early on.

On a visit to Rosemary Crowley's ministerial office, I notice the poster in her waiting room: 'The freedom of women is the measure for freedom in every society'. Sounds good, of course, unless you are a poor bloke with the arse hanging out of your pants. I have always believed in freeing the poor from poverty.

Tuesday, 25 July

As part of my re-election campaign for Werriwa, I've been holding constituent interviews on Saturday mornings in community halls across the electorate. It has been a real insight into how people on the urban fringe see the Keating Government. They don't complain about our economic management but, rather, our political priorities. Basically, they don't want to pay taxes to fund opportunities and choices for others, especially when

---

Jack Lang NSW Premier 1925–27, 1930–32, who then split from the ALP to form the Lang Labor Party; Fed. member, Reid 1946–49; mentor to Paul Keating in the 1960s
Rex Connor ALP member, Cunningham 1963–77; min. in Whitlam govt 1972–75;

mentor to Paul Keating during his early years in Parl.
Suharto Indonesian Pres. 1967–98
Rosemary Crowley SA ALP Sen. 1983–2002; Family Services Min. 1993–96

they are struggling in their own lives with the demands of commuting, raising kids and finding decent services.

Is this a new generation of Australian whingers, or are their complaints valid? Is this just a perception problem for the Government, or is Keating out of touch, having lost the energy and inclination to interact with the electorate, Caucus and Cabinet? Whatever the answer, you would not put money on our being re-elected. The swing is on.

With the extensive media coverage of modern politics, the public now has a heightened sense of the spending priorities of governments. Dole-bludger images are quickly implanted in the public's mind. The Rawlsian veil of ignorance has been lifted. It is not just a question of what governments spend on each individual, it is what the individual *thinks* about the spending on everyone else. What started out as ALP support for the disadvantaged is now perceived as funding for minority groups and so-called elites.

But hey, we are all part of minorities of one kind or another. Outer suburban electorates like mine are a minority in Parliament. That's why we're always getting stuffed over for funding and services. In Werriwa, the feeling is that the money is going to the wrong minority: the unemployed, the arts community, blacks, migrants and any other group that can con the Government into giving them a grant. It's a really punishing mood. I've got to make sure they don't give me too much punishment on polling day.

Tuesday, 22 August

Another blue with Michael Lee, this time over the (046) telephone zone in the southern part of my electorate. Whitlam and Kerin banged on about this for years with no success. Why should people in outer metropolitan areas have to pay STD rates when the unit cost to Telstra is the same right across Sydney? It is very unfair, plus it's a barrier to economic development in places like Campbelltown. Just look at the Minto industrial estate—built-out on the (02) side of the zone line but vacant on the more expensive (046) side.

Yes, it's unfair and uneconomic. It's also of little concern to our Communications Minister, who has failed to use the telecommunications review to solve this or any other problem. He reckons it's a matter of thick

Rawlsian veil of ignorance American social theorist John Rawls has written extensively on the theory of social justice, arguing that the principles of justice are those that would be agreed to by rational citizens calculating their own interests from a position of relative ignorance (the veil of ignorance)
John Kerin ALP member, Macarthur 1972–75; ALP member, Werriwa 1978–93; min. in the Hawke and Keating govts, incl. Treas., 1991

routes versus subsidies for thin routes. My electorate, however, wants to be long and thick.

Gough once told me the story of an ALP National Executive meeting in the early 1970s when, as they waited for someone to turn up, the conversation at this all-male gathering inevitably turned to dick sizes. As they went around the room, some blokes claimed to be long, others claimed to be thick. Until they got to Hawke, who yelled out 'long and thick'. Whenever Gough was unhappy with the Hawke Government he would say, 'Comrade, neither long nor thick'. The same can now be said of Michael Lee.

Michael is the Minister for Guaranteed Income: Telstra, Australia Post, the high arts, media rules creating a concentrated pay TV industry, and a music industry protected from parallel imports. Monopoly and protection all round. The micro-reformers must have been asleep during those Cabinet meetings.

Thursday, 26 October

After nearly two years in the place, the novelty of Federal Parliament is wearing off. How did Weber describe politics: slow boring through hard boards. That's how I feel now. The media and the public have little understanding of just how boring this business can be. Invariably, the same issues, the same people and the same rhetoric, all recycled.

The only way to stay interested is through some adventurism— thinking aloud, tossing around ideas, taking some risks. I suppose that's what makes Keating such an attractive character. If we ever lose him the ALP will be as boring as bat-shit.

My belief in adventurism means that I will always have an uneasy relationship with the NSW Right. Even though I am part of it notionally, its mind-numbing authoritarianism is hard to cop. I joined the Right in the mid-1980s for pragmatic reasons: in a two-faction State you had to join one of them to have any hope of preselection. And the Right seemed to be more realistic on economic issues than the Left.

The faction, however, is based on a culture of anti-intellectualism. Policy is made through a series of deals, rather than the public interest. Power flows from the top down without any debate, goodwill or generosity of spirit. Maybe this is why people like Richardson call me mad. It's synonymous with being hard to control. If so, I should wear it as a badge of honour.

Bob Hawke ACTU Pres. 1970–80; ALP member, Wills 1980–92; PM 1983–91

Max Weber German sociologist and political economist

In practice, the so-called intellectuals of the NSW Right are frauds. Just three years ago Bob Carr was threatening to expel me from the Party for daring to write a paper advocating the redistribution of health resources to Western Sydney. He preferred the status quo, which is no answer at all in Campbelltown and Liverpool.

For me, probably the best thing to do is ignore them. Go to their meetings, listen to their crap and do my stuff anyway. Mate. The NSW Right is a subset of the Party's broader structural problems:

- Our trade union base is in steady decline.
- The transition from Industrial to Information Age politics means workers are becoming capitalists and enjoying every minute of it.
- The Party's local branches and rank-and-file participation are an empty shell.
- State Labor governments have become an exercise in managerialism, lost without a cause.
- Federally, we have become a one-man-show, with a ministry reliant on the bureaucracy and a backbench obsessed with electoralism.

Saturday, 11 November

Twenty years since the *coup d'état* and a commemorative dinner in the Old Parliament House dining room says it all about the ALP. June and John Kerin arguing that Labor has to lose the next election in order to properly renew itself. Neville Wran going berserk and banging the table in delight at the mention of Lionel Murphy's name. Margaret Whitlam calling out 'This is all crap' as Gough gives an 80-minute speech about everything. That's one of the things everyone likes about her, her honesty about Gough.

It reminds me of Lindsay Tanner's story about a meeting of his Melbourne Federal Electorate Assembly to organise a fundraising dinner. One of the delegates suggested Gough as the guest speaker, to which Tanner cautioned that he might speak for a couple of hours. In unison, the rest of the meeting replied, 'What's wrong with that?' They love the old man.

Neville Wran ALP NSW Premier 1976–86
Lionel Murphy NSW ALP Sen. 1962–75; Attorney General in Whitlam govt 1972–75; High Court judge 1975–1986

Lindsay Tanner ALP member, Melbourne 1993–

Friday, 15 December

Louise Webb from Ross Free's office tells me that, as a matter of course, the NSW Teachers' Federation lodges an objection to every Government grant for a non-government school. This is the sort of thing that drags down the Labor movement in the suburbs. When will the Left ever learn? They have come no further than Clyde Holding's story about sectarianism in the 1950s.

Keating remains focused on his 'big picture' strategy: APEC, the Republic, a new defence treaty with Indonesia and so on. But all the public wants to talk about are local equity issues—evidence of how leaders gravitate upwards in politics, while the public remain at ground zero. The next election will be won and lost on the hip-pocket nerve.

A telltale Keating interview in the *Australian Financial Review* today, setting out his credentials as a conviction politician. He has a compelling message about the standard of public life in Australia:

> People of my ilk drift into public life for the public good of it, and for the corporate advancement of the country. But the system is so loaded with disincentives now. We're very zealous about it, and we'll wear the discomforts and setbacks to get the results, but I don't think the Australian community should assume the system's going to keep throwing up people who will do it.

He says it is the 'Low-rent mocking of the political system, as if we're all here for our travelling allowance or our free flight to Sydney or something' that gets to him: 'When people are, in fact, foregoing incomes five and ten times what they're getting here, it becomes a joke … One of the things I think people don't understand is that the conversation in this office over the course of the week would be completely different to the conversation in the media offices over the same week'. Too right, the gap between media perceptions and political reality is huge.

The challenges of political leadership are becoming tougher. Economics has gone global yet people still live in local communities, producing new political tensions. The politicians are in the middle, trying to resolve these issues while still winning elections. It is very hard, especially for parties of social reform. We now rely heavily on inspirational leadership,

---

Louise Webb Schools policy adviser to Ross Free

Ross Free ALP member, Macquarie 1980–84; ALP member, Lindsay 1984–96; min. in Hawke and Keating govts, incl. Schools, Vocational Education & Training Min. 1993–96

reforms that appeal to idealism and goodwill in the electorate. The status quo can never inspire. It just turns us into an insipid version of the conservative parties.

The only changes worth making are the big ones. Left-of-Centre parties need to redefine the role of government and inspire a new generation of supporters. Richard Nixon once scribbled 'Government doesn't work' on one of his briefing documents. From what I can see, these days the welfare state doesn't work. It's the logical place to start in rethinking the Labor project: showing our supporters how market-based economic policies need not be incompatible with equality of opportunity, how the welfare state can lift the poor into a new world of skills and work. The Government is trying with Working Nation, but we need to go further.

Richard Nixon US Pres. 1969–74

1996

*The Keating Government was routed at the election on 2 March, losing 31
seats and winning just 49 in a Parliament of 148. Some of the seats lost were
similar to mine in their socioeconomic profile, such as Lindsay in outer
Western Sydney with a 12 per cent swing against Labor. So I was happy to
retain Werriwa with a margin of 6.2 per cent. My hard work had paid off.*

*The demoralised Labor Caucus gathered in Canberra later that month
and elected Kim Beazley as its new Leader unopposed and Gareth Evans as
its Deputy Leader. In a tight ballot, Evans, who had moved from the Senate
to the Victorian seat of Holt, defeated Simon Crean by two votes. I voted for
Evans. The meeting also elected a new frontbench and I became the Shadow
Minister for Competition Policy, Assistant to the Shadow Treasurer and
Shadow Minister for Local Government.*

At this point in the Diaries, *Beazley becomes a dominant figure. For the
next nine years he was either ALP Leader or striving to regain that position. He
was at the centre of major policy debates and then the internal instability that
damaged the Party after the 2001 election. I made many entries about him
because of his prominence and my belief that he was taking the ALP in the
wrong direction, both in terms of its policies and with its organisational culture.*

*During my eleven years in Parliament, I preferred to drive to Canberra
rather than fly (from my home in Campbelltown, it is just two hours door to
door). The drive took me past Lake George, after which the seat of Werriwa
was named. ('Werriwa' is the Aboriginal term for the lake, which formed
part of the electorate when it was created in 1901.) Along the Hume Highway*

between Goulburn and Lake George is a fine stand of poplars—lush green in summer, but bare and bleak-looking in winter. They always marked the change of seasons for me, and also the change in our political fortunes. In mid-1996, I looked at them and saw our winter of discontent, wondering how many more times the leaves needed to fall before we would be returned to government and I became a Federal Labor Minister.

By the end of 1996, the signs were still discouraging. The new Liberal Member for Lindsay, Jackie Kelly, had been disqualified in the Court of Disputed Returns and a by-election for the seat was held on 19 October. Kelly increased her margin with a 5 per cent swing; compared with the 1993 result, this represented a combined swing to the Liberal Party of 17 per cent. I should have known then that many more winters of discontent lay ahead.

Tuesday, 19 March

The first Caucus meeting since our election defeat. Keating goes through the motions of reporting to the colleagues and then gives the media the slip by going out the back door while the Caucus Returning Officer, Michael Forshaw, distracts them out the front. Paul's had a gut full of this place. He reckons the result is not as bad as 1975, 'the like of which we will never see again'. The result, in fact, is only marginally better—another wipe-out.

But what the hell, he's been a magnificent reformer, running the gauntlet and only getting caught after thirteen years of a nation-building Labor Government. Sounds all right to me. But the media jokers don't get it—Laurie Oakes on Channel Nine wonders how the Caucus could possibly have given him two standing ovations. Because he did great things for the movement and the country, often at great personal cost. That's why. He didn't spend his public life vegetating in a little cubicle in the press gallery, trying to fit his head onto the TV screen every night with smart-arse commentary. That's why.

All Labor leaderships end in defeat or death. But Paul has ended up better than most. Watson and Hughes turned to the dark side. Fisher left politics in disgust. Tudor and Charlton are all but forgotten. Scullin was

Laurie Oakes Channel Nine political correspondent in Canberra, nicknamed 'Jabba the Hutt', a character from the *Star Wars* movies
Chris Watson Fed. ALP Leader 1901–07; PM 1904; later he left the ALP and became associated with conservative politics
Billy Hughes Fed. ALP Leader 1915–16; PM 1915–23; he left the ALP in 1916 during the split over conscription and became a long-serving conservative MP
Andrew Fisher Fed. ALP Leader 1907–15; PM 1908–09, 1910–13, 1914–15
Frank Tudor Fed. ALP Leader 1916–22
Matt Charlton Fed. ALP Leader 1922–28
James Scullin Fed. ALP Leader 1928–35; PM 1929–32

broken by his Caucus and then flogged by the electorate. Curtin and Chifley died on the job, exhausted by public office. At his funeral, a woman asked if Curtin was going to heaven, to which her friend replied, 'I know he's there because Labor leaders have their hell on earth'.

Evatt and Calwell were three-time losers. Gough was a magnificent martyr to the cause, but badly smashed in 1975 and again two years later. Hayden was robbed of the top job and then so embittered by the experience that he became a conservative. Hawke was humiliated by Caucus and then by his own stupidity in the media. And Keating? The True Believers will always love him, and as for the rest of the place, he probably doesn't care anyway.

Keating's a conviction politician. There are two types in this business. Those who refer issues to the opinion polls and those who refer issues to first principles. Politicians who see a public misunderstanding and try to exploit it versus those who try to correct the misunderstanding and advance public debate.

The Keating experience highlights the great question of leadership: how hard to push the reform agenda. I liked the way Henry Kissinger expressed it when he was out here in November:

> The hardest problem for a leader is to take his society from where it is to where it has never been, and that is a lonely task. If he gets too far ahead of his people he will be destroyed. If he is too cautious, problems will overwhelm him. How to find that middle ground is the overwhelming problem of politics. It is a problem I do not believe any society that I know has solved.

What is the answer? Two steps forward, one step back. Explaining and re-explaining to old constituencies why change is inevitable, while generating new support from the beneficiaries of reform. We lost the election because we did not do enough explaining and re-explaining. Economic restructuring in Australia has led to political restructuring. All the old institutions of Labor are under pressure: the union movement, the public sector, the traditional working class.

All Howard did was sit back and take advantage of these pressures, milking the time-for-change sentiment for all it was worth. Despite a big

---

John Curtin Fed. ALP Leader 1935–45; PM 1941–45
Ben Chifley Fed. ALP Leader 1945–51; PM 1945–49

'Doc' Evatt Fed. ALP Leader 1951–60
Henry Kissinger Head, US Nat. Security Council 1969–75 and US Sec. of State 1973–77

parliamentary majority, he still doesn't get it. He's an old fogey in an era of non-stop change. This is Howard's fatal contradiction: the tension between being an economic reformer and a social conservative.

But how seriously will the Labor movement remake itself post-Keating? Not a lot, if you listen to Leo McLeay, who tells me not to worry too much about new ideas: 'They only matter if they can win votes for us'. Still, he's keen to advance greenhorns like me through the system. He reckons if we had won the election, Keating would have put me into Cabinet in Brian Howe's old job of Housing and Regional Development.

Thursday, 21 March

The first meeting of the new Shadow Ministry. If I felt tired and daunted by the task ahead, as I did for 30 seconds, how must these former ministers around the table feel? Beazley tells us to do lots of community functions, but by this he means ethnic communities. No wonder the ethnic associations have good access to the system. Unlike the Anglos, they suck up to the politicians at organised events.

Had lunch with Gareth Evans, who is struggling with his new responsibilities. He finds it hard to think in terms of economic linkages, rather than the one-off events and facts of foreign affairs. I took him to the staff cafeteria, the first time he had been there after eight years in the building. Couldn't half-tell, he didn't have a cent on him. Who said we got out of touch during our time in Government?

Still, he was very frank, bagging Beazley for his habit of slipping off the main game and returning to his comfort zone: 'He would be as happy to be Leader of the Opposition as Prime Minister. That's what I can do, prod him along'. It sounds like an interesting relationship between our new Leader and Deputy Leader.

It also raises doubts about Beazley's reliability. After the election, he was wrapping me all over the place, building up expectations about my role on the frontbench, but then he tried to slot me into Aboriginal Affairs. After Robert Tickner's experience, it's a death seat for Labor MPs. With Leo's help, I got out of there to take on some economic jobs. A much better fit with my background and interests.

Leo McLeay ALP member, Grayndler 1979–93; Watson 1993–2004; House of Representatives Speaker 1989–93; ALP Chief Whip 1993–2001
Gareth Evans ALP member, Holt 1996–99; Dep. Opposition Leader and Shadow Treas. 1996–98

Kim Beazley ALP member, Brand 1996– ; Opposition Leader 1996–2001
Robert Tickner ALP member, Hughes 1984–96; Aboriginal Affairs Min. 1990–96

Thursday, 18 April

I've started the grinding cycle of an Opposition frontbencher. A bizarre lunch at the *SMH* last week, organised by its editor, John Alexander, to work out ways of lifting their circulation in Western Sydney. It is not exactly rocket science. How about reporting some stories from the region? Alexander put an elitist point of view, saying that he 'doesn't want any losers in the paper', stories about poverty and social justice. Well, there goes the West.

The media try to pretend that they do things in the public interest. In fact, they are just another form of commerce, beating up stories and sensationalising the news to sell papers, lift ratings and make profits. I won't be holding my breath waiting for the *Herald* to make money in Western Sydney.

Yesterday's Shadow Ministry had a robust discussion on Aboriginal affairs. Most of the Shadows want to join the Government in putting the blackfellas out to dry—give them a bit of a kicking to win votes in middle-class suburbia, Queensland and WA. And I thought I was a hard bastard.

After the meeting, Peter Baldwin and I went to see Beazley to get his approval for the book we plan to write on a new policy agenda for Labor. Beazley's very happy with the project, especially given his concern that 'We are five to ten years behind in policy development'. He reckons that Baldwin and I are the only two Labor MPs thinking on a different plane. Or maybe he says that to all the boys.

Earlier today the mighty Gareth told me that 'I want to go back to Foreign Affairs'. He's trying to rote-learn the economy and it's not working. He knows nothing about National Competition Policy and Hilmer. It's really quite scary, shattering the image I had of super-competent Hawke and Keating ministers. The more I see of the frontbench, the more sceptical I become.

Tuesday, 23 April

Paul Keating resigns from Parliament. The term commonly used to describe his career is 'intensity'. No one in this place pursued what he believed in with as much drive and intensity. He believed in Labor as a cause for the good society, not just some naked grab for power.

Peter Baldwin ALP member, Sydney 1983–98; min. in Hawke and Keating govts; Shadow Education Min. 1996–97

Monday, 27 May

Beazley tells the Shadow Ministry that 'Opposition is all about pissing on them and pissing off'—a hit-and-run style of politics. He sees our political recovery as hinging on the exploitation of the Government's failings and public discontent, issue by issue. I've got that sinking feeling that, for all his rhetoric, Kim is not going to deliver a new, modern Labor agenda. That's his philosophy: piss on them and then piss off.

It will never suffice. Even in Opposition, a political party needs a philosophy of government, a set of ideas that inspires our supporters and gives the show some purpose beyond an opportunistic grab for power. At the end of the day, only the big things really count. It's the cause, comrades, it's the cause that matters.

If you listen to the debates and amendments in Federal Parliament, all they are doing is tinkering at the edges with the trademarks established by Keating on economic policy, and by Whitlam and Howe on social policy. The only people who make a difference in this place are the agenda-setters.

Thursday, 13 June

I've been drawn into an unbelievable drama about a draft speech on competition policy to the NSW Labor Council. Having briefed the Shadow Ministry on my approach, I set out a position that embraces competition policy while also demonstrating greater sensitivity to public-interest issues in the non-traded sector. There's not much to be gained in efficiency and GDP from the application of Hilmer to small domestic industries. The big gains are in the traded sector, as the tariff reductions have already shown.

And the reaction to this unexceptional position? Hysteria from Evans and harassment from Beazley. Gareth was in Tokyo, taking a break from his grief therapy after our election loss, yet sending back corrections to the speech like a schoolmaster. Christ, this is a bloke who knew nothing about Hilmer a few weeks ago. Egged on by his economics adviser, Paul Grimes, they have put me through the wringer.

Beazley called me on the mobile while I was out doorknocking in Blaxland (the by-election caused by Keating's resignation), telling me to cave in to Gareth's instructions. How reliable is this big bloke? A few weeks ago I was in his office and he was saying that I would be the next Labor Leader, 'sitting in this chair eight years from now'. But under pressure from Evans, he had me scribbling down changes on a piece of paper in the back streets of Bankstown. I've gone from would-be Leader to Gareth's steno. Thanks, Kim.

In truth, the longer the Party takes to redefine itself, the harder it will be to mount an effective attack on the other side. Most of our people are still walking around like zombies, trying to figure out what went wrong. It is now eighteen months since Labor topped 40 per cent of the primary vote in the polls. Maybe it would have been better if Keating had stayed on for nine months to allow a proper review and rethink of what we are about. From there, we could have repositioned ourselves for an effective attack on the Government.

Tuesday, 13 August

A Shadow Ministry meeting in Perth and things get worse. Beazley never talks about the future. He makes speeches and briefs the media as if he is scared of the future. Everything is about today's political opportunity, today's piss. I suppose that's how opportunists live: just for today. A leader's role should be to lead, to show people what can be.

The meeting receives a briefing from Gary Gray, who tells us that all Shadow Ministerial speeches need to be read and checked by David Epstein and Greg Turnbull in Beazley's office before they go out. Great, now we have a thought police with no thoughts of their own. And Epstein of all people, who got Ralph Willis into so much trouble with the fake Kennett letter in the last campaign.

This really is hard-going. Here I am, working my ringer out, wandering all over the country listening to other people's plumbing in over-rated hotels, while MPs like Ted Grace (one of the Opposition's Deputy Whips) get paid more money. Those Whips are special—highly paid loafers who hate it when the Shadow Ministers call divisions in the House and make them do a bit of work. I call a fair number of divisions—I have to, given all the legislation I handle in the House, yet they chip me for it. Now Gray, the mastermind of our 1996 campaign, has ordered the degrading experience of a staff veto. Opposition politics feels like dog shit on the boot of democracy.

Gary Gray ALP Nat. Sec. 1993–2000
David Epstein A senior adviser in Kim Beazley's office
Greg Turnbull Kim Beazley's Press Sec. 1996–2001
fake Kennett letter In the last days of the 1996 Fed. election campaign, Ralph Willis released a letter supposedly written by Jeff Kennett to John Howard, indicating Howard had a secret plan to cut Fed. funding to the States. David Epstein and Gary Gray were involved in the decision to release the letter as quickly as possible before it could be comprehensively checked for authenticity. The letter turned out to be fake, an embarrassment to the Labor campaign
Ted Grace ALP member, Fowler 1984–98; ALP Deputy Whip 1990–98

Tuesday, 20 August

The first Budget of the Howard Government and they have slashed everything. In the chamber, before Costello's speech, our people who had been in the lock-up were cock-a-hoop. Yet the likes of Tim Fischer on the Government side were not taking any crap—they seem to think they are on a winner.

Yesterday I wandered around to the front of the building to have a look at the union protest/riot. Part of me wanted to join in, to grab a sledgehammer and rip and tear against the Tories and their tin-pot Parliament. But I walked away, all neat and respectable. Still, I know how those blokes feel, and good on them for having a go. The shame is they have copped it in the media big time.

Talking of storming the citadel, it was a different topic of conversation at today's meeting of the NSW Right. The main agenda item was the Government's move to reclaim frequent flyer points from MPs. The complaints went on forever, as if the world were ending. I chipped in facetiously, 'Gee, this must be a bad government'. But the rotten rorters agreed, they thought I was being serious!

This is what the Bourbons must have been like at Versailles on Bastille Day—self-indulgent and arrogant. A thousand cuts in the Budget affecting the poor and disadvantaged, but the NSW Right is only worried about one thing. This is not a political organisation, it's a pocket-lining society.

One of the programs abolished is Better Cities, dashing my hopes for the redevelopment of the public housing estates in Campbelltown (in Werriwa). A pox on Howard and Costello and their stinking, rotten Budget. When we were in Government, I convinced Brian Howe to fund the redevelopment and make it a whole-of-government exercise—upgrading the housing stock, but also introducing private ownership and overhauling the education, employment and welfare systems on the estates.

Suburbs like Claymore, Airds and Macquarie Fields have 40 per cent unemployment and 80 per cent welfare dependency rates. Placing so many disadvantaged people in a disadvantaged place multiplies and compounds the problems. The location itself—just living there—makes people worse off, more disadvantaged than they would otherwise be. They have lost the self-esteem and positive life messages that come from living in a normal suburb and holding down a regular job.

Peter Costello Lib. member, Higgins 1990– ; Fed. Treas. 1996–
Tim Fischer NP member, Farrer 1984–2001; NP Leader 1990–99; Dep. PM 1996–99

Better Cities program An initiative of Brian Howe under the Keating govt to provide additional funding for urban redevelopment projects

Often bureaucrats or community workers come into the estates and launch an innovative program for a single service. But it's never enough. Poverty is a whole-of-life problem, a state of chaos and despair that requires a whole-of-government and community solution. That's what I wanted Better Cities to be: an innovative, poverty-busting scheme that brought all the service-providers together. A role model for overcoming the tragedy of underclass in this country. A great Labor thing to do. But now it's gone, and all the NSW Right can do is talk about frequent flyer points. Somebody save me.

Wednesday, 18 September

Little Michael Lee takes a shot at me for advocating the redistribution of health funding in NSW in a speech on the State Grants Bill. The equity arguments are overwhelming. My electorate has 130 000 people, most of them young families, but not one public hospital within its boundaries. The Federal electorate of Sydney has seven public hospitals. Health spending in the centre of Sydney is $948 per person; in Western Sydney it is less than $400. I made my points in the House, reminding them that most of Sydney's public hospitals are located where the people used to live, not where they live now and the suburbs to which they are continuing to move. Every year close to 80 000 patients leave Sydney's Greater West to receive basic care, often travelling for more than three hours to do so.

How could a Labor MP be silent about such an imbalance, especially when his own electorate is being ripped off? Easily, according to Lee, because it might upset people in the inner city. I put to him the argument that it might help us with the Lindsay by-election, where obviously the people in Penrith want Federal Labor to do more for them. His response: 'I just want a policy to elect Ross Free (the former Labor Member), not start World War III in health funding'.

Lee's such a flogger, typical of the culture of the NSW Right: always trying to control things, always trying to narrow the debate, always trying to stand over people. He prefers a political fix to a political fight. The irony, of course, is that one of the things hurting us in Lindsay is our failure to do anything about the (047) telephone zone during thirteen years in Government. That would have been a policy to get Ross Free re-elected in the first place.

Michael Lee Shadow Health Min. 1996–98

Tuesday, 8 October

There are two types of people in politics: the goers and the blockers. Unfortunately, our Party has too many of the latter: quasi-conservatives who missed their real calling in life. They have no claim to being prominent at all. Their miserable role is to hold down ideas and block progress. They should have got jobs as book-keepers or spec-holders, instead of hanging around here.

Monday, 28 October

A terrible result for Labor in the Lindsay by-election, with no rebound from our flogging in March or backlash against the Costello Budget. The scary thing is, on all the demographic figures provided by the Parliamentary Library, Lindsay is very similar to Werriwa—outer suburban, young families, upwardly mobile working class. Western Sydney is changing and the trends are against us.

In the Shadow Ministry post-mortem, Duncan Kerr made a telling point: 'We must recognise that Howard is talking in code to our supporters, and our views are seen as part of an elite'. Many of the Shadows seem to think that we lost the last election because of economic issues, but Duncan has hit the nail on the head. Our problems relate to social issues and values. Whether we like it or not, the mob see us representing the so-called minorities and Howard standing for the silent majority (as Nixon used to call them).

Earlier in the day, Duncan told me that during the truck blockade of Parliament House in early 1995, Keating wanted to call in the army to clear them out of the place. Sounds pretty radical. Mind you, it would have fixed up the protestors, watching their logging trucks being blown away by tank-fire!

At Shadow Ministry, Beazley tells us he is worried about an early double dissolution election and that we should start developing policy. He's a funny sort of Leader: no guidance as to what these policies might be, no philosophy to direct and shape the process, no ideas of his own, just an order to commence. He's like a general ordering his army to march, but not saying in which direction. Last week Maxine McKew told me that at a recent Fairfax lunch, Beazley declared himself to be as socially conservative as Howard. Well, that's more philosophy and direction than he has given us.

One of the hardest things about the frontbench is handling Parliament—getting the mood and atmospherics right, especially during

---

Duncan Kerr ALP member, Denison 1987– ; min. in Keating govt; Shadow Immigration Min. 1996–97

Maxine McKew ABC journalist

Question Time. Earlier in the month I launched an attack on John Fahey over a pecuniary conflict of interest, but it fell flat. Howard succeeded in reducing my claims to their weakest point. The lesson is: always target the weak ministers. Don't give the Government's best performers like Howard and Costello a chance to defend them. Only attack the strong ministers with quality material and an element of surprise.

The House is a chamber of assertion, not explanation. Even with a weak argument, a confident, assertive speech can carry the day. Question Time requires a cool, analytical approach, the ability to anticipate various scenarios and not to be deterred by the Government's bullshit and bravado.

I seem to be doing quite well within the Party. The media have tagged me as one of our 'rising stars', along with Lindsay Tanner. It's a trap for young players, however. As Daryl Melham said to me, 'Understand that you are surrounded by assassins'. It's a lovely business, politics. The established players never miss a chance to keep you down, to remind you of your place in the pecking order. It's never overt, but it's always there. Surrounded by assassins.

Contrast, for instance, my struggle to change our petrol policy with the way in which Beazley's leadership group does business. Whatever they want to push through, they just announce it, without consultation. When I put forward a policy for lower petrol prices by opening up competition at the wholesale and retail level, it took me five Shadow Ministry meetings to get it through. It was like pulling teeth, getting past a thousand questions and tiny objections from Crean and Evans.

When they are not in competition with the young guys, Crean and Evans are at each other. Each morning, the Question Time tactics meeting is dominated by these two jostling for the best material and questions, with Big Kim sitting in the middle, trying to look neutral. It may fuel their egos, but for the rest of us, it's becoming a joke.

Wednesday, 20 November

Bill and Hillary Clinton are visiting Australia to rest up after their recent election campaign. He's an amazingly charismatic speaker, as he showed in

---

John Fahey Lib. NSW Premier 1992–95; Lib. member, Macarthur 1996–2001; Finance Min. 1996–2001
Daryl Melham ALP member, Banks 1990– ; Shadow Aboriginal & Torres Strait Islander Affairs Min. 1996–2000

Simon Crean Shadow Industry & Regional Development Min., Manager of Opposition Business 1996–98
Bill Clinton US Pres. 1993–2001

his address to a joint sitting of Parliament. He has the gift of being able to give each person in the audience the impression that he is speaking to them and them alone. In an age of mass media, he is the ultimate personal communicator.

Beazley gave a nice welcome speech in the House. On the other frontbench, the infantile Downer refused to join in the applause—so typical of the Tories' lack of generosity. I may be a hard and intense person, but even I know that generosity matters. The two traits are not necessarily incompatible. In fact, they are the best combination for public life: a hard head and a warm heart.

Behind the scenes, the Coalition are a dirty piece of work. Downer's spite reminds me of the shit-sheet on Paul Keating I found earlier in the year, left behind on our side of the chamber in the desk used by Neil Andrew from the previous Parliament. For all their talk of God and family, the Tories are a bunch of grubs—one hand on the Bible and the other up their clacker.

Tuesday, 3 December

A few beers after work and a chat with Syd Hickman, Beazley's Chief of Staff. Other Opposition staffers have no idea what Syd does of a day, joking that he plays battleships at his desk. Hopefully that's right and he doesn't run our political strategy. Syd reckons, 'The good news is that Howard has lost the elites, the opinion leaders. Without them the workers don't know what to think and we are a good chance of getting them back'. What patronising nonsense. Howard is doing well because of the gap between elite opinion and working-class commonsense. If this bloke is a battleship, then it's the *Belgrano*.

Last fortnight I did a listening tour through Mackay, Rockhampton and Whyalla, a good cross-section of regional Australia. The workers have their opinions, based on personal experience and an earthy, practical view of the world. I'd say they regard the elites as a bunch of wankers. What they want from Labor is a problem-solving approach to government: decent services, a good education for their kids and a public sector that offsets the inequality of the open economy. They want us to take the old statism (government-led solutions) of Labor's origins and make it modern and relevant to their lives.

When it comes to the elites, I don't blame people for being disillusioned with the media. Just look at the parliamentary press gallery. Very

---

Alexander Downer Foreign Affairs Min. 1996–   **Neil Andrew** Lib. member, Wakefield 1983–2004

few journalists do any digging or original research on public policy and Government administration. Most are just a funnel for Government press releases. Because they rarely check their material, they always assume that the Opposition is engaged in scare-mongering and point-scoring, marking us down before we even start. The system is geared against Shadow Ministers who take public administration and policy seriously.

1997

The major political event of the year was the rise of Pauline Hanson after her xenophobic maiden speech to Parliament on 10 September 1996. The Labor Opposition was practising its own slice of Hansonism, with a strongly protectionist stance in the tariff debate. I was opposed to this repositioning on economic policy and argued against it in Shadow Cabinet. It was the catalyst for my disillusionment with Beazley and belief that he was an opportunist, rather than a conviction politician.

I was growing unhappy in my role as a Labor frontbencher but paradoxically also received a significant promotion that took me closer to the frontline of national political debates. On 27 March, Beazley made me Shadow Minister for Education and Youth Affairs. I was tasked with lifting our profile in this important area and taking on Minister Amanda Vanstone. Perhaps I had some success, as the Prime Minister demoted her on 9 October and appointed David Kemp as Minister for Employment, Education, Training and Youth Affairs.

This was also the year in which my marriage to Gabrielle Gwyther ended. (We separated at the end of 1997 and were divorced at the beginning of 1999.) The diary mentions our marriage problems in passing—I only ever recorded personal matters if they had a direct impact on my work. Gwyther comes back into the diaries in 2003 and 2004, when she tried to cause me political grief. In these later entries, I mention the reasons for our marriage break-up and how I decided to handle the matter publicly.

Tuesday, 4 February

Part of our problem is that Howard has inverted the politics of envy. Traditionally, Labor has benefited from the Australian ethos of cutting down tall poppies—it matched our passion for redistributing resources and attacking inequality. But now the middle class is more inclined to look down the social ladder (at the small poppies), envious of the (undeserved) government money paid to the unemployed, migrants, Aborigines and the rest of the underclass. The long-running sensationalism of the tabloid media on these issues has had an impact.

Our challenge is to focus attention back up the ladder at the corporate chiefs ripping off the tax system, at the banks ripping off their customers, at the worst excesses of global capitalism. At Shadow Ministry I put this strategy to Bob McMullan and Carmen Lawrence, both of whom understand the importance of upwards envy. That's our slogan for the future: Beazley bashes banks, bowsers and bosses.

We also need a new communications strategy. Whether we like it or not, the Parliament has become irrelevant—people get their political information elsewhere. Current-affairs programs and talkback radio have become the natural forums for public discussion. Our democracy is now in the hands of media moguls and shock-jocks. Politicians no longer need to win the Parliament to win elections. They need to win talkback radio. It's horrible but true.

Friday, 14 February

Ross Cameron, the brilliant but creepy Liberal Member for Parramatta, has talked me into participating in his youth leadership forum in Canberra. I rather suspect it's a front for mobilising young Christian soldiers, plus some quality box for Ross. Thank goodness I wasn't the only one sucked in. Howard and Beazley addressed the opening session yesterday and gave some interesting insights into their background.

As the youngest child growing up in an ultra-conservative family, Howard was fearful of social change, not knowing what to do about it when it came. To my ears, it sounded a bit pathetic, so insecure and inward-looking. Beazley is very much his father's son. His formative experience in

---

Bob McMullan ACT ALP Sen. 1988–96; min. in Keating govt; ALP member, Canberra 1996–98; Fraser 1998– ; Shadow Industrial Relations Min. 1996–98; nicknamed 'Comb-over'

Carmen Lawrence Shadow Environment & the Arts Min. 1996–97

politics was tagging along to meetings to hear people attack his father. He would sit outside ALP State Executive meetings in Perth 'feeling very depressed' while Kim Senior faced condemnation and disciplinary charges inside. That says a fair bit about Junior: his natural pessimism in politics, his dislike of conflict, and his determination to redeem and honour the Beazley name.

Earlier in the week I had a sharp reminder of how anti-intellectualism is still alive inside the ALP. I spoke in the House on the limits of the Productivity Commission and its over-reliance on neoclassical economics and rational economic behaviour. I drew on the work of Robert Putnam and Francis Fukuyama (of *End of History* fame) in highlighting the importance of social capital and cooperation to the creation of prosperity. Economic activity is now far too complex for the reductionism of general theories. The problem with the assumption about rational economic man is that it underrates the potential of cooperation as a productive force in our economy. It may well be that competition is the best way to induce economic efficiency, but cooperation is also needed to lift productivity and efficiency in the production of economic and social goods.

My speech didn't impress Ralph Willis, who told me that it sounded like a 'high-falutin' speech, and anyway, 'Who is this Fucking-yama?' Obviously someone who didn't have much impact on the last Labor Treasurer.

Tuesday, 25 February

There is no quality journalism in Australia, only the pretence of it. Earlier in the year, *Four Corners* asked me to cooperate with a show they were doing on the Federal ALP. No worries, I did a long interview and they followed me around the electorate a bit (I was their outer-suburban specimen). On Australia Day they came to the local park for the Campbelltown Council festivities and citizenship ceremony. I was there as the local member. It all seemed straightforward until the program aired last night. It was mainly an exposé on ethnic branch-stacking, replete with voice filters to protect the identity of their star witnesses.

Disgracefully, the footage they used to highlight the branch-stacking came from the Campbelltown citizenship ceremony. These poor, innocent

---

Kim Beazley (Senior) ALP member, Fremantle 1945–77; Education Min. in Whitlam govt, 1972–75
Productivity Commission A Fed. govt agency producing reports and recommendations to the govt on economic reform

Robert Putnam American academic and leading authority on social capital
Francis Fukuyama American author on foreign policy, democratic capitalism and social trust

constituents, who were filmed walking up to the stage to collect their citizenship certificates on Australia Day, have been portrayed on ABC television as ethnic stacks, ostensibly collecting their rorted ALP membership. What a gross defamation. I rang the program to complain and asked for an on-air apology but they couldn't care less, they see no harm in reporting of this kind. And this is the national broadcaster.

Well, as long as my arse points to the ground, I won't have anything to do with *Four Corners*. It is easier to respect the tabloids and talkback radio. At least they know that the modern media has degenerated into just another form of commerce and infotainment, and cater for it accordingly. The ABC still tries to justify itself in the so-called public interest. Ask the new citizens in Campbelltown about that.

Monday, 3 March

If the greed and avarice of Labor Caucus members are representative of social values in this country, then the cause of altruism and socialism is well and truly lost. Everywhere I turn in this place, colleagues are talking about trips, travel allowance and other entitlements. The show is finding its comfort level—accepting our lot in Opposition and milking the largesse of the parliamentary club for all it's worth. If Labor MPs are a bunch of greedy bastards, what hope is there for personal sacrifice and collectivism in the rest of society?

Bad news on the policy front. Beazley, Evans and Crean have appeared on the front cover of *Business Review Weekly* under the banner 'Keating Is Dead' (subheading 'Labor's new guard rejects his faith in free markets'). The article is a long advertisement for so-called industry policy—throwing subsidies, bounties and tariffs at companies that are not good enough to compete successfully in the market economy. This is the mug's game that Keating used to talk about: businesspeople who reckon the world is full of bludgers and hippies, yet want the taxpayers to subsidise their company to the eyeballs, then trot off to vote for the Coalition. Social welfare is bad. Industry welfare is wonderful.

Parts of the article are frightening:

While both sides (of politics) talk about intervention in situations of market failure, the definition being applied by Labor is broader than even the wettest of Government Ministers is willing to propose. Labor now considers it a market failure if opportunities to develop new industries are missed ... Industry spokesman Simon Crean says that the fiscal implications of industry and regional policies are secondary to getting successful programs working ... He is not worried by arguments that his vision for regional development and industry policy could be achieved only at a high price.

Lindsay Tanner also gets in on the act, bagging the economic management of the Keating Government because 'It retreated from job creation, industry assistance, infrastructure building and Keynesian pump-priming'. Good grief, when the three senior Right-wingers in the Party combine with a Young Turk on the Left, maybe Keating is dead. Mind you, this industry policy pap has been around for a while—Smith and Swan were always pushing it during our last years in Government.

As ever, Big Kim has gone along for the ride. One of the golden rules of Australian politics is that every successful ALP Leader has confronted the Party, slaughtering its sacred cows. Now Beazley has embraced one of the shibboleths of the 1970s: government subsidies and central planning of the economy. To paraphrase Keating, these blokes can't plan for what happens in Caucus, let alone plan a complex and dynamic information-based economy.

I always thought the role of modern Labor is to make the private sector compete, to keep the capitalists honest, using the benefits of market competition to drive down prices for working-class consumers. Beazley and co. have gone back to the caveman policy of propping up producer interests, at a huge cost to taxpayers and consumers. Old Labor, indeed. Keating must be off his tree with anger.

Friday, 14 March

A great day's cricket, playing for the Parliamentary XI against the Crusaders at Albert Park in Melbourne. Our side was reinforced by (former Australian fast bowler) Merv Hughes and the middle-order batting wizardry of John Howard. Actually, he's hopeless. A real rabbit with the bat and The Man From Unco with the ball, the sort of player who was an automatic selection as scorer in schoolboy teams. I walked away from the ground thinking, there goes John Howard, a man of few obvious talents.

He's also a smelly little bastard. The rest of the boys tubbed up with a group shower after the match, but not the PM. He was last seen heading off for his plane in his full cricket kit. He must have thought Big Merv was a soap-catcher.

Lindsay Tanner Shadow Transport Min. 1996–98
Stephen Smith Shadow Trade Min. 1996–97;
Shadow Resources & Energy Min. 1997–98

Wayne Swan Adviser to Kim Beazley 1996–98

Thursday, 27 March

Parliament closes down for Easter and Beazley makes me Shadow Minister for Education and Youth Affairs, with Peter Baldwin moving to Finance. The other winner in the reshuffle is Jenny Macklin, who takes on Social Security. Beazley had a nice line at his press conference: 'Some of you may think that Vanstone is her own worst enemy. She has not yet met Mark Latham … Mark is a very aggressive political personality. More aggressive than myself even. Hard to imagine, that'.

For weeks, Leo McLeay had been saying that these changes were in the pipeline. Beazley wants me to give the Party a higher profile in education. The Government has made huge cuts, especially to the universities, but the Democrat spokesperson, Natasha Stott Despoja, has been getting all the media. My performance measures are simple enough: get on TV and radio ahead of Natasha. It's a chance to join the frontline of the big national debates and advance one of the great Labor ideals—equality of opportunity through education.

Monday, 12 May

BHP has announced the closure of its steel plant in Newcastle and the Shadow Ministry is considering our response. It's another chance for Crean to push his industry policy line. In truth, the Hunter region is better off shedding its smokestack image and continuing to diversify into tourism, health, education and high-tech jobs. But Opposition has little to do with the truth. Under Beazley, opportunism always knocks—milking the issue in the media, maximising the public's angst and then moving onto the next opportunity. Pissing on them and then pissing off. Thousands of words have been written about Beazley and his character, but I think just four will suffice: he is an opportunist.

The Shadow Ministry debate on the BHP closure is surreal. We all know nothing can be done and this is simply a point-scoring exercise. It was left to Gareth Evans to drop the clanger, when he said, 'I know this is like farting in church, but what are the makings of a comprehensive steel plan?' He's rooted as Shadow Treasurer, but the old Gareth still has a great turn of phrase. Crean reckons an ALP committee including (backbenchers)

Jenny Macklin ALP member, Jagajaga 1996– ; Shadow Aged, Family & Community Services Min. 1996–97; Shadow Social Security & the Aged Min. 1997–98

Amanda Vanstone SA Lib. Sen. 1984– ; Employment, Education, Training & Youth Affairs Min. 1996–97
Natasha Stott Despoja SA Dem. Sen. 1995–

Colin Hollis, Allan Morris and Rod Sawford will produce the steel plan and 'get the company to invest in new technology'. We might as well ask them to cure cancer while they are at it.

Monday, 2 June

Beazley is the first Labor Leader to take our thinking backwards. A reform party must always look to the future, not the retro-economics of tariffs and industry subsidies. Blind Freddy can see that these are no longer effective policy tools in the modern economy. International competitiveness is being determined by workforce skills and the quality of a nation's education system, not the size of its tariff walls.

If Beazley reckons we are ten years behind other social democratic parties in policy development, why is he taking us back twenty years in economic policy? I don't see any difference between him and Malcolm Fraser: both patriarchal social conservatives and supporters of the post-Federation settlement—protectionism and centralised industrial relations. For the ALP, this is impossible to justify; we're ending the twentieth century with the same framework as when we started. Beazley and his cabal must see this as a big vote winner, but that's their mistake. Keating didn't lose the last election on economic policy; he lost it on social issues, on social values.

Tuesday, 24 June

Is there no end to the Beazley/Crean campaign on tariffs? First it was cars, then textiles, clothing and footwear, and now we have moved onto sugar. Beazley says that reducing the sugar tariff is a big job-security issue when, in reality, no jobs are threatened. It reminds me of Bert Kelly (the former Liberal MP and devout free trader) in his book *One More Nail*: 'There is something frighteningly cynical about a leader who can speak with such conviction when he must know that he is talking economic nonsense. This is even worse than not knowing he is talking nonsense'.

That's our Kim. He complains about the Hanson effect in Asia, but our message on tariffs is no better. Hanson says that Australia shouldn't take their people. Labor says that we shouldn't take their products. Yet we have the hide to call her racist.

Colin Hollis ALP member, Macarthur 1983–84; Throsby 1984–2001
Allan Morris ALP member, Newcastle 1983–2001
Rod Sawford ALP member, Port Adelaide 1988–

Malcolm Fraser Lib. PM 1975–83
Pauline Hanson Independent member, Oxley 1996–98, Founder of Pauline Hanson's One Nation Party

On sugar, our position is pure nonsense. Beazley and Crean are arguing for import protection for an industry not actually threatened by imports. It is already operating at international best practice, with the cost of transport from overseas acting as a natural tariff. On top of that, the industry has single-desk marketing arrangements to eliminate domestic competition. And now Labor wants to provide the equivalent of a $26 million subsidy, all for a bunch of farmers who traditionally have been hostile to us. It's a mug's game and we are playing it to the death.

John Kerin once said to me that if Queensland, with its brilliant sunshine, cannot make sugar at an internationally competitive rate, they should give it away. The industry is quite basic and only requires one resource: sunshine. I put these arguments to the Shadow Ministry but nobody is listening.

Wednesday, 25 June

Lunch with Malcolm McGregor, Bob Carr's former Chief of Staff, who ended up working for both sides of politics. At the moment, he's trying to get a gig in Beazley's office but reckons that John Della Bosca and the NSW Right machine have vetoed him. He's a very funny person with a galaxy of stories, the ultimate political raconteur.

Here are his best from lunch today. Malcolm did a fair bit of work for the Housing Industry Association and campaigned against the re-election of the Keating Government in 1993. After the election he ran into Laurie Brereton at the airport but Laurie kept on ignoring him. Malcolm persisted and followed him onto the plane asking, 'Mate, mate, why won't you talk to me?' Eventually Brereton turned around and, with that raspy voice of his, said, quite coolly, 'Because you're a cunt'.

Malcolm was working for the Libs when Downer challenged Hewson for the leadership in mid-1994. Hewson put out a letter attacking the old Tory Establishment (including the Melbourne Club) and, by inference, Downer's association with it. Malcolm compared it to Richard Nixon's Checkers speech (in 1952): 'Hewson was saying he was down-to-earth. Like Nixon, his wife only ever owned a respectable cloth coat, not a mink coat'.

John Della Bosca NSW ALP Gen. Sec. 1990–99
Laurie Brereton Shadow Foreign Affairs Min. 1996–2001
Richard Nixon's Checkers speech As Dwight Eisenhower's running mate for the 1952 US Presidential election, Nixon was embroiled in a secret slush-fund scandal. He got himself out

of trouble through a brilliant televised speech in which he referred to his wife's respectable cloth coat and the donation to his family of a cocker spaniel called Checkers. Nixon said his children loved the dog so much, they were never giving it back

The letter sent Liberal Party President Tony Staley into a spin, telling Malcolm, 'Hewson is out of control. What, attacking the Melbourne Club like that!'

Wednesday, 23 July

I've just finished a long meeting with the ALP National Platform Committee in Melbourne to consider my draft document on education policy for next year's National Conference. It was surreal. The Committee hears all the submissions from Party members, yet I do the draft as Shadow Education Minister and then the factional hacks and union operatives on the Committee get to pick at it.

So, effectively, the Party consultation process was sidelined. I had to do most of the work, but at the meeting itself, the Committee members had the luxury of sitting back and pushing their petty sectional interests. I was quickly jack of it and basically told them to nick off. Not exactly a productive day of ALP policy-making. I reckon the Shadow Ministers should refuse to cooperate until such time as Beazley fixes up the process and does some work of his own, like developing a policy direction and philosophy to guide the Party and the Platform.

Wednesday, 6 August

A phone conversation with Gareth Evans in which he tells me that he has fourteen of the fifteen sections of the new National Platform drafted, 'and that leaves the introduction on values and principles, which needs to be done last'. Is it just me or would it make more sense to set out our values and principles first and then build detailed policies around them? Wouldn't this produce a more coherent and cohesive document? As it is, we are going to end up with a grab-bag of portfolio policies and spending programs, pulled together with a bunch of motherhood statements on Labor values.

This is how the social democratic project has become overloaded, with so many worthy ideas and spending promises that we cannot possibly fund them all. In government, the resources end up being rationed and most of our constituencies are disappointed. We have learned nothing from the Keating years, especially the problems of downwards envy and a disaffected middle class.

We would be much better off with a hard but rational assessment of the programs that are essential to the Labor cause, thereby giving the electorate a realistic assessment of what we can achieve in office. So much of modern politics is a bullshit exercise in falsely raising expectations and being all things to all people. Over the years, I have grown to despise the intellectual dishonesty of it.

Friday, 8 August

A demoralising defeat at the Shadow Ministry meeting at Rockhampton, voted down eighteen to one on protection for the textile, clothing and footwear (TCF) industries. Crean put forward a recommendation for a tariff freeze and I moved an amendment reflecting the recommendation of the industry's representative on the Productivity Commission inquiry (Philip Brass)—that is, to phase down tariff levels between 2000 and 2005 with an industry adjustment package (bounties awarded for value-adding, regional adjustment programs and special support for companies complying with employment and outworker agreements).

Tactically, I knew I would be shot down if I moved a gung-ho, free-trade amendment. I thought I was on safe ground advocating a policy that the industry itself had asked for. But even that didn't satisfy the protectionist sentiment around the table. Only Peter Cook expressed any sympathy for my position, saying how bad it would be if Labor abandoned its commitment to meeting the Bogor targets for APEC. Normally, Shadow Ministry debates do not go to a vote, but this time Beazley asked for a show of hands and I got done like a dinner.

For me, it didn't feel as embarrassing as it might have looked. I'm on the right side of this argument, intellectually and politically. The day will come when the Party regrets embracing this Creanite populist claptrap. As it stands, the Shadow Ministry policy is to freeze the tariffs between 2000 and 2005, and recognise that the APEC target for the clothing industry will not be met under a Labor Government (a 25 per cent tariff will still apply in 2005, but we need to reach 5 per cent in 2010 to comply with APEC). We have just thrown away our credibility on one of the great reforms of the Hawke and Keating governments, opening up free trade in our own part of the world. An act of lunacy.

Tuesday, 26 August

Crean puts in a shocker at Caucus, saying the media perception is that we have gone backwards on industry policy but he reckons that's wrong. This

Peter Cook WA ALP Sen. 1983–2005; Trade Min. 1993–94; Industry Min. 1994–96 in Keating govt is the same bloke who goes to car and TCF rallies and laps up the applause of workers who definitely think we have gone backwards (after all, that's why they are supporting us). But that's wrong—we haven't gone backwards. Now, why would anyone be confused?

It is impossible not to be downhearted about the Party's lurch into retro-economics. All my life I've believed in the cause of Labor and it's terribly sad to see the show go backwards. It makes you wonder what hope there is in other policy areas. And how do I handle this in terms of my own standing inside the Caucus? Just let the ball go through to the keeper, wait for Beazley, Evans and Crean to fall over so that the younger brigade can have a go? Or keep on fighting and getting smashed at Shadow Ministry?

Either way, it's given me a big dose of the melancholies. There was a time when I couldn't imagine not wanting to be part of the House of Representatives. That time has now passed. I can see the futility of walking alone, all that wasted time and effort, trapped inside a show with really bad instincts. And I'm not afraid to let people know how frustrated I am.

Two weeks ago, the young, hustling Rima Barghout (a Green Valley branch member) came to see me in the electorate office, looking for my support for her to get the preselection to take over from Ted Grace in Fowler. I think she got the shock of her life—I told her it was a wasted ambition, that Federal Caucus is a pile of rubbish and I was thinking of getting out. She didn't know what to say. At least she won't come back and bug me any more.

Saturday, 13 September

Recognition at last: Craig McGregor's lengthy profile of me makes the cover of the *SMH Good Weekend* magazine. It's a blockbuster of a piece, putting the weights on me as a future Labor Leader and Prime Minister. McGregor made the same prediction about Keating twenty years ago, so he's not afraid to have a punt on young Right-wingers from Western Sydney.

One thing is for sure, the senior colleagues will hate it. McGregor actually knows where I'm coming from: a rethink of the social democratic project. He also understands my impatience with the ALP machine and our lack of policy direction. As he sees it:

> There are a lot of hopes riding on Mark Latham. With others, he's got
> to turn the Labor Party around. Then he has to turn the electorate

Craig McGregor Author and freelance
journalist

around. And then, like Gough Whitlam, he has to try to overcome the immense inertia of the socio-political system, and the bloody-minded resistance of the conservative hegemony, to turn the nation around. It's a big ask.

Too big, of course. The first thing I have to turn around is my enthusiasm for Labor parliamentary politics. McGregor has got a sniff of my mood: 'Right now, he's frustrated. Disengaged. Battling incipient boredom and impatience'. And thinking of telling them to jam politics up their date.

What I like about the article is the way in which it deals with the politics of paradox. I'm not some one-dimensional, cardboard cut-out politician. I've actually got my own personality and character, as complex as the rest of society. McGregor says that 'intellectually, he's off to the Right, a hardline economic rationalist; but emotionally, he's a Green Valley radical who got into politics because he couldn't stomach the inequality that confronted him every day and, so, decided to do something about it'. Spot on.

So, too, he portrays me as colloquial in my language, yet widely read. Someone with a 'Hoges-like' sense of humour, yet an upfront and abrasive attitude. A gregarious 'blokey bloke', but also a bit of a loner. I wouldn't have it any other way. It's not the best way to further my career, of course. The media prefer the one-dimensional characters—they are easier to describe to the public. But you have to be true to yourself and make your public life as natural and interesting as possible. Adventurism all the way.

The worst thing about the article is the gruesome photo on the front cover. It makes me look like Colonel Walter E. Kurtz (from *Apocalypse Now*)—no hair and plenty of menacing intent. The horror, the horror. At least I'm not like the rest of them in Parliament House, errand boys sent by grocery clerks to collect the bill.

Saturday, 11 October

I'm writing this note on a Qantas flight bound for Sydney, after a therapeutic four weeks in Europe: meetings in London, studying the Mondragon cooperatives in Spain (mutualism in practice) and then a busy program touring through Madrid, Tuscany and Athens. Not a bad lurk for a Valley boy. The best part of it? Not a Caucus colleague in sight. No industry policy debates. No Shadow Ministry meetings. Just a chance to reflect and have a serious think about the future.

In truth, when this plane thuds back onto the runway at Sydney Airport, I'm also going to thud: into reality, personal and political. The sense of dread is right through me. On the personal front, my marriage has effectively ended in circumstances too embarrassing to report. If this were a personal diary I could write up the drama of how it fell apart. But all that emotional stuff in print—it never looks right. Hey, it was bad enough being married to Gabrielle Gwyther without having to write about it. So let's stick to politics.

I dread facing the colleagues in meeting after tedious meeting. But there's also an opportunity to do something special. The post-Keating generation of Labor leaders have conceded the intellectual leadership of the Party with their tariff bullshit. Nobody takes them seriously. Now my generation has its chance—new ideas and new thinking for modern Labor. This is what I've always wanted to do, an opportunity I would have killed for once. It's time to take it.

Hopefully, my book *Civilising Global Capital*, due out next year, will do the trick. It's been a battle to get it finished—a terrible, demented time trying to write the conclusion—but it will be done. And I'm sure it will make an impact, one way or another. From here on, everything in public life is a bonus, a chance to do things on my terms. That's the key: politics as a job, an interest in life, but not my whole life. I've got to broaden out—catch up with the five-eights (mates), learn something new, take on a postgraduate course, think the unthinkable. See every crisis in life as an opportunity. Socrates was right: 'Know thyself'.

Monday, 17 November

More hypocrisy at a Shadow Ministry meeting. How do these people live with themselves? There they sit, complaining about protectionist policies in the US Congress, then they confirm our own terrible, ultra-protectionist decision on sugar. Bob McMullan is the greatest disappointment of all. In private, he is always telling me how he supports my arguments (this time on sugar), but in meetings, he always remains silent. He's got a PhD in unreliability—a backer-and-filler.

1998

After four years in Parliament, my career trajectory nose-dived. It became clear to me that I was not of the modern Labor culture. I was interested in developing new policies, in thinking aloud about new ideas, in reworking the social democratic project in response to social and economic change. My colleagues, led by Beazley and his inner circle, had a different set of interests: the new Party professionalism of polling, spin-doctoring and temporary, artificial political tactics.

As a single man again, I also found myself subject to the relentless rumour-mill in Canberra, mostly from the Labor side of politics—another sign of the cancer inside our culture. I don't mind telling people what I think of them, but that's the point: do it to their face, don't engage in the politics of personal destruction through rumours behind someone's back. I grew up in a larrikin culture that always called a spade a spade. I thought it was a true Labor Party value, part of working-class solidarity in Australia—that is, until I ran into the machine men of the modern Party, who prefer to call a smear a smear, and spread it as widely and viciously as possible.

Confronted by these realities, I was prepared to walk away from a bad political culture and take an independent approach to my work. After the Federal election on 3 October, I did not recontest the Labor Shadow Ministry, instead going to the backbench to write about policy in newspapers and books. In April 1998 my first major book, Civilising Global Capital, *was published. I valued the experience: the research, the intellectual enquiry, the challenge of testing myself in the realm of ideas. I wanted to do more and further develop my skills in this area. I wasn't worried about careerism—I was motivated by job satisfaction and what I regarded as the true cause of Labor.*

Politically, the Howard Government struggled during its first term in office, with ministerial scandals and resignations, and a general sense of incompetence and drift. To recover some momentum and purpose, Howard went to the electorate with a tax reform package, including the introduction of a 10 per cent GST. This suited Beazley's style perfectly; he's always more comfortable campaigning on the things he opposes than the things he might propose. By election night, he had given the Party an impressive comeback from the ruins of 1996, winning eighteen extra seats and putting us within striking distance of victory for 2001. After the election, the main change to the frontbench was that Simon Crean replaced Gareth Evans as Deputy Leader and Shadow Treasurer.

With Labor on the ascendancy, many people thought I had chosen a poor time to go to the backbench. But I was deeply disillusioned and saw Beazley's election result as a false horizon; it related more to the unpopularity of the GST than the quality of Labor's policies or campaign. I was convinced that we could not win in 2001 without a radically different approach, one based on political conviction rather than opportunism.

Friday, 23 January

My first ALP National Conference as a frontbencher, a chance to push through a progressive education platform and put down some markers for further reform. I've busted a boiler in the education portfolio over the last ten months—racing around the country, meeting the interest groups, winning the media battle against Natasha and Junket Guts (Amanda Vanstone) and also writing my book. So it's nice to see some finished product on the table.

My speech to the Conference set out the agenda for educational opportunity and lifelong learning:

- substantially increasing the public resources available to education as the best investment we can make in Australia's future—in particular, regrowing the university and TAFE sectors. Over the next decade, the national government should take full funding and legislative responsibility for all forms of post-secondary education
- making the HECS system fairer and giving students greater flexibility with their income-support entitlements
- supporting the expansion of adult and community education through a new system of learning accounts

- reforming the school funding system to take greater account of socioeconomic need, and ending the cost-shifting between the Federal and State governments
- establishing an innovative School Equity Program for disadvantaged neighbourhoods, along with homework centres and the Parents as Educators' scheme (linking the home and school learning environments)
- effectively resourcing the early years of learning—building a national preschool system.

All underpinned by mutual responsibility: unless people are willing to study hard, to strive for excellence, to accept responsibility for hard work, then the power of education is lost. The speech was well received.

This is where Labor should be putting its money, not into the industry pot. I'm losing the battle against Crean on that front, but at least the Conference was a chance to argue for a modern approach to public policy. That, if nothing else, makes me feel better. A reason to bat on and keep making the case. Labor must ensure that the inequality of the old economy—based on class, wealth and income—is not simply transferred to a new type of social divide between the information-rich and the information-poor. We must socialise the public's access to knowledge and learning. Such an approach also gives Australia its best expression of economic nationalism. Whereas nations once relied on machine power to generate new industries and jobs, they must now harness their citizens' brain power. The only lasting sources of sovereignty and security come from the skills and insights of a nation's people.

One black mark, however. The Conference dinner was held downriver from Hobart and delegates piled onto boats to get there. On arrival, we were ordered to stay on board while Princess Cheryl (Kernot) and her two fawning courtiers, Kim and Gareth, disembarked first. The Labor Royal Family. I hate it when we mimic the hierarchy and snobbery of high society. In Australia, socialism has always been a social habit, much more than a political program. We are all equal in our mateship group. Now, unhappily in the ALP at least, some are more equal than others.

Friday, 30 January

Another Shadow Ministry road show, this time to Bendigo. It's a beautiful old town, full of colonial buildings preserved from the gold rush days. Politically,

Cheryl Kernot Qld Dem. Sen. 1990–97; Australian Dem. Leader 1993–97; joined the ALP and became the ALP candidate for Dickson in late 1997

it's another waste of space. At the evening fundraiser, Beazley gives a rambling speech on regional Australia. There is no structure or purpose to his ideas. He only sounds believable when he's talking about moral issues and his conscience wells up inside him. He would have made a damn fine priest.

The highlight of the night was to be an appearance by our star recruit, Cheryl Kernot, who looked very uncomfortable just sitting in the crowd, having to listen to Beazley do the talking. This ain't the Democrats, baby— get in line and do your apprenticeship along with the rest of us poor, suffering fools. I must say, I'm not a convert to the Kernot strategy. Labor culture is so unique and demanding that she is going to have a terrible time adjusting. If anything, we debase our culture by looking for a quick fix from outside the Party. This new Labor face is a soft option, helping the leadership group avoid the need for new Labor policies.

Earlier in the day, Beazley and Crean announced Labor's support for a book bounty and then came to the Shadow Ministry to get approval for their announcement. What's the point in having these meetings if the press release has already gone out? A complete perversion of process. Crean reckons that a bounty of $13 million per annum will save 450 jobs, some of them in the Bendigo electorate. That works out at $30 000 per job, a tidy wage by today's standards. I pointed this out to the meeting and said that we might as well give the money directly to the workers so they can go and enjoy a quiet life. For once, I got some support (from Brereton). Needless to say, Crean was not amused.

Crean's full of nonsense, arguing that Australia's competitors provide more assistance to their book industries, listing Indonesia, Korea and Thailand (not exactly big players in the English-language book-publishing industry). Then he claimed, 'Singapore has found a clever way of funnelling industry assistance', as if they are the only ones that do it. In fact, most of the industry-support policies he itemised from the Asian nations apply equally in this country. We don't need a Creanite top-up with $30 000 taxpayer-subsidised jobs, thank you.

Tuesday, 24 March

At Caucus this morning there was a stony, almost fearful, silence as Beazley half-heartedly congratulated me on the publication of my book. The colleagues were much more comfortable with news of Nick Sherry's wedding,

Nick Sherry Tas. ALP Sen. 1990– ; Dep. ALP
Leader in Senate and Shadow Finance &
Superannuation Min. 1996–97

giving him a nice round of applause. At least I know where I stand in the pecking order. But in all fairness to Nick, it sounds like he's got his act together after trying to top himself last year. It's hard to imagine feeling that much despair, wanting to kill yourself. Poor bastard, now he's got to spend the rest of his time in public life with people looking at him thinking, 'That's the guy who tried to top himself'. Some people call it gutsy, but I'm not so sure.

An interesting conversation with Leo McLeay, who reckons that Martin Ferguson will be the next Labor PM: 'Kim will lose twice and then Ferguson will take over—he's got the working-class credentials and the support of the unions, just like Hawke'. I don't see it myself. Marn has the public appeal of a wet sandshoe and often talks like one. As much as I disliked saying it, I told Leo that Crean is perfectly positioned. He works the members of Caucus non-stop, using his role as Manager of Opposition Business to good effect. He'll have the numbers when Beazley goes. Howard will run out of puff after two terms and Crean will get his chance as PM. Not the greatest of thoughts, but at least we'll be back on the ministerial carpet.

Wednesday, 8 April

Excellent coverage of my book—it's the talk of the opinion pages, article after article offering positive reviews. People seem to be energised by the realisation that Labor is still alive, offering new ideas and hope. That's what the Party needs, a sense of movement and passion to fire up our beliefs and conviction. Sure, the book is too long and heavy (140 000 words, I must be a maniac). As Carmen Lawrence said, it needed more editing. But it gives the Party something to debate and wrestle with.

After all the publicity it didn't really need a launch, but the mob at Allen & Unwin had one organised at the National Press Club. Unfortunate timing, as we are likely to be swamped in the media by Peter Reith's big blue on the waterfront. It was good of Beazley to do the honours and launch the book, even if he did nick off at the beginning of my speech, ostensibly to get back for Question Time but, in truth, to avoid questions from the press about the controversial stuff.

I've given him a bagging in here, which he deserves. But the good thing about his being so conflict-averse is that he will do anything for

Martin Ferguson ACTU Pres. 1990–96; ALP member, Batman 1996– ; Shadow Employment & Training Min. 1996–98; nicknamed 'Marn'

Peter Reith Lib. member, Flinders 1982, 1984–2001; Workplace Relations & Small Business Min. 1997–2001

anyone. He can't say no. I call him an opportunist but maybe it's the people around him suggesting opportunities that he can't refuse. That settles it then: he's a weak opportunist. (And I'm a slack bastard.)

My speech was too long and turgid for the Press Club, and in my nerves and excitement, it was delivered too quickly. The main thing, however, was to provide a summary of the book. It was heretical stuff: 'the need to abandon the old ideological boundaries and think radically about the organisation of our society'. Reviving Australia's reputation as a social laboratory. Praising Keating and his big picture in Parliament. And a lovely sledge on the Tories: 'To watch John Howard, Tim Fischer and Peter Costello in Question Time each day is to be reminded of Donald Horne's haunting depiction of Australia as a lucky country run by second-rate people'.

Too heretical for my colleagues—some of them would like to burn me at the stake. As I left the Press Club, it occurred to me that I received many more congratulations and requests for book signings from members of the Coalition than from members of my own Party. In fact, there have been no signings for Labor MPs. So much for a Party five to ten years behind in policy development, needing someone to aid its relevance and direction. I'm a sheep man in cattle country.

Thursday, 7 May

The power of ideas in public life: before his hearing with the Financial Institutions and Public Administration Parliamentary Committee, Ian Macfarlane, the Governor of the Reserve Bank, said to me that chapter one of my book should be compulsory reading for anyone interested in globalisation. He likes the arguments. Governments should avoid a bidding war for footloose capital by throwing subsidies and tariffs at companies. They should make capital compete and build national advantages through the quality of their education and training system and industry innovation. This is the new growth theory of modern economics. Nations should also cooperate through multilateral forums to find new and effective ways of regulating global capital.

In politics you can cop a lot of ridicule by running apart from the herd. So it's nice to receive praise at such a high level. Maybe the hundreds of hours researching and writing were worth it. That's the thing about a book, I suppose: you put part of yourself on public display, your ideas and thoughts to

---

Donald Horne Leading Australian author and commentator, best known for his seminal book *The Lucky Country*

be tested (and possibly torn apart) by time. I like that, the self-challenge in life, always more important than the armchair critics and enemies.

Friday, 15 May

A cracker of a speech at a Christian Schools' Conference in Canberra, not normally my cup of tea, but they really responded to a passionate message about the importance of schooling and state aid. These days, I'm treated much better outside the Parliamentary Labor Party than within. The book has put a huge gap between the Labor mainstream and me. As these Christians might ask, am I a prophet in my own town or a leper waiting to be touched and reformed?

My original goal coming into the Parliament was to make better public policy according to Labor principles. I've now concluded that the Shadow Ministry process is external to this process. I've to adjust down my expectations about the ALP. The task is just too hard amid the true conservatives of Australian politics. So, too, I've to adjust down my expectations about Parliament. The artificiality of the place is killing my enthusiasm: all those Second Reading speeches in an empty chamber, the play-acting called Question Time. If this is the centre of our democracy, no wonder the Australian people have grown to hate politics.

Or maybe it's not a question of expectations. Maybe I need to get used to the mood swings of public life, the semi-permanent imbalance in everything. How I can find inspiration and joy in some speaking events (like today), yet boredom with the work inside Parliament House. How my book can be received exceptionally well in public forums, yet be seen as threatening inside Caucus. In truth, the colleagues are terrified by agenda-setting, paralysed by the prospect of a real debate. Caucus meetings are a joke, with everyone just going through the motions, the bare essentials of Opposition. It's not a debating forum. It's a slow-motion replay.

Saturday, 23 May

The Australian Education Union holds a big conference at Darling Harbour in Sydney, a rally against the Government's policies in the lead-up to the next election. I had to sit there and learn of the contents of Beazley's speech as it was delivered. He was talking schools policy, without ever talking to his Shadow Minister. I haven't had one education policy discussion with him in the past twelve months. I've lodged 60 pages of policy submissions to his Kitchen Cabinet, the subcommittee trying to make our finances add up, but with no feedback. So, why bother?

Beazley's Labor is based on industry policy bullshit and Kernot's defection. He talks non-stop about intervention in the market and 'active government'. Stripped of its bullshit, what does this mean in practice? It means that Labor's election policies are based on $1 billion in new money for the 1999–2000 Budget, funded by the Government's surplus. That is, the only active thing we are doing is bludging off Costello's work in repairing the Budget. We will have $1 billion in new commitments, versus the Coalition's $60 billion: $30 billion from the GST and $30 billion from the Telstra sale. Sixty plays one, and we are the Party of active government. Yeah, and I'm Mary Poppins.

Tuesday, 2 June

High farce in the Parliament, as Crean pushes the closure of a paper mill in Burnie (Tasmania) as Labor's issue of the day. No doubt he has some high-cost plan to bail out the failed business. As the Manager of Opposition Business it was his job to ensure that a backbencher lodged a Matter of Public Importance motion so that the issue could be debated after Question Time. But the motion never went in and we were left stranded. So much for industry planning; these jokers can't get a letter around to the Clerk's office on time. It's a replay of Keating's story about the old Senators and their TA forms, and just as funny.

My book continues to stand up well, the only harsh newspaper review coming from Terry McCrann on the business page of the News Limited tabloids. I don't know anyone who takes him seriously. The reaction from academics and policy boffins (such as Race Mathews and Bob Birrell) has been great. They say it's easy enough to follow and full of creative policy work. Most likely, its reception depends on the reader's prior knowledge of issues such as globalisation. The intensity of the book is particularly appealing for young fanatics and policy specialists.

Most politicians and journalists would have expected me to write a book designed to win the hearts and minds of the mob. But I took a different starting point, the challenge John Paterson gave me fifteen months ago: the intellectual reconfiguration of social democracy to deal with the new realities of economic and social change. No one has the full answer, of course, but I feel like I have gone part of the way. A useful contribution.

Race Mathews Former Fed. ALP MP and Vic. ALP Min.; head of the Australian Fabian Society and Monash University academic
Bob Birrell Monash University academic; immigration and population policy expert

John Paterson A senior Victorian public servant and health economist

Monday, 22 June

Shadow Ministry debates our policy on the introduction of digital TV and the fix is on. Beazley makes it clear that this is not a policy decision but a political one, openly trading our position for the support of the big media proprietors in the forthcoming election campaign. I'm used to it by now. With the advent of industry hand-outs as Labor policy, it is hardly surprising that Packer and co. also receive a sweetheart deal to guarantee their income. Once more, competition and the interests of Australian consumers go out the window.

The weirdest part of the meeting was a debate about the potential impact of New Zealand television content in Australia. Who's ever heard of the Kiwi TV juggernaut putting our people out of work? Anyway, we are moving into a world where the flow of investment, products, information and cultural values has become oblivious to national boundaries. Politicians and their laws are lagging behind these changes. For Australian Labor, it's a case of playing the electoral margins instead of telling people how and why the world has changed.

Thursday, 9 July

What sort of Party is this? I was the guest speaker at Robert McClelland's fundraiser at Brighton-le-Sands (in the seat of Barton) at lunchtime today and Gough Whitlam took me aside for a word. And the conversation went like this (my recollection from a couple of hours ago):

> **Whitlam:** Comrade, there's something I need to raise with you. Gary Gray called on me and asked me to pass on his concerns that you are coming on too strongly with the women in Canberra. He seems to think there is a sexual harassment claim against you. Now, it sounds unlikely to me, comrade. I've seen you in action and you are quite prolific. If anything, the women come on strongly after you. So, as I say, it sounds like bullshit but he asked me to raise it with you and now I have.
>
> **Latham:** Well, it's bullshit. I don't know what to say. I've known you a long time and I can assure you it's rubbish. I've never laid a hand on a woman, never. It's true, I haven't been a monk since my marriage broke up, but nothing like this has happened. Sexual harassment? They've got to be kidding. Anyway, what's it got to do with Gary Gray? Why couldn't he talk to me directly? We're about the same age, I know him well enough. What's he up to?

Robert McClelland ALP member, Barton 1996–

Whitlam: I don't know. He came to see me and said he thought I was the best person to talk to you. I know it's not the sort of conversation we would normally have, comrade. But he asked me to do it. It didn't sound right to me, but now it's done.

It's done all right. The embarrassment of an old man—for Christ's sake, Gough's 82 in two days' time—having to talk to me about sex. A former Labor Prime Minister sent out to raise with me something that, if it were true, would end my career in politics. That's a story in itself, ripe for all the gossips in Canberra—the fact that Gough spoke to me on such a subject. Gutless little Pugsley was not man enough to talk to me face-to-face. Gough couldn't give me any details or a specific incident. It's a nightmare.

Wednesday, 15 July

Leo McLeay raises concerns with me about my role on the frontbench, saying that while he thinks the Party can have a decent debate about its direction, others want me to focus solely on attacking the Government. He sounded like a proxy for Beazley's office. What's wrong with these people, why can't they ever talk to me directly? In my defence, I said that the colleagues couldn't ignore the interest and ideas in my book. Leo replied, 'Mark, most of them wouldn't know what was in your book. They haven't read it'. That says it all, doesn't it? Why bother with them?

Saturday, 18 July

With an election likely before the end of the year, I'm hitting the shopping centre in Werriwa. The problem of downward envy is worse than ever. The punters hate it when one characteristic of life (such as race or gender) determines access to government support, regardless of the poverty and disadvantage people face across their entire lives. It's the folly of segmentation: policy-makers looking at just one segment of life instead of the whole situation.

At Glenquarie shops this morning, which services the Macquarie Fields public housing estate, I was given two stories that confirm the mood. I don't know how true they are, but the perceptions are powerful. A grandmother claimed that special education at the local school was available only to Aboriginal kids. A mum enrolled for a TAFE cooking course said that the form asked if she was Aboriginal. 'I wish', she said, because

---

Pugsley A nickname for Gary Gray

this would have given her an exemption on the $60 enrolment fee. She's got the arse hanging out of her pants and wants to know why poor people are not exempt. Fair play, fair question.

No wonder Hanson is doing well. She has a galaxy of real-life grievances to work off, with both major parties doing very little to address the public's complaints, real and perceived. Major welfare reform is needed in Australia. There can only be two purposes to the public provision of welfare: to move people back into work and to develop their skills and self-esteem. Offering incentives for an active life—lifelong learning, personal savings and the social status of work—while also demanding individual responsibility in return. If we made those reforms, plus ended the segmentation of government programs, Hanson would be stuffed.

Welfare dependency can kill a society, suffocate self-esteem and the stability of a normal life. Business welfare can kill an economy, suffocate innovation and the competitive spirit of the private sector. It's the perpetual dilemma of Centre–Left parties: supporting the active role of government but not knowing when to stop.

Sunday, 19 July

Earlier in the week I had a good tip-off from a senior Fairfax journalist (who said I could never use his name anywhere) that Beazley's office was tipping dirt on me around the press gallery. And, right on cue, a snippet appeared in the Sunday papers today. First Gray and now this: the arseholes are really coming after me. I can't help but compare this treatment with the way Bob Hawke supported Beazley when his first marriage broke down circa 1989.

I've also picked up some information about the Gray rumour, and the story gets worse. Apparently the thing started in Howard's office. And was passed on through (Labor Senator) Robert Ray to Gray. It's unbelievable. Our political opponents start a rumour then our people pass it around the Party, right up to a former Labor Prime Minister. I'm the victim of a Chinese whisper from two voyeurs, Ray and Gray—one's Beazley's best mate and the other, his National Secretary. It's the revenge of the fugly faction.

It says a lot about Gray, as a man and as a Party official. He's paid good money to advance the ALP's interests. Yet here he is taking bullshit from the Libs, retailing it through the system and expecting Gough to do something about it. All of it false, a dirty little rumour designed to damage me. I've never been so angry about something in all my life.

Robert Ray Vic. ALP Sen. 1981– ; min. in Hawke and Keating govts

Friday, 24 July

Lunch in Beverly Hills with Leo McLeay, who is working overtime to get me to be 'a team player'. We talk about the change factor in Australian politics—how to deal with people dislocated and disadvantaged in an era of permanent change. My view is that our message should be—prepare for it—a Labor Government will help you get ready for the challenges of change. Leo reckons Beazley's answer in the election campaign will be to slow down the pace of government. If we win, he will say, 'See you all in three years' time'. How mad can our show get? It's absurd for the Labor Party to think this way.

Anyway, with the crap that's being thrown at me, they can all get stuffed. I'm going to continue to talk about new ideas, whether on the front or backbench. Surely it's useful for the Party, among 80 MPs, to have one or two engaged in the contest of ideas (such as it exists in Australian politics). In particular, it's not a bad role for the Shadow Minister for Education. The so-called intellectuals, Beazley and Evans, don't offer any encouragement to others—just look at the treatment of Baldwin, Tanner and me in this term of Parliament. I have been forced to go it alone and will continue to do so.

I'm disillusioned with Beazley on three fronts. First, on Labor policy, especially TCF, cars and sugar tariffs. He's an opportunist who avoids conflict and conviction, leaving the Party empty and without belief. Second, the backgrounding against me. One thing's for sure, being a high Anglican doesn't make for morality in politics. And third, the persistent word about Kernot's future is that she'll get the education portfolio in government. It must have been raised at the time of her defection. Again, he's too scared to talk to me directly.

Saturday, 1 August

Unfortunately Labor has contributed to the Hansonite surge with its populism on tariffs. We should never have let the protectionist genie out of its bottle. Economic isolationism is the flipside of social racism, encouraging people to think the worst of other nations and people. It also has a domino effect—just look at the special pleading groups that have jumped out of the ground in recent times. I never realised how correct Peter Walsh was in this argument.

I'm taking flak in the media for standing up to Beazley's economic irrationalism. His mate Oakes bagging me in the *Bulletin* last week: 'It is not a good time for any politician in any party to be marked with the economic rationalist brand. Labor's Shadow Education Minister, Mark Latham, is a case in point'. Beazley's people fed him a crazy critique of my proposals for welfare reform by the Queens Beach ALP Branch in North Queensland (of all places). Make no mistake, Beazley and Hanson are singing from the same economic song sheet.

I take up these themes as one of the speakers at a Centre for Independent Studies conference in Moss Vale. It's a collection of Right-wing businesspeople and media types—not normally my go, but it's an outlet for original thinking and getting a message across. After my talk, I handed over my paper to Paul Kelly from *The Australian*, who should give it a good run.

The CIS has done a lot of interesting work on the social capital debate, so it's been quite useful to me. It also has a lot of interesting, wacky characters attached to its caravan of conservative ideologues. My favourite is Frank Devine. He reminds me of my grandfather—always at odds with the world, always having a crack at people, but in a very stylish, witty way. I have even heard Frank bag his own daughter (Miranda Devine, a prominent Sydney journalist): 'Miranda, you know, is a tabloid journalist, but we were never surprised by that. The rest of us are so much smarter, we're with the broadsheets'. Frank knows no limits, telling strangers like me what he thinks about his daughter. The Right-wing commentators bag everyone, even their own kids.

But back to my speech. Other than getting stuck into populism and protectionism, I offered a harsh critique of the political system. Politicians are adding to the culture of complaint, exploiting public misunderstandings rather than correcting them. Modern politics is locked into a corrosive cycle of inadequate information, political opportunism, broken promises and public cynicism and apathy.

When I first got involved twenty years ago it was still seen as an honoured profession. Now the public hate us. At best, they tolerate the system for what they can get out of it. Question: if I had been able to predict the public's dwindling faith in politics and politicians, would I have got involved in the first place? Answer, probably not. My original career ambition was to be a Treasury economist—and there I would have stayed.

Monday, 10 August

Beazley is interviewed by Ray Martin and reveals a Defence Minister's mentality about Australia—always under siege, always needing protection. He is psychologically incapable of making hard decisions, as his record as a Minister over thirteen years showed (Defence, Communications,

---

Frank Devine Senior columnist at *The Australian*

Ray Martin Host of *A Current Affair*, Channel Nine

Education, Finance). We shouldn't be too surprised that he's become a populist Opposition Leader.

Another session with Leo, who thinks I'm not interested because I don't arse-kiss the colleagues. Maybe I just don't like most of them. It's like something Joe Klein wrote about Al Gore in *The New Yorker*, 8 December 1997: 'He tends to make intellectual rather than emotional connections with people'. The article also said that Clinton picked Gore as his Vice-Presidential candidate because 'he took issues seriously—that he didn't just take politically convenient positions, and he loved talking about complicated problems'. I can relate to that: it's a virtue, not a vice.

Try making intellectual connections with Caucus members—it's pretty hard-going, I can tell you. I've got to take comfort from my own beliefs and principles, not those of my colleagues. Like my recent chat with Helen Trinca, who said that my book 'is the bible of the (Federal) bureaucracy'. That has to count for more than the whingeing of Leo's mates.

Wednesday, 12 August

The problem with the Shadow Ministry is that it doesn't take issues seriously. This was one of the strengths of the Hawke Cabinet: it was made up of problem-solving politicians—Dawkins, Keating, Walsh, Kerin, Blewett and co. There is no comparison with the Beazley mob—Lee, Smith, Crean, Bevis and the rest.

The paradox of leadership: Hawke opened up his vulnerabilities to the public—it was seen as insecurity, but really it was inner strength. Keating, by contrast, never opened up—perceived publicly as strength, but in practice it was personal insecurity. I was in Harry Quick's Franklin electorate today and he told a story that highlighted this. He was campaigning with Paul before the 1993 election, taking him to a straightforward community function. He reckons Keating was really worked up about it, asking, 'Will they like me?' People are never as they seem in politics—very often the reverse is true.

Tuesday, 15 September

The straw that broke the camel's back. Yesterday, on the way to Melbourne for the launch of our education policy (for the election on 3 October),

Joe Klein American political journalist and author of *Primary Colors* (Random House, New York, 1996)
Al Gore US Vice-Pres. 1993–2001
Helen Trinca *SMH* journalist

Neal Blewett ALP member, Bonython 1977–94; min. in Hawke and Keating govts, incl. Health Min.
Arch Bevis Shadow Defence Min. 1996–98
Harry Quick ALP member, Franklin 1993–

Louise Webb (my policy adviser) rang to say that John Angley and Mike Pezzullo from Beazley's office had rewritten the policy document. Butchered it, actually. They know nothing in this area, yet they had the hide to delete major sections and rewrite others, and only tell me after the event. They had me trapped, with all the final policy documents being cleared out of Beazley's office, under Bob McMullan's supervision, but there was nothing I could do about it.

Not surprisingly, the fools stuffed up big time. The document allocated $500 million in new funding for government schools, $255 million for Catholic schools and nothing for anyone else. Yet they have the gall to say that a Labor Government will 'develop a new, needs-based schools funding system'. What, with no money for other Christian and independent non-government schools?

Ultimately, they have produced a sectarian-based definition of school need—apparently only Catholic schools have needs in the non-government sector. The other systems will be livid, rightly so. And the irony of it: McMullan, who started out in WA as a protégé of Joe Chamberlain (a strong opponent of State aid), has sent us back to a sectarian schools policy. In practice, the cause of the problem is obvious: they didn't know that there are non-government schools other than those in the Catholic system, so they did not allocate any money to them. The incompetence is breathtaking.

I wanted to take the money the Government announced for the reclassification of Catholic schools and put it into the central pot, allocating it to schools (whether government, Catholic, other Christian, Muslim or anything else) on the basis of need. But no, Beazley had done a sweetheart deal with his WA mate Peter Tannock (head of the National Catholic Education Commission) and the Catholics got a specific allocation from both sides of politics.

When Labor ended the State aid debate in the 1970s, we effectively created a monster. The Catholics now have the funding and the electoral power to play the politicians off a break, creating a bidding war between the parties at election time. As ever, the opportunistic Beazley was happy to play this game, even though it wrecked the credibility of our policy.

Still, I put on a brave front at the launch today. None of the media has any idea of the drama behind the scenes. I introduced Beazley and talked about the importance of education, using some compelling case studies, like the woman in Kiama (NSW) who got back into learning through a horticulture course and ended up doing a pure maths degree at

Bob McMullan Shadow Industrial Relations, Finance & the Arts Min. 1997–98

Wollongong University. Greg Wilton reckons that our Leader looked quite impressed.

But that's it for me. I'm getting off the frontbench—win, lose or draw this election. I've had it on every front. This election campaign has been the most miserable experience of my life. Sitting on planes with a broken back (the result of a slipped disc in 1996). Travelling around the country non-stop, all for nothing. Tedious event after tedious event, with candidates who can barely string two words together. Listening to piss-heads outside my hotel room all night in Alice Springs. And then done over with my education policy, my sculpture smashed to pieces.

I talk about the need for lifelong learning—the freedom of enquiry and expression in society. Well, what about my freedom? Taken away by the system. This follows the absurd, drawn-out saga of my attempts to put into Labor policy the funding of computers in local libraries (the Crean surrogates were coming in and out of my office like a Marx brothers movie). And my attempt to apply mutual responsibility principles to our Parents as Educators program, done over by Jenny Macklin.

Without freedom of enquiry, research and expression, you are only half a person. I've got to find a way of enjoying my politics again. The power of ideas and truth now outweighs any ministerial pretensions I might have had. I've got to find the strength to get outside the system.

Friday, 18 September

Peter Crimmins, the head of the Australian Association of Christian Schools, and his colleagues visited me in my electorate office yesterday. He had tears in his eyes as he spoke about the funding needs of their schools and the lack of vision in ALP policy. He knew it wasn't my document that was released three days ago. Today he sent me a letter that summarises the travesty:

> The ALP's education platform is a revisionist and sectional collection of tired policies in so much as it addresses the needs of Australia's schools. We are disappointed it does not reflect the visionary perspectives and statements often expressed by you in varying forums/conferences over the last eighteen months. As stated to you, these views received wide acclaim.
>
> It defies logic for the ALP to advocate and support 'a new needs-based method of distribution of school funding' while at the same

---

Greg Wilton ALP member, Isaacs 1996–2000;
a good friend of mine

time pre-empting the assessed needs of the Catholic sector by guaranteeing them Category 11 funding from 1999. Is this assessment equitable in terms of the rest of the schools in the non-government sector? Or is this decision to allocate a further $255 million politically motivated?

The 217 Christian schools that we represent are the Protestant equivalent of the Catholic schools that have been guaranteed an increase … As you are aware, our schools serve predominantly working-class communities. We do not want our schools to be only accessible to the wealthy. A genuine needs-based funding policy should direct the highest level of funding from governments to those schools serving the neediest communities. We do not see these announcements reflecting this principle.

So much for being a party of social justice.

Wednesday, 23 September

In the news: Clinton, Blair and Prodi have held an international Third Way seminar in New York, the same day Beazley delivers the ALP policy speech in Brisbane—the least inspiring, interesting and creative Labor policy since Arthur Calwell in 1966. He's turned us into a conservative party, defending the old economy and the old welfare state. What he and his dad have always wanted for Labor: social and economic conservatism.

I didn't go to Brisbane. I told them my back is stuffed, which is true enough. But the bigger reason is that I couldn't give a stuff. Why sit there in agony, physical and political, when I'm about to pull the pin on the whole stinking wreck of a Party?

Earlier in the week, I was in Tasmania with our candidate for Braddon, Sid Sidebottom (that's his real name, not his stage name). And what did he have me do? Judge a lasagne-cooking competition at the university campus in Burnie, including a purple lasagne. There has to be a better life than this.

Saturday, 26 September

The shit has hit the fan over the education policy stuff-up. Sharan Burrow from the Australian Education Union is ticked off by the special deal for the Catholics. The Christian and Independent associations are in a state of

---

Tony Blair UK Labour PM 1997–
Romano Prodi Italian Socialist PM 1996–98

Sid Sidebottom ALP member, Braddon 1998–2004

disbelief. It's a rare achievement, getting the Left and Right offside in the school funding debate.

I put the weights on McMullan, Pezzullo and Angley to find a solution with a sharp memo on 17 September. Three days later they still hadn't responded, so I tried again: 'Another triumph for the floggers who fucked over the education policy. Can I please have a written response to my memo. It would cost $20 million per annum to assist needy Christian schools the same way as ALP policy treats Catholic and government schools.' This did the trick. They decided to make the $500 million in funding for government schools available to needy non-Catholic non-government schools as well. Needless to say, Burrow was not impressed.

Gray has drafted letters to the interest groups trying to explain away the calamity: 'I regret that the version of the policy document provided to you contained a literal error which indicated incorrectly that this funding ($500 million) would be restricted to the government sector only'. That's a good description of my time on the frontbench: a literal error.

Wednesday, 7 October

I pulled the pin on the Beazley show, and gave him a good spray on the way out. People say it's a big call for someone my age to get off the frontbench, but my reasons are sound.

On the personal crap that's going around, there's yet more evidence of Beazley's people's involvement. Gough spoke to John Flannery (Beazley's press secretary), who confirmed a backgrounding campaign against me by their office. My friends in Parliament House are adamant that Beazley's staffers Epstein and Justin Di Lollo have been spreading shit about me all over the place. Race Mathews tells me that a senior Right-wing Victorian told him that I have been stalking a young woman and the police are involved. Things are out of control.

Things have been just as bad after the election. I told Louise Webb I wouldn't be recontesting a frontbench spot. She went down to Beazley's office to put her name on the unattached list for policy advisers. Within an hour, four journalists rang, wanting to know if I was going to the backbench. The next day the Poisoned Dwarf, Glenn Milne, rang to ask: 'Is it true that you are not running for the frontbench because you are facing sexual harassment charges?' When I asked him for the source for this claim, he replied, 'It's from people close to Beazley'.

Glenn Milne Political reporter for Channel Seven in Canberra and columnist for *The* *Australian,* given the nickname 'the Poisoned Dwarf' by Paul Keating

People think Beazley is a big angel, but behind the scenes, he's in the gutter. He and his allies reflect the worst instincts of the Labor movement: all gossip and muck. He's the good Christian who has done a job on my good name. I'm not going to respond in kind. One day I'll let him know what I think about him as a man. Until then, I've got every right to let the world know exactly what I think about him as a politician.

On the policy front, Beazley is the least likely Labor Leader since Calwell. He launched a 263-page policy document during the campaign without his input or conviction. He's sent the ALP into an intellectual black hole, compared with the lively Third Way debates overseas. He's turned us into the conservative party of Australian politics, dominated by minders, pollsters and spin doctors, all too scared of putting a foot forward for fear of putting one wrong. We lack a serious policy culture. Everything we do is disposable—just look at the rewriting of my education policy.

At the beginning of this century, G. D. H. Cole proposed that the British Fabian Society should disassociate itself from the Labour Party on the grounds that 'It had ceased to be capable of formulating a policy'. That's what I've done to Beazley and his frontbench—disassociated myself from people who have no interest in public policy.

Beazley and Crean don't have a policy direction, other than feeding off the Government's mistakes. Having won seats at this election, they will now try to feed off other problems: a slowing economy, the implementation of the GST, plus Howard's leadership woes. It's a replay of Bob Carr 1991–98, the gutting of Labor belief and purpose. The Liberal pollster Mark Textor says that the ALP didn't win because the voters were worried that the same old Labor faces would make the same mistakes again. That's a sound analysis. Until we show the electorate that we have something new to offer, they will keep on rejecting us.

Why does Carr bother? His staffers tell me that he calls himself the Mayor of NSW, so he must hate the job. All he's doing is running the State the same way as Greiner, but with a smarter media strategy. He's always saying that he wants to leave Parliament, but he doesn't have the bottle to do it— nothing else to do in life. David Britton tells a hilarious story of Bob trying to teach himself how to swim, battling to put on goggles (which were five sizes too small for him), looking like a frog. If it weren't so funny, it would be sad.

So, what's my plan for the next three years? I'm better off doing my own thing—the work satisfaction that comes from researching, thinking and writing. I'm better off staying away from people I don't like and can't

---

G. D. H. Cole Prominent British Labour historian
Nick Greiner Lib. NSW Premier 1988–92

David Britton Bob Carr's adviser and Press Sec. in the 1990s

trust. I've got nothing to lose. If I had stayed on the frontbench, they would have tried to constrain and frustrate me, keeping me outside the inner circle, but still locked into Shadow Ministerial discipline. But now I'm free.

Friday, 9 October

A meeting in Sussex Street of the NSW Right to elect its Shadow Ministers for the coming term of Parliament. There were eighteen votes and two of them were informal, failing to number eight squares. The consensus is that Michael Forshaw and Frank Mossfield were the culprits. Really, what hope is there? This group should be renamed the bonehead faction.

It's the ultimate bunch of anti-intellectuals, no different from the Left on policy (embracing retro-economics and the old welfare state). It used to be known for sticking to its mates, but now it doesn't even have a premium on loyalty (replacing Forshaw with Steve Hutchins on the Senate ticket).

I caught the train home to Campbelltown and, as I got off, Beazley rang to talk about my exit from the frontbench. I gave him the full, angry burst on the reasons why, including the personal stuff. He was very defensive and in denial: 'Mate, I don't know anything about this'. A Beazley special, trying to make out he knows nothing about nothing. Good old Sergeant Shultz, he doesn't know what his office, his National Secretary and his best mate have been up to. Well, now he knows what I'm up to. I'm up him for the rent.

Sunday, 18 October

Some more reflections on the election campaign. For all the Chicken Little performances in Caucus, my book did not cost us a vote or even rate a serious mention in the campaign. The Lib scare campaign was directed at Gareth Evans and his retrospective capital gains tax. Another triumph for the brains trust. When this was discussed at Shadow Ministry, I asked Gareth if the policy document could be changed and he replied that it was already on its way to the printer. I then asked why we bothered having a meeting at all.

Yet another triumph: the Australian Chamber of Commerce and Industry bagged our industry policy when it was released. Why did we ever think the views of business mattered, or that these jokers would ever support us?

Sussex Street Location of the NSW ALP office and major trade unions; home of the NSW Right faction

Frank Mossfield ALP member, Greenway 1996–2004
Steve Hutchins NSW ALP Sen. 1998–

This is what happens when the Party's leadership loses its rudder. Beazley is a totally reactive politician, never an agenda-setter. He has allowed the throwbacks in Caucus to react to Keating's economics (with tariffs and industry policy) and the trendy Left to determine our reaction to Howard on social policy.

Politics aside, one of the biggest problems Australia faces is a lack of talent at the top of its major institutions. I was generally optimistic about Australia's future until I met its Vice-Chancellors. What a drab lot. I expected a group of dynamic heavy-hitters to lead the nation's universities, but the standard is very poor. For all the debate about resources, 30 top individuals would actually make a bigger difference.

Beazley is fortunate to have a weak press gallery. With five of Australia's top seven trading partners in recession, he was able to promise Budget surpluses, $3 billion per annum in extra outlays, a 5 per cent unemployment rate plus tax cuts, and get away with it. Some of these characters have been here too long. The likes of Michelle Grattan and Laurie Oakes have been institutionalised into Canberra culture—they can never leave the place and survive. Reminds me of the old guy looking after the library in *The Shawshank Redemption*. He left gaol and hanged himself.

In an era of temporary and artificial political communication, leaders can get away with using issues like railway platforms: solely to get on the train. And then forget all about the issue when the train has pulled out. Beazley's intellectual interests are in the past, not the future. He's a master of the railway platform technique. He made a big deal of community politics in his National Conference speech but never followed up. He spoke a lot about new ideas/new faces, without ever helping them out. He released a 263-page document without developing any of it. He talked non-stop about security without ever defining it realistically. He visits issues but then never returns.

Modern campaigning is like *The Truman Show*. It's easy to hate the artificiality of it, the control freaks and spin doctors without genuine beliefs (and the political 'leaders' who foster this system). The campaign events are choreographed for television, an exercise in battling and controlling the media, all of it divorced from public interest. The media and politicians are trapped by their own silly games. In Christof's words, 'We accept the reality of the world with which we are presented'. Except for Truman.

Michelle Grattan Political reporter for the Fairfax newspapers

Christof Character in *The Truman Show* played by Ed Harris, the producer and manipulator of Truman's world

Monday, 19 October

Beazley reports to the first Caucus meeting since the election. Having campaigned tooth and nail against the GST, he says that we can't abolish it because of the implications for State finances—absolute rubbish. He shows some sensitivity about the Third Way, saying that his staff tell him not to quote Tony Blair, but often he would like to because Blair talks about industry policy—absolute rubbish.

One refreshing note: he reckons the Party needs to reinvent itself, but he leaves it at that, without any detail. The old Kim quickly re-emerged: 'We have one task, to get into government, and that is not an intellectual or academic task. Anyway, we don't know what the issues will be three years from now'. We will never know what the issues are if we don't promote them ourselves. The best way of predicting the future is to create it.

In my new role I can't afford to react to Beazley or his Shadows and look like a maverick. I've got to talk about policy action, not reaction. In politics, one can compromise on the timing and detail of policy, but not the principles. There are plenty of precedents in our show for speaking out, so I shouldn't be deterred. I'll be putting my stuff on the record through speeches and newspaper columns, unlike Caucus members who are always off the record with the media. Like everyone else, I've done a bit of that over the years, but I've never hopped right into it.

I reckon if something is worth saying, you should put your name to it. That's what I plan to do. The precedents: Kernot spent ten years bagging us and then we signed her up as our star recruit. Roger Price and Janice Crosio are addicted to breaking the Party line on Badgerys Creek Airport. Just this morning, George Campbell was in the media saying that our Shadows were not up to the policy task, yet this afternoon he was elected Chairman of Caucus. When he first got the job, Beazley said, 'Let a hundred flowers bloom'. Let's see how he handles my little rose garden. Beazley's people will hate it now that they cannot doctor my words.

Wednesday, 21 October

Lunch with the *Daily Telegraph*'s Col Allan, Malcolm Farr and Piers Akerman at the swank Lucio's in Paddington. It's a marathon session—

Roger Price ALP member, Chifley 1984–
Janice Crosio ALP member, Prospect 1990–2004
Badgerys Creek Airport The site in Western Sydney for Sydney's second international airport. Throughout the 1990s it was ALP policy to support the construction of the airport

George Campbell NSW ALP Sen. 1997–
Col Allan *Daily Telegraph* Editor in the 1990s
Malcolm Farr *Daily Telegraph* Fed. political reporter
Piers Akerman *Daily Telegraph* Right-wing columnist

these guys can really hit the piss. They want me to write a weekly column for the paper and I'm happy to oblige. It's a good forum and, after the turgid prose of *Civilising Global Capital*, a chance to simplify my writing and message for a popular audience.

They have no problem with me also writing for the *Australian Financial Review* at the rival Fairfax stable—the audiences are totally different. This way I'll have all bases covered: the pointy-head audience in the *Fin* and the mob who read the *Tele*. An ideal opportunity for political agitation from the backbench. Plus I'll be earning a few extra bob, much needed for the property settlement with the ex.

The lunch conversation is a long way from policy debate. Running the *Tele* is about good food, good wine and good hatchet jobs. These blokes have scores of public figures they hate, and the purpose of the paper is to do them in. I joined in the spirit, boasting that my first column would out Bob Carr as a Western Sydney hater. When I worked for him he would often say, 'You must feel stupid living in Western Sydney, so far from the coast'. I won't do it, of course, it was just the piss talking.

The lunch finished at 5.30 p.m. and then it was back to News Limited for an hour of work, blind as bats. Col wanted to kick on, but I bailed out. A five-hour lunch is about my limit these days.

Friday, 30 October

My first column for the *Tele*, a tidy effort outlining the weaknesses in Labor's policy culture. As Exhibit A, I used Bob Ellis, speechwriter and court jester to Carr and Beazley. I didn't miss him: 'Trading in gossip and smut, he has sent us further down the American way, where all that is private is ultimately made public … [He's] a dangerous lard of political poison'. Specifically, I referred to the pulping of his book because of its slur on Costello, Abbott and their wives. I also had my own recent nightmare in mind: 'As it is, enough people have been hurt by Parliament House's culture of small talk and smear'.

Sunday, 1 November

Lunch at Paul Kelly's house in Hunters Hill with David Hale, the international financial guru. He's a real Dr Knowledge. The Fabians are often accused of an international conspiracy to run the world. If they ever

Tony Abbott Lib. member, Warringah 1994– ;
Employment Services Min. 1998–2001

succeed, this is the bloke they need—he knows everything about the world of finance. The best I could do was tip Champagne and Jezabeel for his trip to the Melbourne Cup on Tuesday.

John Edwards is also there, and he tells an important story from his time working (as an economics adviser) for Keating. The boss was just back from a Cabinet meeting where he had pushed through a new deregulatory policy and he said, 'Yeah, I got them to agree to it, but they don't really believe in it'. That sums up the dilemma perfectly. As soon as Keating left, Caucus lurched back to the Left on economic policy. They never really believed in it.

Sunday, 8 November

I'm still seething about the rewriting of my education policy. It was an affront to my hard work and diligence in the shadow portfolio. But the more I think about it, the more I worry about its broader significance. There is something about the parliamentary system that narrows down the individual. It takes committed people—complex and passionate by nature, which is why they got into politics in the first place—and turns them into one-dimensional robots.

All the signals and messages in modern politics are about conformity. Playing the media game, milking the electoral margins on an issue, fitting in with the demands of the party machine, waiting your turn for promotion. Never taking a risk, never striking out, never really being yourself. Anyone who breaks this mould is demonised by the system as mad, maverick or erratic. In practice, we are the only real people, the ones who have kept our passion.

In this environment, compromise comes too easily, junking principles and conviction in order to run comfortably with the herd. The original purpose of public life is lost. It's a scary thought, something to guard against, always. But this is what the Beazley operation is on about: conservative control of the parliamentary party. I'm sure I have done the right thing, going to the backbench. Better to die on your feet than to live on your knees. Like Smith, Swan, Lee and the other robots.

The only good news is that the public is on to them. The electorate has worked out the artificiality of it all. They can see through the spin doctors,

---

Stephen Smith Shadow Communications Min. 1998–2001
Wayne Swan Shadow Family & Community Services Min. 1998–2004

Michael Lee Shadow Education Min. 1998–2001

the publicity stunts, the polling and the tricks of marginal-seat campaigning. This is why people now talk about politics with a cool anger. They
have a clear feeing that the system is far from genuine. That the robots, in
fact, are tin men.

Friday, 13 November

The end of the first sitting week of the new Parliament. A good chat
with John Della Bosca, who gave me some encouragement. He relayed a
recent conversation with Bob Horne: 'Mark's problem is he is right'. Della
quipped, 'You're just like [Jack] Lang. That's the slogan—Lang is right, Latham
is right'.

Also met with Professor Patrick Seyd from the Department of Politics
at Sheffield University in the UK. A long conversation about the Third Way
and the Australian political scene. He's not impressed with the Labor
machine men he's met on this trip, telling me that Ray and Gray 'would not
last six months in New Labour; the standard of policy debate would leave
them floundering'. Obviously, I wasn't unhappy to hear that. It puts our
little Party into perspective.

The sadness of the week came from my mate Greg Wilton. We call him
Pills because you never know whether his mood is up or down—we joke
that it depends on whether or not he has had his pills. This week it was
down as he caved in to threats from the Victorian Right and dropped out of
the race to be Chairman of the Caucus Economics Committee. He feels like
he's been shuffled down the list, as one of the new MPs, Craig Emerson, got
the job ahead of him. I wanted him to stand and fight the bastards, send it
to a ballot at least, but Pills wasn't up for it. Very morbid.

Thursday, 3 December

Duncan Kerr is a funny sort of bloke, too suave and trendy for my simple
tastes. But he is one of the most thoughtful and philosophical people in
Parliament, floating around the place in a nice, carefree, balanced way
(although, physically, he has an uncanny resemblance to the cartoon character Touché Turtle). Today we had a good talk about the general shittiness
of Opposition and the position I'm in.

Bob Horne ALP member, Paterson 1993–96,
1998–2001
Craig Emerson ALP member, Rankin 1998– ;
nicknamed 'Emmo' or 'Catman'

Duncan Kerr Shadow Justice & Customs Min.
1998–2001

He said the worst thing about Opposition is that all the influences are negative—lobbying against things. Some people like that; others (like me) struggle to put up with it. Duncan reckons, 'You have given up an 80 per cent chance of a significant role in politics for a 10 per cent chance of a very significant role in the future'. The 10 per cent figure was generous, but still, I don't mind the odds. It's never been any different.

Ideologically, I'm a lone wolf around the place. My notional subfaction, the NSW Right, has no interest in ideas, let alone mine. In a funny sort of way, I'm an heir to the Lionel Murphy legacy—an economic radical and social liberal—but this group no longer exists in Caucus. So I might as well do what Murphy did—enjoy myself in the company of a few good mates.

Tuesday, 15 December

A weird experience yesterday—I was the guest speaker at a conference for News Limited editors in Potts Point. I was expecting a high-powered, professional forum in a luxurious venue. Instead, I ended up in this crowded little room with no air-conditioning on the hottest day of the year. This is what my grandfather used to say: the rich stay rich by being tightwads.

I gave a decent speech about future trends in Australian politics and got to meet Lachlan Murdoch for the first time (who doesn't seem like the sharpest tool in the shed, but then again, I'm always hard on inheritance boys). That was yesterday. Today *The Australian*'s editorial is advising Beazley to put a sock in my mouth. Guest speaker one day, deadshit the next. That's media consistency for you.

Lachlan Murdoch Son of Rupert Murdoch; one of the heirs to the News Limited media empire

1999

Free from the demands of a frontbench position, I was able to immerse myself in the international debate about Third Way politics, starting with a trip to the US in January. My relationship with my parliamentary colleagues was, at best, ambivalent, at worst, poisonous. It wasn't just the animosity caused by my independent thinking or the prominence of my newspaper columns. We were poles apart in our ways of thinking about politics.

From my background in community politics and local government in south-west Sydney, I had always believed in the dispersal of political power: re-engaging people in politics through open government and public participation, empowering disadvantaged communities to find lasting solutions for themselves, and rebuilding social capital, the networks of trust and mutual support between people. In short, I believed in politics on a smaller scale— local communities as the key instrument of reform—bound together by the regulatory power and funding of central government. I saw the capacity of the Information Age to create new networks of information and contact between people as consistent with this approach—indeed, as liberating.

The colleagues, however, were grounded in a different, more centralised scale of politics: hierarchical factional machines that told people how to vote (and sometimes, how to think), a background in big, amalgamated unions and a belief in central government and bureaucracy as the primary units of political life. They came into Parliament not to give power away to neighbourhoods and communities, but to exercise it themselves, to get their hands on what Paul Keating called the levers of public policy.

This was one of the curious aspects of my relationship with Whitlam and Keating (the latter relationship started to develop in a serious way in 1999). While I admired them as great Labor reformers and, at a personal level, great Labor characters, I knew that we had radically different approaches to social policy and democratic reform. Whitlam looked at these issues through the power of the Australian Government and the modification of the Australian Constitution. Keating regarded them as matters of 'big picture' leadership. I saw them as a series of smaller scale pictures: a bottom-upwards approach to community-building, poverty alleviation and democratic renewal. This is what I called the new politics.

From the freedom of the backbench in 1999, these differences and tensions started to emerge. I was criticised by Labor MPs for not being part of their culture and political values. In truth, I was heavily engaged elsewhere: talking to policy wonks and academics, learning from the work of so-called social entrepreneurs and listening to the frustrations of those who ran community organisations and mutual societies. I drifted a long way from the traditional parliamentary model of reform, and became increasingly critical of those who subscribed to it. By the end of 1999, I was preparing to leave Parliament.

Friday, 29 January

The fifth anniversary of my election to Parliament and I'm on a United Airlines flight from San Francisco to Sydney. A four-week study tour to the US, funded by their government (jokingly known among Laborites as the CIA trip). It's been a great opportunity to shake off the cobwebs from last year and bury myself in the big issues. I'm much happier thinking and writing about public policy than dealing with the processes and personalities of politics.

Washington, New York, Princeton University, New Orleans (a big disappointment—the famous jazz bars of the French Quarter have disappeared), Boston, Harvard University, Madison, Wisconsin to study welfare reform, San Jose, Stanford University, San Francisco, UC Berkeley and, finally, the Nixon Presidential Library and birthplace at Yorba Linda. What a highlight: you can walk through the old Nixon house and imagine Hannah Nixon whispering to her son, 'Richard, don't you give up. Don't let anybody tell you you are through'.

In New York I met with Clinton's campaign adviser, Dick Morris, who has an amazing instinct and feel for politics. I explained my situation in Australia and he got it straight away. He reckons that 'This period of ostracisation is essential to your success'. We also talked about the Third Way and the triangulation of policy. He sees it as a spin-off from Hegel's dialectic interpretation of history—out of two conflicting positions a synthesis or settlement emerges.

Take welfare reform. The Right has always stressed the importance of individual responsibility and effort. The Left has pushed for welfare rights and the expansion of government services. The Third Way policy combines rights and responsibilities. Simple but smart. Plus, it has worked for Clinton and Blair.

Morris believes in micro-politics, the small but significant issues that matter to people in their daily lives. He calls it 'stooping to succeed' in politics. They made the same point at the New Democrat think-tank in Washington, the Progressive Policy Institute. The family-friendly issues that journalists and academics snigger at are actually the ones that resonate with ordinary voters. Issues like childcare, checking the credentials of people who work with children, literacy programs and urban congestion. That's the best summary of the Third Way technique: take the best of Left and Right and make it practical to people's lives.

This is why the Third Way is so politically useful: it brings Left-of-Centre parties into the mainstream of electoral success. But I see it as more than that. It also has a radical, even subversive, purpose: empowering people, changing the pattern of influence and control in society. What a great Labor ambition, breaking down the concentration of establishment power and enabling the disenfranchised and the disadvantaged to do more for themselves in life. A wolf in sheep's clothing, if you like.

In Washington I had a chance to see a New Democrat in action when Vice-President Gore hosted a Global Forum on Reinventing Government at the State Department on 14–15 January. He's one of the few politicians I've met whose public image matches the private reality: a stiff and awkward dude, super-serious about himself. I was rung in to the conference as the Australian representative and even asked to make a presentation on something I knew nothing about, a new electronic driver- and motor-registration system in Victoria. I quickly got off on a tangent, arguing that the reinventing government agenda needs to be more than just a technocratic exercise in efficiency. It needs to empower people and address the basic inequality in society. This was very well received by the delegates. It was seen as a counterpoint to Gore's technocratic approach.

The highlight of the conference was an address by Bill Clinton. With just a few notes he wowed them with his unique combination of charisma and serious content. There it was again: he was talking to an auditorium full of people but it felt like he was just talking to me. The other delegates I spoke to said they felt the same way. I would happily give years off my life to be able to speak like that.

The trip was also a chance to talk to some of the academics whose work I'm interested in: Amitai Etzioni, founder of the communitarian movement; Alan Wolfe, author of the outstanding *Whose Keeper? Social Science and Moral Obligation*; Paul Romer, the Adam Smith of Silicon Valley with his new growth-theory economics; and David Card and Alan Krueger, who have found that minimum wage increases do not necessarily have a negative impact on employment levels (due to the boost in spending power in personal service industries). That's the best thing about American politics, it's much deeper than our system—a think-tank on every corner in Washington, every debate reinforced by academic opinion and research.

Etzioni and Wolfe are working on a Third Way approach to the sickness of our society: record rates of family breakdown, domestic violence, youth suicide and community decline. It is such an important project, recognising that not all issues are economic. And the state does not have all the answers to the breakdown in social relations. Social democrats need to reach out to social movements and try to re-equip our citizens with the tools of a good society: trust, mutuality and a moral obligation to each other. This is going to be my big theme for 1999, researching and writing about welfare reform and social capital.

The conversation with Card was really interesting at a personal level. He resents the way in which his research has been drawn into a political and economic bunfight: 'If I had known this was going to happen, I would never have got involved. Krueger is a street fighter who can handle it, but I'm a wimp who hates arguments'. He has concluded that the economics debate is, in fact, 90 per cent political. Wages, in particular, are such an emotional issue it is impossible to shift opinions, even based on sound empirical research.

A rollicking story from San Jose. The first Californian State legislature met there on 15 December 1849. The first session of the newly elected members became known as the Legislature of a Thousand Drinks. The members were bored, a long way from home and with not a lot to keep them occupied (sound familiar?). The Speaker adjourned each day's meeting of the legislature by proclaiming, 'Let's go have a drink, boys, let's go have a thousand of them'. At least he was honest about it. My mate Joel Fitzgibbon would love to have been there.

Joel Fitzgibbon ALP member, Hunter 1996– ;
Shadow Small Business & Tourism Min.
1998–2001

Sunday, 21 February

I must be careful in my relationship with the media. Too many press gallery types are trying to set me up as the opposition within the Opposition, a daily commentator on everything we do. They love beating up stories and personalising conflict. It is not only competition between media outlets, but also within the outlets. Every journalistic ego wants to secure the lead story or, at a bare minimum, ensure that their byline makes the paper.

I need to be cautious, stick to the big policy issues, not personalities. I need to talk about the future, not play to the short-term agenda of the press gallery. Remember, always remember that great quote in Nick Greiner's article about the media (*SMH*, 11 December 1992):

> A commitment to the truth is one of the things most obviously lacking in Australian journalism. An amazing but correct piece of self-analysis by Richard Glover was: 'The reporter's commitment is to boosting the significance of the story, and not to giving us an accurate sense of a lived and fluid reality. The answer to the question, "how bad?" is inevitably bloody bad. Reality, of course, is a world of moderate successes and failures but journalism continues to prefer life at the extremes.' Conflict is the basis for news coverage. It is exaggerated where it exists and created or simulated when it does not.

Glover, of course, knows these things from experience: excitable and extreme in his own work. I suppose that's the only way to survive in the hysterical world of talkback radio. No extremism—no ratings—no program—no job.

Wednesday, 24 March

Beazley and Crean have been forced to switch direction on economic policy, supposedly abandoning the retro-economics of the last three years and re-embracing the virtues of the market. I hope it is true, but am yet to be convinced. An Oakes article in the *Bulletin* today captures the dynamics:

> Simon Crean is drying out. According to Beazley: 'In Treasury Simon will have a much broader set of views about the world. He's a very adaptive guy.' ... [Crean] sings the praises of the

---

Richard Glover ABC radio journalist in Sydney and *SMH* columnist

Simon Crean Dep. Opp. Leader and Shadow Treas. 1998–2001

free-market economic policies which after the 1996 election wipe-out, he seemed determined to back away from ... The party's election post-mortem found that what cost Labor government, what stopped it getting the last few seats it needed, was a perception among voters that it lacked economic management credentials.

People are not silly. We gave away our economic legacy and the voters marked us down. They stuck with Howard, even though he was promising a taxation monster. Now Crean is going to be adaptive. The brains trust has finally worked out we can never restore our economic credentials by banging on about tariffs and subsidies. So adaptive Simon and opportunistic Kim are drying out. They should never have got on the industry policy piss in the first place.

As ever, it's just a convenience for them. It is hard to believe they will convince the electorate of their market credentials when they don't really believe in them themselves. They have wasted three years sending the Party in the wrong direction and, even now, it is doubtful we can recapture our legacy. No wonder Beazley's leadership is being questioned.

That's phase one of my three-year plan: a stunning U-turn on economic policy. Phase two will see Beazley and Crean mess up this new agenda because they don't understand it or believe in it. Then I will be vindicated for my policy stance and return to the frontbench—phase three.

Monday, 29 March

How to win friends and influence people in a ten-minute Grievance Debate speech. Today I unloaded on the Packers and other assorted enemies in Paul Keating's defence. The *Sixty Minutes* program has done a bucket job on him over his piggery, relying on information from the notoriously unreliable Al Constantinidis. The segment was presented by the funny-ha-ha man, Paul Lyneham, which made it look even sillier. I'm from the Whitlam school of sticking by great Labor Prime Ministers, so I came out all guns blazing, pointing to the errors in the program and then getting into the politics of it—the Packer organisation's ambition to own Fairfax and the way in which Keating's cross-media laws stand in their way.

Al Constantinidis Keating's former partner in the piggery business, and Sydney businessman; nicknamed 'Fat Al'

Paul Lyneham Former ABC journalist who moved to Channel Nine

While I was there, I also touched up Brian Toohey. He's following the dictum that my enemy's enemy is my friend. He used to bag Packer but now he's cheering on the Packer allegations against Keating. Gough once told me about Toohey's indiscretions while working for Lance Barnard during the Whitlam Government. I gave the details in the House.

Tuesday, 30 March

Keating calls, very grateful for my intervention. He gives me some of the history of his run-ins with Kerry Packer. Before the 1993 election, Graham Richardson (now working for Packer) said to Keating, 'At least we still have Packer on side'. But Paul reckons, 'That was bullshit. Anyway, what was he going to do, get Laurie Oakes to fart twice instead of once on TV every night?' Classic stuff.

The Packers have always been Tories and 1993 was no different. According to Paul, Packer Senior wanted John Singleton to drop the ALP advertising account for the election campaign. James Packer, in his best tuxedo, went to the InterContinental Hotel in Sydney on election night to meet the new Prime Minister, John Hewson, but then left by the back door once the results were known.

I was the only Labor MP to defend Paul against the Channel Nine muck. And after our conversation I was extra glad that I did. Keating is a mighty tribal warrior. It gives me heart just listening to him. It will cost me dearly with the Packers, of course, but who cares?

Wednesday, 31 March

This Keating and Packer thing has really taken off. Paul Lyneham called around to my Parliament House office, looking ruffled and nervous. Maybe he didn't expect anyone to counter-attack. Or maybe he's in too deep, putting his reputation on the line for the sake of the Packer/Keating feud.

He tried hard to convince me that I was on the wrong side of the argument: 'I'm surprised that someone with your reputation as a thinker in this place would defend Keating. We have more to come in this story, a lot more to come. I'm telling you, we are going to put him in gaol'. I replied, 'Well, that's a big call to make; you are going to put a former Prime Minister in

---

Brian Toohey Senior columnist for the Fairfax newspapers in Sydney
Lance Barnard ALP member, Bass 1954–75; Dep. PM 1972–74; Defence Min. 1972–75 in Whitlam govt

John Singleton Prominent Sydney racing identity, businessman and advertising executive
James Packer Son of Kerry Packer and heir to the Packer media empire

gaol, based on the word of Fat Al. The dogs are barking about him. And you, my friend, are up shit creek without a paddle'. Lyneham left looking nervier than when he came in.

A better conversation later in the day with Mike Keating, who was part of a delegation of ANU economists talking to the Caucus Economics Committee. He said that he found *Civilising Global Capital* easy to follow, the best outline of globalisation he has seen. Colin James, the New Zealand commentator and policy wonk, said much the same thing to me. So the big book is holding up quite well.

On the broader front, Beazley has had a bad start to the year. He has surrounded himself with process people (Crean/Evans/Smith/Swan) and now they are turning the process on him. He's well liked in Caucus and by the public, but he doesn't command respect. He has always fought against things and never staked his career on fighting for something he actually believes in. That's the problem with someone who has taken over the family business.

The lack of respect is hurting him, even with his own people: Smith and Conroy running amok on forests policy, with Swan doing the same on GST policy. The only thing holding up Beazley is his polling numbers. If they fell away, the so-called loyalists would probably turn on him.

Tuesday, 6 April

One thing about elected office, you get used to the barbs and jostling for position. You don't like it, but you get used to it. Not so the media. They have the luxury of sitting back, taking their pot-shots and never expecting a reply. Most politicians allow themselves to be punching bags for the media, too timid or ambitious to ever take them on. Well, bugger that, I like to give as good as I get. If they whack in, whack back. Invariably, the journalists don't know how to handle it.

Just look at Toohey. The day after I got into him in Parliament, he faxed me a letter of complaint: 'What is your proof for your claim [for the matter you raised in Parliament]? I would be grateful for your faxed reply by noon, Wednesday, March 31.' Who does he think he is? Perry Mason?

Today it got even funnier. The editor of the *Financial Review*, Colleen Ryan, has written to me on behalf of her mate saying that she was taken aback by the ferocity of my attack on Toohey. She regards it as an attack on

---

Mike Keating ANU academic and former head of the PM's Dept under Paul Keating | Stephen Conroy Vic. ALP Sen. 1996– ; Shadow Financial Services & Regulation Min. 1998–2001

her newspaper, so she is obviously very sensitive about it. She wants me to send her any evidence substantiating the material in my speech.

What are they going on about? Gough Whitlam is adamant that the matter I raised in Parliament is true. The Toohey and Ryan letters are headed for my pinboard, highlighting all the absurd things I have come across in Parliament. At this rate, I will need a bigger pinboard.

Friday, 16 April

A corker of a day—a briefing and then lunch with Keating at his Sydney office. The man is a comic genius. Best to record his observations in his own words.

On the restoration of the heritage building in which his office is located: 'The National Trust sent around an adviser, a bloke in a turban, telling me what to do. I said to him, "Listen, mate, I first visited this building when I was seventeen years of age. You would have been selling pappadams in Bombay back then"'.

On his economic legacy: 'This bloke Costello got hit in the arse by a rainbow. He's just got to wake up every morning and take credit for the economic outcomes I created'.

On Kerry Packer: 'He falls out with all his close friends, you know. Look at the list—Trevor Kennedy, Malcolm Turnbull and on it goes … He came to see me at Kirribilli in 1994, said he had something big to discuss. He wanted to carve up the pay TV cable, create a cosy little monopoly for himself. He stood there on the verandah of Kirribilli House, looking across the harbour, telling me the areas he wanted. I told him to piss off, I believed in competition and that was not going to change. He looked at me and said, "I knew you'd run out of ideas eventually" and then he left'.

On Stephen Smith (Shadow Minister for Communications): 'How could he ever handle Packer? He's always between a shit and a shiver'.

On Beazley: 'What would he know from roaming around the Western Australian branch and visiting Pommies in nursing homes? He came to see me for advice, you know. Well, Kim and I have totally different views of politics. Look at him, he lost an election and he's still walking around like a big cuddly bear. I told him I see it like the *National Geographic* ad, where in slow motion the wildebeest grabs the lion on the arse, with blood and fur and dust and shit flying everywhere. That's what the mob wants in the last fortnight of a campaign—a sign that you really want it. Kim didn't give that to them last time. He's fucking hopeless. I went and saw my accountant after the election and asked him how he voted. He said that he voted Labor but he didn't think Beazley really wanted it. That sums him up. He won't kill for it'.

Keating had plenty of other colourful commentary about the Packers, Brian Toohey and Toohey's protégés at Fairfax. He wants me to work this stuff into my speeches, but the language and nicknames are red hot, even for me.

Wednesday, 28 April

I'm part of a dying breed in the ALP. Whatever happened to the Party's interest in ideas and reform? It has been sucked dry by the machine professionals and smarties. Also, whatever happened to Labor's knock-around culture? It has been sucked dry by the self-conscious careerists—Smith, Swan, Beazley, McMullan, Macklin, Faulkner, Ray et al. We have too many Christian-icon collectors, bushwalkers and trivia buffs and not enough drinkers/punters.

Face the facts: Labor is stuffed. Its branches are rorted and its membership base is a joke. A party wanting to represent a majority of the electorate itself needs to have a representative membership base. We will never have the new aspirants—IT workers, small businesspeople and consultants—attend our branch meetings unless we give them a real say in the way in which the Party is run. But the factions and union bosses hate democracy, it takes power away from them.

We are supposed to be a worker's party, yet 70 per cent of Australian workers are outside the union movement. The unions in this country are a minority grouping with a majority complex, and they take out their angst on the ALP. They maintain 60 per cent of the delegates to Party conferences and throw their weight around as part of the factional system. If the trade unions want a majority of votes in the Labor Party, why don't they go out and win a majority of support in the workforce? Can't have that, their officials might have to get out of their Chinese restaurants and actually do some work.

Despair on all fronts. Party democracy, policy debates and knock-around types—we are bankrupt at every turn. Time to call in the receivers.

Monday, 17 May

I'm on a Commonwealth Parliamentary Association junket to England, a gathering of MPs from across the empire. The official program is useless, but it gives me a chance to line up meetings to study the Third Way in the

---

Bob McMullan Shadow Industry & Technology Min. 1998–2000; Manager of Opposition Business 1998–2001

Jenny Macklin Shadow Health Min. 1998–2001
John Faulkner NSW ALP Sen. 1989– ; min. in Keating govt; ALP Sen. Leader 1996–2004

UK. There's some impressive stuff going on. The Blair Government is implementing a program of political and social devolution—new regional assemblies, abolishing hereditary peers and empowering community leaders to get stuck into welfare reform. That's what I like about the Third Way, it's based on the dispersal of power and privilege.

Until now, the Left has been obsessed with the economic levers, trying to change the distribution of material goods. This has left untouched the other pillars of inequality in society: political access and social status. Traditional class struggle has faded away. The new struggle is about access and power, breaking down the Establishment's monopoly on social privilege.

The Third Way is more interested in the relations between people than controlling economic relationships. Blair calls it social-ism. It ends the Left's 200-year obsession with the means of production, distribution and exchange. It also marks a change in political technique, away from empowering the state and towards dispersing power to regions, communities and citizens instead, giving people the raw materials with which they might build a more mutual, caring society.

I saw an example of this at Bromley-by-Bow in London. The local clergyman, Andrew Mawson, has transformed a poor neighbourhood by inspiring new confidence and creativity among its residents. He's what the British call a social entrepreneur, a leader who is willing to take risks, who finds clever ways of using abandoned community assets and encouraging people to develop their skills, self-esteem and full potential in life.

On the ground, the results are striking, with new enterprises, jobs and training. This is the best answer to poverty: government support, yes, but resourcing rather than directing neighbourhood initiatives. Too much reliance on government means too much power for government and its bureaucracies. The solution to welfare dependency lies in empowering individuals and communities. The Blair Government is now looking for 2000 social entrepreneurs nationwide.

I had a good talk about this approach with Geoff Mulgan over dinner. He reckons the reforms are encouraging but is not convinced they can adequately reshape the bureaucracy and its hierarchical style. On a lighter note, I asked for baby potatoes to go with my duck and Mulgan corrected me, saying they are called new potatoes. I said, 'Isn't that going too far—New Labour, New Britain, new potatoes?'

The junket ends in three days' time when, hopefully, the Pakistani delegates will rejoin us. It is a standing joke at the CPA: the Pakistani MPs fly

Geoff Mulgan Third Way author and Tony Blair's policy adviser in, disappear into the suburbs of London for two weeks and then rejoin the delegation at the departure gates at Heathrow. This year, one of them actually made it to the orientation session on day one. Poor bastard, he was so nervous when he stood up to talk about his background that he pissed himself, literally! Then we never saw him again.

Tuesday, 1 June

A Beazley classic in Caucus today. He was waffling on about the sins of the Government's GST package and how there was ample room for the ALP to fix it up. Then Sid Sidebottom, a well-intentioned but naïve fellow, jumped up and asked, 'How? How are we going to fix it up, Kim?' As Gareth would say, it was like farting in church. Beazley stuttered and spluttered for a while before finally replying, 'We don't want to give out too much detail just yet'.

Translation: he has no idea.

Tuesday, 8 June

Napoleon once described Britain as a nation of shopkeepers. Today's Caucus meeting was a reminder of how Labor has become a Party of retail politicians. Beazley told us that 'Labor people are always putting themselves on a cross, asking what needs to be done. What we should be doing is pointing out what the other side has already done'. Yeah, but if we go down that path far enough, we will end up just like the other side—a bunch of scragging conservatives, living in the past and never talking about the future.

It's so disappointing. A Labor Leader complaining that Labor people are always asking what needs to be done in society. Well, root my boot, that is what makes us Labor! We care about the needy and want to develop the vision and reality of a fairer society. Beazley should be encouraging the Party to talk more about what needs to be done, not disparaging it.

He's followed Bob Carr's way, a retail politician, running the family business, the family shop. Perhaps it's just the way the system has evolved. Television is the ultimate retail medium, suited to short, sharp images and stunts, never any policy detail or ideology. And television dominates this place—just look at Beazley tossing around cans of tomato soup at his morning doorstops outside Parliament House. It's *The Truman Show* for egomaniacs and opportunists. Marshall McLuhan was right: the medium

Marshall McLuhan Prominent American academic and media theorist is the message. And Australia's great party of social reform has become a retail party, a tomato soup party.

Wednesday, 23 June

The tribe gathers for a tribute dinner to Leo McLeay at the Kurrajong Hotel, celebrating the twentieth anniversary of his election to Parliament. He's been good to me, so I went along, but the sad thing was, it could just as easily have been a Liberal Party function. It was just a series of good fellow stories.

Beazley spoke of Keating and Whitlam as if they were mad. He sees them that way because they believed in things and fought for them. That's not the Beazley way of doing politics. It is typical of the modern ALP—those who believe in things and interfere with the easy path of electoralism and negativity are labelled as weird and disruptive.

That wonderful line in *Alice in Wonderland* captures Beazley's leadership: 'If you don't know where you are going, any road will take you there'. He has prepared none of the ground needed in public opinion to deal with the big issues: structural reform of the health system, our own modernisation of the tax system, the creation of lifelong learning and the rebuilding of community life and compassion in society. Any old road will do.

Friday, 25 June

A telltale conversation with Dick Scotton, one of the founding fathers of Medibank and Medicare. My column in the *Tele* today promotes his proposals for a new round of health reform: ending the gross inefficiency and inequity of the current system by moving to a series of risk-rated capitation payments. That is, every Australian resident would be allocated government funds to cover their basic health insurance, weighted to reflect their exposure to health risks. Universality would be maintained while opening up greater choice, contestability and cost savings in the system.

I asked Scotton what interest Jenny Macklin had shown in his scheme. The answer was 'none'. Moreover, he was scathing about her. He recalled seeing her in the 1980s when she was an adviser to the Victorian Health Minister, David White. She asked him about the future of health policy and he replied that the Government needed to introduce casemix (funding hospitals on the basis of patient treatments—outputs rather than inputs—a system that has now become the orthodoxy in State hospital funding).

Dick Scotton Monash University health economist who, with John Deeble, helped | Whitlam create ALP's Medibank policy in the late 1960s

Macklin replied, 'We don't believe in casemix'. Scotton reckons 'This was one of the more fuckwitted things I have ever heard. I'm afraid she is a person I don't want to have anything to do with'. Great, one of the authors of Medicare has blackballed our health spokesperson. So much for Macklin's reputation as a policy guru.

Tuesday, 29 June

For a while Leo McLeay has been trying to organise a dinner with Beazley and me, his personal effort to see if our differences can be reconciled. Tonight we had a go at it but with no great success. I wrote down a long list of issues I wanted to raise with the Leader—general strategy, economic credibility, employment policy, education and training, mutual responsibility policies and the Scotton health plan—but it was hard getting him to focus on any of them.

Kim has a really annoying habit: whenever the conversation looks like turning into a disagreement or something controversial, he starts staring off into the distance. Time to change the subject. And the bottom line? Where there is no interest in policy reform there can be no activity or progress. The only issue we discussed in depth was Badgerys Creek Airport (one of Leo's favourites), and even then, Kim concluded that we needed to do some opinion polling in Western Sydney. All very depressing.

In a world of constant change, it is better to be always expanding your mind and ideas than to end up like Beazley. There are two types of people I like: those with a deep personal interest in public policy and the larrikin/knockabout characters. No wonder I don't get along with Kim Beazley Junior.

Monday, 12 July

Beazley's letter to the editor in today's *Daily Telegraph* is a good guide to our economic credibility problems. He writes, 'What is required to get the unemployment rate to 5 per cent is a multi-dimensional strategy that invests in the skills of the unemployed, reduces labour costs through wage subsidies, increases work incentives through tax credits, and reduces the costs of working through child care'. Four very expensive commitments in one letter.

Add to that the cost of GST rollback, Research and Development incentives, industry policy handouts, increased hospital funding and our education commitments, and the Liberal attack is obvious: where is the money coming from? These days, policy-making has to be more sophisticated than simply advocating more money for more programs. The public is very cynical about this old Left approach. That's why we should be talking about structural and institutional change, smarter and more effective ways of using public money. We should be advocating a mixed social sector, with increased interaction between public and private service-providers.

And we should be releasing our cost savings upfront—if we have any. Transparency is the best political strategy. There is no way of skating through our credibility problems. That's how we got into trouble in the first place, with Beazley's black hole and the public fear that interest rates will increase under Labor. We need a hard bastard like Peter Walsh to give us fiscal grunt and credibility.

I am afraid Tanner is not in the same league as Walsh. Around the place, I refer to him as 'the ever helpful Lindsay Tanner'. When my book came out last year he helpfully told the press that he was saving his for after the election. When Beazley backgrounded the travelling media pack during the campaign that Tanner and I 'were too intellectually proud for our own good', Lindsay told the media that he 'wears it like a badge of honour'. He should have ripped right into Beazley. Not someone I can rely on; he won't stand up to Beazley or the spending Shadows.

Saturday, 31 July

Last Monday, I gave a big speech on welfare policy at the Brisbane Institute, sharing a platform with Noel Pearson, the charismatic Aboriginal activist from Cape York. I stressed the social dimension of poverty, the need for self-esteem and community-building, using the example and inspiration of social entrepreneurs in south-west Sydney.

The similarities between Pearson's conclusions and mine were striking: welfare dependency is a social, not financial, issue. The welfare state works under the assumption that the poor are hopeless and only government intervention can solve poverty. In fact, this 'pity the poor' ethos is the real problem—it sees welfare as an equation in dollars and cents, instead of an equation between people. Basic self-esteem and trust have broken down. The state needs to find new and innovative ways of rebuilding social capital by identifying community leaders and backing successful projects. It needs to be a junior partner to communities, not the reverse.

These are radical conclusions that challenge the legitimacy and culture of Left-of-Centre politics. Publicly, I have been talking up the prospects of Party and policy reform, but realistically, it is highly unlikely. Labor's culture is based on the authority of government, getting into office and telling people what to do. It relies on the methodology of bureaucracy:

fitting people into categories, standardising problems and trying to mass-produce solutions. Governments cannot legislate for social capital and expect it to happen. The top-down approach does not work.

The requirements of community life are totally different: devolving power, enabling people to make their own decisions, recognising the diversity of individuals and communities, finding unique solutions to localised problems. Government bureaucracy and social capital are a poor fit, a square peg in a round hole. And that is not going to change.

The horse bolted in the first half of the century when Labor abandoned its mutualist traditions—socialism in the relationship between people—and embraced the welfare state—socialism in the relationship between government and its citizens. We can talk about the Third Way, a fourth way, a fifth way. In practice, it will take a miracle for the control freaks and power junkies of the Labor movement to reform their ways. I'm pissing in the wind.

I think we have to get used to the idea of a troubled society. Record levels of GDP now sit alongside record levels of crime, mental illness, family breakdown and social stress. People have had the zap put on their heads.

We talk about globalisation—trusting in strangers—but people don't even know the names of their next-door neighbours. Just look at the suburb I live in (Glen Alpine): double-storey houses, manicured lawns and no community. In fact, when Campbelltown Council asked people what sort of community facilities they wanted, they said none, it might attract undesirables into the area (code for the public housing residents over the hill at Ambarvale and Rosemeadow).

Thursday, 12 August

Another blue with another sanctimonious commentator, this time Gerard Henderson from the Sydney Institute (an old Grouper, one of Santa's little helpers and Howard's former Chief of Staff). He's made a career out of pedantry, pulling apart other people's mistakes. I have now committed the mortal sin of finding a galaxy of errors in one of his projects. Earlier this year he helped his wife write a femocrazy book called *Getting Even*. I wrote a critical review in which I highlighted dozens of rudimentary mistakes, and now the Hendersons are bombarding me with letters and faxes.

You wouldn't believe the sensitivity of these people. They are wrapped too tight. But from where I sit, that's the good thing about Gerard, he's so easy to bait. Say 50 words about him and he will write 50 000 in reply. As they say in the classics, any publicity …

This is the style of political commentary in Australia. It's not considered opinion or analysis but personal payback. Grumpy old men slagging and re-slagging each other—a war of words (usually the same words) between the likes of Henderson, Piers Akerman, Paddy McGuiness, Christopher Pearson, Frank Devine and Phillip Adams. An American wag once described politics as showbiz for ugly people. In this country, political commentary is payback from ugly old men.

My dilemma is this: do I keep on racking up enemies in the media (Packer, Lyneham, Oakes, Toohey, Henderson and so the list grows) or do I bite my tongue and suck holes? Stuff it, it's too much fun baiting the tossers. I say 50 words about them and they write 50 000 words about me. That's the deal.

Saturday, 28 August

Joel Fitzgibbon and I are still cacking ourselves about Michael Lee's adjournment speech two days ago. It was a shameful but hilarious example of the things politicians will do to milk a vote. Lee complained that one of his constituents, a 25-year-old man with a mild intellectual disability, racked up a $2000 phone bill by calling a sex chat line twelve times in one day. He ended up with a bad case of blisters and a bill he couldn't pay.

The bloke's mum approached Lee, who took up the case, telling the House 'it is a social obscenity' that Telstra refuses to waive the bill. Sounds like the obscenity was down the phone line. Lee finished his speech as follows:

> Tonight I appeal to Minister Alston: pick up the phone, ring Ziggy Swikowski and demand that Telstra wipe this bill and that of any other parent of a disabled person out there who has been affected in a similar way. Thank God we are now bringing in the system that requires written requests before these services are hooked up because families like this will no longer be terrorised by Telstra and Card Access in this way.

Terrorised by Telstra! The 25-year-old had access to a phone and he used it. No one held a gun to his head. Anyway, Joel saw Lee after the speech and tried to make light of it, expecting little Michael to laugh and

---

Paddy McGuiness Right-wing commentator with the Fairfax newspapers
Christopher Pearson *Adelaide Review* Right-wing editor

Phillip Adams Left-wing social commentator and journalist
Ziggy Switkowski CEO, Telstra

fess up to his rank populism, as most of us would. Not on your Nelly; he was very narky, insisting that phone sex bills are a serious issue. Obviously a case of one wanker defending another.

Someone with a better sense of humour: I talked to Keating, following up the *Sixty Minutes* stuff. He reckons he saw Brian Toohey in a Sydney restaurant and said to him, 'What's wrong Brian, you're not into me in the paper today. Well, that Latham fixed you up. And do you know what he did with that letter you sent him? Do you know what he did? He wiped his arse with it and pinned it on his toilet wall'.

Tuesday, 31 August

Caucus today and the earth has moved on Beazley. We have fallen 10 per cent behind in Newspoll (Coalition 47 per cent primary, ALP 37 per cent) and the Party is looking for leadership. I have never seen so many heads down at a Caucus meeting. But Big Kim still bellowed away at the front, the emperor with no clothes. He reckons that after the Government's deal with the Democrats to get the GST through the Senate, 'We have been liberated from the Democrats. We are now free to do our own thing … Sure, there is an economic boom underway but we will be out there asking the question of the Australian people: do you feel better off?' That's the best the BLF, the Beazley Liberation Front, can do these days.

The economic indicators are so strong that the only way in which we can win the next election is to generate new issues. But Beazley is yet to get up an issue in his own right. Now that the Government's failures are drying up, he has no issues or appeal of his own. He's a purist in what we oppose, not a purist in what we can advocate. He was the perfect leader for the Party's purposes in 1996–98, but the worst kind for the challenges of 1998–2001.

Could the machine men who back him be losing their faith? Perhaps the two cultures in Caucus are about to collide. The NSW Right culture is to win at all costs. The Beazley culture is scab-lifting—see an issue, a public sore, and try to lift the scab without offering your own remedy. The latter is losing us votes, and the former won't tolerate another election defeat.

So, how does he get out of this? I don't think he can. Kim's advisers are trying to turn him into a tough guy, raising his voice in the House, trying to be more aggressive with the media. But putting a tough surface on a blanc-mange is bound to backfire. What they should do is pick an issue and fight for it, to the death. A big, bellowing cow in Parliament will never fool the public. They want to see the character and conviction of an issues-based Leader.

Thursday, 2 September

The things you do in Parliament House. At midday I went to a meeting of the ALP Status of Women Committee, our frontline femocrat cadres. Now I know how Martin Luther felt, pinning his thesis to the church door. A heretic in their ranks, I advocated an overhaul of the Committee to take account of men's issues. We should call it the Status of Gender Committee, taking account of both genders, a genuinely inclusive approach. After all, the main social indicators now show that men are more disadvantaged than women in life expectancy, school retention rates, university entry to professional careers, youth suicide rates and so forth. We need to address the problem of downwards envy, of angry white men turning against the ALP. Male and female issues should be treated on their merits.

Needless to say, I didn't get very far. If looks could kill. Some of them had technical and historical reasons why my idea was inappropriate. Then Senator Brenda Gibbs, one of the intellectual powerhouses of the Queensland ALP, said what they all thought: 'I knew it would be a mistake to let men onto this Committee. Why did we ever do it?' That would be right, a segregationist approach to the Committee's membership as well as its policies. Ah, Labor, the party of social equity.

But they are not all bad. Give me (Senator) Rosemary Crowley any day of the week. What a trooper. She told me a story about the American writer Dorothy Parker, who was asked to use the word 'horticulture' in a sentence, and replied, 'You can lead a horticulture but you can't make her think'. Years ago, Joel's dad and predecessor in Hunter, Eric Fitzgibbon, told me the story of Rose visiting a colleague's electorate and getting into a discussion with some of the locals about their cars. She floored them by pointing out, 'Listen, you blokes, I have had more rubber up my cunt than you've got on those tyres'. Rose for PM.

In the evening, I went to a dinner in the Great Hall to listen to John Anderson open proceedings at Ross Cameron's youth leadership forum (roped in again). It was one of the wackiest speeches I have ever heard. He attacked humanism, the power of reason and rationality, on the basis that he once spoke to a humanist who didn't know whether he believed in positive or negative humanism. He said that 'nineteenth-century European man' experienced a loss of Christian faith and this led to World War I. He's got to be kidding: what's he saying, that religion has never caused any wars?

Brenda Gibbs Qld ALP Sen. 1996–2002

John Anderson NP member, Gwydir 1989– ; min. in Howard govt 1996–2005; Deputy PM 1999–2005

Anderson found his own faith as a young man when he accidentally killed his sister with a misdirected cricket shot to the head. What about those of us who haven't had this experience? He expects us to share his faith, but with none of his background and his obvious, desperate attempt to find meaning in his life after a shocking tragedy. When I hear stories like this it makes me more convinced about the myths of religion and the spurious grounds on which Bible-bashers promote their faith.

Poor old Ando, he should have just played a straight bat and ignored all this pagan idolatry masquerading as religion, all these kiddie-fiddlers masquerading as priests. Latham's first law of the church: the greater the degree of fanaticism in so-called faith, the greater the degree of escapism, either from addiction (alcohol, drugs, gambling or sex) or from personal tragedy. My evidence? I was at a function listening to John Anderson, organised by Ross Cameron. The prosecution rests.

Anderson went on to talk about our 'shared humanity' and how our morality must come from a higher existence, almighty God. If we share our humanity then, surely, our morality must also come from these shared social experiences. That's the problem with these high-horse Christians, they have no language or dialogue about the real-life relations between people. For them, it is entirely functional. The Council of Nicaea sorted it out nearly 1700 years ago and we should simply follow its orders. Organised religion: just another form of conservative command and control in our society.

Thursday, 30 September

At last, we've seen the back of Gareth Evans, who resigned from Parliament today, ostensibly to chase the top job at UNESCO. The speeches in his honour highlighted the hypocrisy of this place. All the bunkum about Gareth being our greatest ever Foreign Minister (Gough was much better in 1973), yet two weeks ago, in 60 ten-minute speeches by Labor MPs on the big foreign policy issue of the day (Timor), I was the only one who mentioned him.

All the stuff they trotted out about a man of ideas and intellect. Sure, he did some good things, like the Cambodian settlement and getting Mabo through the Senate, but our standards are too low in this country. Gareth was a solid Foreign Minister and a hopeless Shadow Treasurer. Hardly a

---

Council of Nicaea A reconciliation by Christian powerbrokers of competing strands in church doctrine

genius. As a personality, he always reminded me of Bob Carr—it was all about him.

Last night the Party gave him a send-off at the Kurrajong Hotel. It would have been a bit rich of me to attend, so instead I went to dinner at the Chairman & Yip Restaurant with Joel, his brother Mark, and the love of my life, Janine Lacy. We spent the night aching with laughter. Mark Fitzgibbon told the story of when he was working at Cessnock Council in the early 1980s and went to a word-processing course. When he got back to work that afternoon, the head accountant, Stan Neilly (who later became the State Labor member for Cessnock), asked him where had he been. Mark said, 'I've been out learning about word processing', to which Stan responded, 'Sounds okay, but it will never catch on'. One of his best.

We also put in a few calls to the Kurrajong. In my best, deep African accent I convinced the hotel reception that I was Kofi Annan and needed to speak to Gareth Evans urgently: 'This is Kofi Annan, this is Kofi Annan, I need to speak to Mr Evans straight away'. They told me that wasn't possible because he was on his feet speaking to a Labor Party function. I insisted that they interrupt him, but they resisted. In the end I left a message: 'Please call Kofi Annan urgently in New York. He has good news about the African votes for the UNESCO job'. I also put in a call to our mate Bobby McMullan's voicemail, asking a few questions about his comb-over. He never got back to me—totally humourless.

I need nights like this: they keep me going in Canberra. It reminds me of the story about the great British Labour thinker and Minister Tony Crosland. His colleagues used to protest to him about his reputation with women and constantly turning up drunk in the Commons. Crosland replied, 'How else is one to endure being here?'

Saturday, 9 October

Keating phones with another grand tour of events and personalities. Howard wrote to Indonesian President Habibie, urging him to act on East Timor. The US Deputy Secretary of State, Stanley Roth, told Keating of his conversation with Habibie about the Howard letter. Habibie said, 'I was very upset with the letter. I woke in the middle of the night and thought, I must give them their independence'. He then showed Roth the notepad on which he scribbled this note to himself. So, in Keating's mind, Howard is to blame for the shit-fight in East Timor.

Paul explained his strategy with Indonesia, the purpose of his 1995 defence pact: 'What I wanted to do was put their 200 million people in the frontline—their army, our weapons. This was our frontline defence of Australia if China ever went as bad as some people said it could'.

He is ticked off with Brereton over East Timor, pointing out that even McMullan consulted him on the Party's change to enterprise bargaining policy, but Laurie didn't do the same on Timor. If they weren't mates, he would go for him publicly.

He reckons that Richo and Peter Barron worked out a counter-attack strategy against him after his sensational speech last Sunday at the ALP State Conference, when he laid into Packer. They did the media rounds, claiming that Keating did not support the Australian peacekeepers in Timor.

He ran me through the history of his battle to introduce foreign banks and greater financial competition in Australia. At one point Jack Ferguson said to him, 'The Australian banks might be bad and run by the other mob [the Tories] but at least they are our banks'.

He's still very impressed with my parliamentary counter-attack on Packer. He finished by saying, 'Mark, you're the only one in the Caucus who backed me. You're our only hope down there'.

Monday, 11 October

Further defence of the great men of Labor. My *Financial Review* column today makes a spirited defence of Whitlam and Keating's record on Indonesia and the Timor question. I'm swimming against the tide, of course. Brereton has screwed them over by acting as a mouthpiece for Fretilin. I'm the only one in Caucus still holding the line:

> The history of East Timor is a history of moral wrongs: in centuries of Portuguese colonisation, in the 1975 civil war, in Fretilin's unilateral declaration of a Democratic Republic of East Timor in November 1975, in the manner of the Indonesian invasion and occupation and then the recent tragedy. There is no need for Australia to rack itself with guilt over the long history of these events. In fact, the first and most enduring guilty party is Portugal, especially given its disgraceful abandonment of East Timor in August 1975. Yet this is rarely mentioned in the Australian debate, largely due to the partially Portuguese origins of the East Timorese leadership.

Peter Barron Former Hawke adviser who then worked for Kerry Packer

Jack Ferguson Father of Laurie and Martin; former NSW Dep. Premier in the Wran govt and a leader of the NSW ALP Left in NSW

Gough rang, delighted with the article, particularly its use of the term 'partially Portuguese'. He said, 'You have a good way with words, comrade, the way you didn't call them half-castes'.

In faxes to the office, he has started calling me Justinian and himself Solomon—a reference to Emperor Justinian's words as he entered the great church at Constantinople: 'Solomon, I have surpassed thee'. It is ridiculous, of course. Maybe Gough has run out of historical analogies, so he's making them up as he goes along.

Keating also rang, very downcast, on a flight to China. He said, 'This Caucus meeting tomorrow, they're all against me now [on Timor]'. I suppose they are, but all the more reason why he's right and they are just a pile of pissants. No consolation for me, however. Late in the afternoon, I put the Whitlam/Keating arguments to a meeting of the National Right. This was a signal for most of them to start leaving the room, ending the meeting. I felt about two inches tall.

That's the paradox I work under. Encouragement from the likes of Whitlam and Keating, nothing but disdain from my so-called colleagues. Forget about Justinian; when it comes to the Federal Parliamentary Labor Party, I should use Disraeli's declaration: 'the time will come when you will hear me'.

Some comic relief later in the day, as Pills relays a story from one of Wayne Swan's former staffers, now based in Isaacs. The office was working on the weekend to finalise a big project, so Swan brought in one of his children. But things went wrong with the project. Swan flew into a mad fit of rage, slamming closed the compactus (vertical filing cabinets on roller-wheels). After a short period of silence, an agonising scream came from the middle of the compactus—the kid was in there! A few days later, the staffer saw the child again, this time with a pair of black eyes. Now Swan gets around the country lecturing other people about family policy, that's his job.

Tuesday, 12 October

Keating calls from Shanghai and tells me about Tony Benn's categorisation of politicians. There are three types: straight men, fixers and maddies. He puts Hawke and Richo in the fixer category and declares, 'Only maddies can lead this country and get things done. Look at me, I'm as mad as a cut snake'. He ended the call by telling me to 'stay in a crouch', as if we were

Tony Benn Long-serving UK socialist Labour MP

commandoes in the jungle, waiting for something to happen. I might be known as a maddie myself, but I am nowhere near this guy's league.

Tuesday, 19 October

Beazley tells Caucus that his guiding electoral principle is the huge gap between the elites and ordinary Australians. Despite 'our problems and inadequacies as an Opposition, the electorate has made us surprisingly competitive in the polls because they think our heart is in the right spot'. He points to 'the worsening struggle to gain access to education, health, childcare and other services. The mob feel that government is working against them'.

You need to listen carefully to this man. This was not a speech about problem-solving. That's the difference between us. I see a problem in the public arena and think: how do I solve it and explain the solution to people. Beazley sees a problem and thinks: how do I analyse it and exploit it. I've listened to hundreds of his speeches now and not once have I heard anything interesting or provocative. Could he make Opposition any more uninteresting?

That's the big difference between him and Keating and Whitlam. He's a boredom machine. I sat next to Joel during the meeting and he summed it up perfectly: 'You know, Beazley reports to Caucus like it's a branch meeting'. That's right, he's always dumbing down the debate.

And at today's meeting, he also made a fundamental mistake. Beazley fancies himself as an outsider but he doesn't recognise his own background as a political insider, as part of the elites. Nor does he understand that more money for more government programs is not the outsider's answer. He underestimates Howard, particularly on the economy. Howard always looks vulnerable—that's his greatest strength because people in the outer suburbs and regions do not see him as one of the elites.

All the signs are that our policy work will fade away. We are going back to the low-risk 1996–98 agenda. Come 2001, we won't have enough to offer the electorate; we're up against a booming economy and a perceived outsider in Howard, who won't do a Kennett/Goss/Greiner and look arrogant.

Thursday, 21 October

I've been critical of Beazley, very critical, but I was watching him in Parliament this week and thought to myself: he has to master so much

Jeff Kennett Vic. Lib. Premier 1992–99　　|　**Wayne Goss** Qld ALP Premier 1989–96

information every day—the scandals and issues of the moment—is it humanly possible for one person to find the time and resources to also master policy development? Beyond the individual, Labor has a cultural problem, a cancer through the Party: the rise of machine politics and the demise of the True Believers.

The faction bosses see power as an end in its own right, a chance to dispense patronage and entrench their position at the top of the Party hierarchy. They see policy as a vehicle to achieve power, not as a reform tool for a better society. The methodology is simple: use opinion polls and focus groups to find out what the public thinks and then tell them we think exactly the same way. Attack the Government, avoid creative or controversial policies, and make the Party a small target in the media.

This cultural habit has spread through our ranks. Where are the young radicals, the tearaways joining the ranks of Federal Labor? They are not to be found in the class of 1998. Who are we talking about? The likes of Kevin Rudd, Craig Emerson, Anna Burke, Nicola Roxon, Michael Danby, Sid Sidebottom, Steve Gibbons, Julia Irwin, Kelly Hoare and Kim Wilkie. The list goes on: more careerists, more technocrats, more plodders. But no independent thinkers, no maddies, as Keating calls them.

Yet this is the moment when the maddies are needed—a time of constant change and political realignment, the advent of the Information Age. It is quite surreal that Labor is not taking this challenge seriously. For some of the new cadres, it is an act of treason to even raise the possibility of new policies. This is what Roxon said to me last week: I am a traitor to the unity of Labor. This from someone who has only been in the Party five minutes, shoe-horned into the safe seat of Gellibrand through a last-minute factional deal.

The culture is bad and Beazley tolerates it, even fosters it. That's his sin. It's a way of public life for him and those around him. Gary Gray and Kim's staff believe in negative campaigning, never the positive politics of conviction. They plan to delay all our major policies for the election campaign. This is bad policy and bad politics.

Surely, if the Party has something significant to say, it is best to have our policy proposals in the public arena as early as possible. This is the best way of setting the agenda, winning the debate and persuading the public.

Kevin Rudd ALP member, Griffith 1998–
Anna Burke ALP member, Chisholm 1998–
Nicola Roxon ALP member, Gellibrand 1998–
Michael Danby ALP member, Melbourne Ports 1998–

Steve Gibbons ALP member, Bendigo 1998–
Julia Irwin ALP member, Fowler 1998–
Kelly Hoare ALP member, Charlton 1998–
Kim Wilkie ALP member, Swan 1998–

In some areas, such as higher education, the Government has no policy program. All the more reason to fill the gaps with our policies.

If we have nothing significant to say then, yes, our policies will be delayed until the chaos of an election campaign. This is what the brains trust calls the small-target strategy. It is, in fact, the tactic that put the last election out of reach and, if repeated, will cost us the next election as well.

Tuesday, 23 November

My conference speeches and newspaper columns are driving the Tories inside the Labor Party mad. They hate policy being debated and contested at any level, even by a lone wolf backbencher. It was said of Churchill that he always thought aloud, putting all his ideas into the public arena. He felt the need to constantly define and explain his position. That's a good description of my position now.

Sure, some of my proposals may need more work—I haven't got a research department working for me, I'm a one-man think-tank—but at least they are stirring interest in the possibility of Labor innovation and reform. They also challenge the Party's control freaks and their dead hand on debate. Today in Caucus the empire struck back, with the Party establishment trying to put me in my place. They came at me on two issues: higher education policy and the halving of the capital gains tax.

Recently I have been advocating a shift from the unified, national system of universities to a mixed system. That is, give universities greater freedom to pursue their own unique mission and purpose, within national guidelines for funding and equity. In disadvantaged regions, for instance, the universities would operate free of charge, backed by strong public budgets. The major research universities would focus on international excellence, with deregulated fees and publicly funded scholarships to help the needy. Other universities would be funded as per the existing HECS system.

I have no doubt that this reform would lift both the quality and equality of higher education in Australia. Labor needs to abandon the status quo, which gives students from wealthy suburbs five times the level of university participation of those from poor suburbs. We need to entice disadvantaged students to university by making it free. A solid proposal, built on international best practice, and worthy of serious debate in this country. But not for Michael Lee.

At Caucus, Lee took a pre-arranged question from his mate Steve Hutchins. When the Chairman, George Campbell, asked Lee (in jest) if it was a Dorothy Dixer, he replied, 'Yes, it is'. He did not debate the merits of my proposal but tried to rule it out by exclusion: 'When the media ask me about it, I will tell them that only one person in Caucus supports that policy, unless anyone else comes to see me in my office after the meeting'. In my defence, I pointed out that when I held Lee's position I was willing to foster debate and dissent, such as launching a radical set of ideas by Peter Baldwin in his discussion paper 'The Lighthouse'. I assume that nobody entered Lee's confession box after the meeting.

This was a low moment in the history of the Caucus. Imagine Curtin, Chifley or Whitlam handling debate this way, by exclusion. As Leo McLeay said to me later in the day, 'A real smart person would not be threatened by other smart people around him'—an interesting reflection on Lee. Leo explained the hostility towards me this way: 'Our Shadow Ministers see the Government get 80 per cent of the media time, Beazley and Crean get 15 per cent and the other 5 per cent, which is supposed to be their moment in the spotlight, they spend it answering questions about you'. Whenever egos are bruised in politics, the system is very hard and unforgiving.

On capital gains tax, Beazley and Crean have put in a shocker, backing the Government's proposal to open up a new tax break for the land specu-lators and other spivs. I saw these people every day when I was in local gov-ernment and they are not worth a cracker. It's the great Australian economic disease: distorting investment decisions by rewarding the quick gains of property development, while punishing patient capital in the manufacturing and information economies.

It is another example of Labor abandoning its economic legacy. In Government, our reforms were designed to create an economy in which you could turn a dollar by being creative, not by being a speculator. Now the brains trust is supporting changes that, on average, are worth $149 a year for people on taxable incomes below $20 700, but $6500 for those earning between $100 000 and $500 000. A disgustingly inequitable and irrational piece of public policy.

I put these arguments to the Caucus meeting but got nowhere. A bit of back-up from Barney Cooney, and that was about it. The ever-reliable Tanner, the lion of the Left, made a lengthy speech in favour of the changes. The most bizarre contribution came from Conroy, who spoke in favour but then came over to where I was sitting and said, 'I didn't believe a word of what I just said'. I can't believe that he would admit that.

My only consolation: Crean was ropeable at my contribution. I fin-gered him badly in front of his Left-wing mates. They saw first-hand how

---

'The Lighthouse' The title of Peter Baldwin's 1997 discussion paper on the reform of ALP education policy

Barney Cooney Vic. ALP Sen. 1984–2002
Lindsay Tanner Shadow Finance and Consumer Affairs Min. 1998–2001

he has turned us into a corporate welfare party for the benefit of the big end of town.

As usual, opportunism carried the day. In his report to Caucus, Beazley said he was following his pollster's advice: the GST is more unpopular than ever and he wants to keep the focus on this issue. But if the GST is so unpopular, why have we been behind in the polls for twelve months? In truth, Beazley and Crean are heading back to their comfort zone, a scragging, negative attack on a single issue. They have intellectually bankrupted our Party. It is just a matter of seeing if they do the same to us electorally.

Beazley cannot win. Since World War I, there has never been a change of national government unless one or a combination of three factors is in place: an economic downturn; an 'it's time' factor after three terms; and/or a distinctive/attractive Opposition agenda. None of these factors will be evident at the next election. That's the truth of it.

Wednesday, 24 November

Who will guard the guardians? Every now and then I read something that, instinctively, I feel is hopelessly wrong. I hate the way the media get away with it—they churn out their stuff, all their pious commentary about politicians, but then their forecasts are forgotten. No one holds them to account.

Here's a piece from today's *Bulletin* that is going on my pinboard. I want these predictions by Jabba the Hutt to be judged over time:

A great deal of nonsense is written and spoken in the name of political commentary ... Labor is getting smart. It wants to be able to grab political opportunities as they arise, rather than help the Government by making a target of itself ... Expect Labor to show political nous when it comes to announcing detailed policies in a whole range of areas. They will not be dribbled out a long way ahead of the election, as the government and sections of the media are demanding, but held back until much closer to the event—in many cases, until the campaign itself.

Oakes is part of the protectionist Packer organisation. I remember two years ago, when I told him I was writing a book on globalisation, he said, 'Wouldn't it be good if we could stop globalisation'. That's why they hate Keating—he believes in economic openness, not backroom deals, especially their deals. So today in Parliament I let fly, putting everything I know about the Packer family history on the record.

Tuesday, 7 December

The slow-moving fools. At Caucus today the colleagues were lining up to question Crean's deal with Costello on business taxation. Apparently this was the big item at the Left Caucus meeting last night. But where were they two weeks ago when I moved that we oppose the halving of capital gains tax? George Campbell and the other Lefties have been telling me that the Third Way does not address the question of fairness. After the capital gains sell-out, it should be the last time I get that lecture.

Beazley has got himself into a terrible mess on this issue. He's been in the media saying that 'We can fix up the unfairness (of the package) in government'—an acknowledgement that the changes are flawed but he hasn't got the guts to oppose them. Today he told Caucus of his determination 'not to mention the term "capital gains tax" at the next election'. But what if the Coalition promises to halve the tax rate yet again? What will we do then? Beazley doesn't understand that opportunism causes its own problems in politics—it always comes back to bite you on the bum.

Just look at his record on health funding. He told Caucus, 'There is a $1 billion shortfall in public hospital funding and this is where the Government's Timor levy plays into our hands'. But he said the same thing last term about the guns levy, that we could use it as a precedent for permanently lifting the Medicare levy and putting the money into public hospitals. He's like a broken record, always promising decent policies but never delivering.

I continue to get mixed reviews among the colleagues. Encouragement from old romantics like Barney Cooney, who said to me, 'You know that all your stuff will be claimed by others twenty years from now. It's where the debate is headed'. I also ran into Barry Jones outside the Parliamentary Library, who lamented the drift in Labor policy under Beazley, citing the capital gains decision. But he also warned, 'Where else do we look for leadership? Crean is worse, and so is Lee'.

I'm afraid the majority view in the Party has been summarised by Sue West. Last month, when asked by a lobby group about my views, she advised them to 'Ignore Mark. We all do'. That's my unhappy fate in life: a Caucus Cassandra.

Thursday, 9 December

Some encouragement from an unexpected source. Yesterday John Flannery, one of Beazley's press secretaries, called into my office to tell me to

---

Barry Jones ALP member, Lalor 1977–98; min. in Hawke govt; ALP Nat. Pres. 1992–2000

Sue West NSW ALP Sen. 1987, 1990–2002

persevere: 'Keep on stirring the pot, it's good for the Party'. It must be hard-going in Beazley's press office, more so if they have anything to do with Craig Emerson's press releases.

This bloke is a fair dinkum goose. I've been keeping a collection of his media statements. Today Emerson put out a release entitled 'Twelve Christmas GST Porkies—to be sung to the tune of the Twelve Days of Christmas'. He's the ultimate stuntman, anything to get his name in the paper. On 20 October he announced that 'The legislation for the Treasurer's so-called "streamlined new tax for a new century" now weighs in at 4.4 kilograms following an extra 454 amendments rammed through the House today'. Often when I turn on the House TV monitor, he's in the chamber with a set of scales weighing the GST.

His public life is like a long game of trivial pursuit. On 31 March he announced that 'Since the beginning of the year, the Prime Minister has spoken almost 4000 words in response to questions without notice in the Parliament on the GST, but has mentioned "GST" only six times'. Hey Emmo, how much paper have you wasted with your press statements this year? A lot more than 4000 words and 4.4 kilos.

Tuesday, 28 December

It's time to draw some conclusions after four years of analysis and jousting over Labor's policy directions.

The Labor reform task is insoluble. The guiding reform principle of our time is the dispersal of economic, social and political power. But this is antipathetic to Labor's culture of machine politics, trade union bosses and power hierarchies. The ALP is an Industrial Age institution, poorly suited to social justice issues in the Information Age. It is impossible to see this changing.

Parliamentary politics is no longer a viable instrument of social reform. The big issues are social—the breakdown in trust and compassion between people. But the state has no compass or toolkit with which to handle these issues. It relies on the exercise of centralised, hierarchical power: law-making and bureaucratic control over people. It is institution-ally incapable of dealing with the big social policy questions: mutualism, devolution and civil society.

Most of the reform action is external to parliamentary and party poli-tics: the information revolution, innovative small enterprises and new social movements, such as social entrepreneurs. Government bureaucra-cies hate innovation—it's a threat to their conservative system of com-mand and control. This is also the case with the Labor movement. We draw our talent and thinking from the old institutions of the Left: trade unions, political families and rorted branches. As a Party, we are disconnected from the new sources of radical thinking and reform in society. If the Third Way is to have a lasting impact, it will be as a non-parliamentary movement, led by people like Andrew Mawson.

The Australian people hate organised politics. It is now part of the general malaise and distrust of all things public. Even if Labor developed a modern reform program, the electorate would be reluctant to embrace it and trust in it. Under a barrage of media ridicule about politicians, people have become very cynical. They assume that new proposals have been devised solely to win votes. As the public becomes more cynical, the politicians become more opportunistic—a vicious circle. New ideas have become incompatible with the demands of daily politics (finding out what the public will support right now). Proposals that might command majority support years or decades from now are dismissed as useless.

An honest assessment? My position is untenable at every level. I'm out of step with the scab-lifting culture of Federal Labor. I'm trapped in a machine political party far removed from social reform. I have concluded that the best prospects for equality and social justice in Australia are likely to come from the work of social movements. I need to start making plans for my transition out of Parliament as follows:

- I need the parliamentary pension for my financial security, but I'm also on the way out. I've contested three elections and need to try for a fourth to qualify for my super. Therefore, I won't mind if the machine men disendorse me in Werriwa.
- I should disappear from the public debates next year—controversy is starting to follow me. I'm becoming too much of a punching bag for pissants.
- I should write a book about Third Way politics instead. It would be an exit statement from the Labor Party, like Vere Gordon Childe and his 1923 classic, *How Labour Governs*, a commentary on the internal malaise of the Party.
- I should get out and head to London or Washington, go with Janine and start a family.

Disendorsement in Werriwa Under the rules for parliamentary superannuation, MPs need three terms of Parl. and an attempt at securing a fourth term. If they are unsuccessful, either because their Party has disendorsed them (they lose preselection) or they lose on election day, they still qualify for superannuation

2000

A sad and dispiriting year, with the suicide in June of Greg Wilton, my friend and parliamentary colleague. While the breakdown in his marriage traumatised and depressed him, Greg was also deeply upset about the political manoeuvres against him for his seat of Isaacs. My diary entries record the brutality of Labor machine politics towards a colleague desperately in need of personal and political support. While the Labor Caucus recognised the tragedy in what had happened, no one openly confronted and dealt with the Party's role in Greg's death.

This was a mistake as it allowed the worst elements of the machine culture to continue to fester inside the ALP. In fact, the following year, one of the culprits, Stephen Conroy, was promoted to the position of Deputy Senate Leader. Never has the ALP been so insensitive to the tragic death of a colleague and the need to reassess its methods and values. Looking back, this was the point at which my emotional commitment to the ALP and parliamentary life started to weaken. Things were never the same without our mate Greg.

On the broader political scene, the main event was the introduction of the GST on 1 July. The Government crashed in the opinion polls, encouraging Kim Beazley to adopt a so-called small-target strategy. In a number of areas, this involved adopting Coalition policies. In others, it meant delaying the release of Labor policies until late in the electoral cycle. The objective was to keep the pressure on the Government and minimise opportunities for the Coalition and the media to attack Labor. For most of the year, this looked like *a winning tactic, but at a significant cost to the Party's policy principles and commitment to social reform.*

In other respects, it was a year of contrasts: dismal at work but incredible joy on the home front. On 22 April Janine and I were married in Fremantle, and on 7 November (Melbourne Cup Day) our first child was born, the magnificent, effervescent Oliver Latham.

Thursday, 6 January

Tony Abbott visited Claymore to look at two of our social entrepreneurial projects: Argyle Community Housing, where Brian Murnane is working wonders, and the Laundromat Group, a bunch of enterprising women who want to set up a laundromat small business on the estate. It was good of Abbott to accept my invitation to come out and see if he can help in securing government grants.

Maybe it's his background in the Catholic Church, but he seems strongly committed to the principles of social self-help—not rampant individualism, but a revival of old-style mutualism in society. The Laundromat Group is assisted by some of the local nuns, so they had Tony eating out of their hands.

For all his enthusiasm, he also showed a depressing ignorance. His first question to Brian Murnane was 'How do you get on a public housing waiting list?' and then he wanted to know 'Why don't they rent something better?' Hey, this is Campbelltown public housing. It's not about job snobs but sheer survival. Abbott finished the day by saying to me, 'I didn't know that places like this existed'. I suppose if you live your life on the North Shore and represent the seat of Warringah, you wouldn't know about them.

All this talk about Sydney as an international Olympic city. We are actually a segregated city where the tragedy of entrenched poverty is tucked away and forgotten in places like Claymore. And who's the State MP representing Claymore? The Minister for the Olympics, Michael Knight, who's spending billions at Homebush but not a brass razoo of his budget in the public housing estates of his electorate. He was a lion of the Labor Left but now he swans around with the IOC and lives on the North Shore. A man of deep and abiding principles.

Abbott's naïvety about public housing reminds me of that great story by Nugget Coombs about Harold Holt when he was PM: 'Holt could not

Nugget Coombs Long-serving Commonwealth official and supporter of the arts and indigenous community

Harold Holt Lib. PM 1966–67

believe the result of the 1967 referendum recognising Aborigines as Australian citizens. It was just after the referendum and he said, "You know, Nugget, I've never spoken to one, I don't think I've ever met one". But he was sympathetic and wanted advice about the institutions the Commonwealth should establish'. For the Tories, ignorance is bliss.

Wednesday, 16 February

Dinner with Stephen Loosley and Michael Costello (Beazley's Chief of Staff) at the Fringe Benefits restaurant in Canberra. Loosley organised the night as an attempted rapprochement between Beazley's office and me. It didn't work. Costello spent most of the dinner bullshitting to me that the Beazley operation is about radical social reform and that I should be part of it.

He reckons Beazley often says to him, 'When I'm Prime Minister, I'm going to turn this country upside down'. Yeah, sure. He also regards Michael Lee as a great innovator in education policy: 'I've got his full policy draft in my top drawer; it's an amazing effort'. Lee has watered down the education platform for the National Conference, taking out the best of my stuff. Costello was unaware of this. Also unaware that Beazley promised to rewrite the platform, Whitlam-style.

An inkling of what's really going on: Costello says that sometimes he finds it hard to engage Beazley, complaining about his 'thousand-mile stare'. Instead of staring out the window, it might help if they told people where we stand on the GST. Costello reckons 'The policy is all worked out. We'll have a public commission after the election where people can air their complaints and we'll promise to do something about it'. Not exactly the politics of conviction and radical reform.

Some good news, however: Beazley is going to take on a free-trade fight at the Conference, plus make some major policy statements. For instance, he is going to scrap Howard's rotten private health insurance rebate. The timing is right for some boldness from Opposition, unlike the announcement of John Hewson's 'Fightback!' So we will see at the National Conference whether Costello is all talk or if there is some substance to Beazley's bluster.

Stephen Loosley Former ALP Sen.; corporate lawyer and lobbyist

Monday, 21 February

Beazley stumbles on income tax increases to pay for changes to the GST. Last week he guaranteed the Labor Premiers their GST revenue, and now he's refusing to rule out tax hikes to pay for our policy. No one can say that Labor is unaware of the budgetary position. Lindsay Tanner has already spelt out the tightness of the finances to Caucus. The truth is that we have opposed the GST for the past two years but have failed to develop a fiscal framework for dealing with it.

Our position is totally confused. When it first went through the House in December 1998, Crean put out a press release (a classic I immediately placed on my pinboard) describing the GST as the most 'misguided, inequitable, regressive and socially and economically damaging proposal [to ever] pass through the House of Representatives'. But our policy is to keep it. Beazley talks about GST rollback but can never explain how we might fund such a commitment. No wonder the media are onto him.

That's his main political problem: fiscal irresponsibility and the legacy of the 1995 Budget black hole. He knows how to spend money—through tax credits, GST rollback, industry welfare, employment schemes and health and education funding—but not how to save it. All this confusion on something for which Michael Costello said we will hold a public commission in government.

Tuesday, 22 February

Beazley says it is 'impossible' to scrap the private health insurance rebate, yet six days ago Costello told me it would be one of the first things abolished in our promises. Macklin must be beside herself with anger. She despises the rebate and wants to pole-axe it. At different times Beazley has boasted to Caucus that it will go. Where there is no belief and conviction in public life, there can be no real purpose.

Friday, 25 February

A fascinating week for Federal Labor. Beazley has melted down but the Party professionals are trying to get out the line that it's because he's a windbag—he just talks too much and gets off-message. The fact that he's unscripted is one of the things the mob likes about him: he's not your typical politician. They like his avuncular, free-wheeling style.

The real problem lies elsewhere. He is weak—he agrees with everyone and avoids conflict like the plague, such as guaranteeing the Premiers their GST revenue. He has no interest in our policy structure and framework. He has done nothing to repair the problems in our policy culture. His problems are structural and cultural, not stylistic.

This is why he has had a week of policy contradictions. The GST is a disaster for the country but we cannot abolish it. The private health insurance rebate is a 'monumental failure' but we cannot abolish it. The Government's capital gains tax changes are hopelessly inequitable but we must support them. What is the point? He must see government as an end in its own right and will do and say anything to get there.

Beazley used to tell Caucus he didn't like talking about the GST because it obscured the crucial national debate we needed to have about skills and education. He dropped off the GST after the 1998 election and told us the end of that debate was good: we could focus on our positive issues. But then, late last year, as soon as his pollster told him the GST was still a hot issue, he was back into it like a rat up a drainpipe.

Friday, 17 March

You have to laugh in this place. On Monday, Leo McLeay said to me, 'The most horrible bunch of people I have ever had to deal with are those elected in 1998'. I hope he was not talking about Craig Emerson. I will not hear a word said against Catman. He may not realise it, but he is a comic genius with a legion of fans.

On Tuesday, Emerson was giving one of his long and repetitious speeches about the evils of the GST. But he has obviously been watching Crean use props to illustrate his case and attract media attention. So po-faced Emmo pulled out a cardboard cat, a saucer and a container of milk. Apparently milk for human consumption is GST-free but milk fed to your cat is GST-payable. Away he went, pouring milk for the cat on his desk as he addressed the House:

> If you knowingly buy that milk for your cat, you pour out the milk for your cat into a bowl and the cat drinks the milk, then either you or your cat will have avoided the GST ... The VAT Man might just be there at your home having a look at whether you are drinking the milk or whether the cat is drinking the milk or whether the milk went off.

It looked like the Mad Hatter's Tea Party. Naturally, Joel and I organised a replay screening in my office and got Alan Ramsey involved. We were

Alan Ramsey Legendary *SMH* journalist based in Canberra

crying with laughter. To make things worse, Emmo asked me about his stunt and, with a perfectly straight face, I told him it was excellent, that he should bring the cat into the House more often to remind the Government of this shocking GST anomaly. He followed my advice, sitting the cat on his desk during Question Time on Wednesday.

Today the *SMH* reported: 'Clearly Emerson a) loves his cat tenderly; b) is deeply afraid of a shadowy figure he knows only as VAT Man; c) is possibly as mad as a banana'. I don't know whether to laugh or cry. I bet Bob Hawke feels the same way—Catman is his protégé.

Yesterday Beazley cancelled his visit to Claymore (scheduled for next Tuesday) due to 'a problem with a trade union'. What about the problems of a suburb with three generations of long-term unemployment and the newfound hope of finding a solution through social enterprises? He was going to drive up from Canberra, stop at some of the bookshops in the Southern Highlands on the way through, and then check out the projects. A real disappointment. I can get Tony Abbott interested in poverty in my electorate but not the Leader of the Labor Party. The system has gone crazy.

Tuesday, 28 March

Attended the launch of Paul Keating's book on Australian–Asian relations. One of those funny Sydney nights, with plenty of hangers-on at the Café Sydney in Circular Quay. At the end of it, I said to Paul, 'The bottom line in Australian politics is this: we don't have an agenda and it makes Howard look like a leader'. Paul agreed. He can see his legacy slipping away and he hates every minute of it.

Thursday, 6 April

John Kerin, pissed and bitter, gives me a good old bagging while sitting next to Joel at the farewell dinner for Gary Gray at the National Press Club. His wife, June Verrier, said that 'Gabrielle is a good friend of ours'—a sign of where they stand in the scheme of things.

Politics has some interesting characters, but not that many go out of their way to say they are sticking up for you (as Kerin did last year) and then knife you while talking to your best mate. If John had lifted a finger to help places like Claymore during his eleven years in government, then maybe I wouldn't need to be so outspoken about the ALP's neglect of poverty.

But, as Joel reminds me, he's not all piss and wind. He also has a biting wit. I still credit Kerin with the best line I have heard in politics. In the late

1980s, Stan Knowles, a State Labor MP in our area, was caught stealing three drill bits from the Casula K-Mart. Stan has still got his first dollar, so it was not that surprising. Politically, however, it was scandalous: he had to leave Parliament (handing over to his son Craig) and was then convicted of theft. When he heard about it, Kerin said, 'Well, we shouldn't be too hard on Stan, at least it shows he's not a two-bit thief'.

Tuesday, 11 April

I'm getting married again in eleven days' time, so Joel and Leo organised a few drinks with the colleagues. Beazley came along, pontificating about our education policies: 'Higher education requires a lot of thought. We will probably have a different policy in government to the one we take to the election'. I would like to know what he has got in mind. Hopefully, my policy for a mixed university system.

In the parliamentary dining room, I copped a ribbing from a bunch of Coalition MPs about my isolation inside the ALP, joking that I only had one vote for a leadership challenge. What do you do during moments like these? Think of Churchill and the way he was mocked in the Commons by young Tory MPs during his long period in exile? I'm sure many politicians around the world think of Churchill, but it never changes things in practice.

No option but to grin and bear it. In my private life, I have found happiness at last. In politics, these are my dog days—a comeback to the frontbench looks impossible. Beazley and his gang are probably right: the Government is killing itself on the altar of the GST. After the next election I'm going to be a government backbencher again—back to square one. Let's be honest: quitting the Shadow Ministry eighteen months ago wasn't the smartest thing I have ever done.

Everyone quotes Churchill. I prefer a different member of the House of Commons, the political author and academic David Marquand (first elected in 1966). He later described himself as 'singularly ill-suited to the feverish inconsequence of parliamentary life'. I can relate to that. All the tossers racing around—what will they ever achieve?

Tuesday, 18 April

A conference at the ANU on the future of governance and Mike Keating tells me something insightful about his namesake, Paul: 'He was always suspicious of the things he could not control. Working Nation was a perfect Keating operation—putting his department head in charge to write it'. Yes, Keating as the ultimate centralist, so typical of modern Labor culture.

This is why I'm struggling so badly with the colleagues. They think my proposals for transferring power and responsibility to local communities, for backing the work of social entrepreneurs are madness. They came here to run the place, not to give power away. A century ago, the Labor movement was interested in mutualism. Its MPs were community-based. But those habits are long gone, wiped out by the post-war welfare state. We are now a party of centralists. And then there's me.

Wednesday, 10 May

Last month Geoff Walsh said it might be good to have a talk. I told him I thought Beazley was getting the wrong advice from the machine men in Caucus. Today he called around my Parliament House office to hear me out. While Howard appears to be in strife, we need to be wary of his underdog look—it makes him more dangerous.

The Government is going to come at Beazley on two fronts: he spends too much, and he caves in to the unions. He seems like a nice guy, but it's deceiving. Kim's key task is to prove to the public that he is hungry and tough enough by taking on one of our sacred cows: welfare reform, Aboriginal affairs, the rights agenda or the unions. Michael Costello has got him yelling at the despatch box, but it won't work. He needs to improve his content, not his volume.

This is what the new politics is all about: defining yourself by provoking the right kind of opponents. That's when a cynical electorate knows you mean it. It's the real deal—belief and conviction as public virtues. Walsh said he could see my logic but he didn't think it would happen in practice: 'Kim is very mindful of taking the Party with him'.

Well, that's it: he's dealt himself out of the equation. Our fortunes are entirely in Howard's hands. We would be crazy to think we can maximise our support by mimicking Howard's small-target strategy from 1996. The circumstances are totally different.

Saturday, 20 May

Dinner with Dick Morris and his wife in Sydney. He's here as part of the Sydney Writers' Festival, plus to promote the possibilities of his new system of Internet democracy. Australian politics, however, hasn't impressed him much: 'It seems stereotypical and boring. There's too much energy, which the system here can't absorb. I suppose that's why the bright people, like

Bob Carr, turn to the United States instead'. He had dinner with Carr the previous evening, swapping historical anecdotes and stories about American politics, giving him a big wrap: 'It was as bright a political discussion and as entertaining a night as I have had since I left Clinton'. High praise, indeed.

Morris argues that the Internet will liberate public opinion, taking politics back to the Jeffersonian ideals of direct democracy. People have grown cynical of the recycling of opinion polling by their political leaders. They want to cut out the middle man and make these decisions themselves, voting online on the issues that interest them. If he is right, this has the potential to revolutionise the system, wiping away the shallowness of representative democracy and directly empowering the voters.

Cutting out the middle man seems to have been the impact of the Internet in other walks of life, so why should politics be any different? Morris also sees it as a lucrative commercial venture, and has his own vote.com site in the US. Along with Craig Knowles and David Britton (who came to dinner with us), I'm keen to explore the potential in Australia. Make a few bob and open up the Australian political system along the way. Sounds like paradise.

Monday, 29 May

Pills has done something really silly. Last Friday he grabbed his kids and took them to a national park outside Melbourne. He was in a distressed state, stuffing around with his car, in a funk of depression, thought about killing himself, but couldn't go through with it. Thankfully, the coppers picked him up and now he's in a hospital clinic in Geelong. The children are back with their mother, Maria.

I knew he was struggling with the marriage break-up; his fault, his guilt. He said it was too much for him to come to Fremantle for my wedding last month. Then he bailed out of the Reserve Bank hearing last Monday in Melbourne. I couldn't even track him down for a bite to eat. Poor bugger, he's got himself into a terrible mess. I've been trying to tell him that eventually you come out of these marriage bust-ups and things get better, as they have for me. But he's fallen apart, he really has.

Spoke to him this afternoon. He sounded okay, hasn't gone crazy or anything. Gave me an outline of what happened. His big worry is what

---

Craig Knowles Alderman, Liverpool City Council 1982–87, 1988–94; ALP member for electorates covering the Fed. electorate of Werriwa in the NSW Parl. 1990– ; min. in Carr govt 1995–

the police are going to do now. Just wants to get out of the clinic and get things sorted out. What do you say to a mate in these circumstances? I've no experience with anything this bad. Christ, he thought about topping himself, how serious is that?

Met with Beazley to discuss the situation. I know politics is a tough game but I am still unnerved by the conversation. Kim was more worried about the possibility of a by-election than Greg's wellbeing—he doesn't know him that well and seemed distant from the problems Pills has to deal with. He also displayed a surprising lack of confidence, saying, 'We would be slaughtered on the character question [in a by-election]'. So much for the rhetoric that 'Howard's gone' because of the GST. The Leader has given me the job of ensuring that Pills stays in Parliament.

Read the *Herald-Sun* coverage in yesterday's paper. There are some real bastards around—a so-called 'MP friend' said that Greg was a loner, highly strung and in a 'depressed state'. If he was a friend, he wouldn't be saying those things and not off the record. Sounds like Conroy, still annoyed that Greg has shown a bit of independence—he's supposed to be with the Victorian Right but he hooked up with Joel and me in Canberra. Joel and I didn't talk to the papers—they must have fallen for the line that Conroy's a mate. Apparently he introduced Greg to Maria way back when.

Monday, 5 June

One of my heroes when I joined Parliament was John Dawkins, the tough reformist Minister in the Hawke and Keating governments. Unfortunately, my first Caucus meeting was his last—we passed like ships in the night in Canberra. Good to catch up with him for lunch in Adelaide today. He's very experienced with the Beazleys, having represented the seat of Fremantle for decades.

He reckons that Kim Junior's big issue when he first joined the Western Australian branch was abortion. He was always scared of what his dad might think if he took a progressive stance on issues. Dawkins and others used to joke that it took Kim Senior 60 years to become ultra-conservative, so Junior had nowhere to go ideologically from the age of 25.

John is scarifying in his criticism of Beazley's leadership: 'He's the first Leader since Calwell not to take on the Party, in either its structure or policy direction'. He compares him unfavourably with Keating: 'Paul always had to have a model in mind to structure his ideas and policies. Beazley has got nothing'. I wish Dawkins had stayed and become Leader of the Party. I suppose the smart guys in the Keating Government got out when they saw the writing on the wall (1994–95) and left the dross behind.

Tuesday, 6 June

Spent the day with Pills in Melbourne—coffee in Malvern, lunch in South Yarra. He's very twitchy, looking around all the time, struggling to focus on the subject at hand. Lots of worries weighing him down: never seeing the kids again, it's all over with Maria, uncertain if the cops will charge him, plus moves to take away his preselection in Isaacs.

More than anything, he wants to be a father to his children. He blames the Canberra lifestyle for dragging him away from his family. 'Being a part-time dad is not being a dad at all'. He's sick and tired of the rumours and speculation about what happened: 'People in Canberra think they know everything—wrong, they know nothing. A great rumour mill, that's all'. He hates them and, quite honestly, I can't see him coming back any time soon.

But he's shit scared about losing his seat. That's the one tangible thing he's got left at the moment, the one thing propping him up. He's disappointed, even bewildered, that he hasn't heard from Conroy or Beazley, both of whom could put his concerns to rest pretty quickly.

He was vague about it, but it sounds like Greg Sword is trying to help him out. Poor bastard needs it. I mean, it's unbelievable that he hasn't heard from the Leader of the Party. How hard is it to pick up the phone and talk to a colleague in this much strife? Maybe Kim thinks he needs to distance himself from the 'character question'.

I felt helpless through most of our long talk. There are no immediate answers for him. He's just got to guts it out, try to stabilise his life and then see if he can get back into the saddle politically. The only positive example I could give him was Nick Sherry's comeback. We were walking along the street talking about Sherry when, out of the blue, he said he had to go and ducked into a guitar shop. That was it—see you later, he was off into his own world. I felt terrible for him.

Saturday, 10 June

The State Labor Conference has voted to save me as the Member for Werriwa. A long story. It started when I went to the backbench—I made many enemies, especially among some of the control freaks in the NSW Right. Then the electoral redistribution in NSW gave them a chance to have a go at me—it radically redrew my seat, making me vulnerable to a pre-selection challenge. Redistributions are bloody horrible things, out of your

---

Greg Sword National Union of Workers Gen. Sec. and Right-wing ALP powerbroker

control. This one has pushed Werriwa north into the new suburbs out the back of Liverpool.

Not a problem electorally, the margin should stay the same. But a big problem internally—I lost Labor preselection voters at the Campbelltown end of the seat and picked up two of Paul Lynch's stacked Left-wing branches in Liverpool. On the old boundaries, I would have walked in on a rank-and-file ballot. On the new ones, it would have been touch and go.

My argument: the Party has a tradition of re-endorsing Members stuffed around by redistributions, giving them a chance to establish themselves in new branches. The counter argument: my enemies in the NSW Right (Hutchins and Lee) want me to run for Macarthur (now notionally a Labor seat with a 2 per cent margin), claiming that my profile would help us win it. Earlier this year they formed an alliance with the Soft Left, who wanted Lynch to move from State politics to Canberra. Lynch has been invisible in Macquarie Street, a non-event. The Fergusons just want him as an extra number in their struggle for factional supremacy in Caucus against the Hard Left.

To complicate things, Colin Hollis (Soft Left) is retiring in Throsby and the Right reckon that Sharon Bird (ex-Hard Left, a defector to the Right) would win a rank-and-file ballot. But the Hard Left wants to get Jennie George into Federal Parliament and sees Throsby as the logical place to do it. Another factional and subfactional mess to be sorted out by the power-brokers.

Leo and Della Bosca have backed me inside the Right. Yesterday on the way back from Canberra, I had a long blue with Roozendaal, who had all sorts of stupid reasons and scenarios to get me out of Werriwa. His plan was Bird for Throsby, George for Werriwa and me for Macarthur. I told him I wouldn't wear it, that I would resist George at every opportunity: 'Eric, if you think you're going to give away this great Labor seat to a blow-in from Manly, where George lives, all to help your mate Bird, who five minutes ago was in the Left, then I will fight you every step of the way, inside and outside the Party'.

It must have worked, because this morning Della and Leo stitched up a deal with Albanese (Hard Left) to do over the Fergusons. I stay in Werriwa, George gets Throsby, and the Conference, for good measure, also confirmed Irwin in Fowler and a bunch of sitting State MPs affected by the

---

Paul Lynch Left-wing ALP member, Liverpool 1995– ; brother-in-law of Martin and Laurie Ferguson
Jennie George ACTU Pres. 1996–2000; ALP member, Throsby 2001–

John Della Bosca ALP member of NSW Leg. Council; min. in Carr govt 1999–
Eric Roozendaal Gen. Sec. NSW ALP 1999–2004
Anthony Albanese Left-wing powerbroker and ALP member, Grayndler 1996–

scourge of branch-stacking. A close shave. Wise to keep my head down for a while. I looked into the abyss and was too proud and determined to let go of Gough's old seat, that's the truth of it.

Wednesday, 14 June

How do you write this, how do you explain that someone thinks so little of his life that he decides to end it? Greg is dead. He drove out to a national park last night and ended it—an escape from the pain and loss. That's the only way to explain it. He left a message on my mobile yesterday afternoon, saying that things were going to be okay, not to worry about going to Melbourne again. I felt encouraged when I heard it, but now I know what he really meant. Things are okay because people can't hurt him any more. His pain is gone. Unbelievable grief for those he has left behind.

Tuesday, 20 June

On the way back from Melbourne, having given Pills his send-off at Monash University and out in his electorate. This has all the elements of a Greek tragedy. Broken relationships, a shattered family, two little children left behind, broken hearts and bitterness behind the scenes, and the ALP's betrayal of one of its own.

His sister Leeanda gave a stunning speech at the service today, captured all the characteristics and things about Greg we love: his knock-around nature and compassion, always fighting against the odds, his wry sense of humour and love of family. Leeanda has no doubt about what finished him off, blaming Conroy and that wretched, cruel article in the *Herald-Sun* last Tuesday. Greg was staying at her place, so she must have seen the crippling impact on him.

It was another hatchet job: 'Some Labor Party chiefs are keen for Mr Wilton to resign so a by-election can be called'. Full of speculation about who would take over as the Labor candidate, the last thing Greg needed. How low can these animals go? Hounding a bloke already in deep shit, treating him as just another factional number, not a human being. This is not the Labor Party I joined, not the Labor Party that's supposed to be about compassion and social justice. Where was the justice, the fair go, for poor old Pills?

Across Caucus, Conroy is copping the blame, with Anna Burke leading the charge, the last one of us to speak to Greg. And there he was at the funeral today, striding around in a big black coat, like something out of a mafia movie. Yesterday in the condolences in Parliament, Anna said she was 'angry at those who play politics with human life'. Kelvin Thomson also pinged Conroy:

> People can proclaim their compassion for humanity in the abstract as loudly as they like but there is no such thing as humanity in the abstract, there are only people. If you treat people in your life with contempt, then your great compassion for humanity in the abstract does not mean a lot.

After I spoke in the condolences, Graham Edwards said to me, 'That was the best speech you'll ever make in this place'. I hope he's right. I wanted to let Greg's children—the big fella Lachlan and the little sheila Eliza—know how much he loved them. Hopefully in the years ahead, they will read the Hansard and not the dickheads in the media. Their dad was a good man, a great mate—a victim, yes, at his own hand, but also in the hands of others. The sewer we belong to called the Labor Party.

And what about Beazley? He had two weeks in which to call Greg and never did. The family know the truth: that he never had the decency to pick up the phone to give one of his MPs a bit of comfort and security about his political future. It confirms my worst thoughts about him.

All we have left now are memories—our tears, our sadness and our memories. Joel and I have been swapping our best Pills stories. He had a great wit, like his description of Costello as 'K-Mart Keating'—very funny, very apt.

Our best story: last year we had a night out in Melbourne and ended up in one of those places in King Street with dancing girls wrapping themselves around silver poles. Pills didn't say much until he declared, 'In the next life, I'm coming back as that pole'. Matey, better that than the shit you had to put up with in this life.

Wednesday, 28 June

The last week of the Parliament before the introduction of the GST (on 1 July). My researcher, Sam Rosevear, came back to the office today shaking his head. He had been at the Opposition staff meeting, where Michael Costello told them that Beazley plans to get up at 5.30 a.m. for a month to destroy this new tax. That's right, the one we plan to keep. Kim says things because they sound good, not because he means them. We blocked the

---

Kelvin Thomson ALP member, Wills 1996– ; Shadow Asst Treas. 1998–2001

Graham Edwards ALP member, Cowan 1998– ; nicknamed 'Stumpy'

Senate amendments to the GST because 'this tax cannot be made fair' but now, this is the whole basis of our Rollback policy.

Yesterday Crean gave the Leader's report at Caucus (Kim was at the ACTU Congress). He was brazen about our tactics on the GST. So far, he has been holding back the release of any policy details for Rollback, boasting that 'we are getting away with it'. Crean seems to think he has the media wrapped around his finger: 'Last year I got Laurie Oakes to write a piece on petrol pricing'. It sounds too smart by half to me. We have spent four of the last eight years concentrating on a GST scare campaign, and people wonder why we have no policies.

Thursday, 27 July

Beazley has been talking about the importance of a knowledge nation, but so far, there is no sign of what this might mean in practice. Today I tried to fill in some of the gaps with a speech on education policy to the Fabian Society in Melbourne. The key conceptual breakthrough is to abandon the old ideological struggle between public and private money in education. If one accepts the logic of lifelong learning—the massive task of embedding learning opportunities in all parts of society, in all parts of the lifecycle—then we need to mobilise more learning resources from all institutions, public and private.

Governments, corporations, individuals and communities need to do more. If the task is left to the scarce resources of government, then education will continue to be under-funded. If it is left solely to the private sector and funding deregulation, then low-income people will miss out. We also need to advance our concept of learning beyond the formal institutions of the education system. Lifelong learning needs to flourish in the civic institutions of everyday life: in homes, in workplaces, in clubs, in shopping centres, in the places where people gather for a social purpose.

The speech seemed to be well received, notwithstanding the concerns of the old Lefties who normally infest these gatherings. This is one of the striking divides in modern politics: the oldies locked into the standard ideological struggle, but younger people with an open and fresh attitude about the big issues. Good feedback from the students present, especially on my proposals for a mixed system of university funding and the introduction of Lifelong Learning Accounts—tax incentives to help families save for the education of their children, established as sub-accounts to the existing superannuation system.

Rollback policy ALP policy to remove the GST from an unspecified number of items

Also an important speech for clearing the decks on my time as a front-bencher: 'I have been as guilty as anyone in falling for the old agendas. During my time as Shadow Minister for Education I should have done better. Nonetheless, none of us should be ashamed of mistakes in public life—the point is to learn from them'. More than any other profession, politics punishes mistakes harshly. The media and machine men demand perfection, so when you inevitably fall short, it is easier to pole-axe you.

That's the paradox I work under: I have learned a huge amount over the past five years (mainly by talking to intellectuals and community groups outside the ALP) and my policy ideas have never been stronger. But inside Caucus, my standing has never been weaker. The colleagues, of course, will vigorously ignore my Fabian speech.

Tuesday, 1 August

The middle of the National Conference in Hobart and it's as bleak and dispiriting an experience as one could imagine. The usual sport of delegates bitching about each other is in full flight: Leo claiming that Tanner and Brereton have formed a leadership ticket to roll Beazley, Kevin Rudd telling me how dumb Peter Beattie is compared with Bob Carr (for some reason, Queenslanders like calling each other dumb), and the NSW Right union delegates ragging me about my newspaper articles.

It's a waste of life. As a movement, we have lost our narrative, our cause for the good society. The decline in unionism and statism is irreversible. Beazley is not prepared to replace it with social-ism—too dangerous for the leader of a hierarchical/statist party. So, instead, we have a policy vacuum, a crisis in Labor belief.

Have a good look at the show: the branches are defunct and the unions are disappearing. The factions are like sheep—if these delegates were told by the factional bosses to vote for their shadows, they would. They care about power and nothing else. The type of mindless drones who destroyed Pills, put him in an early grave. No wonder I find them so detestable.

Politics is no longer a noble profession—its public standing is down there with used-car salesmen. The media are shallow and conflict-driven. The medium becomes the message. Look at this conference and the way it is choreographed for TV. No fire and fair dinkum debate; the factions work out the numbers and deals in advance. It's not really a policy conference, more like the set of a television show.

The things I have to put up with. Foolishly, I went to the National Right dinner last night. What a narky, miserable bunch of sods. I sat there being

---

Peter Beattie Qld ALP Premier 1998–

slagged by John Hogg and that horrible, drunken Christine Robertson. Why the hell am I doing this?

Beazley talks without a narrative or passion. Whitlam had his big idea, the expansion of the social democratic state. Keating gave the nation a modern economic model. Kim just likes being there: politics as a process, not a burning passion in life. The conference was a chance to explain his vision for Knowledge Nation, but all he gave us were two mild announcements in his opening speech.

I must get out of here. All the big agendas are settled anyway: the new economy is here to stay, the importance of education will not go away, social entrepreneurs are our only hope to solve poverty, and the Internet will revolutionise politics, with or without me involved. I have other options in life. I should use them, starting with family. For work, I can join the New Labour project in Britain, part of the Community Action Network in London. I've had enough of this place, that's for sure.

Tuesday, 8 August

Dinner at the Macquarie Bank in Sydney, where the former Howard Government Minister, Warwick Smith, works as an executive (he lost his seat of Bass at the last election). Interesting to hear him talk of life outside politics. He looks and sounds happier, gushing with enthusiasm about his new lifestyle: lives on the North Shore, paid good money, not missing Howard or his Tasmanian constituents one iota.

Best of all, he gets to see his children at night and on weekends. He was very reflective about it: 'A day you miss with your kids is a day you never get back'. I'm about to meet the same challenge. Janine is pregnant with a little boy to be named Oliver, due in November. It's the greatest thrill and adventure of my life, happening at the right time, aged 39. Who would have thought after the trouble I had six years ago? Love the thought of being a dad. Fan-bloody-tastic.

Monday, 14 August

Just when I thought the machine men could not get any worse. A meeting today of the National Right Caucus in Parliament House to discuss the extension of conscience votes (after Howard's success in splitting the Party during the National Conference on the question of IVF access for single

---

John Hogg Qld ALP Sen. 1996–
Christine Robertson NSW Right-wing faction delegate to the Nat. Conference

Knowledge Nation ALP's policy for education, research, science and information technology released before the 2001 election, based on a report written by Barry Jones

women). Wayne Swan made a remarkable contribution, saying that the first consideration for our consciences should be the electoral position of marginal seat holders.

He's worried that Catholic MPs voting according to their consciences in inner-city seats will lose them. So, too, morally progressive MPs in outer suburban and regional seats will be in strife if we have too many conscience votes. He seems to think they would be better off with binding Party votes— they can tell their electorates they were caucused into it, using the ALP as an alibi. A classic piece of political opportunism. He's willing to have the importance of our individual consciences supplanted by the electoral pendulum. Then he wants people to hide behind the Party rules.

No wonder the electorate is cynical: this is the standard methodology in today's politics. No basic principles from which to determine a position, anything will do to paper over a problem. The electorate is not silly, however. They sense that they don't get much value out of the system, so they disengage. At one level, I can't blame them.

The sad thing for society is that we are missing a golden opportunity to help people resolve these moral issues. Many people are confused about the new technologies, such as birth enhancement. They need leadership to guide them through, a process that gives them more information and a chance to have their say. This is the benefit of communitarian politics: a civic conversation to help society resolve the moral dilemmas of our time. That should be Labor policy, not Swanism.

Monday, 4 September

Last week the media carried a report that Kerry Packer lost $34 million on a gambling spree in Las Vegas, and I made a short speech about it in Parliament. Why not? He runs a media outfit that spends its time investigating other people's business; why shouldn't an MP reflect on the morality of hyper-gambling? It set the other media outlets off and even flushed out Packer himself, giving a rare interview to *The Australian.*

Some are suggesting that it's part of Keating's campaign against Packer, but I didn't make the speech because of the Packer–Keating thing. I made it because I find it morally wrong for any citizen to blow $34 million when there are so many better ways of using the money in our poverty-ridden society.

I also flushed out Howard last Friday, who described Packer's behaviour as that of a 'good corporate citizen'. So much for mutual obligation.

Mutual obligation A policy under which the govt provides financial support for individuals or organisations and expects them to do something in return; also known as mutual responsibility

What is more unacceptable: a young kid on the dole going to the beach or a business tycoon wasting $34 million dollars in a casino? Labor MPs should be exposing these double standards all the time, but our people are scared of Packer and co. That's why the Establishment gets away with it, and remains the Establishment.

Australia's business culture is weak and inward-looking, especially compared with some of the great gestures overseas. Bill Gates, for instance, has committed his fortune to the global elimination of polio. Imagine an Australian businessman talking in similar terms about wiping out a debilitating disease from the planet. Now, that's real mateship, something our culture has lost, replaced by the arrogance and greed of corporate power.

Monday, 11 September

A long meeting with Keating at his Sydney office. Two-and-a-half hours and it felt like he had nowhere else to go. Maybe he's getting like Gough, talking the leg off a chair. Anyway, it was all good stuff. He's the true custodian of the Labor legend, a leader who believes in the politics of attack.

He reckons my problems in Caucus can be solved if I take on the role of a storyteller: try to educate Labor MPs, taking the Caucus Committees seriously, make the case for change all the time. He said to treat them 'like flowerpots in the garden—you don't have to live with them, just water them'.

He gives me another rundown on Tony Benn's categorisation of politicians: maddies (the only ones who ever make a difference), fixers and straight men. Hopped right into Beazley: 'Kim's the worst kind of straight man, one surrounded by fixers. His dad was a maddie, you know, but then he took twenty years off politics to do his moral rearmament thing'.

Paul has summed up Junior perfectly: a straight man surrounded by fixers. Matches something Leo told me on Friday: our focus-group polling shows that people see Beazley as a 'gatekeeper'—nice guy but, like the bloke in the white coat at the cricket, he only opens and closes the gate for other people, never has a dig himself.

Also very critical of Smith—sees him as a lightweight. When he worked for Paul in 1992 and they were putting together the One Nation statement, Smith kept walking into his office and saying, 'Mate, make sure you talk about jobs, jobs, jobs'. All the time—'jobs, jobs, jobs'—that's all he ever said. Paul reckons, in the end, he threatened to strangle him if he didn't stop saying it.

Bill Gates Head of Microsoft and international IT guru

One Nation statement A major infrastructure and govt investment strategy released by the Keating govt in early 1992 to lift the economy out of recession

Finally, Richo has got the hook in him—talks and worries about him too much, bagging his performance as Health Minister seven years ago: 'His job was to reduce 100 private health funds down to two, but he fell in love with Brendan Nelson instead'. These days, Richo is irrelevant—just one of those sad cases who left Parliament and became a corporate lobbyist.

Tuesday, 3 October

Caucus discontent about Beazley's announcement that he will retain the 30 per cent private health insurance rebate (made during the Olympics, the day of Cathy Freeman's big race). Chris Fry (from Crean's office) says it was stitched up at a dinner between Beazley and Swan in Brisbane. It's a vote of no confidence in Jenny Macklin's capacity to argue the case against something she described as 'the worst piece of legislation in the history of the Parliament'.

I asked Macklin about it in Caucus today. She agreed with my proposition that the only way in which we can now work the hopeless rebate out of the system is to integrate the public and private health sectors—a major conceptual breakthrough in Labor policy. Her Medicare Alliance policy integrates Federal and State funding. The next step is to integrate the public and private insurance systems into one national program—the Scotton scheme I have written about in the past. At last, I'm making some progress with these people, getting them to think about long-term structural reform.

It is only happening because of the weakness in Beazley's position. A defining aspect of Labor's second term in Opposition has been its adoption of Coalition policy: specifically, the 30 per cent rebate, the halving of the capital gains tax and the retention of the GST. This marks a decline in the Party's pride and confidence in itself. There was a time when the objective of ALP politics was to sell good policy to the public. This function has now been jettisoned in favour of poll-driven policy-making by the machine men.

Tuesday, 10 October

The Government is introducing a new funding system for non-government schools, based on the socioeconomic status (SES) of students and their parents. It's an improvement on the old category-based system, although it

---

Brendan Nelson Former AMA head; Lib. member, Bradfield 1996–

still has too much guaranteed funding for wealthy schools. The scandal in the policy, however, is the exemption granted to the Catholics.

Instead of having their needs assessed and grants allocated school by school, the Catholic Education Commission is going to keep its block grants. That is, it will continue to receive a bundle of money from the Government and make its own school-by-school allocation of funds, with no public transparency. Every other system will receive school-by-school SES allocations from the Federal Government. It's a rort to maintain the centralised power and authority of the Catholic Commission.

The story gets worse. At Caucus today Beazley said he spent the weekend at Notre Dame University in Fremantle (regarding the Republic). Peter Tannock told him that if the Catholics had accepted the SES system, they would have received an extra $240 million in public funding. As it stands, they will get $100 million in additional funding. Incredibly, in the name of centralised power, they have done themselves out of $140 million, much needed in their schools. It's a scandal of the first order.

But get this: Beazley wants to hush it up. He told Caucus, 'I said to Tannock to take his money [the $100 million] and leave the politics to the politicians. We [the ALP] are not going to say a word about it in public'. Beazley reckons he's against the elites in this country but now he wants us to condone a backroom deal to protect the Catholic elite, which costs their school students $140 million. Bugger that, I'll be exposing this big time in speeches and newspaper articles. The Catholic schools in my electorate are grossly under-funded and this will make the inequity even worse.

In his next breath, Beazley told Caucus that he plans to campaign hard on the Government's overall funding package, especially the extra $50 million allocated to the wealthiest 50–60 private schools (the old Category One): 'We will be ruthless on this issue over the next twelve months'. But if the Catholics took their full SES allocation (the extra $140 million) this would reduce the funds available to Category One schools. His position is incomprehensively hypocritical.

And how ruthless is he really going to be? So ruthless as to let the Government's legislation pass through the Senate. The same sort of ruthlessness he showed on the GST, private health rebate, etc. How much longer do we have to put up with this?

Thursday, 12 October

The talk of the Caucus is Beazley's daily strategy session with Smith and Swan over coffee at Ozzies at 8.30 each morning. They must want people to notice them, it's such a public spot. They turn up like clockwork, briefing

Kim on the things he shouldn't believe in that day. It's right up the nose of the Left in particular.

I say don't blame them, look at the general culture of the Party. The Glimmer Twins are merely a product of it. We are now a cause for power and not much else. Power inside the Party has fallen into the hands of machine politicians, committed to exercising authority as a way of masking their own insecurities and inadequacies. Anyone who thinks/creates/innovates is a threat to them. It happens issue after issue, debate after debate. I'm only tolerated because I get good press and there would be a media backlash if they kicked me out of Parliament.

Beazley has surrounded himself with the clerks of the Labor movement: Smith (a former State Secretary), Swan (a former State Secretary), McMullan (a former State and National Secretary) and Ray and McLeay (Right-wing enforcers). It's quite a feat: he's in bed with the worst elements of the Party, manipulative and opportunistic, yet publicly he's seen as a decent and avuncular fellow. Maybe I underestimate him. Maybe he's a polished illusionist and political magician.

Monday, 30 October

Last Friday I wrote a *Tele* column getting stuck into Peter Reith and the Telecard affair, calling for the reform of MPs' entitlements. All the allowances and featherbedding should be bundled together into a capped global budget for managing our offices. It's ridiculous that politicians are elected to run the country but do not have the authority to run their own office budgets.

Labor should be leading the charge in cleaning out the system. We suffer most from the public's distrust of politics. How can we persuade people to support social reform and fairness if we are perceived as the equivalent of used-car salesmen? As I wrote in the *Telegraph*, 'Modern politics is fuelled by disrespect and cynicism all-round. It is slowly bleeding to death. This is why the reform of the entitlements system is so necessary. It is the first step in rebuilding popular trust in the role of parliamentarians'.

Today Joel told me that Marn raised the issue in Shadow Cabinet, complaining that our marginal seat holders are worried about the introduction of global budgets. He's part of the club, one of the shop stewards for parliamentary entitlements, always looking for more. I can't understand

---

Glimmer Twins Nickname for Smith and Swan | **Martin Ferguson** Shadow Regional Development, Infrastructure, Transport, Regional Services & Population Min. 1999–2001

it: like me, he grew up in Western Sydney—he should be a club-buster, not a featherbedder.

Beazley responded to Marn by saying he doesn't support global budgets because imagine the mess politicians would get themselves into if they ran their office finances. Not a great vote of confidence in the intelligence of his Caucus colleagues. But a sign that Kim's also part of the club.

A follow-up to the schools funding debate: Leo told me that Michael Lee is struggling to work out how to amend the Government's Bill. I've sent him some proposals for improving the SES system, but he won't entertain them (mainly because they come from me). This evening at Caucus Committee, Lee admitted that our policy to cut the funding of 61 Category One schools is faulty: 'Some of them deserve the extra money based on need, but we can't say that publicly'. Just when I thought things couldn't get any worse, along came little Michael. Each to their own, I suppose. I'd rather get the policy right in the first place.

Tuesday, 31 October

At Caucus, Kim tried to keep the troops focused on the tantalising prospect of an election win and off the repeated sell-out of Labor principles. He told us the polling was firming up nicely: 'This is an election for us to lose; the electoral bottom line is pretty horrible for the Government'. He's still very cautious about being proactive with our policies, saying there will be no new releases this year: 'We have made announcements which are dramatic enough'. I must have been asleep that day.

Poor guy, he tries hard. Maybe it's just a matter of perspective. He grew up in a conservative environment, so maybe he thinks a 1 per cent change is really radical. Hell, where I grew up we wanted to change things 100 per cent, rip down the whole bloody edifice if we could. Reform energy, that's what this Party lacks.

Thursday, 2 November

A chat with Alan Ramsey, the only journalist in the place with a sense of Labor history. And he gave me a few little stories that are worth recording here. He said that Bob Hawke rang him, worried about Kim and how we're going. He admitted, 'Kim's not much of an Opposition Leader but he will make a great Prime Minister'. Sounds like Hawkie regards it as an improver's handicap.

Ramsey detects disquiet elsewhere in our ranks: 'Mate, senior people think you will be very lucky to win indeed'. My guess is he was talking about Faulkner, to whom he is very close. The Senate Leader down on the Reps Leader—not the strangest thing to happen in our crazy Party. The unity of Labor is the hope of the world. If that's the case, there's no bloody hope.

Thursday, 7 December

The last day of the parliamentary year. No diary entries for a while because of the best thing ever: Oliver's birth on Tuesday, 7 November, at Canberra Hospital. A really tough time for Janine but so much joy when it was all over. The little champion arrived just in time for the Melbourne Cup. That was his first activity in life: resting in my arms watching Brew greet the judge. We backed Yippyio, a gallant second after a chequered run. His grandfather would have been happy.

I took two weeks' paternity leave to help Janine get used to the new routine. Oliver has added a new dimension to our lives, sending me gushy. All parents say this, but I feel something special about him, a special bond. Joel reckons the resemblance to me is scary. What's wrong with that?

Some thoughts on the election year ahead. Our problem is that we have run our agenda in Opposition through political ploys. But our political problem is that the public is seeing through the ploys: GST, SES schools, PHI rebate, etc. The only way to sustain a strategy is to support good policy measures that can also be presented as good politics.

This can't be achieved through opinion polling. The ALP polling is reactive—telling us what people think about current issues but nothing on where the issues are headed. Nothing about the problems the public wants us to solve, such as parental involvement in schooling, the introduction of charter schools.

Next year we will test the rule that the Australian public always gets its election results right. In truth, we don't deserve to win, we've been too opportunistic and cynical. So the Coalition would normally win next year. Howard will then hand over to Costello, who will beat Crean in 2004. A minimum of eleven years in Opposition.

My theory is that Labor's electoral success runs in long cycles. We peaked in 1945, after Scullin's bad experience in the 1930s. Then we peaked again in 1985 after Whitlam's bad experience in the 1970s. If history repeats itself, our next peak is due in 2025, my 31st year in the Parliament. Bloody hell.

PHI Private health insurance

2001

This was a dramatic year in Australian politics, with the Tampa controversy, September 11 and the War against Terror, and the Howard Government's political comeback, which led to Labor's election defeat on 10 November. On election night Kim Beazley stood down as Labor Leader and was replaced by Simon Crean. Jenny Macklin became Deputy Leader and Bob McMullan the Shadow Treasurer.

Crean established a Shadow Cabinet system, an inner core of the Shadow Ministry. Between 1996 and 2001 under Beazley, there was no such distinction—all 30 Shadow Ministers were in the Shadow Cabinet. I returned to the frontbench as Shadow Assistant Treasurer and Shadow Minister for Economic Ownership, Housing and Urban Development, as part of the outer Shadow Ministry. This followed a keenly contested ballot within the NSW Right faction for frontbench positions. My success was due to the support of Crean and Laurie Brereton, with whom I had forged a close alliance after our earlier differences on East Timor. Laurie had retired from the frontbench and became an influential figure on the backbench.

Earlier in the year, my work focused on two important activities. The first was turning political theory into practice by supporting innovative projects in my electorate. This was my strongest period as a constituent MP. I tried to bypass the traditional hierarchies and institutions of politics by backing community leaders who wanted to develop new models of schooling and welfare provision in south-west Sydney. I established a trial program of direct democracy—online voting—in Werriwa.

I also consolidated my policy work and written material into a coherent philosophy of politics. This was set out in a speech at the University of New South Wales in July. I concluded that Labor needed to pursue the dispersal of economic, social and political power, break down the Establishment's control of society and empower disenfranchised citizens in the outer suburbs and regions of the nation. This anti-Establishment approach to politics became my mantra as a frontbencher under Crean.

It also became clear in 2001 that balancing work and family commitments was not going to be easy. My first trip away from Oliver left me feeling guilty and uncomfortable. Fatherhood gave me my strongest sense of responsibility in life, and I started a four-year struggle to give it the time and priority it deserved.

Tuesday, 9 January

The fabled parliamentary study tour, but this one is fair dinkum: India, London, Ireland, Israel and Cairo—all of them for the first time except London. Day six and I've hit the wall in downtown Delhi; walking the streets of this place has been a cathartic experience.

The poverty makes you wonder what sort of world humankind has constructed. The sight of grown men, hundreds of them in one street, sitting on the ground outside restaurants, waiting for scraps to be thrown out at the end of the day. The inhumanity of allowing this to happen to people in a world of plenty. No wonder I felt sombre, like Yossarian on the streets of Rome. The problems seem too big, and Australian politics an exercise in futility. Back in my hotel room I jotted down four things that make social democracy redundant:

- The market won the Cold War and sustains an international system of poverty and inequality.
- Change must come from a community level, but the nature of civil society is largely predetermined by factors more powerful than politics.
- Democracy is rooted: the political class is too cynical and the public too apathetic.
- The managerial class has captured the ALP; it's become a party that manages the existing order, instead of creating a new one.

Yossarian The main character in Joseph Heller's novel *Catch–22*

In these circumstances, why put pressure on my health and family? The week away from Janine and Oliver has been really tough going. The extremes of political life: love the experiences it brings (Agra, the Taj Mahal, Fatehpur Sikri), but hate being away from home.

Thursday, 11 January

I'm in London to deliver a paper to the International Conference on Asset-Based Welfare, hosted by one of the Blairite think-tanks, the Institute for Public Policy Research. It always freshens me up to get out of the country and talk about new social democratic ideas. Perhaps I should have pursued an academic career.

I like this concept of asset-based welfare. The original goal of the welfare state was to solve poverty and to give people peace of mind. In a post-war world of stable employment and steady careers, transfer payments did the trick. If people fell out of the workforce, welfare benefits held them over until they found a new job. But in the new economy, insecurity has become a way of life. People move in and out of jobs all the time, requiring new skills and economic assets to cushion them against the inevitability of change.

The smart thing for our side of politics is to reform the welfare state to meet these new challenges. Transfer payments are still important, but they are no longer sufficient to give people peace of mind about the future. About 60 per cent of the population are participating in the benefits of mass capitalism—the growth in share ownership, economic investments and intellectual capital.

Social democracy needs to spread these benefits to 100 per cent of society. My paper advocates the creation of First Shareowners Schemes, Lifelong Learning Accounts and Family Income Accounts to achieve this goal. It went down fairly well at the conference: the usual scepticism from the social welfare lobby, but interest and enthusiasm from the American and British Third Wayers.

Monday, 5 February

Back in Canberra for the resumption of the Parliament. Lunch with the NSW Right and the Leader at the Kurrajong Hotel. Beazley was surprisingly down-cast about our prospects. Went down there expecting the conversation to

Asset-based welfare Policies that help people save and accumulate assets, beyond the traditional forms of govt income support

focus on gossip, insiders' stories and machine politics/process, with not a policy discussion to be found. Spot on: that's exactly the way it was. This is going to be a long year.

Friday, 9 February

An unbelievable article in *The Australian* today by Michelle Gilchrist entitled 'Good times at the Holy Grail, a Canberra bar that is more than just a drinking hole'. It's a follow-up to the bar-room spat between Pyne and Emerson/Swan, and ends with the following paragraph:

> Canberra hangouts have a code of silence that Christopher Pyne seems to have broken. If Noel Crichton-Browne had threatened to 'screw the tits off' a journalist in Canberra instead of Perth, he might have survived. The MP who told another female reporter he was going home to masturbate did.

That's me! What a stitch-up. About two years ago, I was chatting to a cadet journalist from the *SMH*, whose name I can't even remember, at La Grange in Manuka when things got out of control. She started telling me about how she lost her virginity and how she enjoyed group sex. Now, I don't mind women who talk like blokes but this was ridiculous. She had trouble stamped on her forehead, a real bunny-boiler.

I needed to get out of there, so I said, 'Okay, good on you, I'm going home to masturbate', and ran for the hills. I thought it was funny at the time and would never hear of it again. It certainly wasn't in the cadet's interests to retail the conversation around. But she must have put it through the press gallery. Now the Anti-Christ has put it into print.

There are some strange people in politics, I can assure you, but it's nothing compared with the nutters in journalism. The prudish and spooky Anti-Christ trying to fit me up as another NCB. Honestly, I should never have swapped Western Sydney's knock-around culture for the freaks and weirdos of Canberra.

Sunday, 11 February

A seminar for Labor MPs and candidates in Sydney to get us ready for the forthcoming campaign. These events always provide good insight into the

---

Chris Pyne Lib. member, Sturt 1993–
Noel Crichton-Browne WA Lib. Sen. 1981–95; Independent Lib. Sen. 1995–96

bunny-boiler The Glenn Close character in the film *Fatal Attraction* who boils Michael Douglas's daughter's pet rabbit

true state of politics. The Party officials usually love to dazzle us with their morsels of inside information drawn from the internal polling and new, clever campaign techniques. Today was no different.

Geoff Walsh tossed up the standard lines about the Howard Government being out of touch with the concerns of ordinary Australians. But then he gave us a peek at the real situation: 'Our numbers are soft, however, relayed through minor parties, with big variations geographically. There is a record low vote for the two major parties'. The next election can't be a shoe-in if our primary vote is low and we are relying so heavily on minor-party preferences.

Walsh also said the GST had 'lost its early lustre', and the further one moved from the GPOs of the major cities, the stronger the opposition to it. I'm not entirely convinced. This may reflect a problem with the polling methodology: people like to complain about things on the phone but real life is not so bad. Look at my sister's family next door: with seven kids, they have done so well out of tax cuts and increased family benefits they are now building an in-ground pool. Next summer, we will all be floating in their GST windfall.

Eric Roozendaal's presentation was a bell-ringer. He said there has been a dramatic change in the last five years in the way Australians perceive politicians. Their view can be summarised in five words: distrustful, alienated, sceptical, disillusioned and cynical. How bad is that? Bad, but at least he's honest about it.

He went on: 'Every day there are new allegations in the media against parties and politicians and they have an impact. Political loyalty has become conditional. Political loyalty is evaporating rapidly. In the 1970s and 1980s, 10 per cent of people were swinging voters. Now the figure is 30–40 per cent. The voters are looking to punish politicians'.

Eric's remedy is not about fixing the core problem; rather, it's about how we can squeeze a victory out of a deeply cynical electorate. He recommends the use of what he calls 'relationship campaigning', interacting with voters one-on-one: 'People now expect a high standard of service from all organisations and that is what you must deliver. Research in the United States has shown that if MPs interact three times with undecided voters over a two-year period, they triple their chances of getting their vote'.

This is the new race to the bottom in politics. Give up on policy, give up persuading people about issues, but try to strike up some kind of personal relationship with them—MPs as a cross between social workers and the Avon lady. It's the sad decline in the content and serious intent of our democracy. The hollowing out of high-level trust: people don't believe the major parties and their leaders any more, but they might vote for a smiling face and handshake down at the local shopping centre or train station. How the mighty have fallen.

Monday, 12 February

My love/hate relationship with Bob Carr continues. Sometimes we are collaborating with each other, but more frequently, we are bagging each other. It's a fundamental clash of personalities: the Eastern Suburbs geek versus the Western Suburbs larrikin.

At the moment, we are in a collaborative phase. Today at NSW Parliament House Bob launched my new book from Allen & Unwin, a treatise on education policy, *What Did You Learn Today?* He gave a generous speech, but like Beazley three years ago, was very careful to distance himself from the lively, controversial proposals. His office also minimised media interest by telling the State press gallery there wasn't anything newsworthy in his speech, so only a few journalists turned up.

The book is a program for the creation of a learning society, mobilising new resources from all parts of the nation for its education. I'm particularly keen on the idea of charter schools—local schools run by parents and communities, breaking the centralised control of the State bureaucracy and the Teachers' Federation in public education. Hopefully, Carr will take up my proposal for a charter school trial in south-west Sydney. He's always talking the talk of education reform. This is his chance to walk the walk.

My third book. Gough once told me that Dick Hall's ambition in life was to fill the shelf of a bookcase with his own books. I've got a long way to go, but progressing nicely. My next one, *The Enabling State* (co-edited with Peter Botsman and published by Pluto Press), should be out in April. It's not everyone's cup of tea in the ALP, but I love writing books. The second Leader of the FPLP, Andrew Fisher, once said that he didn't like reading books because they might make him change his mind. Christ knows what he would have made of me.

Monday, 19 February

The things you hear about the Labor movement never cease to amaze me. I was one of the speakers at a seminar in Hobart tonight, discussing the Party's policies and organisational structure. The next speaker was Greg

---

Dick Hall Former Whitlam staffer, ALP activist and author

Peter Botsman Political commentator and head of various ALP-aligned think-tanks

Sword. He said he was reluctant to talk about the reform of the rank-and-file Party because he had only attended two branch meetings in the last decade.

I had to pinch myself to ensure it wasn't a dream/nightmare. What sort of organisation has a President who has barely made it to meetings? He's in the job because of the unions and the factional system—our version of the separation of powers. In effect, Greg Sword and I occupy different political parties. I go to local branch meetings—have gone to hundreds of them over the past decade. He goes to union meetings, where he would never see people like me or local members of the ALP. Yet he's our President.

This is where the factions have got out of control. When I first joined the Green Valley branch of the Party in 1979, the meetings were full of committed trade unionists—committed to local rank-and-file activism and the cause of industrial labour. By and large, they saw them as the same thing. But now power in the ALP rests with the factions; the branches don't matter, so the unionists (those who are left) don't turn up. For those of us romantic about the Party's traditions, it's a terribly sad thing. The gutting of the real Labor Party, the one I grew up with.

Monday, 19 March

A walking, talking example of the need for radical education reform in NSW: Bev Baker, the head of the Parents and Citizens Federation. I debated her tonight as part of the Public Education Lobby in Liverpool. She is incredibly out of touch, claiming, 'There is no such thing as a poor private school'.

She even had the hide to call our Families in Partnership (FIP) charter/community school proposal a clique: 'If they decide on school uniforms, you can't send your child there unless she wears a uniform'. Shouldn't parents who want their children to attend schools with uniforms have an opportunity to set them up? Anyway, Families in Partnership is a cooperative organisation comprising the parents of intellectually disabled children. They want to be closely involved in the education of their kids through a community-run school—not exactly a sin in life. It's hard to knock them and their children, but Baker found a way.

This is the problem with so-called peak interest groups. Because most parents don't get involved in the P & C, unrepresentative people can take control and purport to speak with authority in the media. When I mentioned Bev Baker's name at the Ingleburn ALP branch meeting later in the night, the members booed—an extraordinary reaction.

Tuesday, 27 March

At Caucus today Beazley gave us a guide to his election strategy. He plans to use the Charter of Budget Honesty to his advantage: by holding back the costings on his policies until halfway through the election campaign. Until then he will rely on a list of priorities with a firm implementation timetable. He hopes to win by talking up our issues and intentions pre-campaign, but not putting out any of the details until the five weeks leading up to polling day.

No wonder Caucus has an empty feeling to it. Yeah, we might win, but what is our crusade/purpose? It's a million miles from Kim's promise to totally rewrite Labor's Platform and policy direction.

Monday, 2 April

There are not enough experiments in Australian politics. I've decided to run one, testing the potential of direct Internet democracy in practice. I told my *Tele* readers today that I'm collecting email addresses in Werriwa and, once a week, will ask people to vote on a topical issue. We are converting my website to an electronic voting format—the first MP in Australia to follow the direct democracy advice of his electorate.

It's a radical and subversive thing to do. The rest of the system will hate it. In fact, that's a good reason to do it. Someone needs to try something—anything—to break the cycle of public cynicism and apathy. Representative democracy has failed. We need to transfer power from the Parliament to the people, and see if they are still interested. That's my job and methodology, bypassing the established hierarchies of power:

- bypassing the parliamentary system with my e.democracy trial
- bypassing the traditional welfare state with our social entrepreneurial projects in Werriwa—Claymore, Minto and FIP
- bypassing the school education establishment with the FIP community school proposal
- bypassing Labor Caucus with my Third Way agenda and contacts
- bypassing the media —the press gallery, in particular—by writing my own articles and books.

Charter of Budget Honesty Legislation introduced by the Howard govt in 1996 providing full financial updates on the Commonwealth Budget during election campaigns and the costing of major election policy commitments

Tuesday, 8 May

The night of nights for the Labor establishment, a gala dinner at the tennis centre in Melbourne to mark the centenary of Caucus. More evidence of my double life inside the show: piercing looks and hatred from so-called Caucus colleagues versus encouragement from the camp-followers—calls of 'keep it up' from Dawkins, Cohen, etc.

The Dawkinses are really into Beazley. Not just John, but also his wife Maggie: 'I used to work for Kim and he could never make a decision. If you asked him to, he couldn't reform the colour of the toilet paper'. Also a revealing insight into his true economic views: 'In 1983 he said to me, "I am a protectionist" and it was because of the influence of his dad. Kim was never comfortable with the big reforms of the 1980s'.

John Faulkner put on a great show of Party history. Fascinating to compare the applause meter for the former Labor Prime Ministers. It was in direct proportion to the size of their election losses: subdued applause for Curtin and Hawke, pandemonium for Whitlam and Keating.

The living greats spoke, obviously trying to out-do each other. Gough stuck to his human rights agenda and, thankfully, Freudenberg's speech. Hawke tried to reinvent himself as the father of multiculturalism, with no mention of his greatest achievement: opening up the economy. A trip down memory lane with his speaking style: a tub-thumper who degenerated into a clown. Paul seemed to be down in the dumps; he gave us a bit of economics and then his spiel on national identity.

The Big Man went okay, given the hard acts to follow—his usual mish-mash of issues. As Beazley finished, I scribbled on my program, 'We have never been weaker, we have never been stronger'. That was the mood among the True Believers in the vast crowd: Kim should beat Howard, but it's been a terrible sell-out of Labor's reform traditions to get there. It was striking to have so many people—none of them serving MPs, of course—come up to me and say something along those lines.

Thursday, 24 May

Poor Beazley, he had to do his Budget reply speech against the backdrop of a blooper by Conroy. He was at a Budget forum for school kids this morning and one of them asked him if we would increase revenue to pay for Knowledge Nation. Conroy started speculating about the hard

---

Barry Cohen ALP member, Robertson 1969–90; min. in Hawke govt

Graham Freudenberg Legendary ALP speech-writer from Calwell to Carr decisions we needed to take, possibly increasing some taxes—not exactly in line with the Leader's small-target strategy.

Kim was back on message with his speech, however. He itemised budget savings of $130 million per annum to pay for our spending commitments, the equivalent of just 0.09 per cent of Commonwealth outlays. I say to people the Labor movement limits itself by trying to change the public sector by 2–3 per cent, when the real reform task is to change society by 20–30 per cent.

Well, Kim's not even that ambitious. His Budget reply represents a 0.09 per cent change to the public sector—funding a cancer program, government schools and rollback for charities. Now the media pressure will really be on. He's not going to be able to hold back his other policies for the campaign, surely.

Wednesday, 6 June

A conversation with Cheryl Kernot today: she's as downcast about our situation as I am. She said that her proposals to assist social entrepreneurs were ranked last by the PRC. So much for Beazley's enthusiasm for community-building. Crean said to fund the policy through the REDOs. Cheryl laments the lack of reform energy and drive. Poor woman, she thought she was getting herself into a dynamic social democratic movement. But all she did was join the ALP.

She hates the machine men and they hate her. Her only comfort in the Caucus comes from the ginger group clustered around her: Murphy, Sidebottom, Cox and Danby. She feels hard done by and I think much of what she says is valid. It's a cultural thing: going from the Democrats to the ALP is like the difference between being tackled by John Napper and Les Boyd.

More discontent about Beazley around Caucus. Laurie Brereton, Joel and Carmen Lawrence all talk of Kim's total discomfort in their presence. That's right, he's only comfortable with process people. Yesterday he told

---

Cheryl Kernot ALP member, Dickson 1998–2001; Shadow Employment & Training Min. 1999–2001
PRC Priorities Review Committee of the Shadow Cabinet; the Opposition equivalent of a razor gang
REDOs Regional Economic Development Organisations, first established under the Working Nation statement in 1994
John Murphy ALP member, Lowe 1998–

David Cox ALP member, Kingston 1998–2004
John Napper Played more than 300 games for the Liverpool Rugby Union club (the Bulls) and, legend has it, never made a tackle
Les Boyd The most feared and dangerous rugby league player in the Sydney competition in the late 1970s and early 1980s
Carmen Lawrence Shadow Industry, Innovation & Technology Min. 2000–01

Caucus that we are not doing things for next year or even the next three years; we have a bigger and longer program of change for Australia. Sounds great, but after five years in the job, he just needs to tell us what it is.

Tuesday, 19 June

A big shift in Beazley's rhetoric in Caucus. He sounded downbeat today, complaining/predicting that the Government will not face a critical media in the election campaign. Must be something bad in our polling. He said the public know that we stand for education and Knowledge Nation, even though 'they may not have a clear picture of it'. The vague slogans of Knowledge Nation and Rollback are actually a problem. The public have worked out that Kim stands for nothing and he uses slogans to cover up his policy vacuum.

Thursday, 12 July

Everything I believe in, everything I have researched as a parliamentarian, is in this speech: 'Reinventing Collectivism, The New Social Democracy', delivered today at the University of New South Wales—my most important piece of work in the last three years.

On every front, collectivism is in retreat: state socialism is dead, industry planning is redundant, the welfare state is under siege, trade unionism and working-class solidarity are fading away and people have lost faith in government bureaucracies and organised politics. Our side of politics needs to invent new forms of collective action: rebuilding social capital, creating networks of mutual interest and mutual support—embracing the virtues of civic socialism.

Instead of controlling and directing the delivery of services, government should play the role of a facilitator or enabler. It needs to act as a junior partner to community effort. And it can be done: through service devolution (such as charter schools and social enterprises), by limiting the incursion of market forces into civil society, through the creation of lifelong learning, and opening up new forms of public participation in our democracy.

Unless we do these things, the problem for Left-of-Centre politics is insoluble—my pessimistic outlook. It's a huge reform task. In the Industrial Age, social democracy embraced the politics of bigness. It was thought that large, centralised institutions were needed to stand between the public and the prospect of market failure. Our side of politics became synonymous with big government departments, big trade unions and big protest groups. We tried to create collectivism on a mass scale—a huge, historic mistake.

Big hierarchical organisations—public and private—destroy rather than create social capital. They treat people as clients rather than citizens. Institutional power needs to be pushed downwards, so that a self-reliant public can make more of its own decisions at a community or neighbourhood level. People are longing to belong to something more inclusive than markets and states.

This speech ties my policy work into a common philosophy of governance: supporting the dispersal of power in society. Hierarchy allows power and privilege to be concentrated among the few. A network society disperses economic, social and political power to the many. The new political divide is between insiders and outsiders—those who occupy the centres of authority and influence in society and those who have been disenfranchised by the power elite.

The Third Way is a political cause for outsiders. It aims to democratise power and spread the benefits of ownership as widely as possible. It is against centralisation of any kind, whether in the form of corporate power, super-unions, big government or an out-of-touch political system. This approach is evident in my work program: the devolution of economic power through a system of stakeholder (asset-based) welfare; the importance of competition policy as a way of dispersing market power and economic privilege; the devolution of social power through a community-led approach to public policy; and the dispersal of political power through new forums of public participation and direct democracy.

This should be our new positive agenda. If you listen to the Left these days, they only talk about the things they oppose. Labor needs to get outside the traditional institutions of the Left (trade union bosses, protest meetings and parliamentary speeches) and develop a radical pragmatism—learning from social practitioners in the search for new forms of collectivism.

This is where we can use the Information Age to advantage, to bypass the old hierarchies and open up new opportunities on the fringe of politics. Business and social entrepreneurs talk a language of change, creativity and enablement. Machine politics, by contrast, has narrowed its conversation to an exchange of slogans, spin and electoral manipulation. This is why the old politics is dying and a new paradigm is needed.

That's my task, my political project: a revolution in Labor's philosophy and methodology. But I'm the only one talking about it. Maybe I'm wasting my time—the futility of a minority of one. But, realistically, what have I got to lose? I got into this from a minority position, an angry young man from Green Valley, ripping and tearing against those opposed to change—clubbusting, as I called it at Liverpool Council.

There's no shame in having a go and finding out that you're on your own. The main thing in life is to have a go, even if the system puts you down and isolates you. That's me, in the isolation ward of Labor politics.

Saturday, 14 July

Last month I saw the movie *The Bone Collector*. Last night I met him. I was trying to get home after the big ALP fundraiser for Gough's 85th birthday. I left Darling Harbour at about 12.45 a.m. The Bone Collector tried to take me for a ride. He was driving along Punchbowl Road and I asked him to turn left, down King Georges Road, to get to the M5, the standard way home. He told me it takes 25 minutes to reach the M5 that way. It actually takes five. Then he took me through the back streets of Bankstown, so I gave him a gob full.

The Bone Collector knew I had busted him, so he told me to get out of the cab, thinking I had to walk home. But I pulled out my mobile to phone another taxi and he went berserk. He started yelling that I needed to pay the fare. I told him to piss off, gave him my business card and said that if he wanted to take it further he should contact the police.

The mad bastard then drove onto the footpath, trying to knock me over (I had to jump up onto a brick wall). Bloody hell, I thought it *was* a scene from a movie. Then I crossed the road to get away from him. He did a U-turn, got out of his cab and started to follow me up the road. He ran up behind me, nicked my work satchel, the 1985 UNESCO one from Gough, and then tried to race back to his car.

Well, stuff that. I'd taken enough shit from him, he wasn't going to steal my property as well. So I turned and chased him—and got the shock of my life when I caught him and brought him down with a copybook tackle. I'm happy to report the old skills are still there.

I grabbed my satchel and got out of there. I thought his next move might be to get a gun out of his taxi—how mad was he? So I hid in a block of flats and eventually hailed down another cab to take me home. On the way back, I called Combined Taxis and lodged a complaint. They said I had done the right thing in not paying (once he told me to get out of the cab, I was under no obligation to pay) and that the cabbie should have followed my instructions to go down King Georges Road. No worries.

Until I had a knock on my front door just before dawn this morning. Janine and Oliver are in Perth and I had left my glasses in the kitchen, so all I could see out of the bedroom window was a sedan with a white light on top. I shat myself: thought the Bone Collector had tracked down my address and was here to clean me up. I didn't answer the door and eventually the car drove away.

Scariest night of my life, I didn't sleep a wink. Then, this morning, another knock on the door: the Campbelltown police wanting to know if I got rolled last night. Turns out the cabbie went to Bankstown Police Station and told them someone had robbed an MP called Mark Latham, and then that person tried to pass himself off as me (with the business card) to avoid his cab fare. It was the cops knocking on my door in the early hours checking to see if I was okay. What a shemozzle.

I told the policeman it was me, not a robber/impersonator, and gave him the full story. He was cool, as was Inspector Nadazdy from Bankstown Police, who said not to worry, sounds like the taxi driver was in the wrong. Bloody oath, he was.

Called Joel and told him what happened—he thinks it's the funniest thing he's ever heard. Certainly one of the weirdest things to happen to me. We talked about the politics of it—could be a sensational story in the media. Maybe I should pre-empt it, write it up in my *Tele* column as a real-life nightmare on the streets of Sydney. But why draw attention to it? If the cops aren't worried about it, why should I be?

Monday, 30 July

An email exchange that perfectly describes my dilemma inside the ALP. I sent Vern Hughes a copy of my UNSW paper and he emailed back:

> Your last two papers have been particularly sharp and I agree with every point in them. The trouble is, when I look at your Labor colleagues, they are not on the same planet as you. They're still into unreconstructed state paternalism and proud of it, aren't they? How do you see this problem, Mark? Do you think you'll win them over in the end, or will it be necessary to part company in some way? If it is the second, I'd join you in a flash.

My honest response: 'Yes, you are right, they are quite proud of state paternalism. I'll probably end up in London working for Demos and CAN. Nobody can bash their head against a brick wall forever'.

Vern Hughes Executive Officer of the Social Entrepreneurs Network, a coalition of social and community workers who believe in an innovative approach to solving poverty, based on the establishment of social enterprises

Demos A London-based Left-of-Centre radical think-tank
CAN Community Action Network, the British equivalent of the Social Entrepreneurs Network

Wednesday, 8 August

The ever-reliable Tanner gave me a little lecture in today's *AFR*: 'I'm a believer in trying to contribute to public debate and trying to influence outcomes—I don't think spending my life on the backbench would be the most effective way of doing that'. Lindsay is living proof that the centre of politics can melt your brain—his thinking has not advanced in three years. Most of the interesting ideas are on the edge of politics, away from the dulling impact of a thousand process-driven meetings. The backbench is far from perfect, but at least it's an opportunity to engage in some creative policy work, free from the control freaks at the centre of the system.

Tuesday, 21 August

Kim really struggled at Caucus today. After six years of trying to work it out, he said that our policy is to offer relief to families and oldies under pressure, the same policy as Howard via his tax cuts. He said that small, inexpensive policies are enough to satisfy the public, such as our $51 million redirection of Category One school funding. Plus he suggested some strange policy linkages: 'To get into the law and order debate, every electorate should cobble together an Education Priority Zone'. What could he mean by that?

Here are my election predictions:

- The GST is fading as an issue. After all our complaining, Rollback will be a molehill.
- The polling is false: people will go for Howard's tax cuts, as opposed to Beazley's limited spending plans. The elites like government spending; the public likes Bugs Bunny in its pocket.
- The rural backlash will not eventuate at the ballot box. They are professional whingers who stir up the system to get more grants and government assistance, but then vote conservative.
- The Aston by-election on 14 July showed that Howard is right in it. His underdog status helps him, as does our domination at State/Territory level. He will win the campaign and win the election.

Closer to home, my Internet polls in Werriwa have been disappointing—a failed experiment. On average, only 300 people have been

---

Education Priority Zone An ALP policy to provide extra funding and innovative projects for disadvantaged schools in disadvantaged communities

Aston by-election Caused by the death of Lib. member Peter Nugent, which resulted in a disappointing result for the ALP and the election of Chris Pearce as the new Lib. member

voting in each ballot. Sure, the technology is new and it's an outer sub-urban seat where people are busy with family commitments, but I was hoping for at least a thousand participants.

For those who do vote, the results and feedback have been good. But we have a long way to go before e.democracy takes over from the traditional system. The interest is not there. Dick Morris's promise of a political revolution has stalled at the gates of the Bastille. Not a good time, I must say. Despair on both fronts, nationally and locally.

Monday, 27 August

Popped into Old Parliament House this evening for the launch of the C. E. W. Bean Foundation, honouring the work of Australia's war correspondents. The driving force for the Foundation is Tony Walker from the *Fin Review*, labelled 'the big swinging dick' by his workmate Paul Cleary. If you know Tony, it's a corker of a nickname—he's very self-assured, a larger-than-life character.

Clem Lloyd gave an entertaining talk, pointing out that, since the 1830s in this country, his profession has carried the description 'working journalists'. The only other way this term has been used in Australia is in relation to 'working dogs' and 'working bullocks'. An apt label, given the way the media move as a pack.

A basic truism of our society: people who communicate regularly with one another think similarly. Press gallery journalists are exposed to the same information—it's risky for them to break the orthodoxy and leave the herd. Group-think is an obvious human tendency. In politics, it is a powerful institutional force for conservatism. That's how Parliament House works.

It also makes some journalists incredibly precious. Exhibit A: Phillip Adams. Last month I wrote a *Tele* column parodying Howard's oft-quoted desire to find a Right-wing Phillip Adams at the ABC. Harmless enough. I thought it was humorous. But not for Phil. He wrote me a long, rambling letter in reply, telling me his life story (very strange, I've never met the guy). Some really sad and brutal things happened to him when he was young. No wonder the slightest hint of criticism sets him off.

Today he was at it again. Yet another letter, this time going in hard and dirty. He says he's discussed with 'some senior colleagues' the circum-stances of my resignation from the frontbench in 1998. He reckons there's

---

Clem Lloyd A long-serving Australian journalist, particularly associated with the Whitlam years

another version of these events, which doesn't cast me in such an 'heroic light'. He ends the letter by saying that he regards this other version of events as very plausible.

You don't need to be Einstein to work out what he's referring to. Adams loves the smutty rumours and innuendo of Labor politics. He would have been lapping it up: the retailing of the Ray/Gray smear around the Party, turning it into folklore. The black man and his bullshit. But what can I do? Best to follow the advice of his erstwhile friend, John Marsden, who said, 'Don't worry about Adams, he thinks his shit doesn't stink'.

Tuesday, 28 August

Beazley in Caucus continues his small-target approach, this time on the latest refugee boat and Badgerys Creek Airport. At least he's consistent: the bigger the issue, the smaller our policy. It's amazing he has lasted this long. He can't get a message out. For example, he was going okay on health care in the Parliament and then the fiasco about his daughter's appendix stuffed it. Now the tactics committee is back onto a Crean/GST scandal.

Whatever happened to the Party of big dreams, big ideas and big vision? On every progressive issue that matters, he has made us a small target.

Wednesday, 29 August

Is this what it was like when Menzies made his surprise parliamentary statement on Petrov just before the 1954 election? That's how it felt today: high drama as Howard and Ruddock rushed in special legislation (the Border Protection Bill 2001) to make sure the Government has the legal authority to turn around the Norwegian flag vessel, the MS *Tampa*, with its cargo of asylum-seekers rescued from an over-crowded Indonesian boat trying to get to Christmas Island.

All week Beazley has been offering support to the Government on this issue, but this evening, without time for a Caucus meeting, he decided to oppose the Bill and we all voted accordingly. Well, root my boot, I've no

---

John Marsden Well-known flamboyant Sydney lawyer who lives in the electorate of Werriwa Bob Menzies Lib. PM 1939–41, 1949–66 Vladimir Petrov A Soviet diplomat/spy who defected to Australia in 1954 and sparked the Petrov Royal Commission at the height of the Cold War

Phillip Ruddock Lib. member, House of Representatives 1973– ; Immigration & Multicultural Affairs Min. 1996–2003

idea what's going on inside his head. I sat next to Joel during the division and said I could easily vote for this, what's the problem? Sounds like the Bill will be blocked in the Senate and Howard has got himself a winning issue. What was the point in being a small target for three years, only to take a U-turn today?

Confusion among the colleagues. I went to the Caucus Committee earlier today and the views were diametrically opposed. Leo McLeay, forever the control-meister, said that we can't do anything about the issue, 'the election will be won or lost in the next three months'. He sounded paralysed.

Duncan Kerr offered a powerful critique of Beazleyism: 'We have been in a crouching position on immigration for quite some time. We need to be honest about this: we have not offered an alternative and the vacuum has been filled by Hanson and Howard. We have been unable to guide the public debate, crouching in the grass'. Then Craig Emerson said something nonsensical and I stopped taking notes.

But Duncan is right. This was always the problem with being a small target. The electorate is volatile and our support is soft, channelled through minor parties. The Government can find an issue and harden up its support at any time. Kim took our destiny out of our hands and now look at him.

Thursday, 30 August

A special meeting of Caucus first thing today to confirm Beazley's decision to vote against the Border Protection Bill. He could have been Evatt talking the day after Petrov, as he told us: 'We may have the public against us, but we will win the next election on this once we get our message out'. Overnight he has become a big, big target. I have always thought the historical parallel was between Beazley and Calwell, but I was wrong. It is between Beazley and Evatt.

After Caucus, the Leader started getting 'our message out'. Here is the first transcript sent through from his office, his first answer on the John Laws program this morning:

> We have been supporting them (the Government) all week. But this is a piece of draconian legislation dropped on us at about 40 minutes' notice prior to its debate which basically suspended all laws. It

---

John Laws Long-standing talkback radio host

doesn't provide a solution to this because the solution to this particular problem is unquestionably providing a safe haven for these folk outside Australia—and it's got nothing to do with that. It doesn't stop a ship going out and doesn't stop a ship going out and coming back in and going out and coming back in and playing some form of legal yo-yo with us. It doesn't stop any of that. But what it does do is suspend the application of all law. And it's extraordinary legislation—law of murder, assault and all civil and criminal and liability associated with it.

I'm glad he cleared that up. But I can't believe he is banging on about the law of murder. It's a bit late in the story for a military buff and former Defence Minister, someone who will sit around for hours talking about the slaughter of war, to be complaining about the legalisation of murder. It's the whole basis of the coercive power of the state.

Has Kim met any coppers lately, young guys without much status or hope in society until the government gave them guns to point at people? Same with the meatheads in the army. That great line from *Apocalypse Now* by Captain Willard: 'Charging a man with murder in this place (Vietnam) was like handing out speeding tickets in the Indy 500'. Kim loves all that SAS crap, stormtroopers shooting at will. Why, all of a sudden, has he turned against it?

Saturday, 15 September

Learning by doing. Turning my ideas into practice. I have been talking and writing about the importance of mentoring, giving troubled boys decent role models in life, teaching them the difference between right and wrong. Now I'm doing something about it. I've been helping a young fella each weekend, taking him up to Sweeney's riding ranch where they have given him some part-time work.

In a few weeks you can see the difference in him. Poor bugger doesn't know his dad. His family is always on walkabout through the public housing estates—they have lived in Ambarvale, Lurnea and Cartwright in the two months I have known them. When I first took him up to Sweeney's, we walked past the parked cars and he told me how to break into them. I said the best thing is to own a car—great way to impress the girls. Today he told me that he's banking his money to buy a car asap. Felt good to hear him say it.

Mentoring works, but it's hard-going to get people involved on a mass scale. I can feel the time pressures myself. I don't see enough of my own son and with an election coming up, I won't see much of this young bloke. But he's got his start, working with men, good earthy blokes at the riding ranch. All those books and articles I write—nothing beats putting your knowledge and convictions into practice.

Monday, 1 October

That's it for me with the *Daily Telegraph*. I lodged a tidy piece on Noel Pearson and Aboriginal welfare for today's paper but it has been butchered—bits left out, bits in the wrong place, barely readable the way they have presented it. I can't work out who's running the place any more. I used to deal with Cookie (Ian Moore)—he was good. Now the management has fallen to bits. Three years of columns is enough, anyway—I'm out of there. Never again.

Saturday, 20 October

The set-up of the century. I hadn't heard from the Bankstown coppers for months about the Bone Collector. Then they called on Monday, saying they needed to interview me urgently. I said they had to be kidding, it's the middle of a Federal election campaign and anyway, why was it urgent when I hadn't heard anything since July? Turns out the bloke doing the report on the incident took a seven-week holiday in Greece.

I tried to fob them off until after the election but they kept on calling. Eventually, I agreed to see them at Bankstown Police Station last night, with an assurance that there would be no media involved at any stage. Stupid me. At eight o'clock this morning, Oliver in my arms, I answered the front door: it was a reporter from the *Sun-Herald* barking out questions, less than twelve hours after I left the cop shop. The abuse of police power—it's endemic.

And the only thing that changed between Friday 13 July and now? I wrote a *Tele* column with follow-up radio interviews in late July critical of Peter Ryan and his police force.

Sunday, 21 October

Front page of the *Sun-Herald*: 'Police Quiz Labor MP, Latham Broke My Arm, Claims Cabbie'. The media are all over this like a rash. The Bone

---

Ian Moore Opinion-page editor at the *Daily Telegraph*

Peter Ryan NSW Police Commissioner

Collector's real name is Bachir Mustafa, who has been on compo since I tackled him, so he got his money after all. He's not complaining too much, and even fessed up to his theft: 'I did something I should not have done. When he was walking away from me, about 15 metres ahead of the cab, and I thought I was not going to get my money back, that's when I snatched his bag'. Not that the wallopers or the media are interested in that. They just like the story, nice and sensational.

Monday, 22 October

Keating calls, despondent and resigned to our election defeat. He's also lining up some retribution: 'I know I've been out of it for a while, but I still carry the flame for our side. Like Clinton and the Democrats in the US, I'm the last one to win a national election. And I tell you one thing: when this is over I'm going to barrel those close to Kim: Smith, Swan and McMullan'.

Serious shit. He also had some serious advice for me: 'You've got to get away from this "hear ye, hear ye" approach to policy, yelling out in the town square. You've got to get into the persuasion business, talk to Caucus until you turn them around. You know, I had to do it with the likes of Russ Gorman (the former Member for Greenway). I mean, just imagine the fucking indignity of it—Russ Gorman! So get into the persuasion business and if you bag someone, makes sure it's one of those miserable cunts on the other side of the House'.

Friday, 26 October

Is this the low point in our five wasted years? A Crean/Swan press release today announcing that our election policy on poverty is to convene a summit. How can a Labor Party not know what to do about poverty? This is the issue that should make us radically different from the other parties— an intense and burning passion for the elimination of poverty, defining our sense of purpose in a fast-changing world.

They announced it at the ACOSS Congress, so it's not hard to guess what sort of summit it will be: Left conservatism, ACOSS whingeing about all the things they don't like in the world. But not offering any answers, other than increased transfer payments. They just don't get it.

The first task in ending poverty does not relate to material goods. It is a social task—connecting people with others, rebuilding their self-esteem and confidence, creating a new common purpose in their lives. The core demand in poor suburbs is not for more government spending or more market forces. It is to make the neighbourhood normal.

This means getting the social dimension right—through mentoring, helping parents to be better educators in the home, backing innovative community leaders, social entrepreneurs. Every time I think about our mutualist traditions as a Party, I feel sad that we have lost them.

Thursday, 1 November

Is this Australia's first emotional election campaign? Howard has the electorate's emotions running his way on refugees and terrorism. Beazley is not making the same connection with his campaign on health and education. Emotions matter in an era of uncertainty (September 11, etc.) and total disengagement by the electorate. You need to say something stunning/meaningful to punch through the media clatter.

Our problem is the collapse in our heartland vote after Tampa. Electorates with high NESB are fine—the ethnic groups are jumping out of the ground to back us, thinking that Howard is about to bring back White Australia. But the Anglo seats (such as the Hunter and outer Sydney) are in deep trouble. They think Howard's a national hero for turning that boat around. Two Australias, with ethnicity as the real (but unspoken) electoral divide in this campaign. Told Ramsey my views and he wrote them up in his column last Saturday.

My barometer in this campaign has been the Green Valley Shopping Centre. A month ago the Anglos had their heads down, avoiding me like the plague as they walked past my stall—I was Tampa-infested. Now they are starting to engage, slowly drifting back. Beazley has fortified our vote after his success in the leaders' debate. He can't win but the underdog effect is helping him. Still, he must be poison in our polling—Mark Arbib advised me to take his photo off my how-to-vote cards.

Beazley is attempting to be the first person to win an election having become Opposition Leader straight after his party had been thrown out of government. It has never happened before in 100 years of Federal politics—the first Leader in Opposition has never taken his party back into office. And, I'm afraid to report, Kim Beazley Junior is not about to rewrite history on Saturday week.

Sunday, 11 November

Another Beazley defeat. Another wasted opportunity for the ALP. It will be known as the Tampa election but our problems run deeper than that. After

Mark Arbib NSW ALP Asst Gen. Sec. 1999–2004

six years of Beazley's small-target strategy, we face an identity crisis. The True Believers don't know what we stand for and the swinging voters have stopped trying to find out.

Howard has become the first political leader in the Western world to win consecutive elections while promising and then implementing a broad-based consumption tax. With this issue out of the way, the Coalition will be harder to defeat in the future. That's the Beazley legacy—two missed opportunities when the Government was vulnerable to defeat. Four years banging on about that bloody tax and we went backwards.

This was supposed to be the unlosable election but Kim lost it. And now he's gone, handing over to Crean. He couldn't get out of the job fast enough last night, it was almost like he was relieved that the campaign was finally over. Here's my post-mortem on his leadership.

Our big problem is we have lost the outer suburbs, the traditional middle ground of Australian politics. Just look at the seats lost in this campaign: Macarthur, Dobell, Dickson and possibly Canning. Over the past three elections, seats like Lindsay and Hughes in Sydney have moved against us by more than 15 per cent. Our economic policies have failed to back the legitimate aspirations of working families for greater ownership and opportunity.

To some extent, we have become victims of our own success. In the 1970s Whitlam gave the working class an education. In the 1980s Keating gave them economic openness and opportunity. Not surprisingly, this has produced a surge in working-class aspiration. And the policy response by Beazley Labor: to head in the opposite direction.

Just as the aspirationals were getting into full stride, Beazley, Crean and Evans gave away our economic legacy and credentials by declaring that Keating was dead. After six years of growth and prosperity under Howard, the bird has flown. It is now exceptionally difficult to restore our achievements in the public's mind, even if the Party was willing to try. It's a fair dinkum tragedy.

In the last term of Parliament, Crean kept on saying, 'we're dry, too'. But, in fact, we were dry first. The open growth economy used to have a Labor brand on it but then the brains trust gave our brand to the Tories, free of charge. If the economy stays strong, Howard will be odds-on to keep on winning. Thanks, Kim.

And that's just part of our problem. Our social values have also deteriorated, embracing social rights at the expense of social responsibility. This is out of step with suburban attitudes and expectations. As soon as Beazley wobbled on the Tampa legislation it was all over. The boat itself was not the problem. It was Beazley's response that killed us politically. It said Labor was willing to tolerate people doing the wrong thing, that we are a soft touch.

Nobody doubts our compassion to care, only our toughness to govern. People in the suburbs respect the rule of law. For them, letting people break the immigration laws willy-nilly is like saying to the young punk who wants to climb through your bathroom window and ransack your house, 'Welcome, come on in, help yourself'. As soon as you say to the suburbs you're weak in one area, they assume you're weak across the board.

After years of embracing the rights agenda, the electorate now see us as behaviour-neutral. This is a betrayal of the Curtin and Chifley tradition, which took a tough but fair approach to social behaviour. Our former leaders knew that a good society relies on a certain level of order and cohesiveness. They recognised that one of the pillars of social justice is the shared expectation that people are responsible for their own behaviour.

State Labor has been able to convey these values through the law-and-order debate and win government across the Commonwealth. Federally, Beazley created a vacuum, which Howard readily filled. Our only response to wedge politics was to crouch in the grass, hoping the issues might go away. This was the folly of the small-target strategy. We abandoned our dialogue with suburban Australia, while the gentrified Left abandoned us for the Greens and the Democrats. A wedge has been driven through the middle of Labor's ranks.

We need to close the gap between our dual constituencies. This can be achieved by rebuilding our agenda for mutual responsibility. Again, this was something we started in the Keating years (through the Working Nation statement which placed sanctions on loafers) but then we stopped talking about it under Beazley. Work for the Dole now has a Coalition brand on it.

Our silence on these issues is Howard's greatest asset. He is very good at defining himself through his weakest opponents. In a debate between him and the likes of Phillip Adams, he cannot lose. Wedge politics only works when the Left find excuses for people who are doing the wrong thing.

The underlying battle in Federal politics is about economic aspiration and social responsibility. Everything else is just a distraction to fill up the

Work for the Dole A Howard govt policy that requires young people to undertake community work in return for their unemployment benefits

24-hour media cycle. Until Labor learns this fundamental lesson, Howard is sitting pretty. He has the discipline and savvy to ignore the media's hysteria about trivial issues and stick to the basics—economic growth and the rule of law.

Thursday, 15 November

A ballot today within the NSW Right to elect its Shadow Ministers. I'm back in. And over the moon about an unlikely victory. Here's how it happened, blow by blow.

On election night I told my supporters in Werriwa that I would be standing for the Opposition frontbench. With Beazley gone, it's a good time to come back. Not that you can be optimistic about Labor politics. Intellectually, my conclusions are on the dark side: the reform task is incredibly difficult. But this parliamentary term is a good chance to test myself and see if I can make a difference in practice.

Or, to use the Napoleonic maxim: commit and see what happens. I never want to die wondering. Never want to sit on the porch of the nursing home, some silly old prick dribbling on myself, wondering what would have happened if I had had a proper go at parliamentary politics, a bit of adventurism against the odds.

This meant getting the numbers inside our group. A tougher assignment than I expected. My first ring-around produced just a handful of supporters—Joel, Laurie Brereton and Steve Martin. Most see me as a troublemaker. Janice Crosio must have used the term 'team-player' a dozen times, meaning that I'm not one of them. I'm paying the price of three years of agitation and freedom on the backbench.

The big disappointment was Leo McLeay. After eight years of telling me that he's my strongest supporter, he dropped me like a bad habit. But he didn't even have the guts to tell me straight. When I called him on Monday, he said, 'I don't know who I'm voting for just yet; I've got to see the full list of who finally nominates'. In fact, as the group's convenor and numbers man, he was already organising his own ticket for the four spots: Steve Martin, Robert McClelland, Mike Forshaw and Steve Hutchins. Leaping Leo, I'm afraid, is not much of a bloke.

Joel Fitzgibbon Shadow Min. for Resources 2001–04
Steve Martin Shadow Trade & Tourism Min. 2001–02
Janice Crosio Chief ALP Whip 2001–04

Robert McClelland Shadow Attorney Gen. 1998–2003; Shadow Workplace Relations Min. 2001–03
Steve Hutchins Pres. NSW ALP 1998–2002

The objective of this little exercise was to roll him and get Joel and myself elected at the expense of Forshaw and Hutchins. Steve Hutchins— it's an insult to our professional integrity. He's a slow-talking, slow-moving Sussex Street clone. His sole claim to high office in the Labor Party was that he ran the truck drivers' union in NSW. He's a machine man, so they made him a Senator and President of the NSW Branch.

The turning point in the ballot was Simon Crean's intervention. First I spoke to Martin Ferguson, who said that Crean was interested in getting me back on the frontbench. Then I spoke to the new Leader himself on Tuesday. Despite our many past differences, he was willing to support me, providing I become a team player. In effect, he placed me on probation: 'Nobody doubts your ability, just your loyalty to the team. I'll back you, but the first sign that you are playing up again, you'll be back out'.

That suits me fine. I'm sick and tired of writing newspaper articles and stuffing around on the sidelines. If Crean is willing to give me a chance, then I'm willing to leave the past behind. I know, it's convenient for me to say that, but what's the alternative: another three years on the backbench? I'm taking my chance, just like the rest of the place. The old saying: there are no permanent friends or enemies in politics, just permanent interests.

I'm determined to prove the critics wrong. I can show my loyalty and value to the Party by fighting the other side: attacking the Tories, standing up to them in Parliament, giving the True Believers something to cheer for. A bit of fibre in the Labor spine. Keating is right: work harder to persuade the colleagues to my point of view, plus give the other mob some curry.

The rest of the lobbying in the NSW Right was a frenzy of calls and cajoling, scraping together the necessary nine votes. Crean's calls on my behalf were vital, especially with the likes of John Murphy, Frank Mossfield (the Member for Greenway) and Annette Ellis. They are loyal to the Leader and rely on his word.

Laurie Brereton did a great job backing us in, organising the numbers. He got Keating to lobby his successor in Blaxland, Mike Hatton. It was hard-going, with Paul telling me, 'Mate, he's brain dead. What can you do with a poor silly bastard like that? I spent 90 minutes on the phone with him—90 fucking minutes—and I barely got him to add up two plus two'. Hatton came good in the end as part of a complicated vote-swapping deal with McClelland, so the Great Man didn't waste his time.

Martin Ferguson Shadow Regional & Urban Development, Transport & Infrastructure Min. 2001–02

Annette Ellis ALP member, Namadgi 1996–98; Canberra 1998–
Mike Hatton ALP member, Blaxland 1996–

Some Sussex Street treachery also helped along the way. Eric Roozendaal soft-pedalled in his support for Hutchins, even though he's a fellow Party officer. When I told Eric yesterday that I thought Hutchins would be defeated in the ballot, he replied sarcastically, 'That would be sad, wouldn't it'. He's a snake in the grass, our Eric.

The group met earlier today at the Randwick Labor Club. Typically, Leo tried on a couple of rorts, giving a vote to Michael Lee (even though he has no hope of holding Dobell in the final count) and trying to give votes to both Sue West and Ursula Stephens, even though they represent the same seat in Parliament—West as an outgoing NSW Senator and Stephens as the incoming Senator for that spot in July. Leo wanted two for the price of one. The meeting allowed Lee to have a vote but knocked out the Stephens rort.

But mission accomplished. Our ticket was comfortably elected—Martin, McClelland, Joel and I are Shadow Ministers for the next term of Parliament. And the best thing about it? Hutchins received just six votes out of seventeen—a terrible outcome, a landslide against the State President, the titular head of the faction. Leo couldn't believe it. Under pressure, he normally has a red melon, but today he looked like an exploding beetroot.

McLeay's authority within the group has collapsed like a house of cards. It was great to watch his enemies grow a heart and some courage as soon as they worked out he was vulnerable. All their grievances and mis-treatment in Leo's hands, but they were only willing to act when they saw others doing it. You can never underestimate the impact of herd behaviour in this business. At our next meeting, Laurie should replace the Leaper as the faction's convenor.

How good is this—the elation of an unexpected victory, coming from behind and knocking over the party machine. The NSW President, no less. It's a measure of our joy that Joel declared, 'Mate, this is better than sex'. It must be good.

Wednesday, 21 November

Last Saturday Alan Ramsey wrote up the details of the NSW Right ballot, accompanied by a great cartoon of me holding Hutchins's head on a platter, with two forks sticking out of his skull. Every time I look at John Murphy he mimics this look with a huge grin on his face. He's a madman, Murph, who just loves the competitive atmosphere of politics.

Ursula Stephens NSW ALP Sen. 2002– | **the Leaper** Nickname for Leo McLeay, as in 'Leaping Leo'

An interesting talk today with David Epstein, Beazley's former Chief of Staff, who gave me a fair bit of encouragement while I was on the back-bench. I think he felt guilty about the sexual harassment rubbish. He says that after the 1998 election defeat, he advised Kim to have a big reshuffle and create a whole new agenda for Labor. Specifically, he told him to set out his ideas and vision for Australia in a book, to which the Leader replied, 'Forget about that, I'm going down to the bookshop to buy a few'. Hopeless.

Thursday, 22 November

The first Caucus meeting since the election, and Beazley's last report as Leader. He spent most of his time complaining about the media not giving his policy announcements a big enough run. But increasing spending by 0.5 per cent on a program first announced twenty years ago is hardly news-worthy. Nobody, least of all the media, knows what he believes in.

We need to regain our reputation as a serious party of conviction rather than a machine party of opportunism and oppositionism that relies on the Senate to do our work. We need to avoid the Kernot syndrome: new faces are a soft option compared with new policies. We have set ourselves the task of varying by 2 or 3 per cent the way in which government works, when the real challenge is to change by 10 to 20 per cent the way in which society functions.

We need to make some 70:30 calls—invite controversy so that we can define ourselves by our opponents (the 30 per cent), and prove our convictions to our supporters. It might help if we had a few policies that made an impact without needing a dollar sign next to them. Like reinventing democracy, embracing community politics and cleaning out all the parliamentary rorts.

This is urgent work. Everyone can identify Labor constituencies that are fading away but not new groups of supporters. We must appeal to the fastest growing group that still carries Labor values—the new aspirational class. Aspiration is not new but economic mobility is. Our people now have a taste of success and they want more.

They want a Labor Party that offers more than just symbols and safety nets. A Party that moves beyond the politics of envy. These days, we are just talking to ourselves. So, what should be the rhetoric of a modern social democratic party? How about reward for effort, rungs on the ladder of opportunity, rights and responsibilities, building a stakeholder society—civic socialism?

Whitlam used to call the Victorian ALP 'impotent but pure'. It's not a bad description of Beazley's impact on Federal Labor. I can think of five big policy areas where Kim has gutted us:

- We love the symbolism of the Republic, reconciliation and immigration (so-called population policy), yet at election time we know these issues are uncampaignable. We treat them like a mad uncle in the attic.
- We want more government spending on education, health and just about everything else, yet the fiscal well has run dry. Beazley's frontbench only had one policy—how to spend more money—but ultimately, they could not campaign on it.
- We look to the welfare state to solve poverty, yet it has no answers to the social dimension of the problem, say, when bad parents pass their dysfunctional lifestyle on to their kids. The big issues are social, but Beazley Labor had nothing to say about social capital.
- We want to plan and control industries, yet the complexity of the new economy makes this impossible. Our attempt ends up looking like Barry Jones's Noodle Nation.
- We want to run the country and modernise its institutions, yet our own structure is moribund—trade unions, local branches, Party conferences, preselection processes, plus our policy-making culture.

I've set some personal goals for the next three years. I want to get the margin in Werriwa back up to a double-digit figure (it's now down to 8.5 per cent). I want to give the Party some policy direction, to fill the Beazley vacuum. And I want to stabilise my career; play a team game and climb through Caucus ranks. Since 1996, NSW hasn't held a leadership position in the House of Reps, so feasibly, I should aim for the Deputy Leadership after the next election.

As ever, Keating has been useful with advice. He seems mindful of my reputation as a bit of a wild man: 'You've got to water the plants in Caucus; we've all had to do it. And remember, no jerky movements. That's what Beazley's dad used to say, the party of social attack must be exemplary. Those Liberals get away with it, playing up all the time, but not us, we are expected to be exemplary.'

Yeah, that would be right. Lecturing us on family values and then straight onto the ran-tan. Another shocking double standard by Australia's ruling-class wankery.

Noodle Nation Nickname given to the Knowledge Nation policy because of the ludicrous Barry Jones diagram

Wednesday, 28 November

Crean is proposing Party reform but it's not clear how far he is willing to go. The fact that he has even placed it on the agenda is remarkable enough. Who would have thought? The son of a Whitlam minister, a former ACTU President, a Beazley loyalist talking as if he wants to shake out the machine and democratise the Party. He's got my support simply because he's having a go. Anyone who has the machine men shitting themselves must be okay.

Crean is certainly not afraid of making enemies. First he took on the factions to get new blood onto the frontbench, and now he's threatening the power of the State-based machines. Already as Leader, he's made enemies of Con Sciacca and Arch Bevis, two Queensland duds he kicked off the frontbench; McLeay and Hutchins, the Sussex Street gang; plus Ray and Conroy from the Victorian Right.

The Fat Indian is bagging Crean because he didn't consult him about the Shadow Ministry—supposedly the first Leader in twenty years not to do so. But why should Crean talk to him? His main contribution is to play factional games and spread rumours about me.

One thing's for sure, the factional warlords will strike back. That's the whole point: they haven't grabbed so much power inside the Party to just hand it over one day without a fight. Already the dinosaurs are digging in. Greg Combet is in the media saying that he opposes reform because it might mean having small business representation at Labor Party conferences.

No, no, you wouldn't want the great growth sector of the economy, the emerging entrepreneurs, to feel welcome inside the ALP and have a say at our conferences. We should just leave it to a bunch of half-pissed union officials with a declining membership base. Actually, the day we have small business delegates at the National Conference is the day we will start to look like a modern, effective political party.

The most discouraging aspect of Crean's agenda is that he has appointed Bob Hawke and Neville Wran to conduct the Party review. In their day, they were both parachuted into parliamentary seats and never attended branch meetings, so they have little knowledge of the rank-and-file Party. It's the same problem as Greg Sword and most of the union officials. They belong to a different party from the one I've been involved with for twenty years. If Crean is going to take on the factions and the union powerbrokers, he should go the Full Monty and put some radical reformers in charge of the process.

Fat Indian Nickname for Robert Ray given to him by Paul Keating

Greg Combet ACTU Secretary 2000–

Thursday, 6 December

Geoff Walsh briefs the Shadow Ministry on the election result and the Party's marginal seat polling. It was a nervous and clumsy presentation. He started out by mixing up the polling for 2001 with 2000. Kelvin Thomson is not normally known for his wit but it was very funny when he said, 'That was the first problem: we had the wrong year'.

As it turned out, we faced a 4 per cent swing at the start of the campaign and finished 2 per cent at the end. So much for the spin that Beazley brought us back from an absolute catastrophe. The net gain in the campaign was just 2 per cent.

On the key issues, the Liberals led 48 to 25 per cent on economic management and 49 to 20 on industrial relations. When asked about the five things Labor would do in government, 46 per cent of people said we would be controlled by the ACTU and 53 per cent said we would increase taxes. That's a stunning snapshot of our economic credibility problem.

By the end of the campaign, the GST had dropped out of the list of the top five election issues. What a waste of the four years we spent campaigning against it. This was supposed to be the one big issue to put us back on the Government benches and it fizzled out. At the end of the day, the public is not stupid. They know a political scare campaign when they see one, and the caravan moves on.

Beazley's small-target strategy also flopped. By the time of the campaign, Tampa and terrorism were the only issues in town, obscuring whatever polices we had to present. The embarrassment of it: Beazley having to use our ads to tell people what he stood for. Six years in the job, and nobody had a clue.

Post-Tampa, Kim's popularity numbers were inverted, as people thought he was playing politics with the issue. This was when the small-target tactic killed him. Our lead in the polls in early 2001 was based entirely on preferences, mostly from Hansonites disenchanted with the Government. This was obviously a soft and dangerous position to be in, especially when Howard pushed the immigration button. Our position in the polls will only be solid if we lift our primary vote.

Walsh then gave a breakdown of the demographic groups. We lost more women (2.7 per cent swing) than men; young families in the 30 to 39 age group were the biggest movers against us (with a 3.9 per cent swing); the worst regional result was metropolitan Sydney (5.3 per cent), while every income group above $30 000 per annum moved against us. In fact,

Kelvin Thomson Shadow Environment &
Heritage Min. 2001–04

the higher the income, the bigger the swings against Labor—a bad sign in a growth economy.

The debate that followed the presentation was very disappointing. Most of the Shadows just wanted to talk about technical issues: Chris Evans on direct mail, Martin Ferguson on MPs' entitlements and Carmen Lawrence on the need for more research on voting trends. You wouldn't have thought we had lost three elections in a row. Only Thomson and I spoke about the need for policy change and to address the values debate. Welcome back to the Shadow Ministry, old son.

Thursday, 13 December

A beautiful Sydney night, one of those pearlers you only get in the emerald city, and it's a chance for Christmas drinks under the Harbour Bridge with the Tourism Taskforce, John Brown's outfit. Bob Hawke is the star turn, especially after his shocker on Victorian Derby Day. Some photos have just appeared on the Internet showing a shit-faced Hawkie leering and lurching at some young sheilas after the races. Board odds! He's 73 years old going on seventeen.

Benny Humphries reckons that Hawkie is shitting himself about the photos, with good reason. And this is the bloke who is conducting our Party review. What is it about older guys in politics? They either act like teenagers or bitter has-beens. Give it a break.

Sad news in the electorate. Bob Carr has abandoned the FIP community school proposal. How unreliable is he? He told me he would support the project—he wanted an innovative charter school to break the mould and achieve something special in NSW education.

Along with the FIP Committee, I went away and organised something special. The Pratt Foundation was going to donate $100 000. The University of Western Sydney was going to donate land and its teaching and research expertise at Campbelltown. The local health services were committed to working with the school. The parents were super-keen and energised by the prospect of being on the board of governors—they have been poorly treated by the State system and passionately believe they can do a better job themselves.

Chris Evans WA ALP Sen. 1993– ; Shadow Defence Min. 2001–04
Carmen Lawrence Shadow Reconciliation, Aboriginal & Torres Strait Islander Affairs and Arts Min. 2001–02
John Brown ALP member, Parramatta 1977–90; Tourism Min. in Hawke govt

Benny Humphries ALP member, Griffith 1977–96; min. in Hawke govt
The Pratt Foundation The philanthropic trust established by Melbourne businessman Richard Pratt

All we needed was State Government support to set up the school and help these disabled kids. But Carr went to water, scared of upsetting the interest groups (the Teachers' Federation and the P & C), scared of doing something different. It makes you wonder why he bothers. This is what he said in his rejection letter:

> Government support for a community school would constitute a significant policy shift. While the Government remains open-minded about innovative ways to deliver quality public education, it is important that reforms are understood and supported by key interest groups and the wider community. As I'm sure you are aware, a number of high-profile stakeholders are highly critical of the community school model.

I bet they are. They don't want to give up their centralised control of the system and allow some parents in Campbelltown to have a go. I replied to Carr today, summarising the anger and disbelief of the parents:

> Your decision is an enormous setback for Families in Partnership and will jeopardise its future viability and enthusiasm. Like all community groups, it needs to put runs on the board just to keep going. The parents feel that they have wasted fifteen months of high hopes and hard work in trying to make the community school a reality.
>
> At a personal level, I am sorry that you did not persist with your stated support for the community school model. It is just wrong, bordering on evil, to put the views of out-of-touch, ideological obsessives like the NSW Teachers' Federation and Bev Baker ahead of the interests of intellectually disabled children. No parent who truly loves children would ever do such a thing.
>
> I am afraid that when history records the story of your administration, it will see a lot of publicity but not much public policy ... You should have been better than that.

I hate it when Labor turns into a do-nothing, good-for-nothing, conservative outfit, frozen by a fear of change. But that's the man I used to work for.

2002

Another disappointing year for the ALP, dominated by a lengthy debate about the organisational reform of the Party that produced only minor improvements at a Special National Conference in October. Two weeks after the Conference, the Party suffered a crushing defeat in the Cunningham by-election, following sitting member Steve Martin's resignation.

As expected, Simon Crean's leadership came under pressure from the factional and union interests opposed to organisational reform. They used Crean's poor standing in the opinion polls to undermine him in Caucus and the media. I regarded Crean as a big improvement on Beazley and resented the motivations and tactics used against him. I resolved to remain loyal to his leadership, mainly on principle but also out of self-interest, as this assisted my rehabilitation in Caucus after three years on the back-bench.

During this period the media started to talk about me, yet again, as a future Labor Leader. Like all parliamentarians, I wanted to serve in the best way possible, but I never had a clear and consistent view about the leadership. I moved between three positions: seeing it as a ridiculous proposition, that it would never happen; an inkling that it might be possible down the track, but I needed more experience in junior leadership positions, such as the Deputy Leadership; and finally, a concern that even if it were possible, it would be incompatible with my responsibility for raising a young family. In short, I was ambivalent. I never mapped out and stuck to a predetermined career path in politics.

In August 2002 Crean promoted me into Shadow Cabinet to fill the vacancy left by Martin. I became the Shadow Minister for Economic Ownership, Housing and Urban Development and Community Security. Part of my role was to stand up to the Government and take on its head-kickers, such as Tony Abbott. This aggressive role also helped my rehabilitation within the Party. I ended the year satisfied with my work and, at home, buoyed by the arrival of our second son, the angelic Isaac Latham.

Sunday, 3 February

The Hawke–Wran review meets at Penrith RSL in the seat of Lindsay. The rank-and-file in Western Sydney have a chance to put their views directly to Neville Wran. There's a wide range of opinions, often contradicting each other, so it's hard to know what he made of it all. He's probably just glad to go home to Woollahra.

It's the great dilemma of ALP politics. Over the past twenty years, the Party has become more hierarchical, concentrating power in the hands of a few factional chiefs and union bosses who are always self-serving and often corrupt in their methods. Yet if power were decentralised and transferred to the rank and file, this can hardly be regarded as a representative group.

The dedicated branch members who turn up to our monthly meetings tend to be obsessive types who bang on about the same issues. I often joke that they mustn't have a TV at home, so they go to Labor Party meetings on a Monday night for a bit of entertainment. But there's a sad element of truth in this.

In fact, the majority of branch members are ethnic stacks, the lost souls who can barely speak English, organised into the Party by property developers interested in municipal preselections, or Lebanese hustlers looking for community grants, migration assistance and an easy life. They never attend any meetings but end up in the attendance book courtesy of the rorting of branch officials. And most of them do it. That's the sorry state of workers' representation in the modern Labor Party.

Actually, there is little workers' representation left. In NSW we have fewer than 4000 branch members who also belong to Labor-affiliated trade unions. These affiliated unions represent less than 10 per cent of the Australian electorate—a political rump. Yet this tiny group controls 60 per cent of the delegates at State Labor conferences.

This is the key to the factional system. The union secretaries have little interest in local branch activities or in encouraging their members to join the rank-and-file Party. Their power base lies in determining the block of union delegates and factional representation at our conferences. This is why the ruling faction in each State puts so much time and resources into union elections, siphoning off Party funds to keep their factional mates in key positions. This way, the State Secretary and a handful of union secretaries can run the entire State branch.

Anyone who criticises this system is labelled as anti-trade union. In fact, the rank-and-file union members are just as disenfranchised as the rank-and-file Party members. The problem is the concentration of power in the hands of a few stand-over merchants. This system has led to machine control over preselections and, increasingly, the Federal and State Parliamentary parties. ALP conferences are all stage-managed events, with a loss of open debate and voting. Factional patronage and career systems, based on loyalty rather than merit, have emerged. All this, alongside a sharp decline in rank-and-file activism within both the local branches and trade unions.

When I worked at NSW Party headquarters in 1987–88, I remember the General Secretary, Steve Loosley, saying to me, 'The big decision we need to make is whether we actually need a rank-and-file membership'. It took me a while to work out he wasn't joking. With modern fundraising capacity and campaign technology, it is possible to run a successful political party without any local branch members. That's what Labor has become, a virtual party controlled by a handful of machine men.

I'm still finalising my submission to the Hawke–Wran review: how can we cut the Gordian knot? The State machines are crook and will never surrender power. Even if they did, our rank-and-file forums are moribund. Still, something needs to be done. The best option is a bold experiment with the democratisation of Labor: the direct election of parliamentary leaders, State officials and conference delegates by the Party membership.

A last-ditch attempt to revitalise our grassroots. It's hard to see it happening, of course. Like all hierarchies, the system needs to fall over before it fundamentally changes.

Friday, 8 March

A meeting of the Centre Unity (NSW Right) group in Sussex Street. Normally this mob listens obediently to lengthy reports from Roozendaal and Della Bosca and then trundles off to the pub. But tonight there is actually debate on Labor's refugee policy, with John Robertson arguing for an open-door approach. The ethical decline of our Party is complete.

John Robertson Sec. NSW Labor Council 2001–

Imagine having to convince the so-called hard heads of the NSW Right of the need for a responsible position on this issue. But that's what I am forced to do at the meeting. Labor's constituency expects us to uphold the rule of law and not make excuses for people who are trying to break the law. An island continent like Australia needs vigorous border controls and a mandatory detention system. If asylum-seekers were released into the community they would simply shoot through—I know I would in their circumstances. Robertson's position is ridiculous.

And what's it got to do with the trade union movement anyway? Last time I listened to them, they were complaining about a flood of illegal workers into Australia undermining their wages and conditions. No wonder union membership is in free-fall. People work hard, pay their dues and then watch union officials spend all day playing internal Labor Party factional politics and funding Free the Refugees campaigns, instead of representing their members in the workplace.

All this rhetoric about unions being the backbone of the ALP is tosh. Worker representation is a great socialist ideal. But in practice, it has produced a cohort of union officials who are out of touch with their membership and undemocratic in their values. The average union member couldn't give two hoots if their union sends delegates to Labor Party conferences. The officials, however, use this unrepresentative power to throw their weight around inside the Party and try to run the parliamentarians by remote control. It's a house of cards.

So, too, the NSW Right. At this meeting, it hit me like a silver bullet: I've got no chance of ever leading the ALP. It's a lost cause. An insider's Party under the control of out-of-touch unionists like Robertson. The best I can do is provoke some debate, develop some policy ideas and stand guard against the ethical erosion of the show.

Thursday, 21 March

What am I doing here? Caucus and the National Executive have organised a tribute night for Beazley at the Lobby Restaurant in Canberra and somehow I've lobbed into the audience. Completely surreal. A bit like the reason politicians turn up to their enemies' funerals—just to make sure they have gone.

Bob Hawke gave a long, ranting speech, talking about Kim as if he were dead. Totally embarrassing, and the poor bastard just had to sit there and listen to it. Hawke called him the most 'decent loser' in the history of Australian politics. I've never heard a speech supposedly praising someone actually put him down so often. In fact, the speech wasn't really about Kim; it was, as ever, all about Bob.

Then it was Beazley's turn to talk and talk. The bottom line of his par-liamentary career? He said that he always wanted to be in that big white building because his dad told him so many stories about the characters in it. I think I'll stick to *Green Eggs and Ham* with Oliver.

Wednesday, 17 April

Called in to see Keating in his Sydney office this afternoon. Reminiscent of the way he used to call in to see old Jack Lang in the 1960s—the wheel has turned full circle. He's a moody guy, up and down throughout the conver-sation. He's still obsessed with the Federal Parliament—quite sad, in a way. Reminds me of my worst feelings about Gough—they can't let go, politics as an obsession, instead of an achievement in life from which you move on.

Spent most of our time talking about superannuation. Paul wants us to go back to his policy of 15 per cent contributions—reckons Crean should have given me the superannuation shadow portfolio instead of Sherry, of whom he has a poor opinion. To demonstrate his argument, Paul kept on pulling old newspaper clippings out of his filing cabinets—he must have hundreds of them stored away. Every time he did something noteworthy as Treasurer or PM, he must have ripped out the newspaper story that day and put it away. I suppose it was his equivalent of keeping a diary like this.

One point really struck home: the Party's commitment to the open, competitive economy needs to be a passion, a crusade, not some off-the-shelf convenience at election time. This is Keating's critique of Crean and McMullan: 'They don't get it, they don't actually support the model I put in place. Fancy making McMullan the Shadow Treasurer. He used to sit there in Cabinet waiting to see which way the debate was going before speaking in support of the majority. You watch him in your meetings, that's what he does—trying to make it sound like he invented the decision that people are about to make anyway'.

He's picked him like snot. Poor old Comb-over—he would keel over if he heard someone talking about him like that. But that's Paul's genius, an instinctive feel for how the show works. And how to cut people with lan-guage. He's not interested in the small talk of Labor politics—who's up whom, who's rooting his secretary and all that—it's all policy analysis and advocacy, the flow of ideas and personalities. That's why I like him. We lost too much when we lost him as Leader.

Nick Sherry Shadow Retirement, Incomes & Savings and Consumer Affairs Min. 2001–04

Bob McMullan Shadow Treasurer 2001–03

Why doesn't everyone see him this way? In the arts, academia, even the sporting world, people like him are seen as geniuses: passionate, unpredictable, but utterly brilliant. They see things others can't. Only in politics are they seen as unusual, and belittled and denigrated. One-dimensional characters are the norm: inside the Party, little Comb-over clones; in the media, Grattan and Oakes clones (a truly horrible thought).

Public life narrows you down. The system is geared to preserving the status quo, the imbalance of power. The ALP is caught up in this culture now. Well, bugger that—I'm with Keating, all for cutting loose.

Monday, 6 May

I'm fighting on two fronts. The first is to advance asset-based policies inside the Party. Crean launched my discussion paper on economic ownership at Liverpool Council earlier today. He's come good as Leader, growing in the job: talking about the modernisation of the Party, defining ourselves by the things we propose, not the things we oppose—a clean break from Beazleyism.

Part of reclaiming our economic legacy is letting the public know we support the ownership revolution—the explosion in share ownership, small business ownership and housing values in this country over the past decade. We need to take the revolution a step further, and ensure that all Australians have opportunities to save and accumulate assets. That's what the discussion paper talks about: First Share Ownership Schemes for low- to middle-income earners, Employee Share Ownership Plans, Matched Savings Accounts to help the poor save, Nest-Egg Accounts to help people save for the future needs of their children, and Lifelong Learning Accounts to cover the costs of education.

It makes sense for people to save and accumulate assets during the good economic times to minimise their vulnerability during a downturn. My objective is to provide savings and ownership opportunities across the lifecycle: as families plan for their children's future, as young adults enter the home-ownership market, as people pursue lifelong learning, as workers move in and out of jobs and then into retirement. As the superannuation experience has shown, the best way of reducing economic inequality is to make savings and assets available to all Australians.

The NSW Labor Council has been bagging me, of course. They hate the idea of people being owners, not just workers. If people are economically self-reliant, they don't need to waste their money on the union fees that fund long lunches and piss-ups in Sussex Street. The poor can save— that's what Matched Savings Accounts are proving in the US. With a little incentive and guidance, they spend less on grog, drugs and gambling, and put the money into owning a car, a home or supporting their kids' education. This gives them the self-esteem and confidence to get out of poverty altogether. It's commonsense.

My second fight is with the Tories and their mates in the media. I hopped into the Liberals in a speech to the NSW Young Labor Conference on Saturday, defining the narrowness of their culture and the hypocrisy of their methods. This is what we need to do to combat wedge politics. Andrew Norton, a former adviser to David Kemp, let the cat out of the bag when he wrote that 'The purpose of wedge politics is to define and limit the political space within which Labor must operate'. We need to counter this approach.

Abbott has been making speeches at Young Liberal conferences for years, attacking our culture. So I returned the favour. In 1997 he got his mate Christopher Pearson to write up the details of his illegitimate child. But still, he's got the hide to attack father–son relationships on our side, calling people like Joel and Crean 'Hereditary Peers'. So I gave Abbott a touch up and a nice new nickname: the Hereditary Disappear. Plus I outed the rest of Howard's muckraking squad: Heffernan, Baume and Staley.

All good stuff, only one problem. On Friday night on *Lateline*, when debating Chris Pyne, I called Staley a 'deformed character'. It wasn't deliberate: I had this vision of him lurching around on his callipers and it spilled out as a word picture. Sloppy language, very unfair to the disabled. Howard, Costello and the media have been at me ever since.

Glenn Milne was hovering around at the launch with Crean today. Liverpool is not usually his scene. He wanted to be part of my political execution, but had no such pleasure. Thank goodness I was standing next to Crean and not Beazley. Simon was firm and direct, putting the media tarts back in their box.

The Dwarf is just a frustrated politician; fancies himself as a player, not just a commentator. Circa 1997, he told me how he backed Keating over Hawke and planned to do the same thing for Costello over Howard. He should stick to his day job. Word is, Channel Seven is not too happy with him—why does he save his best stories for his column in *The Australian* rather than the nightly news?

David Kemp Lib. member, Goldstein 1990–2004; Environment & Heritage Min. 2001–04
Tony Abbott Employment & Workplace Relations Min. 2001–03; Leader of the House 2001–

Bill Heffernan NSW Lib. Sen. 1996–
Michael Baume Lib. member, Macarthur 1975–83; NSW Lib. Sen. 1985–96
Tony Staley Lib. member, Chisholm 1970–80; min. in Fraser govt; Fed. Lib. Pres. 1993–99

At least Keating is happy. Staley has been pursuing him for more than a decade about his piggery. How's this for a classic with the Great Man this afternoon:

> **Keating:** Mate, mate, now you're heading in the right direction; you've got the right enemies, mate. Forget about arguing with Phillip Adams and Anne Summers, this is the mob you want to hate. They'll come after you, just like they came after me, but that's good. You want them to hate you, just like you hate them. Now you've got the right enemies. Jack Lang told me that you've got to polarise them, split 'em up. He said when you've got the right enemies, that's when you're making progress in politics. Mate, you're onto it now. Anyway, what did you say about Staley?
>
> **Latham:** I called him a deformed character.
>
> **Keating:** That's okay, mate. I said twisted in body, twisted in mind. Anyway, he's not really deformed. I mean, you're deformed when it comes from birth. This bloke only had a car accident, he's not really deformed. Stick on him, mate.

Good reception this evening at Sydney Town Hall for the launch of Don Watson's book on Keating. Noel Pearson did the honours, but spoke for far too long, giving us a lecture, not a book launch.

One thing about attacking Staley and the other Tory grubs: our people love it. The place was packed and at least 30 True Believers came up to me offering congratulations. Their common theme: 'It's about time we gave it back to them'. It's rugged, sure, but magic for my rehabilitation inside the Party.

Wednesday, 8 May

The end of a two-day seminar for Shadow Ministers at Leura in the Blue Mountains, universally described as a 'love-in'. We meandered around, trying to find some common theme and purpose to our work, but the seminar only highlighted the many conflicting agendas and priorities in the group.

I think it also showed that Crean is tougher, more active and more determined than Beazley but he lacks spark. Is he going to inspire enough people to be Prime Minister? That's his challenge. Among the leadership

---

Anne Summers Prominent Australian feminist and author

Don Watson Prominent Australian author and former Keating speechwriter

group, Macklin has the best grasp of what we need to do. But she needs a policy reference group to help her through the policy review process—a huge task.

For some reason, the Left has more frontbenchers serious about dealing with our issues, our split constituency problem—the inner city trendies versus the outer suburban pragmatists. Macklin, Tanner, Lawrence and Martin Ferguson are right onto this problem, whereas the Right are mostly useless, especially Smith and Swan—their only answer is to follow the polls. Perhaps Rudd and Bishop are okay—more thoughtful and considerate in their views.

You have to wonder what Smith and Swan hope to achieve in politics. When asked about his goals, Smith said he wanted to 'undermine the Government and communicate effectively'. I said I wanted to solve poverty, something Smith described as making us sound 'too lofty'. Better that than an empty shell.

There are some signs of unrest in the Right about Crean's leadership. Macklin reckons that Swan won't fight in the House as the Manager of Opposition Business and protect Simon from Government attacks, calling him a 'wasted resource'. She wants Albanese and me to do more, acting as Crean's bodyguards in Parliament.

As we finished the love-in, I asked Conroy what he thought of it and he replied: 'Bloody useless, but the biggest worry of the lot: Simon reckons he got something out of it'. A look of disgust on his face—not a happy camper. Yes, it had to happen: the machine men coming at Crean because he's a threat, someone who talks about the organisational reform of the Party.

Keating called again in response to Alan Ramsey's excellent article in the *Herald*. He wants me to keep up the attack on the Tories: 'Mate, if you have a go, something always turns up, like this Ramsey piece today. If you're a mouse, nothing will ever happen'. Paul's got the smell of battle in his nostrils; he loves the engagement with the other side.

I'm doing fine, happy to be in the outer Shadow Ministry. It gives me time to be with Ollie, a roving policy commission (as long as I'm careful) and this new attack role I've developed. Post-Staley, I've been transformed

Jenny Macklin Dep. Opposition Leader 2001– ; Shadow Employment, Education, Training & Science Min. 2001–04
Lindsay Tanner Shadow Communications Min. 2001–04
Stephen Smith Shadow Health Min. 2001–03
Wayne Swan Shadow Family & Community Services Min. 1998–2004; Manager of Opposition Business 2001–03

Kevin Rudd Shadow Foreign Affairs Min. 2001–
Mark Bishop Shadow Veterans' Affairs Min. 2001–05
Anthony Albanese Shadow Ageing & Seniors Min. 2001–02
Stephen Conroy Shadow Finance, Small Business & Financial Services Min. 2001–03

from a Labor maverick into a Labor hitman—my rehabilitation is complete. Looking back, it's been a remarkable achievement in the six months since the last election.

Most importantly, I'm enjoying my work again. Has life been better? Not at home, that's for sure. As part of the seminar we were asked where we wanted to be in ten years' time. I think most of them wrote down political stuff. I answered, 'Coaching my son's football/hockey/cricket team'.

Monday, 13 May

Keating has put me in contact with Bill Kelty to talk through my policy ideas—a good chat today. He's on board for the creation of learning accounts, health accounts and the innovative use of superannuation investments for urban renewal projects. All the new ideas you never hear from Sussex Street, Head Office or union leaders. Kelty is savage on them, saying that the NSW Labor Council made itself irrelevant during the big reform period, 1983–96.

The Party has divided into serious policy people versus PR flakes. That's the machine culture: policy soundness and structure do not matter, it's all a convenience to get them through the next power play. Kelty is a serious policy person. He told an instructive story about the Beazley campaign: 'I walked up to our polling booth on election day last year and saw our banner: "Jobs, Health, Education". I didn't think we even had a jobs policy last time, did we?'

Monday, 27 May

A helpful talk with Rodney Cavalier today about the unions' role in the ALP. He wants to kick them out because they form the basis of the corrupt factional system. I like Rodney's strong sense of Labor history and dedication to democratic reform. He also has an interesting view on how the Tories see this issue. Santamaria and Menzies had a stand-off on the union question in the 1960s: Santa didn't want the Liberals to destroy the unions, he wanted socially conservative Catholics (the National Civic Council) to take them over.

In the mid-1970s, after the DLP's demise, Santa declared that his followers might as well join the Liberals, a socially conservative party. This is

---

Bill Kelty Secretary, ACTU 1983–2000
Rodney Cavalier ALP member of NSW Parl. 1978–88; min. in Wran and Unsworth govts; ALP historian and cricket buff

B. A. Santamaria Influential figure in the Catholic Church, responsible for the ALP Split in the 1950s; head of the National Civic Council

how the likes of Abbott and Gerard Henderson got involved, how all these Lyons Forum people and religious fanatics ended up in what had been, almost exclusively, an Anglican party. Santa even wrote a chapter for a Lyons Forum book in the mid-1990s, the ultimate endorsement.

But it begs the question: why don't Howard and Abbott move to destroy the union–ALP link? They probably have the numbers in the Senate to pass legislation restricting public electoral funding to organisations that are democratically constituted, and the ALP would not qualify. Or they could put through a law requiring the unions to hold a ballot of their membership before donating to political parties. In most cases, the members would vote it down.

Cavalier reckons the Government won't do it because, just as it suited Menzies to have the communist bogey in the 1950s and 1960s, it suits Howard to keep the union millstone around our neck. I can see the logic from their point of view. Why destroy one of the greatest handicaps facing the ALP?

Thursday, 30 May

The real union agenda in resisting organisational reform was revealed today. John Robertson has outed himself in an article in today's *SMH*. He's complaining about Crean's plan to water down union voting power at State conferences from 60 per cent to 50 per cent. Such a modest proposal: I'd knock them down to 25 per cent, their level of representation in the Australian workforce. As a trade-off, Robertson wants the unions to have a bigger say in the selection of parliamentary candidates, claiming that:

> This process is [currently] dominated by the factional warlords, whose branch stackings deliver them the ability to anoint their chosen followers. Those involved in the trade union movement who have neither the time nor the inclination to immerse themselves in local branch politics are locked out of these elected positions.

What he's saying is that unionists do not want to belong to Labor branches—the real ALP locally—they just want to run the preselection process by remote control. It's the Greg Sword dilemma. And it's a disgrace—the separation of powers within the ALP, such that the people who

---

Lyons Forum Grouping of socially conservative coalition MPs named after Joe and Enid Lyons. Joe Lyons: UAP PM 1932–39; Enid Lyons: UAP and Lib. member, Darwin (Tas.) 1943–51

actually belong to the Party effectively have no say, while those who won't lift a finger locally run the show through the Sussex Street factions.

Thursday, 13 June

Lunch with Greg Combet in Melbourne, whom I have only met briefly on one other occasion. A chance to size him up and see if he's interested in policy reform, the new Kelty. He's certainly not in that league; a nice enough bloke, but with the grey countenance and intent of a technocrat. He's very cautious about my economic ownership agenda. His ambitions for the union movement extend no further than getting the basics right, incrementally improving its membership coverage.

It comes down to survival for these people—a siege mentality. Take Combet's assessment of Doug Cameron at the AMWU: 'You've got to understand that Doug is losing 6 per cent of his membership each year. He's got to put on a show, jump up and down with his protectionist line, just to demonstrate to his members he's fighting for them. Doug's actually a good person and more sensible than that'.

Maybe so, but why should ALP policy-making be held hostage to the tactical agenda and showmanship of the Doug Camerons of the world? We should be acting in the national interest, not the self-serving parochialism of sectional interests. Combet means well—most of the Left-wing unionists do—but why should Federal Labor be dragged down, handcuffed to the drowning men of the union movement?

Thursday, 20 June

The Catman is under attack left, right and centre. Tom Switzer at *The Australian* has been complaining for ages that Emerson sends him useless opinion pieces and then goes berserk when they are never published. To prove his point, today he forwarded to me one of Emmo's dopey emails:

> Tom, How ironic! *The Australian* carries a front page story on Barry Jones lamenting a lack of vision in the ALP, yet when I have brought vision opinion pieces and speeches to *The Australian* it doesn't consider they're important enough to publish. Regards, Craig Emerson.

Doug Cameron Nat. Sec. AMWU 1996– | **Tom Switzer** *The Australian* opinion-page editor

Vision opinion pieces and speeches? The Catman doesn't lack confidence, just ability. Maybe he needs to suck up to Tom's cat with a bowl of milk. People are still laughing about that speech.

Makes you wonder about the media, doesn't it? Nothing is sacred, not even Emmo's emails. What sort of confidence could contributors to the opinion page have in Tom when he does this sort of thing?

Wednesday, 26 June

Pandemonium, simply because I called Howard an arselicker in today's *Bulletin*. If anything, I was restrained—Howard has got his tongue up Bush's clacker that often the poor guy must think he's got an extra haemorrhoid.

The thing I'm worried about from the interview lunch with the lovely Maxine McKew is some quotes on the politics of hate. I was lamenting the abolition of the Better Cities program in Campbelltown's public housing estates and how much I hated the Tories for it. Needless to say, hatred got a run in the article, but not the policy issue that fired me up. Doesn't seem to matter—the media have gone off about the arselicker.

The papers had an advance copy of the thing, even a chance for the usual suspects to bag me off the record: Swan in the *Courier-Mail* with his mate Dennis Atkins, Rudd in the *Age* with Ab-Fab, prissy Labor blokes complaining that I have had a dig at Howard—the revenge of the whitebreads. Howard hasn't responded, leaving it to Abbott, who reckons I am quite 'vile and scurrilous'.

The hypocrisy of this place is breathtaking. Labor, Libs, Nats, journos—most of them on the tarry-hoot, trying to throw the leg over, into everything but a bath—but today, feigning outrage because I called an arselicker an arselicker. That's what they should stick on my tombstone: Here Lies The Man Who Called Howard An Arselicker—Denounced As Morally Unsound By Tony Abbott In An Article By Louise Dodson, God Help The Poor Bastard.

Anyway, what are the rules of morality in Howard's Australia? Eight months ago, he falsely accused some parents of throwing their children off a boat and has never apologised—and the commercial media could not care less. I call him an arselicker and the shock-jocks are all over it like a rash. This is what we are up against: the shameless double standards of the Australian Establishment.

George W. Bush US Pres. 2001–
Dennis Atkins *Courier-Mail* political reporter

Ab-Fab Short for 'Absolutely Fabulous', a nickname for Louise Dodson, political correspondent for the *Age*, given to her by Stephen Ellis (former *AFR* journalist)

Friday, 5 July

Lunch with the NSW union secretaries in Chinatown to try and settle the recent tensions within the NSW Right. Laurie thought it would be a good idea to calm things down ahead of the Special Rules Conference. Can't say it worked. They are resisting Party reform more than ever. The Labor Council is now the anti-Crean faction.

Greg Donnelly, State Secretary of the SDA, gave a long homily about the relevance of his union and how the FPLP could learn from them. That was enough for me: 'Yeah, sure, Greg, your union is so relevant that all I ever receive from you is propaganda about stem cell research and other religious stuff. Now, mate, I know a little bit about your members in my electorate and I reckon I could visit Woolies and Coles for the next thousand years and those young girls at the check-out would never talk to me about stem cell research. You peddle this religious propaganda oblivious to the views and interests of your members'. Dallas Donnelly almost choked on his dim sim.

Monday, 26 August

Parliament House: a lively debate at a meeting of the NSW Right on Party reform. Joel and I argued for a new way of electing delegates to the National Conference: bypassing the State conferences and factional machines and allowing the rank and file to directly elect the delegates through Federal Electorate Councils. Hutchins and McLeay put forward feeble reasons in opposition to the proposal.

Leo said it would make the Party 'more politicised', speaking as if we were the women's auxiliary at an RSL sub-branch. Too much politics in a political party—what next, people tackling each other in footy matches? This is how the machine men operate: dumbing down the debate, taking participation out of the system, so all that remains is an empty shell, one they can easily control.

Hutchins backed up Leo by predicting 'warfare' if we open up the Party to direct balloting for important positions. Joel cut him down in one blow: 'It's actually called democracy'.

Special Rules Conference An ALP national conference organised in 2002 to consider the recommendations of the Hawke–Wran review into the reform of the Party's rules

Greg Donnelly NSW Shop, Distributive & Allied Employees' Assoc. (also known as the Shoppies) Sec.; nicknamed 'Dallas Donnelly' after the rough-house Sydney rugby league player in the 1970s

Thursday, 29 August

A phone call from a poorly briefed John Hartigan, complaining about Tony Walker's report in the *AFR* yesterday, which said that my attack on the new political correctness singled out the Murdoch press—it did no such thing. I told Hartigan to check his facts before whingeing to me—he's obviously too lazy to read the Hansard for himself. He shouldn't rely on Walker, but go to the source. This is what Paul Kelly has always said about the management of News Limited—they hardly give you confidence in the quality of business management in this country.

On Monday I gave a corker of a speech in the Grievance Debate, criticising the new political correctness of the Fairfax and Murdoch conservative columnists. They have spent the last twenty years vilifying the disadvantaged in society, but now they want civility in the public debate. With Howard in government, they want to quieten things down and preserve the existing social and political order.

The speech hit the mark. Already the Evil Empire has struck back, not just with Hartigan's big whinge, but plenty of rubbish in the *Telegraph*, including a feature article by Rachel Morris yesterday: 'Just before midnight on Monday, Mark Latham gave new meaning to the grievance debate, unloading in a 10 minute tirade against, well, everyone'.

Yeah, sure: my speech was at 5 p.m., and her piece was full of errors. I expect more of it—the Evil Empire will exaggerate and manipulate anything to get at me now. The arrogance of them—they think they rule the country. They might run Howard, but like most Labor people, I still remember what they did to Gough.

The Tory Establishment can't have it both ways: saying that Labor is no longer a working-class party but then complaining when I rip into them, working-class style. Albrechtsen is the worst of them—she complains about my language, but she uses terms like 'fuck-wittage' in her columns. Why does she expect her critics to be prim and proper in return?

Tuesday, 17 September

A rare honour. I'm delivering the annual Menzies Lecture at the Menzies Centre for Australian Studies at the King's College in London. I got here by piggy-backing a parliamentary delegation to Indonesia and Vietnam that

---

John Hartigan CEO News Ltd 2000–
Paul Kelly *The Australian* senior journalist, nicknamed 'the Professor'

Janet Albrechtsen *The Australian* Right-wing columnist

finished last Friday. Also have meetings and seminars scheduled with the British Government on asset-based policies.

I've put a lot of work into this text, learning the lessons of the last election, trying to reposition our side in the culture wars. Howard has done well in the suburbs with his attacks on the so-called elites. We need a framework in which to handle the importance of social values in modern politics. This is the flip side to the economic globalisation debate. Issues such as the mass movement of people, the internationalisation of crime and the free flow of information and cultural products are challenging our sense of community and citizenship.

Howard has responded by feeding off the things he opposes: the Left-wing elites and their rights agenda. We need to reposition Howard as part of the conservative elites—the big business/big media/old money agenda to concentrate power in their hands at the expense of the suburbs. That way, we can create a third choice in Australian politics, beyond the conservative Establishment and the new progressive Establishment, and their insider struggle against each other.

The core argument in my lecture is that at the social centre, people tend to take a tourist's view of the world. They travel extensively, eat out and buy in domestic help. The cultural challenges of globalisation are seen as an opportunity, a chance to develop further one's identity and information skills. This abstract lifestyle has produced an abstract style of politics, where symbolic and ideological campaigns are given top priority.

In the suburbs, the value set is more pragmatic. People do not readily accept the need for cultural change or the demands of identity politics. They lack the power and resources to distance themselves from neighbourhood problems. This has given them a resident's view of society. Questions of social responsibility and service delivery are all important.

The political spectrum is best understood as a struggle between insiders and outsiders—the abstract values of the powerful centre (the conservative and progressive Establishments) versus the pragmatic beliefs of those who feel disenfranchised by social change. This is different from class-based politics. Rather than draw their identity from the economic system, people see their place in society as a reflection of their access to information and public influence.

This is the way forward for Labor. Our values and ideas about social justice still matter, but to win public support they must deliver tangible, pragmatic gains in people's lives. In an era of public cynicism about organised politics, bite-sized changes are more desirable and certainly more credible than big-bang social theories.

The Left needs to personalise its politics. Our commitment should not be defined in terms of ideology or dogma. It should be to good schools, good health care and the other elements of a good society—dispersing power and influence to the outsiders. We shouldn't be afraid to tell the story of our own climb through society. In terms of values: responsibility from all, opportunity for all, community with all and democracy by all.

Between this lecture and last year's effort at UNSW, I've worked out the framework for a modern, successful Labor Party. The challenge now is to hold the line, not be knocked off course either by the conservative or progressive elites. They will come at me, but that's where I want to be, in the middle of the debate. I can't allow them to wear me down, either by personal attrition or policy condemnation. The Menzies Lecture has lifted the scales from my eyes on how to win the culture wars.

Saturday, 5 October

The Special Rules Conference of the ALP in Canberra, and the worst elements of the Party are on full display. The NSW Right Caucus this morning wanted to roll Crean on his limited reform proposals (50/50 at State conferences and the direction election of the National President), with Hutchins and other unionists leading the charge. I made a contribution in favour of the reforms. I also pointed out that this group has historically supported the Party Leader and one of our number, Sharon Bird, is out there trying to win the Cunningham by-election in two weeks' time. The Labor Council mob was happy to cut her throat just as they want to cut Crean's.

As the Conference started, I witnessed the most hypocritical thing I have seen in politics. For months, Albanese has been racing around boasting of how he has established the ABC club—Anyone But Crean. He's been promoting the merits of Macklin and then Lawrence as leadership alternatives. He's an archetypical spoiler in Opposition, Clyde Cameron's heir inside the Party. Yet there he was, flanking Crean as he entered the Conference, like some kind of Left-wing Praetorian Guard.

Not a good sign for Simon's leadership: Albanese on one side of him and the Catman on the other. I'm a member of the CLs—the Crean Loyalists—but that image this morning was enough to make me shudder and look twice at my membership ticket. The poor bastard is surrounded by treachery and buffoonery.

Sharon Bird ALP candidate, Cunningham by-election Oct. 2002

Anthony Albanese Shadow Employment, Services & Training Min. 2002–04

All very depressing for our once great Party. I have been re-reading Vere Gordon Childe's 1923 classic, *How Labour Governs: A Study of Workers' Representation in Australia*. There is nothing new in politics; these problems are an endemic part of our movement. Childe could have been there today:

> The Labor Party, starting with a band of inspired socialists, degenerated into a vast machine for capturing power, but did not know how to use that power when attained except for the profit of individuals, [becoming] just a gigantic apparatus for the glorification of a few [union] bosses. Such is the history of all Labor organisations in Australia, and that not because they are Australian, but because they are Labor.

Saturday, 19 October

A wipe-out in the Cunningham by-election: a massive swing against us, an easy win for the Greens, and Simon is in deep shit. No other conclusion can be drawn. He's lost a seat from Opposition: a traditional Labor electorate, Rex Connor's old seat.

I thought of The Strangler as I was handing out how-to-vote cards on the Woonona East booth, my pessimism about the result growing by the hour. He would barely recognise Cunningham today, with its trendy Greens flocking into North Wollongong's beachside suburbs, driving property prices up into the million-dollar range. Within the space of a generation, coal-mining villages have been converted into a playground for the wealthy. A sign of the times for Labor: squeezed by the new rich on one side and trade union traitors on the other.

Basically, we lost Cunningham to the education unions. The President of the South Coast Labor Council and local Teachers' Federation organiser, Peter Wilson, ran as an Independent and swapped preferences with the Greens. I met him at the booth—obsessive, bitter and opinionated, as expected. I asked him why he was ratting on the Party and he responded, 'I haven't been a member of the ALP for years'.

Vere Gordon Childe (1892–1957) Served as Private Sec. to NSW ALP Leader John Storey (1919–21). Disillusioned with the ALP movement, he left Australia to become one of the world's leading archaeologists. In the renovated Reading Room of the British Museum he is listed among the Notable Holders of Readers' Tickets, alongside Marx, Lenin, Trotsky, Orwell, Russell, Disraeli, Dickens, Tennyson and Wilde. *How Labour Governs* is the definitive study of the corrosive influence of machine politics in the early years of the ALP
The Strangler Nickname for Rex Connor, derived from his time as a member of NSW Parl. when, according to legend, he was found in the corridors one night applying a headlock to a journalist

How did we get into a situation where someone who hasn't been a member for ages and who represents a union that is not actually affiliated with the Party becomes the resident expert/media darling on all things wrong with the ALP in Wollongong?

The Teachers' Federation staffed the booths for Wilson, and funded his campaign. The higher education union supplied booth workers for the Green candidate, Michael Organ, who works at Wollongong University. These are the same people, of course, who will be begging us to block Howard's education reforms. More evidence: the unions are not there to help political Labor, they are in it for themselves.

As for affirmative action, scores of feminists were on the booths working to get the Green man elected over the Labor woman. One of the most instructive days I've had in politics. And one of the saddest in revealing the true state of our movement.

Tuesday, 29 October

A long discussion in Shadow Cabinet about our general political situation and strategy. Between the lines, a lot of criticism of Simon. Tanner made the sharpest point, saying that we should go in harder when attacking the interest groups associated with the Government. He's right, the Liberals have been very effective in shackling us to unpopular causes, such as the unions, trendies and welfare groups. We need to return the favour, and a rich field of material is available: the banks, elite schools, doctors, big businesspeople and the arrogance of US foreign policy.

Conroy supported Tanner with a good example of the problem. The Party is divided between pro-US and anti-US sentiment, but we all go to State and National conferences and vote for the same resolution. No message gets out to the public. We spend too much time pleasing ourselves instead of the electorate.

Crean listened closely, then continued down his well-worn path, talking about the importance of consensus and electoral inclusion. It's not in him to pick a fight to prove his point. He likes long meetings—a process-driven approach to politics.

Tuesday, 12 November

A meandering talk with Professor Paul Kelly—in that thorough, considered way of his, he likes to get inside the latest Party manoeuvres. So I gave him

---

Michael Organ Greens member, Cunningham
2002–04

my latest theory on how it works: forget the factions as an explanation of what people believe in, Caucus has broken into three groups—the Young Radicals, the Young Technocrats and the Hawke-style Corporatists. The first group is in a minority position, the second and third groups share a cautious, conservative approach to Labor politics, the dominant strand of Caucus thinking.

Earlier in the day, a classic example of a Young Technocrat in action. Towards the end of Question Time, Rudd asked Downer a legitimate question about Kopassus: have they been cooperating with the terrorist outfit, Laskar Jihad? But straight after, Rudd raced up to the Indonesian Embassy to explain himself, petrified they might take offence. He's not in this to win public support for Labor. He's just an insider in the Canberra foreign-policy establishment. There was no need to explain himself to the Indonesians. It was just a question, and a good one at that.

Thursday, 14 November

Living on the edge, doing crazy things to alleviate the boredom of parliamentary life. Since my attack on the Tory elites, some of our people have wanted me to go further, to really unload on the neoconservatives. Last night, for instance, Jo Fox, one of Carmen Lawrence's advisers, issued a challenge: to describe Albrechtsen, so heavily loathed by the Labor femocrats, as 'a skanky-ho who must die'.

I didn't understand what 'skanky-ho' meant; it sounded like more American rap rubbish to me. But I can't say no to a challenge, that's my problem. So, away I went this morning, slipping a line into my speech on the Financial Sector Legislation Amendment Bill, which attacked Malcolm Turnbull over the HIH collapse. I described dirty Janet as 'a shanky-ho who will die in a ditch to defend the Liberal Party'.

Hopeless. I used the wrong term, that's how much I knew about it, so I had to alter the Hansard Greens this afternoon, changing 'shanky' to 'skanky'. Maybe not a smart move, as it turns out this is the equivalent of calling someone a 'filthy piece of rugby hot-box' (a time-honoured description from *The Bulls Roar*). Outrageous when you think about it, not that many people noticed, just a couple of journalists, expertly deflected by

---

Kopassus The Indonesian Army's Special Forces unit
The Bulls Roar The official organ of the Liverpool Rugby Football Club
Malcolm Turnbull Lib. Fed. Treas.

HIH One of Australia's leading insurance companies, which collapsed in 2001 in one of the worst scandals in Australian corporate history
Michael Cooney Worked for me in 2002–05 in various senior roles

Cooney. It just goes to show: you can say anything down there, only two men and their dogs are listening. Parliament is a waste of space; tedious and irrelevant.

This is why Labor MPs, from time to time, play word games in the House. The best was in the last term of Parliament, after Rudd said he had received complaints about the GST from a constituent who manufactured products known as Dick Balm and Cock Paste, lubricants that he wanted to be GST-free. Julia Irwin and I managed to enshrine in the parliamentary record the names Dick Balm and Jock Paste. It added to the hilarity of a late night Caucus party. Go the skanky-ho!

Friday, 15 November

Another strategy discussion, this time with the full Shadow Ministry. Simon is standing his ground with his consensus/inclusion line. He told us, 'Some people say I should be picking fights. I disagree'. I've been telling him to pick some fights—he needs to thump through to be heard in the public debate. He's putting out good policy stuff, he works his ringer out, but something is still missing: the thump factor. The public tune out when he speaks—bad feedback in my electorate lately.

But realistically, it's an international problem for our side of politics. How do we energise our supporters, find new issues and causes, a movement that actually moves and encourages people to believe in progressive politics? With the War on Terror narrowing the international affairs debate, we need to be twice as different, twice as radical on social issues—health and education policy and social capital. This is where the anti-Establishment theme is so important—a movement for the outsiders who miss out on social opportunities.

Wednesday, 20 November

A tidy address to the National Press Club, much better than my piss-poor effort four years ago. Summarised and popularised the Menzies Lecture agenda: Howard as an insider, hoarding power for the ruling elite; Labor as an anti-Establishment party, a party for the outsiders in the vast suburbs and regions of the nation. Our goal: the dispersal of power. My example: the creation of Nest-Egg Accounts, so that all young Australians can enjoy an endowment of assets at age eighteen, the equivalent of a financial inheritance.

Inside the Party, there's movement at the station. Last night Swan refused to rule out a leadership challenge to Crean, the first tangible sign that it's on and an ABC candidate has identified himself. Little Swannie has got big tickets on himself. Crean promoted him to Manager of Opposition Business and now he's using it as a springboard into Crean's job. Perfect timing for my purposes at the Press Club. Tonight on the news I'm the public face for loyal Labor, for solidarity Labor, putting down the rebels and defending the Leader. Miracles do happen.

Thursday, 12 December

Out of that place—the last sitting day of the year. I've escaped a late-night sitting to come home to Janine and new baby Isaac (born 6 December). He's going to be a big lad, huge plates of meat. Two boys, hey, who would have thought?

I finished the session strongly, pursuing my opposite number, Helen Coonan, over a range of sins: conflict of interest, avoiding land tax, inappropriate use of ministerial letterhead, various breaches of the Ministerial Code of Conduct. We had a good tip-off about the land tax issue, and it snowballed from there.

A handy ministerial scandal, and I've been collaborating with Mark Riley from the *SMH* over the past month to give it profile. Howard won't sack her. He would let Jack the Ripper off these days, but at least I made her pay the full land tax on her holiday home. What an outrage: a Minister for Revenue who didn't want to pay her fair share of State Government revenue.

Also, an amazing lesson in media practice. As part of his so-called research, Riley went through Coonan's garbage bin at her holiday house in Clareville, handing over soiled documents for me to use in Question Time. Ethically, I suppose I am just as bad as him—he went through the garbage and now I have the documents sitting in my folder. But one thing it does show is that everything they say about journalists who rummage through other people's garbage just to get a story is absolutely, pathetically true. And from what I can see, Riley is one of the better ones in the press gallery.

Saturday, 14 December

A profile on me by Mike Steketee in the *Weekend Australian* today. Keating once told Caucus to be cautious with this bloke—he's a protégé of the Packer stooge and infamous Labor hater Alan Reid. Paul was right: a fairly jaundiced piece by Creeping Jesus, Keating's nickname for him. The guy's not even thorough—the thing is riddled with mistakes, ten errors of fact that I can see.

Helen Coonan NSW Lib. Sen. 1996– ; Revenue Min. and Asst Treas. 2001–04

There's the usual anonymous criticism from so-called colleagues; Rudd this time—his pompous language is a give-away. Worst of all, Steketee recycles slabs of bullshit from Frank Heyhoe, a blast from the past. What a calamity that bloke was. Heyhoe was the worst big-noter I have ever met in politics, obsessively talking about himself. That's how Kerin described him: an obsessive personality. Loosley called him one of the greatest nutters he had ever met in the ALP, and that's saying something. It's a great Labor word—nutter—referring to all the eccentric characters in the Party.

Heyhoe used to be the Secretary of the Green Valley branch. When I first met him in 1979, he told me that Whitlam would ring him at work for advice. When I went to work for Gough, he couldn't even remember Heyhoe—and Gough never forgets people's names. When he was Deputy Mayor of Liverpool, he would talk about it like he was head of the UN—big-noting, always big-noting. Heyhoe came around our place at Ashcroft once just to show me he was driving the mayoral car, a white sedan. Big deal—he created a fantasy world of self-importance for himself.

He's at it again today, telling Steketee he was a great mate of my father. Dad hardly knew him—met him a couple of times picking me up from branch meetings. Before that, when I first joined the branch, Dad had never heard of him. Heyhoe is not the full quid, lying about my dead father—deceitful and offensive stuff.

I made a mistake accepting his charity after Dad died in 1981. Mum didn't want me to do it, but in my youthful naïvety, I didn't see any harm. Often I'm a bad judge of character, too trusting of people and their motivations. Turns out it was just another opportunity for Heyhoe and his mate Casey Conway to big-note themselves. They thought I was their political lackey, that they owned me because they whipped the hat around and helped me through university. Good, decent men like Neville Bates (publican of the Green Valley Hotel) were also involved, but they never made a fuss about it.

We only accepted the money after Heyhoe gave his word that the donors would remain anonymous and it would never be held over my head. But then I got onto Liverpool Council and Conway ratted on the Party in 1989, and started making speeches at Council meetings, saying, 'I paid for this boy's education and now he's opposing my motion'. How bad

Frank Heyhoe Alderman, Liverpool City Council 1980–83
Casey Conway Alderman, Liverpool City Council 1977–91; Liverpool Mayor several times during the 1980s; left the ALP in 1989 to contest the Liverpool by-election as an Independent

is that? Jack of it, one night I tried to give Conway his money back. He refused, so I donated it to charity.

I should do the same for Heyhoe. He's in this Steketee piece complaining that I dudded him for the Mayoral preselection in 1990. Twelve years later, he's still obsessed with Liverpool Council. All I did was return the favour. The previous year, he promised me his vote in the State preselection against Lynch and Conway, but I have no doubt he put me last. He must have known I wouldn't support him in 1990, not after what he did to me.

He had no chance in that ballot anyway. His local government career ended in 1983 when Paciullo and Conway got together to knock him off for North Ward preselection. He busted up with Conway for a while, but now they are back together, thick as thieves. So why complain about me? I didn't do him in when it mattered—his mate did. Loosley was right.

Conway's just as obsessed. Paciullo tells me he's still writing letters to the Liverpool papers about me, fifteen years after I took the Mayor's job off him—his great heartache in politics. But he's more to be pitied than despised. Poor bugger, he spent all that time in local government, only to see one of his kids fall apart. He must have felt guilty about it, time away from home etc. As some parents do in these circumstances, he ended up under the spell of a shonky methadone doctor in Liverpool, a tragedy really.

I'm the same age as his children and the comparison must hurt. Guilt, the guilt that only a parent can feel, every day for fifteen years. He must have thought: I helped Latham with his education, when I should have been at home. The scaggy stuff is a terrible thing in any family.

In the end, I busted up their club at Liverpool Council and they hated it, hated me. But were they ever true Labor men? Heyhoe, with his love of Council robes and the trappings of office, his attachment to the monarchy and traditional institutions. And Conway, employed by the biggest land developer in Liverpool during his time as Mayor. No, they were part of the club that I closed down. Municipal insiders. Now I have to wear their bile and bitterness—the price of doing the right thing at Council.

I can wear it quite easily. I only worry about the things that went wrong and, unfortunately, there were a few of those. Thankfully, Steketee

George Paciullo Alderman, Liverpool City Council 1958–71; Liverpool Mayor 1968–69; ALP member, Liverpool in the NSW Parl. 1971–89; min. in Wran and Unsworth govts; succeeded me as Liverpool Mayor in 1994; served in that position until the Council was sacked in 2004

only makes a passing reference to the 1989 Liverpool preselection—it was a Sussex Street special, real machine politics. Creeping Jesus has crept in the wrong direction. I complain about journalists a fair bit, but sometimes, their stupidity is a blessing in disguise.

Thursday, 26 December

That Steve Waugh is quite a guy. I've been listening to an interview with him on ABC radio. He's been struggling for runs and his place in the side is at risk, sparking media debate about his future. He said that one paper has been campaigning for him (the *Daily Telegraph*) while others have been against him. But then the silver bullet: 'None of them care about me, they only want to sell newspapers.' Exactly. What a great man to call the media for what they are: users who eat people up for commercial purposes. And a terrific poke in the eye for the *Tele*.

I'm taking a long break from work, some paternity leave to help out with the new bub. This is my first decent holiday for a decade, beautiful time with family. But also, some time to reflect on what's happened to our society.

I remember Christmas Day when I was a kid, circa 1970. The streets were full of children on their new bikes, skateboards, a real community event. I went jogging at 11 a.m. yesterday and Glen Alpine was like a ghost town, not a kid in sight. People don't see each other any more, not even on major holidays. No talking, no interacting, no community.

We have become an Inside Society, kids on computers, parents petrified of street crime, unwilling to use their front yards. Social capital is in retreat, even on the best day of the year. If you stand in the middle of Glen Alpine on Christmas Day, you can see what's happened to our society—rows of double-storey houses, material wealth but no social wealth, a neighbourhood of nothingness. In my job, I talk about community, but I live in a place without one.

Steve Waugh Captain, Australian test cricket team 1999–2004

2003

A turbulent and often spiteful year for Labor. Instead of working hard to rebuild our policy credentials after the shortcomings of Beazley's small-target strategy, the machine men in Caucus spent the year undermining Crean's leadership and trying to reinstate Beazley. By the end of the year, against my expectations, I was Leader of the Federal Parliamentary Labor Party.

The year started badly, with the Party failing to clearly define a position on the Iraq War. We failed to vigorously oppose the Howard Government's misguided policy of searching for Weapons of Mass Destruction that didn't exist, and of making Australia a bigger target in the War on Terror. As a result, we lost further ground to the Greens in public opinion. Our stance on the war heavily influenced my views about foreign policy, reinforcing the need for strong and well-defined positions.

This episode was followed by months of speculation about a Beazley leadership challenge. On 16 June, Crean decisively defeated him in a ballot (58 votes to 34) after which I replaced Wayne Swan as the Manager of Opposition Business—a significant promotion into a high-profile position in the House, opposite Tony Abbott. At this point, Crean also abandoned the Shadow Cabinet system, returning to full Shadow Ministry meetings.

This expression of Caucus democracy did nothing to ease the white-anting of Crean. In the second half of the year, Labor MPs devoted most of their time and energy to the leadership struggle. On 2 July, Crean made me Shadow Treasurer, pitting me against the formidable Government team of Abbott and Costello.

Crean's move put me in the frontline of the leadership issue. The Beazley forces knew that if they could damage me they would also damage Crean, and rule me out as a possible leadership contender. Crean's fortunes and mine became interwoven. In late November, senior Party figures—a delegation of John Faulkner, Martin Ferguson and Robert Ray—forced Crean to stand aside as Leader. In the ballot to fill this vacancy on 2 December, I defeated Beazley by 47 votes to 45. The last stage of my parliamentary career had begun.

To help readers understand the two Labor leadership ballots in 2003, I have prepared a table that sets out the factional and sub-factional affiliation of each of the 92 Caucus members (see Appendix 1).

Sunday, 5 January

A huge time yesterday at the Sydney Test, Australia versus England. The previous evening, Steve Waugh had scored a magnificent century. We were there to see him get out for 102 early in the day and then watched Gilchrist rip apart the Poms' attack. Waugh has ended the newspaper debate about his future.

I organised this as a 'Back to the Hill' day with the rugby-club mates—the mighty Liverpool Bulls, reliving our glory days from the early 1980s, on the piss, on the Hill. The Bulls were in fine form, matching wits with the Barmy Army and ending the day legless. It must have taken me an hour to walk to Central Station—two steps forward, one step back. That's one of the good things about being a middle-ranking Shadow Minister: nobody really knows who you are, so you can still do normal things with your idiot mates and nobody cares.

The one flaw in the day can be summarised in two words: Matt Price. It was a big mistake to invite a Canberra type to a mates' day out. The fellas, quite frankly, thought he was a flogger. He didn't fit in, wouldn't have a drink, wouldn't have a go and ended up scurrying off to the Churchill Stand mid-afternoon. He put in a shocker.

Janine put me in contact with Price, through a friend of a friend, when he first came to Canberra from Perth in 2001. In all fairness, she said to be careful. In Perth he was regarded as two-faced. Yes, he can never hold a

---

Adam Gilchrist Australian cricket wicket-keeper batsman
Barmy Army Large group of English supporters who follow their team around Australia with rollicking songs and good humour

Matt Price Canberra-based journalist with *The Australian*

confidence. Like giving away his sources—he told me that Swan is the worst of the Shadow Ministry leakers.

Thursday, 23 January

My beautiful break is coming to an end, back to work tomorrow: Shadow Cabinet in Melbourne. No shortage of politics through January. Two weeks ago, an *SMH* front-page story that Crean is about to make me Shadow Treasurer (not true) and then, a taste of ALP division over Iraq. With Janine and Isaac away in Perth, I took Oliver to Laurie's beach house at Careel Bay. Joel came along for dinner and it turned into a hate-session on the Bush Administration and the folly of invading Iraq.

Laurie believes in an independent foreign policy but even he looked surprised when I said we should rethink the American Alliance. Under Bush and the hard-Right Republican hawks, the US is going to use the War on Terror as an alibi for a new round of expansionist and arrogant foreign policy. Internationally, it's a disaster, feeding the cause of militant Islam and alienating most Western nations. This is not the way to deal with terrorism—weakening the international coalition that emerged after September 11. It's going to turn this decade into an anti-American decade.

The next day, I took Ollie to Barry Cohen's native animal park near Gosford. Here's a Labor man who wants to invade Iraq and blow the crap out of the Arabs. I told him to get used to the idea of an independent ALP foreign policy, starting with Iraq.

Cohen is also a fierce advocate of business welfare policies—for himself. He spent most of lunch whingeing about the lack of government subsidies for his park, so typical of people who have got themselves into flawed business ventures. The place is a commercial disaster—there's nothing there for children except a few scrawny emus and aimless wandering through the bush. No amount of public money can make it attractive for families. It was a stinking hot day and all Barry did was whinge, whinge, whinge—we couldn't get out of there fast enough. The worst day of this holiday.

Friday, 24 January

Crean is bleeding to death on Iraq. He's incapable of coming up with a clean, straightforward position. Everything he says is heavily qualified by a series of caveats. I've never seen policy-making by caveats before—it's the political equivalent of water torture. Simon has come back from his trip to the US with yet another: we might support an American invasion that is not sanctioned by the United Nations if the majority of Security Council members vote to invade but one of the permanent members exercises a veto. Try selling that jumble of words in Western Sydney.

Bob Brown is killing us on this issue through the power of a simple, commonsense message: Bush is an imbecile and Australia should not be part of his war. Mind you, our position could be worse—Conroy could be in charge. At today's Shadow Cabinet he formally moved that we endorse Howard's deployment of troops and an American invasion of Iraq, irrespective of the UN.

Not even the other Big Macs—the US faction of Rudd, Smith and Swan—could support him. All he had was his own vote. Imagine that: the ALP supporting Bush and Howard in the invasion of a country on the other side of the world without UN approval. If we followed the Conroy doctrine, after the next election, Brown would be the Leader of the Opposition.

Monday, 3 February

Seven years in Opposition for our troubled Party. Today was a microcosm of all our woes: personal and factional treachery, policy confusion and plenty of bullshit. We're a Party structurally incapable of governing ourselves, let alone the country. Maybe it was the Christmas break (Parliament starts tomorrow); it gave Caucus members a chance to realise how much they dislike each other. Four events I must record.

Shadow Cabinet met in the morning. We had a long debate and more confusion about our position on Iraq. Rudd reported on his recent trip to Washington and New York, but he need not have bothered, it's all in Glenn Milne's column this morning. As ever, Rudd is insatiable for publicity. He is such a big-noter, telling Milne he held talks with four of the five permanent members of the Security Council: France, Britain, Russia and the US, but not China.

Then his prediction: 'Rudd is convinced a second UN Security Council resolution allowing the use of force against Iraq will be passed without either France or Russia exercising their right of veto … His instincts are the vote will go 13–2 or 12–3. France, Rudd thinks, will either vote for it or abstain'.

Keating, for one, thinks this is nonsense—the Russians sacrificed too much in World War II to be pushovers for the Americans. Brereton is also sceptical: 'Mate, he says whatever the Americans want him to say. They own him lock, stock and barrel'. This has always been Danger's view of Heavy Kevvy—too close to the US. He's certainly part of the foreign policy

---

Bob Brown Tas. Greens Sen. 1996– ; Australian Greens Leader

Heavy Kevvy Nickname for Kevin Rudd

establishment, and yes, there are some missing periods in his CV, plus a general mystery about the guy. If he grew up in poverty in rural Queensland, where did the posh accent come from? But a Maryland candidate in our midst, I doubt it.

At Shadow Cabinet, you could almost feel Crean urging Rudd on, praying that he's right about the Security Council. Simon doesn't want to get between the Americans and their dirty little war—that's what the caveats are about. UN approval is the Leader's best way out of this issue— his ticket to respectability at the next American–Australian Leadership Dialogue, the US-sponsored club that our senior people have signed up for. The US owns more than Rudd.

My second meeting of the day: the mates of the NSW Right, intent on rolling Danger as the faction's convenor. You've got to hand it to Leo, he's a wily old dog. Ever since his humiliation after the last election, he's been working overtime to regain the numbers in the group. He would do and say anything to take his revenge on Laurie.

Just look at the alliances he's formed: in thick with Roozendaal, whom he used to call 'the Jew-boy' (an old-fashioned bigot, our Leo); winning over Irwin and Hatton (both under preselection threat in their electorates, so Sussex Street is standing over them); and offering to back Roger Price for the convener's job—after a decade of hostility between the two of them, he was McLeay's candidate today.

Leo even manufactured an issue with which to campaign against Laurie: Danger's public comments last month against the war. McLeay and Hutchins have got more front than Mark Foy's—undermining Crean at every opportunity but then attacking Danger for supposedly undermining Crean. They got silly Ursula Stephens to sign a letter as the NSW Branch President chastising Laurie, and then leaked it to the media.

A full-on campaign. And they came close, losing by one vote. Joel almost threw it away, initially voting for the no-confidence motion—a brain explosion. They will be back for more, no doubt. This run at Laurie was a proxy for their bigger campaign against Crean. That's the word I'm putting around. Some encouragement from Irwin, who said, 'I don't think they will go after Simon, Mark, but my support is guaranteed, I'll never vote against the Leader of our Party'. A Leo Lackey but also a Crean Loyalist—a unique combination.

My third meeting was at the National Right, with the Big Macs putting the arguments for war but never fully committing themselves. They know

---

Ursula Stephens NSW ALP Pres. 2002–

the full Caucus is overwhelmingly against them. Not surprisingly, Beazley was the worst, claiming that 'We may yet oppose this war, but understand this: when it is over the Iraqi scientists will be on international TV pointing and saying, "there it is, there it is". That is the political price we will have to pay'.

He has no doubt the Weapons of Mass Destruction exist. But where is the hard evidence, other than the assertion of the foreign policy establishment, of which Beazley is a card-carrying member? This is what the Hawke corporatism of the 1980s has produced—a blustering Establishment figure, a man of war. He also blustered away during the Caucus debate, calling for better diplomacy in the region to sell this war to our neighbours. He looked keen to sell himself to the colleagues, actually. Too keen.

A final event: out to dinner at Figaro's in Kingston with Janine, Laurie, Joel and Leah to celebrate Danger's victory. We enjoyed a table outside on the footpath while our rivals Price, Hutchins, Stephens, Irwin, etc. broke bread together inside—quite a set-up. Then, Beazley and Michael Costello emerged from Portia's Place just up the road. They spotted our table and started to panic, turned in opposite directions to try and avoid us, but ended up colliding with each other like a pair of Toltoy dolls. Costello bounced away from us but Beazley was catapulted towards our table. Funny as.

The Big Man engaged in some small talk, never looking us in the eye, of course. Then he spotted the mob inside, and another fearful look unfolded across his face. That was enough for Kim; he shook his head in despair and walked off muttering to himself, 'Price, mmm, Price'. Politics can be hopeless and frustrating, but also totally hilarious on a night like this.

Tuesday, 4 February

With a NSW election coming up, I've thrown myself into a local controversy—can't help myself. Last month Pat Farmer pulled a publicity stunt on the front page of one of the local rags. He was knocking on the electorate office door of the State Member for Campbelltown, Graham West, trying to return his $50 back-to-school allowance because it arrived in an envelope with a letter from Bob Carr, politicising the money.

I've had a lot of fun with Farmer since he was elected in 2001. He's a slow-talking drone who made his name by running around Australia for

---

Leah Ilott A friend of Janine Lacy

Pat Farmer Lib. member, Macarthur 2001– ; former long-distance runner

charity. I've nicknamed him Forrest Gump (as in 'run, Forrest, run') and it has stuck. The Liberal backbenchers love it. Sussan Ley and Sophie Panopoulos tell me they all use it—in fact, it's so good, they reckon I couldn't have invented it.

After Forrest did his little stunt, I rang Graham West to say that we had him on toast. Last year Forrest used his taxpayer-funded newsletter to publicise the State Liberal candidates for Camden (Paul Masina) and Campbelltown (David Wright). I told West to go on the attack, outing Forrest as a hypocrite. Then West replied, 'Sounds okay, but I had better ask Walt'. I said, 'Who the fuck is Walt? You're in the middle of an election campaign and the local Liberal MP is up you for the rent. Have a go and fight back'.

Apparently Walt works in Carr's media office and backbenchers like West are not allowed to scratch their backsides unless Walt gives them the green light. So I decided to hop into Forrest myself. And today he's in the local rag admitting he did the wrong thing and, if the Federal Government guidelines for electorate newsletters have been broken—which they have—he's willing to pay back $750 to the taxpayer.

Delighted, I rang West again, urging him to take advantage of Farmer's embarrassment. His response? He needs to ask Walt. Well, strike me down, what sort of robots are they breeding in the NSW Parliament these days? The conservative clerks of the Labor movement—I'm surrounded by them. Too scared to go to the toilet unless the boss-man says it's okay. Just ask Walt. I did a little thing on the adjournment tonight anyway, rubbing it into Forrest and urging Eric Abetz to recover the money.

Thursday, 13 February

Crean's staffers are enjoying themselves today. His foreign policy adviser, Carl Ungerer, was up in Rudd's office and found Kevvy's eight-year-old daughter wrapping a present for Mr Schieffer, our mate over at the US Embassy. A peace offering, apparently, for the nasty things we said in Parliament about Schieffer's baseball and land development partner, George W. Bush. Sounds like Rudd's part of the conga-line.

Kevvy reckons he got a call from the Embassy asking, 'Mr Rudd, what's a suckhole?' After he gave them a diplomatic answer, the Embassy official wanted to know, 'Is Mr Latham allowed to say that about the President?'

Sussan Ley Lib. member, Farrer 2001–
Sophie Panopoulos Lib. member, Indi 2001–
Graham West ALP State member,
Campbelltown 2001–

Eric Abetz Tas. Lib. Sen. 1994– ; Special
Minister of State 2001–
Tom Schieffer US Ambassador to Australia
2001–04

I suppose it's like wondering whether or not the Queen shits. Hey, Bush works in an office where there has been plenty of sucking over the years. If they elected Billy Clinton twice, they should be able to understand it when an Australian politician places the President in a conga-line of suckholes.

The power of word pictures in the media—they have really gone off about it. A little secret: I adapted the phrase from one of Bob Carr's classics. He used to describe Greiner's ministers as 'a conga-line of rustic clowns'. I always loved the imagery of that expression and now, with the addition of suckholes, it's even more vivid. Why shouldn't Howard be remembered as an arselicker and a hole-sucker? The Tories don't like it because they know it's true. They just can't help themselves, on their knees to the international elites.

Sunday, 16 February

A huge protest march against the war in Sydney, but a missed opportunity for Federal Labor to demonstrate our anti-war credentials. Crean panicked when he heard about the size of the Melbourne rally—150 000 people turned out on Friday evening to oppose the invasion of Iraq. Originally he planned not to take part in any of the rallies around the country. So yesterday morning, he rang Laurie and McClelland to see if he should be part of the protest in Sydney today, taking Danger's slot on the speakers' list. They decided it was too risky, however, as John Pilger was scheduled to speak—he would have denounced Crean and Labor's policy on the Middle East.

Instead, Crean set off for Brisbane—a safer bet because his mate Jim Soorley was hosting the rally up there today. Or so they thought. Simon gave a speech emphasising the need to disarm Saddam and got booed for his troubles. Isn't it obvious what you do at these events: stand up, denounce Howard as a lying suckhole to the Americans, pledge your opposition to the barbarism of war and then sit down? Politics 101. Somehow, we ended the day with 700 000 Australians marching, united in their hatred of Howard, but the Leader of the Opposition gets booed off the stage in Brisbane. Honestly, what hope is there?

John Pilger Australian expatriate Left-wing author and journalist

Jim Soorley ALP Brisbane Mayor 1991–2003

Thursday, 27 February

Day five of a six-day trip to Shanghai and Beijing as part of an ALP delega-tion hosted by the Chinese Communist Party. A good sense of camaraderie in the group—a thousand and one Rudd jokes, of course. In particular, I'm getting on very well with Peter Cook (good bloke—Danger's mate) and Kim Carr—behind the factional façade, he's refreshingly irreverent about Labor politics. We've appointed him the senior Party theorist for heavy ideolog-ical discussions with the Chinese. He loves this style of politics—machine men working out the fate of the nation behind closed doors—as happy as a pig in shit.

We met the Macquarie Bank representatives in Shanghai to talk about the emergence of a private housing market and banking deregulation. Keating is involved with them, trying to develop new forms of housing credit for one billion Chinese—now, that's what I call the big picture. Shanghai is going gangbusters, a permanent construction site.

A fascinating discussion in Beijing with Mr Dai, a senior foreign policy official, about relations with the US. The Chinese are ropeable, not so much about Iraq, but North Korea. Mr Dai said he hosted a visit from Kim Jong-Il eighteen months ago from which it was clear he wanted to open up his country to economic liberalisation, to be North Korea's Gorbachev. Kim's big worry, however, was the reaction of the military hardliners to reform, the risk of some kind of coup against him.

This is why Mr Dai regards Bush's Axis of Evil rhetoric as disastrous. It has sent Kim back into his shell, worried that if he pursued the reform process it would now look like a reaction to bullying by the US. No wonder the Chinese are off their face about the dunderhead Bush. He's not going to get any comfort from them on his other foreign policy frolic: a new UN res-olution on Iraq. Their big issue is North Korea, and Bush has stuffed it and now it's his responsibility to fix it. As ever, there's an old Chinese saying: he who ties the bell must untie it.

A good discussion today with our host, Mr Zhang, about social demo-cratic reform. He reckons the Chinese are interested in opening up low-level democracy, what we call local government. That's encouraging, but when I raised the experiences of Hu Yaobang and Zhao Ziyang—the coups against them when they pushed for democratic reform—Mr Zhang tact-fully changed the subject.

Kim Carr Vic. ALP Sen. 1993– ; Shadow Science & Research Min. 2001–03
Kim Jong-Il North Korean leader
Axis of Evil Defined by Pres. Bush as Iraq, Iran and North Korea

Hu Yaobang Gen. Sec. Communist Party of China, 1980–87
Zhao Ziyang Gen. Sec. Communist Party of China, 1987–89

Geoff Walsh made a good point about our circumstances back home, an insightful summary of Federal Labor's predicament: 'Post-1996, we haven't been able to strike an identity with the electorate that is appealing'. Certainly not under Beazley, and now Simon's efforts are being wrecked by his foreign policy caveats.

Friday, 28 February

My 42nd birthday and Mr Zhang organised a cake towards the end of our lunch at the Hepingmen Roast Duck Restaurant in Beijing. The Chinese are good. In Shanghai I noted that a previous Member for Werriwa had celebrated his 55th birthday in that city in July 1971, as part of the first ALP delegation to the People's Republic, and Zhou Enlai had been good enough to organise a cake. Of course, I let slip that I had a birthday coming up on this trip. This has been the best overseas trip I've had in politics.

Friday, 7 March

The madness of the media. A promo by Ray Martin on Channel Nine at 6.25 p.m.: 'Coming up on *A Current Affair*: dangerous footpaths. Don't trip, the Council will blame you. Plus, are we really ready for war?' No doubt about Ray, he's always got his priorities right.

Monday, 24 March

War in Iraq, and Simon has got himself into a terrible tangle. The basic lesson: never listen to Rudd on foreign policy. If that guy's an expert, then I'm Henry Kissinger. The Americans were humiliated at the Security Council, as they should have been. Whatever happened to a 12–3 vote? Three weeks ago France, Russia and Germany pulled the pin on Bush and the other warmongers. A week ago, the US, Britain and Spain withdrew their draft resolution on Iraq—they weren't within cooee of getting it through.

Last week, as the war started, Crean copped a pounding in the media for not cheering on our troops. In all honesty, how can we be a cheer squad for a war we don't support? It's just the nationalistic jingoism of people looking at Iraq from the safety of their TV screens. Anyway, it sure spooked Simon.

At Shadow Cabinet this morning, he wanted to back-pedal on our call for the Australian troops to come home. He would be happy to see this conflict through to its end, undermining our anti-war principles. Macklin and

Zhou Enlai Chinese Premier, 1949–76

I pulled him up, reasserting the line: a Labor Government would immediately bring the troops home. No Shadow Cabinet sell-out.

At one level, Simon has put in a shocker: eleven months of heavily qualified positions and an endless stream of caveats, topped off by his capitulation in the first week of war. But, in his defence, he was led up the garden path by Rudd. He was sweating on the Security Council resolution that never came.

Today, Rudd was even worse. At 9.15 a.m. he played a role in drafting the troops' resolution at Shadow Cabinet, but at 5 p.m., at the National Right meeting, after Robert Ray attacked the wording, Rudd stood up and disowned it, calling it 'hopeless'. I'm still shaking my head in disbelief that it was the same person at both meetings. He's an incredible piece of work.

All these attempts by our people to glorify the troops, treating them like untouchables—is this what our Party is really about? I said to Laurie today, what sort of person seeks a job that involves killing other people? It's not my cup of tea, I can tell you. And thankfully, not Laurie's either.

Friday, 11 April

My worst fears confirmed: Beazley wants his old job back. Lunch with Max Walsh today at the little Thai place down the road from my office in Ingleburn. First time I have met the legendary Walsh—conservative, prickly, not a Labor man. He's writing a piece for the *Bulletin* on my latest book, *From the Suburbs*, an edited collection of speeches and papers over the last two years, published by Pluto Press.

The conversation was hard-going; we didn't click at all, but then he dropped the clanger: Beazley has done a lunch with Maxine McKew and 'It will be read as he wants to come back. Our people want to go big with it'. I bet they do. I went pretty big with it myself—straight to Crean.

Coincidentally, he was on his way to Macarthur—early evening drinks with branch members on the verandah of Fratelli's (at Clem Tacca's golf course out the back of Raby), followed by the season launch of the Campbelltown Kangaroos AFL Club inside the restaurant. Simon has adopted them as a fraternal club to his beloved North Melbourne Kangaroos.

I sat next to Crean and passed on the information from Walsh. He looked stunned and bewildered, not believing that Beazley would do something like this. I had to keep repeating the point: 'Get ready for a big *Bulletin* article where Beazley directly destabilises your leadership'. I can

---

Max Walsh Prominent financial journalist and political commentator

understand his surprise, I suppose, as he gave Kim six years of tight loyalty, first as Manager of Opposition Business and then Deputy Leader. He didn't expect bastardry in return, but that's Beazley: publicly avuncular, privately a dirty dog, as I found out five years ago.

I picked Beazley first, and now the whole Caucus is going to see him for what he is: a rank opportunist. As I drove home with Janine, we both felt pretty sorry for Simon. He's tried to do the right thing with Party reform and putting out our policies. He works his ringer out—here he was in Campbelltown on a Friday night, trying to help the local footy team—but somehow it doesn't work for him. People chatted away during his speech at the footy function—very embarrassing.

With someone like him, I get the feeling it might click into place one day—the power of perseverance. In Simon's own mind, I reckon it's a question of destiny: son of a Labor Cabinet minister, ACTU President, worked his way through the parliamentary Party. It's his turn, he's done the work. For someone to take it away from him now would be a heart-breaking injustice, that's why he fights so hard.

What are the other factors? He has history on his side: the Party has always given its leaders a shot at one election at least. Beazley wants three. Plus he's a proven election campaigner, towelling up Costello last time. Crean is no world-beater but he deserves a fair go, especially up against the horror of a Beazley comeback.

Not content with gutting us of belief and policy for six years, now the old windbag wants to finish the job, finish off the Party altogether. Up the American clacker one more time, a pale imitation of Howard, coffee every morning with Swan/Smith to find out what he doesn't believe in. It's too horrible to think about.

Wednesday, 23 April

Beazley is all over the *Bulletin*. The front cover reads: 'If I Were PM: Kim Beazley finally takes a stand and ignites the ALP leadership debate'. His big theme? Respect. 'If I was running a Labor party campaign now, I'd run on the word respect.' Not much respect for his chosen successor: the McKew interview is framed around a picture of Simon's face on a dartboard. Not much respect for loyalty and decency there. Gough's right: this bloke is the worst former leader of the Party since Calwell.

Leadership articles by Oakes, Wright and Walsh as well. Even little Richo has a go. All up, ten pages of anti-Crean propaganda. Not hard to tell

Tony Wright Canberra journalist for the *Bulletin*

whom Packer is backing: the compliant windbag from the West. Oakes is on board: 'Beazley is the only alternative to Crean that Caucus heavy-weights such as Robert Ray and John Faulkner would be likely to throw their support behind'.

Wright has framed a bookmakers' market for The Hopeful Stakes. I'm 6–1: 'Has previously crashed through the outside rail, running amok in the Members' Stand and trampled a taxi driver'—how funny is that? He describes Stephen Smith as 'Labor's communications spokesman'. He's so dynamic, journalists don't even know his correct portfolio—Health. Walsh's piece concentrates more on the leadership than my book. He's only good for tip-offs.

I've been looking at the numbers. On a hard count, Crean has got them 52–40. He's strong in the Soft Left and Centre and splits the Right with Beazley. The big disappointment is Albanese and his sub-faction of seven votes. Albo despises Beazley's refugee policy, but still this warrior of the so-called Left is willing to back the most conservative man in Caucus. Uren wasted his time nurturing this bloke—turned out to be an exercise in US compliance and Christian conservatism.

For my purposes, the interesting count is to look at the next genera-tion. I can position myself as next in line on the Crean side, a powerbase at last, versus Swan, next in line on the Beazley side. Looks good, I've got Swan covered 56–36. That's my target: to keep those numbers. If Simon loses the election—the Beazley forces won't let him win one—and the Party jumps to the next generation, they jump to me.

Monday, 12 May

Out to dinner with the Crean Loyalists tonight. Parliament comes back tomorrow for the Budget. I said to Harry Jenkins, 'I used to eat alone bag-ging Beazley, so it's great to see a full table these days'. Harry had a good chuckle, as he always does—a very decent person, always strikes me as too decent for this show.

Simon gave a strong speech to Caucus this afternoon. He's using the advantages of incumbency well. By my count, stretching his lead over Beazley 56–36. If Beazley starts dropping into the low 30s there may not even be a challenge. Irwin is one snake in the grass Simon won't get. She is in the *SMH* today comparing Crean to Calwell and says that, while she was

---

Tom Uren ALP member, Reid 1958–90; min. in Whitlam and Hawke govts and mentor to Anthony Albanese

Harry Jenkins ALP member, Scullin 1986–

raised to always support the Leader, 'At the end of the day the movement comes first'. No Julia, your innate sense of treachery comes first.

Keating rang, describing the Beazley push as 'the revenge of the blancmange'. Magnificent. He also offered a neat summary of the generational issue: 'Of the Whitlam generation, Whitlam was the only good one. Of the Hayden generation, only Hawke could win. Of my generation, now that I've gone, there's nothing left. They have never done much, have they—Beazley, Crean, Evans, Lawrence, all the ones in their fifties? That's why it now depends on the generation in their forties, your generation'.

He also had a piece of advice: if Crean offers me the Shadow Treasurer's job, some people will say don't take it as Simon is a dead horse. Paul reckons I should grab it with both hands. If Beazley gets the leadership, I should dare him to move me, just as Paul stared down Hawke in 1982 when he wanted to put Willis in the job.

Wednesday, 14 May

A nosh-up with the AHA in the Bradman Pavilion at Manuka Oval. Danger joined us, just off the phone with Keating. He reckons Paul phones him every day to get an update on the Federal scene. At the moment he's right into the leadership stuff. Truth is, he would dearly love to come back and be part of it again. He should never have quit Blaxland in 1996. A vital lesson: when you get out of this place, make sure you have no urge left to contribute. Otherwise you end up looking like Paul.

Friday, 16 May

Lunch with Roozendaal at Gemelle's in Liverpool. The Beazley people must be pushing on with their challenge, as Eric had just one purpose: to scare me about the NSW Office polling in Werriwa. If it's accurate, we have a problem. From a sample of 400 voters, the Liberals are ahead on the primary vote 41 to 36 per cent (a 14-point collapse in our vote) and 52–48 two-party preferred (a 10.5 per cent swing against us). My numbers are good: 70 per cent approval, 13 per cent disapproval, with no gender difference.

Simon's, however, are appalling: 74 per cent of voters prefer Howard as Prime Minister, 13 per cent for Crean. As I said to Eric, how bad can it get? We have held this seat for nearly 70 years and now only 13 per cent of people want the Labor Leader to be PM.

How could I defend him in these circumstances? By pointing to his outstanding Budget Reply speech last night and the need to give him some clear air in which to campaign properly. I'm not budging, even in the face of this research report.

I know my seat. It's full of new double-storey housing estates—I've got to work hard to win their support, Crean or no Crean. I know the established areas back to front, but a whole new city has been built through Prestons and Cecil Hills, new residents who don't necessarily know me. That's why I started a program of street meetings and doorknocking through these areas last month. It's going well so far.

It will be a fight to hold Werriwa, no doubt about it. Crean's bound to lift a bit, which will help. Plus the top issues in Werriwa are highly campaignable: defending Medicare, cutting immigration numbers, making neighbourhoods safer, improving living standards and doing something about youth unemployment. These issues are right up my alley as the local MP.

Tuesday, 20 May

More bagging of Beazley, this time at dinner with Daryl Melham and Warren Snowdon in Darwin after a North Australia Policy Forum. Melham told the story of how Beazley almost lost Brand in 1996 and Daryl asked him what he would have done if he had gone down. Kim replied, 'I would have gone to Britain to join the UK Parliament and been part of Blair's team'. He later described the Third Way as an imitation of the ALP but he was willing to leave Australia for good and be part of it—an honorary Pom.

Tuesday, 27 May

After the NSW Right dinner at Portia's Place, an interesting conversation with John Murphy and his wife Adriana. They reckon that Simon won't give me a proper promotion, say, as Shadow Treasurer, because he sees me as a threat. Adriana kept on stressing her closeness to Carole Crean, so I assume that's where the information comes from. Political spouses are always the honest ones.

Laurie has got word back that Richo gave me a bagging at Conroy's Victorian Right dinner last week, running the line that I have a problem with women. The pot calling the kettle black. This is the standard critique from the Beazley people, the so-called gender gap. But Roozendaal's research shows that it's nonsense—70 per cent approval from both men and women in Werriwa.

The more I see of the press gallery, the more I struggle with them. There is a huge disconnection between the electorate and the gallery. The

---

Daryl Melham Shadow Justice & Customs Min. 2001–03 | **Warren Snowdon** ALP member, NT 1987–96, 1998–2001; Lingiari (NT) 2001–

public is deeply cynical about the system—the whitebreads, polly-waffle etc. Yet the media/gallery is the funnel by which these artificial messages and processes are conveyed. They see politics as a game, not real life, and encourage the MPs to play it. Some rules of the game: punish politicians who are 'off-message', even if they are telling the truth. Politicians should always focus on their opponents, thereby 'applying pressure'. Politicians should only create narrow points of difference with each other, and milk issues at the margin. And finally, unorthodox politicians should be stigmatised as 'mad'.

These are the rules of the parliamentary game. But this is not the game the Australian people want their representatives to play. It is, therefore, thoroughly predictable that the public would despise politicians and journalists alike. And they do, with a passion.

Monday, 2 June

The break I have been hoping for has arrived. A clandestine meeting this evening with Laurie, Kim Carr and Peter Cook at Cookie's unit in Civic. Carr instigated the gathering but didn't want any of the colleagues to find out about it, so we met in private, in an atmosphere of secrecy. Laurie was worried about being seen going into the block of units.

Excellent news: Cook and Carr have adopted me as the next Labor Leader, either after the next election or if Simon falls over beforehand. They don't want to be caught on the hop by the Beazley forces. A possible scenario: Martin Ferguson to tap Crean on the shoulder before Christmas; he has been telling people that Simon deserves a fair go up until December.

Our job in the coming months is to position me as a viable alternative to Beazley. Carr wants me to smooth the waters with the industrial Left in Victoria, starting next week. They like my foreign policy stance but are worried about my economic policies. I'm not going to compromise on my commitment to competition and economic openness—it's a matter of explaining the model to them, just as Keating did with Wally Curran and co. in the early 1990s.

For the long term, we all agreed on the need to reform the Right, which has become heavily Balkanised. We need to clean out the non-believers like Swan, Smith and Rudd, and give the faction a purpose beyond political patronage. A long-term project.

Wally Curran Left-wing leader, Vic.
Meatworkers' Union, 1980s and 1990s

The Beazley challenge is going nowhere. Little Swannie and his mate Smith have rooted their reputation with a good part of Caucus. My rehabilitation is going as sweet as a nut. Now that I'm applying myself to the task inside Caucus, I'm making progress quite easily. I made the challenge bigger for myself but now I'm jumping these hurdles like Edwin Moses.

I'm on a real high, despite missing Ollie terribly. I love that boy and hope he is proud of his dad—a dad who might actually make something of himself. I was proud of my father but struggle with the realisation that I never knew him properly, never got to talk to him as an adult about his other life—his first marriage, his daughters, his problem on the punt, etc.

I've been thinking about him a lot lately. Mum was the hero from my childhood but Dad remains my emotional legacy. That's why I hate being away from Ollie. A son must always know his father and never be left wondering. I suppose that's one of the reasons I keep chugging away with this diary, so the boys can read it one day. Even scatty entries like this one tonight.

Tuesday, 3 June

During Caucus this morning, Crean relayed the news that Howard is staying on as Liberal Leader. Smart timing to cover up his problem with Costello. The Rodent announced it in the Government party room, under the cover of our leadership woes. He's drawing the obvious comparison: stability and continuity on the Government side, turmoil within the Labor Party.

It makes last night's discussion seem academic; we are having an early election. How can Howard resist the opportunity of cashing in on our problems? He's a student of Menzies, so the nation will be voting before Christmas. Maybe I can take over after the election, if I hold on to Werriwa. Roozendaal's numbers are still ringing in my ears.

Other news this morning: Smith, Swan and Conroy were busted meeting with Beazley in the Sydney Airport lounge last Friday. The little red roosters were flushed out of their coop by a security alert and evacuation of the airport. What a bunch of amateurs. They should have rented out Cookie's unit for the afternoon.

Edwin Moses Champion US Olympic hurdler

The Rodent Nickname for John Howard given to him by Andrew Peacock in the 1980s; Howard was always gnawing away at Peacock's leadership of the Lib. Party

Friday, 6 June

It's on. After stuffing around yesterday, Simon has called a Special Caucus meeting for Monday week, 16 June, to put down the Beazley challenge. On my count, he should win 57–35, a handsome victory, but not the devastation that the blow-hard Beazley deserves.

The windbag has shat in his own nest. After all this destabilisation, the Crean forces will have every reason to ostracise him in the future, confirming his reputation as worse than Calwell. I keep thinking of that horrible speech he gave Caucus about the search for WMD in Iraq—bellowing about the need to keep the focus on the Government. Kim was more upset about my attack on Bush than the Americans were. 'Dumb politics, dumb politics', he kept on yelling. Well, where will the focus be for the next ten days? On Dumb-Dumb's push to regain the Labor leadership.

Here's something else I should report—the return of Gwyther. Out of the blue, Janine and I received a letter today. Gwyther is complaining that her home has been 'suffused' with images of my family. Apparently these photos are 'so potent' they have made her mother 'literally weep'. She concludes the letter in a really weird way: warning me and Janine not to smile at her from any of these photos.

She's talking about my Werriwa newsletter and invitation for residents to attend my street meetings. If she doesn't like the leaflets, throw them in the bin instead of showing them to her mother, who lives in the Blue Mountains. She says in the letter she's getting on with her life, but clearly she hasn't moved on. She has a new husband and young son—what looks like a new life—so why do a couple of leaflets in her letterbox send her into a spin?

Talked it over with Janine. There's no doubt Gwyther is going to cause trouble in the future. She's so obsessed with the past, she's objecting to a few photos. But I can't understand it. If the truth came out about 1997 she wouldn't look any better than me. The old rule: the only people who really know what happened in a marriage break-up are the two who were in it.

Thursday, 12 June

Come in, spinner. A speech in Macklin's electorate last night, the Melbourne launch of *From the Suburbs*—perfect timing for the leadership battle. Cooney wanted a full-scale attack on Beazley's character but I chose a subtler route, not even mentioning his name. But the message was clear, a neat summary of our struggle against machine politics:

If the push against our Leader were to succeed, it would set a shocking precedent. This long campaign of leaking, backgrounding and sabotage would be legitimised within the ALP. Simon Crean is a tough and determined person who has been willing to stand up to the machine men. This is why they turned against him. They like soft and indecisive leaders with whom their interests will always prevail. A North Melbourne Shin-Boner is a bit too tough for them.

That was Cooney's line, my resident AFL expert. Then I tried to define the contest. The new dividing line inside the Party is now between the True Believers—those who want modern Labor to stand up and fight for our policy beliefs—and the machine men, with their over-reliance on polls, spin doctors, the daily media cycle and a command-and-control style of politics. Machine politics reduces our Party to a bland form of Labor conservatism. It replaces the passion and radicalism of Labor with a 'whatever it takes' approach to public life.

Best of all, Beazley took the bait. He called a press conference earlier today to say that I'm only good at damaging the Labor Party and taxi drivers. That's where we want him: avuncular Kim out the window and a glimpse of the nasty grub that lies beneath.

He's having a bad campaign. He looked like a spiv at the Randwick Races with Hawke, little Swannie hovering in the background as his Press Secretary. Now he's trying to scratch my eyes out. He's trying to run a presidential campaign through the media but it's backfiring—Caucus hates the public damage to the Party. Crean's odds: he's London to a brick on.

Monday, 16 June

Crean in a canter, 58–34. I was out by one in my count—a good sign that I'm getting to know this Caucus and its numbers. Relief more than jubilation on Simon's face as the result was announced in Caucus. His sense of destiny remains intact.

A loss of face for the Beazley forces. Smith has gone to the backbench; he gave his letter of resignation to Simon on his way out of the meeting—a tick for doing the right thing, which is more than can be said for Swan, Conroy and Albanese. Albo let it be known through the media he was supporting Beazley but didn't have the courage to front publicly. He likes to keep his ABC Club as a secret society.

Swan pulled a ridiculous stunt. Fancy calling a press conference at Circular Quay and evoking the foundation of the nation in support of a Labor leadership challenge by Kim Beazley. He tried to sound Churchillian but he just looked silly. Simon punted him as Manager of Opposition Business today and gave me the job. This is the one I've always wanted; I get to hone my debating skills in the House, a real parliamentarian at last.

A margin of 24 sounds substantial, but it may not be as strong as that. It was almost as if Beazley ran dead. For instance, he never phoned Cathy King to canvass her vote, yet she was elected to the Parliament for a marginal seat under his leadership at the last election. Examples like that across the factions. Beazley is fairly lazy but nobody could be that lazy and stupid in a leadership ballot.

The other interesting ploy was Robert Ray's, Beazley's mate and de facto campaign manager. Simon is adamant that he got Ray's vote. One theory: Ray wants to be kingmaker, switching to Beazley later on and giving him momentum. Maybe Beazley's machine men thought they had a respectable tally of votes, in the mid 30s, so they kept some fat up their sleeve for next time. The conventional wisdom is that it always takes two leadership challenges to finish off a Leader. This was just their first strike. Machiavellian, but not impossible.

Monday, 7 July

The machine men love to leak: polling results, the details of private meetings, anything they can get their hands on. At last, a leak that helps me. McMullan has given Milne the truth behind my so-called stuff-up on negative gearing.

Last Wednesday, Simon made me Shadow Treasurer. There was something wrong with him that day, I'm sure; I only spoke to him five minutes before my press conference—chaos in his office. I went on *Lateline* that night and got too chatty with Tony Jones about our plans to reduce the scale of negative gearing in Australia to take the top off the property boom. The combination of negative gearing, the halving of capital gains tax, high top marginal income tax rates and the end of the stockmarket boom has sent the property market in this country out of control—a spiv's paradise.

It's good economic policy to do something about it. But a hairy proposition politically. Costello, ever the opportunist, is trying to run a scare campaign. Crean was asked about negative gearing the next day in Adelaide. His staff had not briefed him on my *Lateline* comments, leaving open a policy review, and he said our policy was to keep it. The media have jumped all over it as a Crean-repudiates-Latham story.

Cathy King ALP member, Ballarat, 2001–   **Tony Jones** Host of ABC TV's *Lateline* program
Bob McMullan Shadow Finance Min. 2003–04

Enter Comb-over, operating under a hierarchy of hatred: he hates Crean more for dumping him as Shadow Treasurer and putting him into Finance than he hates me for taking his job off him. So he wired up the Dwarf with the details of the PRC meetings that looked at cost savings of up to $12 billion. Plus, my office has been working on a plan to cash out the benefit and effectively means-test it, another cost-saving possibility. McMullan's treachery is a bit too late to help me—the public damage has already been done—but at least the truth is out there now.

Tuesday, 15 July

A meeting with Keating and his business partner Mark Carnegie at their office in Park Street, Sydney. Paul wants to ensure his economic legacy is safe with me—that as Shadow Treasurer, I stick to his beloved model. He's got no worries, I'm a True Believer. I have always believed in Labor as the party of productivity and competition policy, pro-market but not necessarily pro-business. We need to stitch up the Liberals as the party of business preferment and special deals—a replay of Paul's strategy in the 1980s.

The bigger challenge is to craft an agenda for the next round of economic reforms. You can only liberalise an economy once, realising a big boost in productivity. After that, you need to keep reforming to keep the economy growing, otherwise the productivity gains start to expire. Paul loves to talk about the history of his model, how he set up the open growth economy. He's not so big, however, on the details of what we need to do next.

That's my job. I've been thinking about economic reform for a long while, but now I need to push my ideas through Shadow Cabinet. Here's the agenda: a new round of trade practices reform, improve the competitiveness of our tax system (Paul wants us to lower the top marginal rate and I think he's right), a national savings strategy to overcome Australia's culture of debt, new investments in education and training (new growth theory economics), new standards for corporate social responsibility, plus asset-based policies, extending the ownership revolution.

The key is updating the *Trade Practices Act*, private competition policy. Big business hates it because it makes them compete, instead of bludging off the privileges of monopoly and oligopoly markets. Competition spurs on innovation and excellence in the market, opening up opportunities for small and emerging enterprises; it disperses economic power to many, rather than concentrating it in the hands of a few companies.

This will be my big push: strengthening Section 46 (abuse of market power), outlawing predatory pricing, divestiture powers to break up cartels, cease-and-desist orders to provide immediate relief from market abuse, and new ACCC powers to deal with the creeping concentration of industries such as the grocery retail sector, and the abuse of franchisees by parent companies, such as my little mate Searley's problem with Arnold's Pizzas.

A long talk with Paul. Two highlights: first, he gave me the history of his struggle with the banks to free up the financial system. The old Martin Place mob loved the protection and preferment of the Menzies era. Keating was their club-buster and he still hates them: 'One of the few things that would tempt me back into Parliament is to fuck the banks'.

And second, his usual condemnation of Beazley: 'That useless fucking windbag Beazley had no indignation, that was his problem'. A beautiful contrast with Hawke, who calls Kim a 'decent loser', as if it is some kind of virtue. Keating, however, despises the idea of a Labor Leader readily accepting defeat at the hands of the Tories. He wants it to torture Beazley, just as it has tortured him since 1996.

Saturday, 26 July

A grand tour through Ballarat, Daylesford and Ararat in regional Victoria. Ararat is in the seat of Wannon, which we have no hope of winning. I was there to support the local Labor branch in its centenary celebrations, and delivered the J. K. McDougall Lecture last night. McDougall was a founder of the branch and Labor Member for Wannon (1906–13), a throwback to the agrarian origins of our Party.

What a great slice of Labor history, a Party presence in this country town for 100 years. And the branch is still going strong—a crowded room for my lecture, Saturday-morning discussion groups and genuine community activism. If only this was the universal state of the Party. Maybe the country branches have kept their charm and community purpose compared with the ethnic stacking and rorting in the cities. I can't imagine a Conroy or an Albanese visiting Ararat—there is no factional advantage to be gained.

Caught the plane home this morning, with Derryn Hinch and Neil Mitchell in the same row. They were on their way to Sydney for a magazine photo shoot for radio shock-jocks. And wasn't Mitchell different away from his microphone—elitist, no longer pretending that he sticks up for the little guy. When I told him where I had been he shook his head in disgust and

---

ACCC Australian Competition and Consumer Commission
David Searle An old school and rugby club mate, who runs a pizza shop in Ulladulla, NSW
Stephen Conroy Shadow Trade, Corporate Governance and Financial Services Min. 2003–04

Derryn Hinch Melbourne radio broadcaster and long-time controversialist
Neil Mitchell Right-wing radio shock-jock on 3AW

said, 'Why would anyone go to Ararat; it's so ordinary there. You people have horrible lives in politics'. I quite liked Ararat: down-to-earth, friendly, fighting back from an economic downturn. Much more agreeable than sour-puss Mitchell.

Sunday, 3 August

Signs of trouble for me this morning on the Sunday TV talk programs. Swan was on Channel Seven with Milne, casting doubt on my proposal to assist essential workers in Sydney overcome the housing affordability crisis. That way, we can still have nurses, firemen and police living in this booming city. On Friday, Conroy sent around a note on the same policy, suggesting it might lead to higher interest rates, with copies to Crean, McMullan, Cox and Griffin, so it's bound to be leaked to the media.

These roosters have not learned anything from the leadership debacle. They are small-minded troublemakers and white-anters who would love to see me fall over to hurt Crean—two for the price of one. Ditto their allies in the media. The three gallery journalists who have run a ten-year critique on me are Oakes, Grattan and Milne. It must be a particular personality type: anally retentive, politics as a game, all about process. Yet they have most politicians living in fear of policy innovation—Canberra's culture of fear.

Swan and Smith are trying to make out around Caucus that we will flounder without their tactical genius. But their only tactic is to do nothing, say nothing other than obvious attacks on the government, and stand for nothing. Take the big burning issue of poverty, for example. Swan's 2001 policy was to have an inquiry. Now he's got a Senate Committee looking at the issue—twenty Swan/Hutchins doorstops and not one mention of a policy to solve poverty. In fact, there is no public awareness that the Senate inquiry is even going on, let alone what Labor might stand for.

Unfortunately, this culture has infiltrated the Party. It stands as the dominant culture in Parliament House and the press gallery. I am so glad not to be one of them. Look at Matt Price on *Insiders* today. Barrie Cassidy raised my performance on the Denton program (one of my best efforts in the media) and Paul Kelly's piece on our economic policy direction. Yet Price, knowing that Gerard Henderson was sitting next to him, ready to have a go at me, responded by soft-pedalling: 'I don't know about Latham, whether it works or not'.

David Cox Shadow Asst Treas. 2002–04
Alan Griffin ALP member, Corinella 1993–96; Bruce 1996– ; Shadow Consumer Protection & Consumer Health Min. 2003–04

Barrie Cassidy Host of Sunday-morning ABC TV program, *Insiders*
Denton program *Enough Rope*, ABC TV program hosted by Andrew Denton

Price makes out he's a mate, all pally, etc., but he's really in it for himself. Two-faced indeed. Sometimes it is impossible to satisfy people in this business. Stuff them all. As I board the plane for Brisbane, on my way to an outer suburban ALP fundraiser tonight, not exactly fun city, I am thinking of how much better life would be if I were like Neville Smith. We had dinner at the Hermitage last night and I walked away jealous of his lifestyle: dedicated to his family and spending all weekend with his children. Sounds like paradise, versus the crap I have to work with.

Wednesday, 6 August

An excellent meeting with Coxie and staff (Alex Sanchez and Nathan Dal Bon from my office, and Silvana Catalano from McMullan's office) to draw up a list of quality cuts to the Budget. I have set a target of reducing outlays by 3–5 per cent to make way for our spending priorities. No small-target politics this time and no prospect of pushing the Budget into deficit. It can all be handled on the expenditure side.

Coxie has drawn up a long list of cuts he wants to pursue—a superb heir to Peter Walsh. The rest of the meeting was spent adding to the list: parliamentary superannuation and other pollie rorts, the Private Health Insurance Rebate, the Housing Depreciation Allowance, means testing the First Home Owners Grant, knocking off golden handshakes, abolishing the Employment Advocate and Building Taskforce, savings on the PBS, ending abuse of the medical rebate, hitting the taxation of trusts, efficiency savings in Defence, selling the Telstra share in Foxtel, rationalisation of regional programs, knocking off concessions for farmers, asset-testing the FTB and raising more revenue from Big Tobacco. Fiscal rigour: I love it.

Tuesday, 12 August

This Parliament desperately needs an independent Speaker to apply the rules fairly and to lift the public standing of the place. Most of the angst and disorder comes from perceptions about the partisanship of the chair. On our side, we reckon a Liberal Speaker is ripping us off, while the other side gets shitty if their bloke doesn't come down hard on us. Institutionalised distrust and chaos.

Neville Smith School cricket coach, mentor and friend

FTB Family Tax Benefit

Neil Andrew knows the score. Today he told me he 'would resign from the Liberal Party tomorrow and become an independent Speaker if not for my seat'. Obviously he wouldn't be re-elected in Wakefield as an Independent. And I suppose he's worried that if he left the Government his electorate would suffer in terms of grants and access to ministers. Realistically, we need some kind of agreement between the major parties to reform the House. Instead of this institutionalised gridlock.

Thursday, 21 August

My campaign against the Government's special deals and cronyism has hit a raw nerve. Abbott tried to hit back in Question Time today, saying that my sister Toni received favourable treatment from Liverpool Council when she became the caretaker for Collingwood House in 1992 during my time as Mayor. She got this position with no pay, just rent-free accommodation in a small flat, entirely on her merits. When the appointment came before Council I declared an interest and didn't vote.

A storm in a teacup, even by municipal standards eleven years ago. But it's revealing about Abbott and the research the Tories put into people. Abbott had his staff sniffing around Liverpool as far back as 1997. These are the fruits of his labour: some dirty old local newspaper clippings and a silly attempt to stitch up my sister.

But his attempts were enough to stoke the weird voyeurism of some press gallery types. I went for a drink in Kingston earlier tonight but had to leave early because of the spooky behaviour of Lincoln Wright and his mate (Luke someone) from News Limited. They kept coming up to me, wanting to talk about the Collingwood House thing, like it was the new Watergate. It's hard to describe how bad they were, like a pair of spaced-out stalkers.

I tried to shake them off politely but, in the end, the only way to get away from them was to leave. One interesting thing they told me, however: Matt Price came back to the News bureau from Question Time very excited about Abbott and my sister, wanting to write it up big. Two-faced indeed.

Wednesday, 3 September

How bad are News Limited and its anti-Labor propaganda? It's a running dog for Howard and the Libs, with its shocking stance on Iraq, the neocon-servatism of *The Australian* and its disgraceful defence of Abbott and his

---

Neil Andrew House of Representatives Speaker 1998–2004. As the Manager of Opposition Business I had a fair bit of contact with | Andrew and he often gave me feedback on ALP's call for parliamentary reform

scam with Australians for Honest Politics. In my experience, it's a company run on personal connections and preferences, not the facts.

I'm embarrassed to think I used to be a columnist for the *Tele*. Ian Moore and David Penberthy have their heads in the toilet bowl over Sandra in my office and this business with her partner, who's in strife over his role in a Port Kembla brothel. In truth, the *Tele* loves brothels, they help to pay their wages and add to Murdoch's profits. Just look down the back of the paper, page after page of brothel advertising. Moralising, hypocritical Tories—is there a worse species of animal on earth?

Tuesday, 9 September

Has there been a lower point in our time in Opposition? Jennie George stood up in Caucus today and said 'Abbott has done nothing wrong' in relation to Australians for Honest Politics. Yeah, sure, he lied through his teeth to the ABC, secretly established a slush fund and went through the back door to deal with a political opponent. Yet this former head of the ACTU is now defending the man who wants to rub out the unions. The confusion within the Labor movement is complete.

Our poor Party. Bob Carr has lifted the scab off the leadership tensions again. He's so self-indulgent, always agonising about coming to Canberra, but too insecure to ever do it. Plus, he's a realist. He would be starting all over again, with no support base and no sympathy in Caucus. He has reached his peak as the time-serving Mayor of NSW.

No, the ABC Club will have to make do with Beazley, the great splitter. He has divided this Caucus more thoroughly than at any time since 1955. The Party gave him unity for his six years as Leader and, in return, he has given us chaos. Crean has tried to appease, consult and include the ABC Club, but in truth, they only understand one thing—political violence.

Thursday, 11 September

A briefing on the Party's opinion polling from Tim Gartrell and Mike Kaiser. That's one of the benefits of this new job, of climbing through the ranks: I get to see some of the expensive research the Party pays for. By the end of

---

Australians for Honest Politics Slush fund established by Tony Abbott in the late 1990s to finance legal action against Pauline Hanson and the One Nation Party
David Penberthy *Daily Telegraph* journalist

Sandra Herbert-Lowe Worked in my Werriwa electorate office
Tim Gartrell ALP Nat. Sec. 2003–
Mike Kaiser Former Qld ALP State Sec.; former ALP member Qld Parl.; Asst Nat. Sec. ALP 2003–04

the meeting, however, I was wondering if it might have been better to remain in the dark. Ignorance is bliss.

We are in a terrible position. Simon is unpopular, but it goes beyond the personal standing of one individual. We have big structural problems that have plagued us for the past decade and remain unresolved. Best summarised by Geoff Walsh's observation in China: we are yet to create an identity that the electorate can relate to and support.

Under Hawke and Keating we became the party of economic liberalisation and the rights agenda, a historic shift away from our traditional working-class identity. This confused the electorate and, unhappily, we have done nothing to end the confusion during our seven years in Opposition. Beazley left a huge vacuum with his small-target strategy by refusing to tell the electorate what we stood for because he didn't know himself. Then we spent the last two years arguing about the post-Beazley leadership—the indulgence of a long-term Opposition talking to itself instead of the people.

If an election were held this Saturday we would be smashed, reduced to a parliamentary rump. Howard is not stupid, he gets the same kind of research—he must go before the end of the year. Look at the fundamentals in our polling.

On which party is best at handling the economy/deficit/interest rates, the Liberals are ahead by a margin of two to one. On defence/national security/terrorism, they have a huge three to one lead, despite the calamity in Iraq. Our strengths are more modest: a healthy advantage in education, but a relatively small lead over the Coalition in health.

The research report says that 'Howard is experiencing a second honeymoon—he is seen as strong, decisive, acting in the national interest'. By contrast, we are seen as 'lacking policies and direction, divided [internally focused] and big spending'.

On voter sentiment, 'From Tampa onwards the national mood has been heavily in Howard's favour (in June, 60 per cent of people said that Australia was heading in the right direction, with only 29 per cent saying we were on the wrong track). This is similar to the State mood measured for Beattie, Carr and Bracks'.

On voting trends, 'The Coalition primary vote is very strong, while Labor's primary is stuck at Tampa levels'. Queensland and WA are our worst States, and outer metropolitan areas are our worst regional result. We are in trouble across all demographics, including our 'loyal base—low-income public servants, renters, etc.'

Steve Bracks Vic. ALP Premier 1999–

The contrast between Federal and State Labor is interesting. The States have the advantages of incumbency in a booming economy. But the other important factor is this: the State parties have not experienced an identity crisis. They still campaign on the staple Labor diet of good schools, hospital care, community services and environmental protection. And they win easily as the natural party of State Government.

Federally, our problems are structural. People don't trust us on national security because they see Labor as a soft touch to the bleeding hearts. That's one of the focus-group quotes: 'You can't trust Labor any more, the bleeding hearts get to them'. This is my point about values: not just zero-tolerance of terrorism, but getting back into the mutual responsibility debate, rewarding hard work—a tough but fair approach.

On economic management, we have got ourselves into a terrible predicament. The Keating model was good for the country but the voters no longer associate us with the model: 'Swing voters associate good economic news with the Coalition—they see the reduction in (government) debt as a key achievement of the Government ... Swing voters generally don't trust Labor to run the economy—there is a particular concern that Labor is the big-spending party'.

This is because Beazley gave away our economic reform legacy post-1996, and Howard and Costello got a big tick from the electorate for overcoming the Beazley budget black hole. Even worse, the one thing people now remember from the Hawke/Keating days is high interest rates. They don't remember the model, just the pain.

Check out these focus-group quotes: 'Over the last few years, I think the economy has been managed better than the way Paul Keating was taking it'. Plus: 'Life's better now. Interest rates were a killer—Labor had interest rates up over 20 per cent'. A killer, all right. We would have been murdered at the 1993 election if not for 'Fightback!'; it gave us a three-year reprieve. Our economic credentials have been shot to pieces at the last two elections, with Howard and Costello looking like miracle men.

A crippling catch-22. If we talk about the success of our economic model, people associate the success with Howard/Costello. If we talk about the Hawke/Keating legacy, people associate it with high interest rates. What can we say about the economy during a record period of growth and prosperity? Have a look at Western Sydney: every second vehicle on the road is a one-tonne truck, tradesmen run off their feet. It's gangbuster city.

The best we can do—and this is what I'm trying to do—is point to clouds on the horizon, namely Australia's debt culture and the risk of the housing boom/bust, and rebuild our credentials through a new reform program. Possibly need to emphasise the need for fiscal rigour—hoe into outlays, attack government inefficiency. The old Bob Carr theme: waste and mismanagement. Encouragement in the research report on this front: 'Swing voters believe savings can be made by cutting government waste'.

One more thing: wait for an economic downturn. People are cynical about politics and political rhetoric, especially the Opposition's predictable negativity. The public pays on economic results, real life experiences, money in their pocket. The research report says, 'Perceptions that Liberals are better economic managers is a key foundation for Coalition support'. Will those perceptions change in a growth economy? No. We have become a doomsday party, waiting for reality to change.

The news is not much better on the personality front. Costello has a love/hate relationship with the electorate—40 per cent approval, 40 per cent disapproval. As one focus-group person said, 'As much as I detest Costello, he's a fantastic economic manager. And the economy is the main reason I vote Liberal'. It's not a beauty contest out there, that's for sure—the new middle class loves the feel of new money in its kick.

My numbers are disappointing: 18 per cent approval, 31 per cent disapproval and a huge 51 per cent undecided—no demographic or gender breakdown in the report. It's tough going in Opposition to get a high recognition level from a disengaged electorate. Those who know me like my independence, straight talking and written work. On the downside, they see me as 'Too aggressive and promoted for the wrong reason, as an attack dog on the Liberals'. The attack dog role was my ticket to rehabilitation inside the Party, but it's become a handicap in the electorate. It's time to round out the image a bit.

Is there any hope in our hopeless political situation? The research concludes: 'We must consolidate our strengths on health and education before opening new fronts. Our success in rebuilding our primary vote and capturing key target groups will depend on this'. In other words, Crean needs to run hard on health and education to minimise the size of our defeat.

Maybe the Beazley people are right. They are getting the line out that after the next election, Smith will lead the Party—the triumph of attrition. They reckon Swan, Rudd, Tanner and I will lose our seats. In effect, the end of Labor as a viable force in national politics. How depressing.

Friday, 19 September

I fired a warning shot across Carr's bow to stop him destabilising Crean and the Federal Party. He's having a big blue with John Singleton about his Government's new clubs tax, so I took Singo's side, endorsing him as my kind of fella. I wiped the memory of the Estonian woman and the Workers Party from my mind for five minutes.

Roozendaal rang me yesterday afternoon to protest on Carr's behalf, telling me that 'It's a sign that you are too easily distracted. You can't say no to a fight. If you want to be Leader of the Party one day, attacking Bob is not the way to do it'.

What a surprise today to read in *The Australian*: "'Latham has demonstrated his major flaw in his aspiration to be Leader—he's too easily distracted and he can't resist a brawl," said one senior Right figure. "He's done a great disservice to his leadership aspiration."'

He didn't even have the courage or sense to put his name to it. Classic Roozendaal, a dumb-arse sneak. Just like his leaking of the Werriwa research and all the NSW polling, and his constant destabilisation of Crean. He works on the basis that the State party can do no wrong and Canberra Labor is a lower priority. A machine man, the most detestable of the lot.

Friday, 3 October

A meeting of the NSW Right on the eve of the State Conference. The main item of business is Roozendaal's attempt to caucus the group into voting for Steve Hutchins as head of the NSW Senate ticket, ahead of John Faulkner, the Party's Senate Leader. It's an act of madness, cutting the throat of Senator Forshaw at number three on the ticket. We need to maximise the Labor vote to get Forshaw re-elected and obviously Faulkner has a better chance of doing this than the hapless Hutchins.

But factional pride will not allow it. Eric is insisting that a Right-winger needs to head the ticket, even one as embarrassing as Hutchins. Faulkner's bid is doomed—the Right-wing union bloc is so strong at Conference that they will simply follow the Roozendaal ticket and vote down our Senate Leader. The stupidity and sheer indulgence of the factional system on public display.

It was sad but also funny when Roozendaal tried to give us a rational reason for accepting his recommendation. The best he could come up with was to denounce Faulkner for not wearing a tie when he worked at Head Office as the Left's Assistant General Secretary in the 1980s. Pathetic. I've told

---

The Estonian Woman Featured in TV advertising critical of the Whitlam govt in the 1974 Fed. election campaign. The ads were commissioned by NSW Lib. Premier Askin and produced by John Singleton

Workers Party Established by John Singleton and others as an anti-Whitlam free-market libertarian party in 1973–74

John that I'm voting for him and will ask the Werriwa FEC delegates to do the same. As a sign of solidarity, we will cast our votes in open-neck shirts.

Wednesday, 8 October

An entry I was hoping I would never have to make. I rang David Epstein earlier today, Kim Beazley's Chief of Staff during 1998 and 1999. Robert Ray is at it again, spreading rumours to Caucus members, repeating the crap that he circulated five years ago: that I harassed an unnamed woman in Parliament House.

Ray spoke to John Murphy in the context of Crean tapping the mat—highly unlikely, but these Roosters are as worried about me as they are about Crean. Murphy and his wife have a social thing going with Ray—they visit each other's homes to cook and swap recipes. Last week Ray told Murphy that if the Caucus contest is Beazley versus Latham, then Murphy should be aware that Beazley has a file on me about my past personal indiscretions Murphy should look at. He also told him that Howard has a copy of the same file.

This is why I rang Epstein, to get to the bottom of this rubbish and diarise the information to protect myself for the future. Epstein said Beazley's office never received any written material or verbal complaints about me. There is no file that he knows of. He said that the rumours in 1998 were based on gossip within Beazley's office about me and Liz Iser in the media office. Gary Gray got involved, over-stepping his role as National Secretary, by taking gossip from a few Caucus members and adding it to the Beazley office rumours. A case of exaggeration and mischief-making.

This really is pathetic stuff. First the Roosters said that I would melt down as Shadow Treasurer, which hasn't happened. Then Beazley tried to appeal to the Left with a tax-and-spend agenda, claiming that I was too Right-wing on economic policy, which didn't work for them. Now they are getting personal, resurrecting a smear from 1998. Beazley and his campaign manager are doing their worst, targeting a good Christian in Murphy.

I don't care what people say about me politically, but it makes my blood boil to think of the impact of this sort of stuff on Oliver and Isaac, especially if Ray tries to feed it into the media. Politics can be a dirty business, but our Caucus is infested with the sewer rats of the movement.

Roosters A nickname I gave to Wayne Swan, Stephen Smith and Stephen Conroy

Friday, 10 October

A footnote to Faulkner's unsuccessful bid to head the NSW Senate ticket. At the conference last weekend, he circulated endorsements from Gough and Keating and still got voted down by the NSW Right—not the rank-and-file delegates, but the union blocs. Roozendaal has responded by taking down Keating's and Whitlam's photos in Head Office, ever the petulant child, unfit to be on the payroll of our Party. Also, confirmation of the foolishness of Roozendaal's plan: Forshaw told me he voted for Faulkner ahead of Hutchins. As number three on the ticket, he wanted to maximise the Labor vote.

Tuesday, 14 October

A meeting with Gary Gray this afternoon in my Parliament House office, and got his version of events from 1998. After Sherry tried to kill himself, both sides of politics agreed to set up an informal and supposedly confidential process 'to monitor MPs who were known to be having problems'. This involved Gray, Ray and Epstein on our side, and Nick Minchin and Tony Nutt in Howard's office on their side.

How did I get on their radar screen? According to Gray, Nutt approached Ray with a story that I was having an affair with Penny Fischer in Senator's Parer's office, plus a concern about a 'risqué telephone conversation' with another Parer staffer. Ray passed it on to Gray, who then decided to speak to Gough. Beazley was aware of it, absolutely. He acted dumb when I spoke to him that time in 1998, but he knew all along.

Gray's story is very different from Epstein's. In both cases, it is ridiculous to think that these stories evolved into a sexual harassment/stalking allegation against me. Just as absurd: they are now being used to support Beazley's bid to come back as Leader. Such trivia, a million miles from sexual harassment. And so much for the confidentiality of their little committee—they have been haunting me for five years.

Nothing ever happened with Liz Iser or Penny Fischer. But what if it did—it's not exactly a criminal offence? I was living by myself at the time. What are we here, the Labor Party or the Fred Nile puritan party? Just because women have no interest in guys like Nutt, Ray and Gray, it doesn't mean the rest of us are disqualified for life. I mean, if they want to start

---

Nick Minchin SA Lib. Sen. 1993– ; Finance & Administration Min. 2001–
Tony Nutt John Howard's principal Private Secretary and long-time Lib. Party apparatchik

Penny Fischer Worked as a receptionist in Sen. Parer's office in the late 1990s
Fred Nile Conservative Christian MP in the NSW Legislative Council

accusing and condemning every bloke in Parliament House who has ever had a 'risqué conversation' with a woman, they will need to build a few more prisons in the ACT.

The only thing I can think of is a light-hearted, even risqué, telephone conversation with Catherine McGovern in Minchin's office around that time. Nothing ever happened between us and she has been friendly ever since; she now works as a lobbyist around Parliament House. But she was in a long-running relationship with Conroy, so maybe that's the link: Conroy and his mentor Ray are trying to cause me grief, while covering Conroy's tracks. Maybe the rumour didn't start with Nutt after all, it started with Ray.

Friday, 17 October

Movement at the station. Faulkner has become disenchanted with Crean's leadership and is looking to replace him. We travelled to and from Melbourne today for Jim Cairns's funeral, in Toorak of all places. On the plane back to Sydney, in his cautious and guarded way, Faulkner let me in on his private torment. He is agonising over whether it is his responsibility to tell Simon to go. Does he pole-axe a Federal Labor Leader or watch the Party get slaughtered at the next election? He was thinking aloud in the seat next to me, perhaps hoping that I would help him with his 'choices to make'.

I told him I still supported Simon but, realistically, I was bracing myself for the terrible prospect of Beazley's return: 'I don't want to be treated like shit, tossed out as the Shadow Treasurer. I said I would do the right thing by the Party when I came back to the frontbench and I have, so I think I've earned a bit of respect'.

John wanted to know if I would contest a leadership vacancy, and I said probably not, conceding Beazley's superior reputation on national security matters for what is bound to be a national security election. I hated saying it, but with John, there is no point in stuffing around. He's an honest person and he deserved an honest answer. But I also told him that, if necessary, I'll fight to defend my position. If I'm under threat, I will stand to put a stake in the ground for the future.

I assume Faulkner will now take that message back to Beazley and we will see how the dark side responds. Smith wants to be Shadow Treasurer under Beazley, no doubt about that. So Beazley can make a choice: keep me or fight me. And I will fight every bit as hard as they have in recent times.

Catherine McGovern Worked in Sen. Nick
Minchin's office in the late 1990s

A melancholy day: sharing John's torment about the leadership and sending off Cairns. I only met him once, when I was working for Gough in 1985. We ran into him at Canberra Airport. Gough greeted him with a kiss on the forehead. So, despite their differences inside the Party, they ended up comrades.

Gough also told me an important story about him. In a state of shock, Cairns called Gough behind the Speaker's chair in the House in 1975 to tell him he had just found out that his dad had not been killed in World War I. He had shot through to South Africa. Cairns then recalled how, after the war, his mother waved away charity workers from their front door, who were trying to help her as a war widow. His mum knew the truth. They weren't eligible for assistance, but she never told her son.

As I said in my condolence speech in the House on Tuesday, 'It is a shocking thing for a grown man to find out the truth about his father. It can change you. It can haunt you for the rest of your life'. That's how I relate to him: the missing piece in life from not knowing the full story about your father until it was too late.

Cairns was a hero, the only Australian parliamentarian to ever lead a social movement, the peace movement in the 1960s. He embodied the great, unresolved tension of Left-of-Centre politics, one that I feel all the time, to pursue reform through the collective power of the state or to change society through the methods of non-state reform: mutualism, community-building and the enlightenment of the individual. He was a great and complex man, hopefully to be remembered for much more than Morosi.

Monday, 3 November

My submission to Shadow Ministry this morning on competition policy—to beef up the *Trade Practices Act*—met with surprising resistance from Tanner. How's this from the intellectual spearhead of the Labor Left? He says we shouldn't touch the supermarket duopoly between Coles and Woolworths because they have an agreement with the SDA, the Shoppies. This is the bloke who made his name in the 1980s by winning control of the Clerks' Union in Victoria from the Groupers. Now he's defending their sweetheart deal with the bosses.

Juni Morosi Cairns adviser for whom he declared a certain kind of love during the Whitlam government

the Shoppies The SDA had an agreement with Coles and Woolworths to maintain unionised workplaces. Inside the ALP the Shoppies have lobbied to protect the market share of Coles and Woolworths against competition from independent grocers and retailers

It's the equivalent of the Government's deal with Manildra. Left-wing cronyism is alive and well inside the ALP, in defence of a Right-wing union. Tanner has lost the plot. And his economic credentials have gone out the window. It's bad enough that he's beholden to the unions, but to go in to bat for the Groupers is unbelievable.

Tuesday, 4 November

Every Tuesday after Caucus, I provide a briefing for the press gallery, part of my job as the Manager of Opposition Business. Today I tried a bit of light relief on the ultra-serious reptiles, starting my Caucus report with a parody on the Melbourne Cup field:

> Kim Beazley said that any leadership push is Distinctly Secret. The Crean Loyalists said that's Frightening. Then Wayne Swan said: listen colleagues, I Ain't Seen Nothing. The Shoppies said we can't change our vote, we're under Holy Orders. Robert McClelland then reported: we're down in the polls due to the ASIO raids on the Mamool and Fawaz families in Lakemba. George Campbell said we're losing votes in County Tyrone.
>
> I chipped in and said don't be silly, the Leader deserves a Big Pat on the back, he's doing really well on Millstreet, where they reckon he's Pentastic. He's even got that Bold Bard, Graham Freudenberg, doing speeches for him. Naturally, the Caucus agreed. These days, they reckon I'm Mr Prudent and we've got the best economic policy since Schumpeter.

Michelle Grattan was sitting next to me and she kept on scribbling, taking down notes until I was halfway through. Then she looked up in a state of confusion, anguish peering out from behind her coke-bottle glasses. They should have a rule that journalists can only work in this place for a maximum of five years. Otherwise they become as humourless as my mate Michelle.

Tuesday, 18 November

A meeting of the Federal Campaign Committee in Sussex Street. Strife across NSW. Head office polled twelve key seats in September/October,

---

Manildra Ethanol company owned by Dick Honan that was the subject of a major political controversy in 2003 about Howard govt policies designed to harm Manildra's competitors

with swings to us in just two: Newcastle and Richmond. We are at serious risk of losing Banks, Greenway, Lowe and Barton, with no hope of picking up the Coalition marginal seats of Eden Monaro, Paterson and Parramatta. More Roozendaal leaks to the media can be expected. The Party pays for this stuff and he gives it straight to the papers; an outrageous waste of resources.

Some good news, however, with an encouraging bounce-back in Werriwa. We are now ahead on primaries: 40.7 per cent to 39.7 per cent and two-party-preferred 52–48. My approval numbers are about the same, while Crean's have improved. Howard's advantage as preferred PM is now 63–18, still massive, but better than the May numbers (74–13).

I might just survive the next election. For reasons I will never understand, Howard has missed his chance for an election this year. Simon is hanging on for dear life. He only has to get through two more Caucus meetings till Christmas. Another polling footnote: the National Office now has my numbers as Shadow Treasurer at 24 per cent approval, 31 disapproval and 45 undecided. They've lifted from when I first got the job, but still net negative.

Saturday, 22 November

I have seen some hatchet jobs in my time, but the piece by Mike Seccombe in the *SMH* today is in a league of its own. A thousand words of anonymous quotes from so-called colleagues, bagging the crap out of me. Whatever happened to the *SMH* guideline about not using off-the-record quotes because their credibility can never be tested publicly? This thing has become a tabloid on a big piece of paper, as bad as the *Tele*.

Maybe the Beazley forces are ready to go again and this is a pre-emptive strike in case I decide to run for the leadership. Just like the Ray stuff with John Murphy. If they want a fight they can count me in now. This is beyond the pale. All the snakes are sliding around in the grass, feeding their poison to Seccombe: Rudd, Swan, Albanese, Tanner and Comb-over.

Seccombe even has a go at my speech to the Press Club annual dinner two weeks ago, saying it was 'dull' to talk about 'politics as a vocation'. That's right, someone like Seccombe is not interested in politics as a vocation, a calling in life to serve the community. His nose is pressed against the window, looking for the inside story. He's written me off in this article, saying I'm a shot bird for the leadership. A good enough reason to run if Simon gets pole-axed.

Ninety-nine per cent of the things I do and say in politics I put my name to, making myself accountable, exposing myself to public assessment. I like it that way: upfront engagement as a way of political life. But some of these characters, the machine men, work almost entirely clandestinely, trying to manipulate events without putting their names to it.

Why do I find it so offensive? It breaches the code of honour that exists—or used to exist—among Australian men. Be frank and upfront with your mates—that's what mateship is about. I still can't believe that so many Labor men dishonour the code so easily. Have our blues, but be man enough to put your name to your views and stand by them. Working-class honour is dead inside the ALP, killed by the machine men and the journalists who live off clandestine politics.

Monday, 24 November

Another Tanner special. He has commissioned research by the Parliamentary Library to identify electorates where more than 10 per cent of voters pay the top marginal tax rate to try to prove that the ALP has no political interest in tax relief at the top end. Then he gave the information to George Megalogenis for today's *Australian*. At least he had the guts this time to identify himself as the leaker/troublemaker.

Tanner is smoking an exploding cigar with this one. The list identifies 24 key seats for Labor: ones we either hold now or need to win off the Government, including his own electorate of Melbourne. He looks like a goose. He's practising bad economic policy and bad politics, so that he can criticise my views on tax and destabilise Crean.

The Beazley mob has gone to town on this tax issue, trying to pick up votes in Caucus from the Left. But we can't win an election unless the new middle class—families on $60–70 000 in the major cities, with high living costs and mortgages—know that we are on their side financially. We should be hammering the need for tax relief across the board, plus the problem of high EMTRs. But instead, Tanner, Swan and Albanese, along with half the press gallery, are hammering me.

My tax strategy is simple. We need to avoid two traps the Government always sets for us. First, running down the surplus and leaving us with no money to fund our social investments, and second, leaving us with no choice but to rubberstamp their tax cuts. The electorate is entitled to ask why they should change governments if Labor's tax policy is the same as the Liberal's. This is the fiscal straitjacket they placed on Beazley.

This time, we need to give ourselves maximum flexibility: $6 billion per annum in budget savings, plus an alternative tax plan that funds itself.

High EMTRs High effective marginal tax rates; refers to the interaction between the tax and social security systems. As people move into higher income bands, they pay higher tax rates and lose social security benefits—a disincentive to work harder

That way we can responsibly meet our health and education commitments while differentiating ourselves from the Tories on tax. I'm not going to wear Costello's straitjacket. That's why I got the Chifley Research Centre to commission Access Economics to look at tax alignment—bringing the top marginal income and company tax rates into line at 30 per cent—funded by a growth dividend, closing down tax avoidance and cutting tax expenditures.

If the research and numbers stack up, it's a good plan. It will catch the Government by surprise, give us economic credibility by improving international tax competitiveness, appeal to aspirational voters, and make the system fairer. As high income earners have incorporated, it is now optional in this country for anyone to pay more than 30 per cent tax—why should honest PAYE workers pay 47 per cent? If the unions knew what was good for them, they would support me. The massive incentive to incorporate is killing their membership. Just ask John Sutton at the CFMEU.

I briefed the PRC about this proposal and got the approval of the Chifley Board, chaired by Macklin. Yet the internal enemies are giving me curry, without knowing the full details. This is the impossibility of fighting on two fronts. I can't fight off the enemies publicly without tipping off the Government about my proposal and jeopardising the Access project and $120 000 worth of research. No wonder divided parties lose elections—they make straitjackets for themselves.

Sunday, 7 December

Unbelievable. Four years ago I was a despised backbencher, making plans to leave Labor politics. Today I'm the Leader of the Federal Parliamentary Labor Party. It just goes to show, there is not much difference between the rearguard and the vanguard in politics. All it takes is a change of direction.

All those years ago, a balmy Sydney night, January 1979, when I walked up to the Dr O'Brien Hall in Miller and joined the Green Valley branch of the ALP. Who would have thought? All I ever wanted to be was a Federal Labor parliamentarian, and now I'm the leader of the show. One day my picture will hang in the Caucus room wall, alongside Curtin, Chifley, Whitlam and Keating. When they grow up, I'll be able to tell Oliver and Isaac how I started out in a public housing estate and became Leader of the Opposition. Maybe Prime Minister.

Chifley Research Centre ALP think-tank
Access Economics Canberra-based economic
think-tank and research organisation

John Sutton Gen. Sec. (Construction div.)
Construction, Forestry, Mining and Energy
Union

Heady stuff, still swirling around us. It will take weeks, months, for the weight of it to sink in. I feel like Muhammad Ali in one of his old film clips, standing on the top rope after a big victory, yelling, 'I shook up the world!' Well, Australian politics at least.

So much has happened. I knew Crean was in trouble, but I never expected it to move so quickly or favourably for me. Best here if I just record the sequence of events.

Two Wednesdays ago (26 November) I was watching the ABC evening news in my Parliament House office. Jim Middleton reported that a group of powerbrokers, including Faulkner, Ray, Martin Ferguson, McMullan and Macklin, were about to move against Crean. I went around to Crean's office straight away, and found him in his press office talking to Frank Spencer about the Middleton story.

Knowing of Faulkner's discontent, I told Simon to start calling around his chief supporters to check on his numbers. He was very dismissive: 'This is more Smith and Swan bullshit fed to Middleton. They are at it all the time. They plant this stuff trying to worry me'. I left him to it, wondering if he was trying to look confident or if he genuinely had no idea about Faulkner's disillusionment with him. I was due in Manuka for dinner with my staff; I had given my advice in good faith, and that was it.

The next morning, I was out for a walk around Lake Burley Griffin and Laurie rang. He said that the leadership was in motion, that last night Faulkner and Ferguson saw Crean and tapped him on the shoulder. I told him I was unsure about whether or not to run, and he said: 'Well, mate, we have been preparing for this all year and people expect you to run. I know it's tough on Simon, but this is the chance we have been waiting for. You have a good chance of winning it'.

I rang Janine straight away and we talked about my doubts. Can we win, what about the impact on the boys, are we ready for this? Momentum carried us forward. We didn't want to give it to Beazley on a silver platter; I was the logical one to run and get the benefit of Crean's numbers. Laurie had placed a lot of faith in me. Even if I lost, it would position me nicely for the future. On balance, it was time to put my hand up.

I kept on walking, back into Parliament House and straight to Faulkner's office. He gave me the bare details of his meeting with Crean. He said, 'I was going to see him this weekend, but that Middleton thing last night, that fucking McMullan, he gave it to Middleton, so we had to do it last night'. I told him I intended to run. Faulkner said he expected Beazley

---

Jim Middleton ABC TV political reporter | **Frank Spencer** Nickname for Simon Crean's Press Sec., Stephen Spencer

to win the ballot but he was willing to support me. He wouldn't be lobbying for me or talking to the media—he said he didn't want his name in the paper—but he was inclined to vote for me.

His main advice was to prepare me for defeat: 'Whatever you do, don't get angry about it and head off to the backbench'. I told him I had no plans to do that, even if Beazley replaced me as Shadow Treasurer with Smith. Apparently, some Beazley backers such as Sciacca wanted to do a deal with me: if I didn't run, I would stay as Shadow Treasurer. But Smith would not have a bar of it. Bad luck for them.

During the day (Thursday, 27 November) we had crisis meetings in Simon's office with his lieutenants: Cook, Laurie Ferguson, Gillard, Kim Carr, Sawford, Emerson and Danger. His support had fallen away in the Centre and the Ferguson Left, and while he could still run and win a ballot, it would only be by a couple of votes. Our count was 48–44.

Crean was brutally honest about his position: 'That's not sustainable in the media. The other leaders will vote against me—Faulkner, Conroy and Macklin—fucking Macklin, she came to see me to tell me she's voting for Beazley. Faulkner said that a majority of the Shadows are against me. I don't see how I can do this'. He was strong and clear-headed under pressure, while the rest of us looked and felt traumatised.

The consensus was that I had the best chance of stopping Beazley, so I went for it. Not with any great joy; the overwhelming mood was that Simon deserved a better fate and the Party was being torn apart by a pack of mongrels. Speaking of which, as a courtesy to the NSW Branch, I rang Roozendaal to let him know I was running and expected to get around 40 votes. He immediately passed on this information to Jim Middleton.

We agreed that Simon would announce he was stepping down at a press conference the next morning, with a ballot for the leadership to be held at the Caucus meeting scheduled for Tuesday, 2 December. We considered a spill for all the leadership positions—a chance to fix up Macklin and Conroy—but backed away when it became clear that this would cost me votes in the contest against Beazley. A handful of Macklin supporters would switch their votes and defend her if she was under attack.

That night Simon had his last supper in Kingston (I never know the name of the place, but it's under the apartment block opposite the newsagent). All the Crean loyalists were there and, after a while, the good food and wine broke the tension. It ended up being a hate session on

---

Laurie Ferguson ALP member, Reid 1990– ; Shadow Citizenship & Multicultural Affairs Min. 2001–04

Julia Gillard ALP member, Lalor 1998– ; Shadow Health Min. and Manager of Opposition Business in the House 2003–

Beazley, and strengthened our resolve not to reward the animals that killed Simon.

After a brief strategy meeting in Crean's office on Friday morning to confirm Thursday's decisions, I drove home and started calling my allies in Caucus. No surprises, all on board, except for Robert McClelland, who was strangely ambivalent.

I publicly announced my candidacy on Saturday, 29 November, in our backyard, stressing the themes that would resonate with Caucus: the need to go forward, not back; that disloyalty shouldn't be rewarded. I tried to position myself as the conviction candidate: 'The Australian people won't ever have any doubt about where Mark Latham stands'. Beazley never talks about policy, so I set out my priorities: eliminating poverty, early childhood education, reinventing democracy and Australian independence through the Republic. Then it was back to the phones.

The turning point was my conversation with Jan McLucas. I had been doing well using the 'don't reward disloyalty' line but it had the opposite effect on Jan. She said, 'I'm actually looking for someone who can bring the Party together. We won't survive unless we are united and people start talking about the future, instead of what we have been doing to each other the past twelve months'. I lost her vote, but thereafter I switched my patter to a more positive theme: taking the Party forward, not back to the future with Beazley. This worked well with the undecided votes. If not for McLucas, I would not have won the ballot.

Late that afternoon, I came out of our office at home and said to Janine, 'I'm lifting well into the 40s, I think we can win this'. There was a lot of dislike and distrust of Beazley and those around him. This was the great irony; smartarses like Albanese had been running around talking about the ABC Club, but now Caucus was going ABB—Anyone But Beazley.

Jann McFarlane, for instance, gave me an hour-long barrage against Beazley and his minders. Incredibly, he didn't pay one visit to her marginal seat of Stirling, just across the river from where he lives in Perth, during her first term in Parliament, 1998–2001. There is no goodwill in Caucus for Beazley from his time as Leader. No one said he was good last time, let's bring him back. I started the ballot behind, but now the younger guy was running past the old failure.

By the time I got back to Canberra on Sunday night, I had 43 hard votes in a ballot of 92. The bedrock of my support was the Centre—there was no way they would support the machine candidate, Beazley. I had

---

Jan McLucas Qld ALP Sen. 1999–

Jann McFarlane ALP member, Stirling 1998–2004

them all bar McMullan. Plus, I had the Ferguson Left, except for Marn, Chris Evans, Kerry O'Brien and Sharryn Jackson (the Miscos group). Good support across the other sub-factions. Crean's backing was vital, hardening up those who might have otherwise forgiven Beazley for his treachery.

The other factor assisting me was Rudd, the pretender. I couldn't have won it without him, good ole Heavy Kevvie. He never had more than six or seven votes at any stage, but he stayed in the ballot until late on Sunday, kicking along the generational-change argument. It is amazing that journalists couldn't see through him. Two factors: they are dumb and lazy, and Rudd is a fanatical media networker. He is addicted to it, worse than heroin.

In the ballot, no journalist tipped me to win. Some, like the Dwarf, tipped a Beazley landslide. It demonstrated how they don't do their research or really understand Caucus. They just hang off the factional chiefs. Having dinner with Smith and Swan or getting on the squirt with Albanese and Griffin is hardly going to tell you what's going on. Then again, some Caucus members don't understand Caucus. The Queensland bird-brain Bernie Ripoll was telling the media, 'Latham won't get more than six votes'.

On Monday, I received commitments from Penny Wong, who was swung over by Gillard; David Cox after I promised him Shadow Minister for Finance; Sid Sidebottom after I promised to visit his electorate first; and Ruth Webber, who sealed it with a bear hug in her office—the vote that tipped me across the line. Come Tuesday morning, I had 47 votes, if they all held.

McClelland, the weak animal, was still wavering. He was worried about my national security credentials—he might lose his seat. I threw everything at him, including a promise to make him Shadow Minister for Homeland Security. He was always telling me that the best barometer of public opinion in his electorate was Robert Stone, the former St George rugby league player. In desperation, I urged him to ring Stone and see whom he would support, Beazley or me.

Incredibly, he did it and Stone told him to vote for me. So I got a commitment out of McClelland on the morning of the ballot, but it was pretty shallow—the sort of thing people tell you to get you off their back.

Kerry O'Brien Tas. ALP Sen. 1996– ; Shadow Primary Industries Min. 2001–03; Shadow Aboriginal & Torres Strait Islander Affairs & Reconciliation and Shadow Tourism Min. 2003–04
Sharryn Jackson ALP member, Hasluck 2001–04

the Miscos group ALP MPs affiliated with the Australian Liquor, Hospitality and Miscellaneous Workers' Union
Bernie Ripoll ALP member, Oxley 1998–
Penny Wong SA ALP Sen. 2002–
Ruth Webber WA ALP Sen. 2002–

Nonetheless, I was able to walk into the Caucus room with 48 committed votes, a sound position. I could drop one and still win.

The other possibility was a tied ballot, 46–all. Under Caucus rules, this meant a draw from the hat. This was untenable; the winner would have been crucified in the media as the Lucky Dip Leader. On Monday I saw Faulkner in his office and warned him of this. He said he had been thinking about it as well and put in place a contingency plan: he would adjourn the meeting, take Beazley and me into one of the offices outside the Caucus room and tell Kim to pull out. Obviously, in his position, he needed a clear victory. For Beazley, a draw was as good as a loss.

So, in effect, I could afford to drop two votes. In the end, it was 47 to 45. The next day, Anna Burke rang me. Before the ballot she told me she was undecided, but now she was calling to say she had voted for me. I tend to believe her. So who were the two rats in the ranks? When I was in local government, John Newman told me a great rule for preselection ballots: no matter what they say and promise, the ones who fail to look you in the eye are the ones who won't vote for you.

By this test, the rats were McClelland and Sidebottom—neither could look me in the eye. Rob showed he lacks character—weak at heart. He's not so silly that he allowed his vote to be determined by a football player, surely? And poor Sid, he was between a shit and a shiver. The other possibility is Emerson—an untrustworthy piece of work. He fancies himself as a future Leader, so he wouldn't want a young bloke like me in the job. All the other leadership aspirants—Rudd, Smith, Swan and the ever-reliable Tanner—voted for Beazley.

The amazing thing about my victory was that I beat the factional system, the power of the machine. Kim Carr was the only factional leader who backed me. Look at who got rissoled: Ray, Conroy, Marn, Smith, Swan, Sciacca, McLeay, Bishop, Albanese, Griffin, plus Sussex Street. Add to them the union bosses who opposed me: Sharan Burrow (ACTU), Greg Combet (ACTU), Bill Ludwig (AWU), Bill Shorten (AWU), Jeff Lawrence (Miscos), Doug Cameron (AMWU) and Joe De Bruyn (Shoppies). Far Left and far Right, they backed Beazley—someone they could control, unlike maddie me.

Hats off to the colleagues who stuck to the independent Crean/Latham side of Caucus. A gutsy bunch, defying the factions, putting their preselections at risk, wanting a Leader who advances real Labor values

---

John Newman ALP member, Cabramatta in the NSW Parl.; assassinated in 1994
Sharan Burrow ACTU Pres. 2000–
Bill Ludwig AWU Sec., Qld branch 1988– ; Right-wing powerbroker

Bill Shorten AWU Nat. Sec. 2001–
Jeff Lawrence The Miscos Nat. Sec. 1992–
Joe De Bruyn Shop, Distributive & Allied Employees' Assoc. Sec. 1978–

and policies, rather than poll-driven opportunism. Maybe there is hope for the old beast yet, with lionhearts like Christian Zahra, Catherine King and Kirsten Livermore in our ranks.

Mind you, it didn't take long for the machine men to extract their first bit of revenge. At the National Executive meeting last Thursday, they rejected my pleas to save Peter Cook's preselection as a Western Australian Senator—Saving Private Cook. So I said to Joel, 'If we win the next election, my first act will be to abolish that horrible, wretched thing called the National Executive'. I will launch World War III on the factional warlords, each and every one of them.

Ringing around Caucus to lobby for votes is a unique experience. Here are the shockers I came across.

Jenny Macklin—I rang her on the Saturday after I publicly announced, as a courtesy to the Deputy Leader. She said that she would remain neutral in the ballot, but by Sunday, it was clear she was lobbying for Beazley among the Caucus women. I fronted her in her Parliament House office that night: 'What's going on, you promised to stay out of it and now every second female MP I call has had a call from you canvassing for Beazley. I mean, you didn't lift a finger for Simon for two years and now you're dudding me'.

She replied: 'What do you mean, I did nothing for Simon? What about the 7 per cent improvement in Newspoll on education issues? As far as I'm concerned, canvassing for Beazley is not canvassing against you. I think it's better if Kim has a clear victory. Anyway, I'm doing it to defend my position, and I'm entitled to do that'.

What's Newspoll got to do with it? Simon needed a Deputy who did some of the heavy lifting for him. But Jenny is totally ineffective. I'm lumbered with her now; might as well not have one. Macklin is as useful as pockets in your underpants.

Jennie George—A big disappointment. She encouraged me to run for the leadership last year but then dogged it, under pressure from Albanese. Too many visits to the Holy Grail.

Anthony Albanese—When I rang him, he said, 'I know Kim is hopelessly conservative but I started the campaign against Crean and I am going to see it through. I wish we had someone else to run, but that wasn't the case. Beazley was the only one who put up his hand'. I told him the vote might be 46–all and he agreed. He said if he thought that was the case on Tuesday morning, he would vote for me to break the deadlock. Not the sort

---

Christian Zahra ALP member, McMillan 1998–2004

Kirsten Livermore ALP member, Capricornia 1998–

of guy you would want in the trenches next to you. Crean calls him a habitual liar, and I think that's right.

Julia Irwin—From the neighbouring seat of Fowler, representing the district in which I grew up. She voted for a Western Australian, rather than the local lad, which really put the hook in me. But then again, it was Irwin, the Dorrie Evans of Federal Parliament.

Michael Hatton—A Beazley voter who gave me this long conspiracy theory, claiming that 'Brereton decided to split the NSW Right to pick up votes from the Left. Very clever'. Very untrue, very bizarre. Hatton also blamed Laurie for the *Daily Telegraph* putting him on its front page as the type of bludging Labor MP that should retire. It is refreshing to know the *Tele* gets some things right. Hatton reflects the worst of our culture—obsessed with TA, wife on the payroll, a sandwich short of a picnic.

Sharan Burrow—Rang around all the Caucus women—a big Beazley weakness—calling me misogynist and threatening their preselections. She left Kelly Hoare crying in one of the corridors. I had to swallow hard to call her after the ballot and pledge a decent working relationship with the ACTU, if that's possible.

Stephen Loosley—Works as a Murdoch operative these days, so he rang Sharon Grierson to lobby for Beazley. This made her more determined to vote for me. Loosley was in Canberra on Tuesday as part of Beazley's 'transition team' but after the result became known, he was around knocking on my door, wanting to see me. As if I would let such an opportunist in my office. No snakes allowed.

A power of work to be done: rebuilding our policy culture, rebuilding Caucus solidarity, giving the show some hope and public appeal. Howard missed his chance of getting an election out of Simon. Gartrell tells me our internal polling is still very bad: 'We would have lost twenty or 30 seats if an election had been held in November. I kept on telling Simon, but he said the polling was wrong, he never believed it'.

At least I have made a decent start. Nervous as hell at Tuesday's press conference, but got through it with no mistakes. I could have started with a long shopping list of issues, but concluded that I was the issue. People would want to know who I am and what I stand for.

So I told them, branding my beliefs as 'the ladder of opportunity'. Plus I drew a line under my attack-dog role, promising no more crudity and a positive contribution to public debate. Followed up with a good MPI in the

---

Dorrie Evans A character in the 1970s TV show *Number 96*, famous as a gossip
Sharon Grierson ALP member, Newcastle 2001–

MPI Matter of Public Importance; a major debate in Parl. after Question Time

House on Thursday, explaining the different rungs on the ladder, and how Howard was taking them away. There was a great reception at the Victorian ALP Conference yesterday—you could feel the relief in the room that I was not Beazley.

Only two dark clouds. As expected, Gwyther is back. I got word on Tuesday night she was bagging me to journalists. So I rang her at around 10 p.m. to find out how far she was going to take it. Never again. It was a weird, weird conversation. She kept on saying, 'Oh darling, don't you worry about things; you have achieved what you wanted', talking as if we broke up five minutes ago. Without a doubt, the biggest mistake of my life and now, like all mistakes, a price will be paid.

I'm in a no-win situation. If I tell my side of the break-up, it will look like an undignified shit fight. I don't want that to be the public's first impression of my leadership. So best to play a straight bat and hope someone gives her the help she clearly needs. Abbott tried a personal attack in Thursday's MPI ('the scorned former mentor, the abandoned first wife, the bashed taxi-driver—a trail of human wreckage') but it seems to have backfired.

Mind you, Faulkner is convinced that Abbott and others will return to the well. He pulled me aside this morning for a chat after I had spoken to a candidates' seminar organised by NSW Head Office in Sydney: 'You wouldn't believe how dirty these Liberals can be. You are a threat to them now. They think you have a reputation and they will do everything to get you into strife—planting women to try and root you, hidden photographers, the works. It doesn't matter what happened in the past, the only thing that will get you into trouble is what you do as Leader of the Opposition. So promise me you'll be careful'.

He's got no worries. I couldn't be happier at home. And anyway, the only problem I've ever had with this sort of stuff came from our people, including John's mate, the Fat Indian.

Everyone has trouble in his or her personal life. Just look at Abbott. But people want their politicians to be constructive and to address the issues that matter. The real test of character is not what you did in the past, but how you deal with the allegations when they are thrown at you. If handled correctly, I might be able to turn Gwyther into a positive.

It didn't seem that way on Wednesday, however. Word came through that she had a shot at my mother on radio. Very upsetting. I went into a meeting with Rudd and lost it, broke down crying. Attack me, sure, but my mother hasn't done anything wrong. She used to defend her.

Rudd and I then had a good meeting with US Ambassador Tom Schieffer. It was an attempt to close down the Alliance issue; I tried to charm the Texan with my knowledge of Landslide Lyndon Johnson, after which we did a press conference in the Caucus room. Unbeknown to me, Malinda Wink from the press office thought it was a good idea to place an American flag behind the podium. I didn't notice it as I walked into the room, too busy concentrating on my notes, and only found out about it as I was walking out, when Rudd said, 'What was that American flag doing there?'

During the press conference, Dennis Shanahan from *The Australian* asked me: 'Mr Latham, aren't you just wrapping yourself in the American flag?' I fobbed him off. If he had asked why I was standing in front of an American flag, I would not have known what he was talking about. Disaster narrowly averted on day two of my leadership. Poor staff work can kill me in this new role.

A footnote to an amazing week. On Friday night I had dinner with Combet and Burrow in St Kilda, Melbourne. The unionists have to grovel a bit now. I said we had to modernise the ALP–union relationship, around what I call the four Ps:

- Pluralism—rebuilding our branch culture, getting trade unionists involved locally
- Partnership—Crean's concept of a 50/50 partnership on policy
- Participation—I'm not opposed to unionism *per se*, just the idea of six union secretaries sitting around a Chinese restaurant table planning the future for everyone else
- Personnel—if they want people like me to take unionism seriously, they need to give us better Senators and stop sending their rejects to Canberra.

Saturday, 13 December

A BBQ at home with Laurie and his wife Trish to celebrate our success and talk tactics for 2004. Danger surprised me by saying, 'This is a four-year

Landslide Lyndon Johnson Lyndon Johnson defeated Coke Stevenson by 87 votes out of a total of 988 295 votes cast in the 1948 Senatorial election in Texas, earning him the nickname Landslide Lyndon. The election was plagued by allegations of vote-rigging against the Johnson campaign. Schieffer knew Johnson as a young man in Texas and ran for elected office himself

Malinda Wink Worked in Simon Crean's press office and then came onto my staff
13 December A small point to assist the reader: in Dec. 2003, I decided to diarise the details of the new ALP frontbench in one entry, rather than stretch them over several entries.

campaign to make you Prime Minister'. Bullshit, I can beat Howard in one. The main thing is competence, showing people you can do the job. It stands you in good stead for the future, no matter what happens as Opposition Leader.

Still, I've got a lot to thank Laurie for. He and Crean were the keys to my victory. Danger is a cool and patient dude, he reads the play better than anyone else in the game. We haven't always been close—he was pretty edgy about me circa 1998—but now he's the man.

And Crean? I suppose his main motivation was to stop Beazley, his burning passion in life. Can't blame him, Beazley's betrayal of Crean still leaves me breathless. How does the Bomber get away with it? People are still writing him up as a decent loser (yet again), but he's one of the most indecent politicians I have come across.

Another good week, after I sorted out the new frontbench line-up. A lot of chopping and changing to get it finally sorted out. Last Saturday afternoon, Crean rang me to say that he wanted to be Shadow Treasurer. We had earlier agreed that he would play a backroom role: watch my back, liaise with the backbench and help out with parliamentary tactics. I had him slotted as Shadow Special Minister of State and Deputy Manager of Opposition Business, had planned to put McMullan back into Shadow Treasury, and Cox into Shadow Finance.

Simon had obviously been stewing on the McMullan factor: 'We can't let McMullan have it. He's hopeless and such a treacherous bastard. I want to step up and have a major role'. I couldn't say no, not after all his support for me and everything he had been through. After lecturing Caucus on loyalty, how could I dud the man who delivered the job to me? Keating wanted me to do the two jobs myself—Leader and Treasury, just like Chifley. That wasn't feasible, so I went with the loyalty option: Crean.

By and large, I wanted to keep the Shadows in their existing positions. We don't have time for major changes, with people having to learn new portfolios. If I make mistakes or the National Conference blows up next month, say, on the refugee issue, Howard will shoot for a March election.

So, minimal changes only in the final line-up. Stephen Smith back on the frontbench as a unity gesture and into Immigration. Let him sort out his mate Carmen on the refugees. Unite the Party. I can't win without uniting the Party—all other feelings must be put aside. I made Roxon the Shadow Attorney General and put McClelland into a consolidated Homeland Security position, as promised, even though I don't reckon I got

---

Bomber Nickname for Kim Beazley from his time as Defence Min. in Hawke govt

Carmen Lawrence Directly elected ALP Nat. Pres. 2003–04

his vote. I gave the hapless Kerry O'Brien Aboriginal Affairs, shifting my mate Gavan O'Connor back into Agriculture.

Gillard replaces me as the Manager of Opposition Business—my de facto deputy. The Deputy by title, Ms Macklin, put on one of her hissy fits about the reshuffle. I wanted Melham to assist her in the employment and training area but she said she was unwilling to work with him and went on strike. Lovely group of people on the Left—they hate each other more than they hate the Libs. In the end, I shifted Melham into Housing and Urban. A hiccup, however, compared to my Nightmare on Rudd Street.

Kevvie wanted his title expanded to the more grandiose Shadow Minister for Foreign Affairs and International Security. No worries, but then he rang me last Sunday to say he objected to McClelland also having the word 'Security' in his title. At first I thought it was some kind of joke, but the crazy bastard was serious: he had a long and absurd argument about the alleged overlap between the two jobs. I suggested he talk to McClelland, hoping to never hear from him again.

By the end of the day, Rudd was threatening to go to the backbench, over a question of semantics. I told him I was willing to accept his resignation and he went away to think about it. The ideal contingency plan was McMullan to Foreign Affairs and then I could save face with Coxie in Finance. Rudd called at about 11 p.m. and backed down, allowing the announcement to go ahead the next day.

Compared to that melodrama, the rest of the week was a breeze: quality visits to Tasmania, starting with Sidebottom's seat, Melbourne, Brisbane and Western Sydney. Excellent media. Even an attempted rapprochement with News Limited: dinner last Thursday at Azuma's in Sydney with John Hartigan, Campbell Reid (editor, *Daily Telegraph*) and Jeni Cooper (editor, *Sunday Telegraph*). Cooper and I once had a fling, so it was weird to see her in such a senior role—who would have thought?

Hartigan raised my joust with the Dancing Bears as 'an unacceptable attack on our people'. I tried to dismiss it as a bit of fun: 'Come on, they dish it out all the time, they must expect something in return; it was a bit of a hoot'. But Hartigan sat there po-faced, the arrogance of the Evil Empire on full display. I'm not backing down, so my rocky road with the Murdoch mob is not about to get any smoother.

Gavan O'Connor ALP member, Corio 1993– ; Shadow Agriculture Min. 2003–

Dancing Bears Name given to Right-wing journalists by the American author David Brock. I applied it to the News Limited columnists Piers Akerman, Andrew Bolt and Janet Albrechtsen

Friday, 19 December

The joy of starting a two-week break. Am off to Peppermint Grove Beach, south of Perth, with the boys, Janine and her family. A chance to draw breath and think about the election year ahead.

Yesterday I had coffee with Beazley in Perth. After the ballot, I offered him a spot on the frontbench, but he said he wasn't interested: 'That's it for me, that was my last shot. I'll just drift away from things now'. That's Beazley code for saying, I'll stay on the backbench to see if you fall flat on your face. Then Faulkner brokered something more realistic: Beazley will help organise a trip to the US for me next year, introduce me to his contacts, reassure the Americans and, in return, if we win the election, we'll make him Ambassador to the US.

He seemed pretty cheery about it over coffee, the old avuncular Beazley. Or, should I say, Ambassador Beazley—he likes the sound of it. Actually, I've put him on a pretty good wicket, much better than he deserves. If we win, he's an Ambassador, and if we lose, he'll have another run at the leadership. I'm a great one for honouring our former leaders, even the Calwell of our generation.

Silly Kim. If he hadn't destabilised Crean and stumbled into the first challenge, he would be Leader right now. All he had to do was wait and accept the call-up of a grateful Party as Simon fell over. For a military buff, especially an expert on the American Civil War, he forgot the advice of Ulysses S. Grant: 'The best man for the job does not go after the job. He waits to be called'.

After the early hiccups, the staff operation seems to be working better. There's not much I can do about it anyway. With the possibility of an early election, I have had to amalgamate my people with Crean's and hope for the best. Michael Cooney didn't feel up to the Chief of Staff position, so I have retained Mike Richards. He gave me one good tip: 'Remember, you have a megaphone in front of you'. Meaning, I don't need to strive so hard to be heard in the media. I think it will work out okay.

My last appointment for the year: a get-to-know you chat yesterday afternoon with the new editor of *The West Australian* newspaper, Paul Armstrong. Well, that's what I thought it would be. But then he turned up with two reporters with notepads and started to badger me about our refugee policy. He tried to turn a polite coffee into a full-on interview, so I couldn't get out of there fast enough.

Ulysses S. Grant General-in-Chief during the American Civil War; US Pres. 1869–77

Mike Richards Simon Crean's Chief of Staff 2003, who continued in that role in my office

But not before the greenhorn gave a lecture in self-importance: 'I can make or break the Western Australian Government, just as I can make or break the Opposition Leader, Colin Barnett, if I choose to'. Well, bully for you. But if he wants to be a politician he should actually put his name on the voting paper. We'll hear more about this guy one day, and it won't be pretty. A suitably surreal way in which to finish off an amazing year of politics.

2004
Pre-election

Publicly this is the best known period of my parliamentary career: the early success of my Labor leadership, the Howard Government's political fight-back after the May Budget, the six-week election campaign, our election defeat on 9 October, the recriminations within the ALP after the loss, and finally, my resignation from Parliament in January 2005. Privately, there were many other issues and considerations that influenced my actions during this period. The Diaries *tell this story. For me it is the most important and powerful part of the book.*

The best summary of what happened in 2004 I can offer is this: I became increasingly disillusioned with the major institutions I had to deal with—the media, the machine culture of the ALP and the prospects of meaningful parliamentary reform in Australia—and was shattered by the impact of work on my health, privacy and family life. My career had come full circle, and I returned to the conclusions I reached in 1999–2000 about the futility of Labor politics. This time, when an opportunity arose to leave the Labor Party behind, I took it.

In the flurry of media speculation about the politics of 2004, the personal side of my experience has never been presented. I kept it to myself, my family and my diary. As the year progressed, the diary became an important outlet for recording the irreconcilable tension between work and family life. The lesson for those who write about political events is this: never underestimate the impact of private factors and emotions on public figures. When confronted by a choice between realising my political ambitions and meeting my personal responsibility to those I love and care for, I chose the latter.

Throughout this hectic period, I maintained a regular series of diary entries except during the election campaign. This was a time-management issue: I was too busy studying policy documents at night and preparing for the next day's campaign to write up detailed diary material. I did, however, keep notes, and as soon as the campaign ended, I recorded lengthy entries dealing with this major event. I had a clear and vivid recollection of what had just occurred, so I felt comfortable with this process. Readers will find this campaign record in mid-October.

Sunday, 4 January

The end of my break, not that I relaxed too much. Spent my holiday thinking of ways to beat Howard. The excitement of getting this job has abated. Now it's down to the nervous reality of wondering if I can do it well, if I can handle an election year.

It's a huge task. We have spent two years arguing about the leadership instead of working on policy and fighting the Libs full on. There are six things I'll need to do to get the Party back on its feet:

- answer the Walsh dilemma. We need to develop a strong and appealing identity for modern Labor. That's the Ladder of Opportunity—the powerful combination of hard work, good families and communities, and the civilising role of government. I've got to energise the Labor movement after the bad experiences with flip-flop Beazley and Crean destabilisation
- unify the Party, try to put Humpty Dumpty back together again. My offers to Smith and Beazley have eased the tension. I want to bring Carmen back to the frontbench, providing this refugee thing goes okay at the National Conference. I can't afford to be rolled by the Left, allowing them to water down our policy. So many grievances and rival-ries inside our show; managing them will be the hardest part of the job
- get us back into the values debate. Policy releases are important, not just for their technical detail, but for the values they convey to the electorate. Everything I put out must be underpinned by the right kind of Labor values: opportunity for all, aspiration and social mobility, mutual responsibility (hard work), community-building (mutualism) and public participation (reinventing democracy)
- emphasise our credentials on service delivery, remind the electorate that we're the party of good schools, good health services, practical

things that make a positive difference in people's lives. No more looking at policy as an abstract exercise in ideological correctness

- overcome Howard's wedge, and anticipate any new wedge issues he may throw at us. No more crouching in the grass. Plus redefine the symbolic issues of the Left in terms of traditional Labor values. We want the children out of detention centres, not because of UN Conventions, but because we care for children, and they deserve a better life. We want to say sorry to the Stolen Generations, not because of indigenous rights, but because of family values. We want to treat same-sex couples fairly, not because of their sexuality, but because they love and care for each other. It's about good values

- wrong-foot Howard by raising new issues, setting the agenda. It'll be up to me to do it. He had a fix on Beazley and Crean—he knew where they were coming from. My values and policy priorities are different. He's never heard a Labor Leader talk about democratic reform, community-building and mutual responsibility. I'll need to test him in the first week of Parliament by attacking the Club—put forward the abolition of the rorted superannuation scheme. It's a time bomb in his lap.

Saw the enemy today in the Trust Box at the SCG for Australia versus India, Steve Waugh's last test. Howard looked constipated as usual—he always has that worried look on his face. His wife, however, seems a nice lady. She gets a bum rap in the media, from what I saw today. Friendly, motherly—why do our people complain about her all the time? I like to take people as I find them.

I had a burst of guest commentary on ABC Radio, organised by Faulkner. It's the world's best job: great view of the ground, chat away about the game, food and grog laid on, and you get paid for it. In my next life I want to come back as the Skull, Kerry O'Keeffe.

The Trust Box is a hoot, presided over by Lord Rodney Cavalier. He attacks the Federal ALP and the corrupt patronage of the factions, but never says boo about State Labor. It's not hard to see why: Carr has given him this sinecure at the cricket, one of the plum jobs inside the system. And he loves to lord it over the assembled guests: a combination of ex-sporting heroes, business donors and political hangers-on, all enjoying the largesse with their nosebags on.

Cavalier is Labor in theory but elitist in practice—a modern Labor trend, common in the likes of Carr, Jones, Evans and Rudd. Give me

Kerry O'Keeffe Former Australian Test legspinner, now cricket commentator | **Rodney Cavalier** Chairman, SCG Trust

Curtin/Chifley-style austerity any day. In fact, give me the SCG Hill any day: a much better day last year tarry-hooting with the Bulls. Better cricket and better company.

Wednesday, 7 January

I moved into my new office in Parliament House yesterday. Since the building opened, it has been occupied by Howard, Peacock, Hewson, Downer, Howard (again), Beazley and Crean—just one happy story out of seven. I said to the staff that the whole purpose of moving into this office is to get out as quickly as possible.

Pulled together my inner circle today for a planning meeting: Gartrell, Faulkner and Brereton, plus senior staff. The Shadow Ministry is too big to get things done, so I need this group as a sounding board. They were warned that all our discussions must be kept confidential; the first time it leaks is the last time it meets. I gave them my strategic agenda:

- The positive candidate always wins. The electorate doesn't hate Howard, so negativity will not work. We need to add value to the debate, encourage people to move past Howard to a better way of running the country. Push the need for generational change.
- The new generation candidate needs to move the agenda forward; campaigns work best when they use ideas to advance the thinking of the electorate. So I have to get off the blocks with a flurry of policy announcements.
- Pursue the politics of personal connection—triangulate beyond Left and Right, using values and instincts to make personal connections with the electorate. My bible is a great article by David Winston in *Policy Review* (June 1999): 'Triangulation is not an exercise in claiming the ideological middle ground. It is a strategy that rejects ideological points of view altogether, concentrating instead on making a connection with people'. Like Clinton in 1992: a caring populist.
- We need mobility: we have to shift the agenda to our social policy strengths and get out of Howard's firing line on the economy and national security. If we campaign on his strengths we will get a Crean-like result.
- Use policies/issues as a way of conveying values. The logic of my approach is this: values—problems—solutions (in the national interest).

That's the strategy, my best thinking for beating Howard. There are six themes that go with it:

- the Ladder of Opportunity, conveying values of opportunity, responsibility and hard work
- a Big Country: Labor as the party of the fair go that reaches out to people. We are the enlargers of public life, the true patriots. We must communicate the rights agenda in terms of traditional Labor values
- the Economy: prosperity with a sound social purpose. A Labor government will do more to create/maintain our prosperity, and create a second generation of economic reform. Plus fiscal responsibility: get our savings cycle ahead of our spending cycle, with all policies fully costed and fully funded. I want a bigger budget surplus than the Government
- National Security: standing up for Australia, putting the safety of our people first, unlike Howard's adventurism overseas. A defence-of-Australia strategy
- Community: work to solve social problems. Conveying values of trust, solidarity and cooperation—Australians sticking together. New issues that Howard hasn't thought about
- the New Politics: openness, public participation, ethics, standards. Labor is for the people, not the powerful. Campaign as an outsider against the insiders' Club in Canberra.

The meeting had no problems with any of that. They looked relieved that I had a plan. In fact, that the Party has a Leader who actually plans ahead. Beazley just meandered along while Simon buried himself in detail and process. We agreed that the best way of handling the next four months, up to the Budget, is to think about it as two different phases:

- from January to the end of the first sitting fortnight (22 February)—milk any honeymoon effect, and the burst of media coverage, plus release policies in each of the six thematic areas to show my values/instincts to the public. A flurry of activity built around the National Conference
- from 22 February till the Budget (11 May)—consolidate on phase one, building a steady and competent profile, showing people I am up to the job. Set the agenda and then ease back, bedding down the policy announcements.

Sunday, 1 February

How good is this? A magnificent Sydney Sunday, strolling through Darling Harbour with Janine and the boys, the *Sun Herald* headlining 'Book Mark' on its front page, a successful ALP National Conference behind me. So far, it's been too easy. Things are going 95 per cent to plan; only a couple of hiccups.

Easy media coverage for re-announcing policies in January: BAS simplification, childhood obesity, an Australian coastguard (a cop on the beat), Medicare teams to save bulk billing and the responsibilities of citizenship on Australia Day. When Simon first announced this stuff, nobody noticed. I put them out during a quiet time and they led the news. Money for jam.

The Conference started on Thursday with my opening address. Nervous all morning; calmed myself by thinking about Ollie and his *Lion King* characters. The speech rolled out my Third Way themes: a positive party, opportunity matched by responsibility, responsive and flexible service delivery, rebuilding social capital, opening up our democracy, and economic policies based on competition, incentive and budget savings. A good summary of my work over the past five years.

Another olive branch to those who were bagging me: I announced Tanner's new role as the Shadow Minister for Community Relationships. I want him to lead the charge on social capital, find new solutions to the problems of loneliness, work stress and community breakdown, starting with a national mentoring program. The next step is to bring back Carmen and put her in charge of the reinventing democracy agenda. It's worked inside the Party: our first directly elected National President. So it can work more generally in the parliamentary system.

Good policy announcements the other two days of Conference: a national dental program and a national reading program, early childhood education as the foundation of lifelong learning. That's today's newspaper headline: 'Book Mark', sensational stuff. Cameo appearances by Neville Smith (mentoring) and Mem Fox (reading aloud) to reinforce our policy themes. It's hard to believe—we are still shaking our heads—but I was the Lion King of this show.

The Party even handled the refugee debate okay, the Left doing what it does best: going through the motions of defeat. I announced a new policy position ahead of the Conference last Friday week—a tougher stance on people smugglers, but a softer stance on TPVs. We caught Howard on the hop and he was slow to attack it. It also took the sting out of

---

Mem Fox Australian children's author and advocate of reading aloud to infant children

the Conference debate. An important lesson: try to do the unorthodox with Howard—he's in the groove, expecting old Labor stoushes and policies. I've got a dozen things in my kitbag that can surprise him.

So, what about the hiccups? It's never too hard to guess who's trying to spike my success:

- Roozendaal leaked my announcement on banning donations to the Party from Big Tobacco, dulling its impact on the first day of the Conference. He will never change: more interested in donations to the Party than Labor values
- Carr bullshitted to the media, saying that his Government had not been consulted about the new policy on Sydney's second airport— sending it to the Southern Highlands. We had extensive talks with Knowles and his office; they helped us define the study area for the new site. Craig tells me Bob knew about this but is just being Bob, making trouble for me. His DNA is programmed for revenge, even at the start of a Federal election year
- One of the business lobby groups in Canberra played computer games with its copy of my opening speech, decoding the various drafts and changes to it, and then gave them to Costello's office. Sloppy staff work at our end, it was sent out in the wrong format. No lasting harm from Costello's quasi-attack, just a nuisance distraction. But a sign of where these business groups line up: acting as research assistants and agents of the Liberal Party. One for the memory bank.

Friday, 6 February

Has my easy run come to an end? I'm sitting in the lounge of Coolangatta Airport (plane delayed) watching the usually unflappable Faulkner get worked up about a political problem. He's on the phone to Lincoln Wright from News Limited trying to talk down the significance of the Liverpool preselection. Wright is investigating it for an exposé in the Sunday papers, based on material fed to him by some of the old enemies inside the Party. One of those horrible moments in politics when your fate is entirely in the hands of others.

Fifteen years ago when it happened, John wanted to fry me politically. It was a classic Left versus Right factional stoush, and he was leading the charge for the Left. Now he's doing the right thing, blaming everything on Head Office. He says that 'I'm doing everything I can to keep this quiet'. At last, he's on my side of the controversy. I can't remember the details, it is so long ago, but John seems to know the story chapter and verse. Machine politics at work in the late 1980s.

Faulkner is so anxious, almost obsessive, that I'm starting to shit myself. He says he doesn't think Wright could be so dumb as to miss the significance of this. I was the beneficiary of the Head Office rorts, with dozens of Party members rubbed out of the ballot. Some big Labor names were involved, people who have gone on to be Federal and State front-benchers, making it a pretty big story now that I'm Leader of the Party. That's why the enemies have leaked it. I had a feeling that things were going too well, that something had to go wrong. This is it.

Sunday, 8 February

Massive relief. It's unbelievable: Lincoln Wright has concentrated on the same old rubbish from the big-noter Frank Heyhoe, relegating the Liverpool preselection to a secondary issue in his story. How good is that? There must be a god and he votes Labor. The journalist's name is not Lincoln Wright, it's Lincoln Wrong. Now I can think clearly again.

Last week looks so much better. We did a bus trip from the Central Coast to Tweed Heads, via Tamworth and Lismore. Three excellent community forums, attendances of around 500 at each—democracy in the raw. Good media coverage, especially compared with Howard's bumbling efforts in Perth, the Seniors' Tour.

Lismore was the highlight. Tony Wright turned up, looking very relaxed and comfortable, boasting about his visit to Nimbin. What's with that guy? He's a social Leftie who idolises Howard. After dinner I dropped in at the local pub, only to be confronted by a mad Indian chief who presented me with a leather scrotum bag. He said he wanted to put my remaining testicle in it. The pub security kept an eye on him while I got out of there. The world has gone mad and I'm in the middle of it, freaked out by Wright, Wrong and Sitting Bull. The whole thing is so crazy all I can do is laugh.

Back in Canberra tonight. Parliament starts on Tuesday. I'm going to roll this parliamentary super bomb down the aisle and watch the Club panic. Crean and Sherry were going to do it last year—close the scheme to new entrants and put new MPs on the community standard—but then Simon got pole-axed. They are still onside, along with Macklin, Faulkner and Danger, so I've got some good back-up to fight the Entitlements Club.

Earlier today Conroy told me that 'This will be a disaster politically. It won't work for you. In fact, it will rebound on the Party'. What planet is that guy from? First he wrecks Beazley's Budget Reply by saying tax increases are on the agenda. Then he tries to convince Crean to support the war in Iraq. Now he's telling me that attacking Public Enemy Number One, the parliamentary super scheme, will be a disaster.

He's part of the Entitlements Club—following the unwritten rule in Parliament House that we all stay silent about the squirreling away of money and benefits for MPs. It's a cross-party deal, threatened only by the likes of Ted Mack and Peter Andren. And now me, a major party leader who'll bust the Club wide open, shake the squirrels out of their tree. You beauty, I can't wait to see the look on the faces of the Caucus Club members: Marn, McLeay, Hatton, Campbell, Ripoll, Bevis, Price, Sciacca, etc.

Friday, 13 February

Last night Howard folded on parliamentary super. The Club has been routed. He only held the line for two days, giving Abbott and Costello enough time to attack me. Now they look like idiots. Abbott is a Howard acolyte and will cop it sweet, but Costello must be beside himself with anger. Trouble in paradise, it seems.

If nothing else, I can tell my grandchildren I achieved one thing in this job: that I got legislation through to end that rotten rort of a scheme. There are some issues where the weight of public opinion is so great that the Club cannot hold out. Howard would have been mad to persist—I would have hammered him every day until polling day.

A big lesson here for the Party. After eight years in Opposition we are back in the business of getting legislation passed by Parliament. Because we had a go and set the agenda. We got off our lard arses and did something that was popular but also consistent with Labor values—Curtin/Chifley-style austerity. This is the way to beat Howard. Follow the advice of the Great Gretzky: always skate to where the puck is going, not where it's been. And remember: statistically, 100 per cent of the shots you don't take don't go in.

A good meeting this morning with Gillard's health experts, Stephen Duckett and Hal Swerissen. We have worked out a way of dealing with the despised private health insurance rebate. We need to kill it slowly; adopt the strategy Howard and Wooldridge used for their attack on Medicare, dismantling it slice by slice.

If the Federal Government takes over the public and private health insurance costs of senior Australians (say, 70 years and above), it can make

---

Ted Mack Independent member, North Sydney 1990–96
Peter Andren Independent member, Calare 1996–
Tony Abbott Health Min. 2003–
Wayne Gretzky Canadian ice-hockey player in the 1980s and 1990s; the Don Bradman of ice hockey

Stephen Duckett Former head of health dept in Keating govt; health policy academic, La Trobe University
Hal Swerissen Health policy academic, La Trobe University
Michael Wooldridge Lib. member, Chisolm 1987–98; Casey 1998–2001; Health Min. 1996–2001

significant savings on the cost of the rebate—an electorally appealing policy that partially pays for itself. This would also be a significant move towards the integration of the public and private health systems in Australia, taking Labor policy closer to the Scotton model. The health economists are going to crunch the numbers/costings and see how they look.

I like Gillard because she has a go. She's the opposite of white bread: feisty, irreverent, good sense of humour, the closest thing we have to charisma in Caucus. Not afraid of policy innovation but also steady and sensible. Look at the way she has walked into the MOB role, the first woman to handle this traditional machine man job in the House. Good humour: she calls Faulkner the Governor-General for the way in which he straddles the sub-factions in the Left. There is something vice-regal about John, the way he presides over Party affairs without going too far into the muck. The perfect nickname.

Wednesday, 18 February

Phase one has gone superbly; my first couple of months in this job couldn't be better. Topped it off today with a speech to the National Press Club, setting out my vision of society. The political system is missing the point. The Right argues for more market forces; the Left wants more government intervention. The people themselves want more society, a new sense of belonging, a new set of social relationships.

My speech was 100 per cent positive—no whingeing about the Government, the traditional curse of Opposition Leaders. It was a synthesis of all my work on social capital: the importance of localism, government as a facilitator/enabler, the devolution of service delivery, a communitarian approach to policy-making (a civic conversation), refocusing IR policy onto the employee–family relationship. Plus Tanner's agenda: addressing the crisis in masculinity, the critical need for mentoring.

If we get into government this is the most important thing we can do for the country: rebuild trust and confidence between Australians, overcome social problems and re-establish the basis of a mutual society. I want to attack poverty and create new opportunities for people, but to do that I need the electorate to be comfortable with helping the disadvantaged. These days, most people don't even talk to their next-door neighbour, let alone reach out to the poor. Overcoming downward envy is a precondition for social justice.

Phase one could not have worked better politically. Personally, however, I feel like shit. The time away from the boys is killing me. The most important part of the speech is the bit I wrote for myself, as a way of getting it out of my system:

> In my own circumstances at home, Janine and I have a non-stop dialogue about work and family. How to turn her legal qualifications into a legal career, how to juggle my new responsibilities against time at home, how to organise childcare for the boys and then how to make all this happen ... I've got to confess, as someone who feels a bit guilty about not seeing enough of my own children, I'm increasingly envious of parents [who stay] at home. They have the wonderful opportunity in life of turning quantity time into quality time with their children.
>
> Women in our society have traditionally taken this role, but I'd expect in the future we're going to have many more stay-at-home dads in Australia. This is an important part of rebuilding male identity, recognising the significance of fatherhood. And big boofy blokes like me, traditionally our role has been based on muscle power and our dominance in the workforce. That's what it used to be, but with changes in technology, many men are calling out for new sources of identity and self-esteem.
>
> Fatherhood, the role of parenting, is absolutely vital in making that transition. And I trust that working men, those of us in the workforce, can understand this new role and, in our friendships and peer groups, give stay-at-home dads as much support and recognition as possible.

As I delivered those words, I wanted to yell out, 'Yes, folks, we need to honour the home-dads. And I'm getting out of here right now to become one. Goodbye and good riddance'. I've got to win this bloody thing. Getting into the Lodge is our work and family solution, the only one I can think of. Otherwise I'm not going to last in this job. I know one thing for sure: I'm not going to be a long-term Opposition Leader.

Friday, 5 March

Lunch with John Laws at his swank Otto's in Woolloomooloo. Never had much to do with this guy, whom Keating describes as 'a fully paid-up member of the white-shoe brigade'. He's certainly got very traditional views about society and gender issues in particular. Lunch was his idea, an attempt to get me to raise matters in Parliament about his radio rival, Alan Jones; the head of the ABA, David Flint; and Howard.

It's a very Sydney story—all about networking, media influence, and who's running the show. This is what these media celebrities are really on about: lots of gossip, and how to fix up their rivals in the ratings and ego stakes. I was fairly cautious about his claims—I won't be raising them in Parliament—but it was fascinating to hear him out. I told him I have had a decent run off Jones, going back to Liverpool Council days. Laws reckons that will change as the election gets closer and he shows his true political colours.

Laws also has it in for Howard big time—nothing wrong with that— and is backing Costello for the Liberal leadership. Another characteristic of media celebrities: they are political players—the great luxury in life of having their opinions aired every day, and exercising public influence, all without having to do the grinding, tedious work of a practising politician.

A very Sydney end to the lunch as well. As I was walking back to my car, a newspaper photographer arrived, five minutes too late to catch me and Laws at our table. I suppose that's part of the game: being dobbed in and then photographed for some pathetic gossip column—the haven of lost and lonely media consumers, just like talkback radio itself.

Thursday, 11 March

Three dinners and a stalking incident. Just another regulation week in the job. Dinner number one last Monday night: Richards and I trekked out to Cavan (took forever to get there from Parliament House) to meet with Lachlan Murdoch and John Hartigan. They wanted a 'get-to-know-you' opportunity, so the Evil Empire must think I have a chance. No harm in turning up to see what they are up to.

Paul Kelly was right about this duo: lacklustre and overrated. Most of the conversation was about children and footy, the pitfalls of Super League and their bum investment in the game. Two main political issues: AWAs and Foxtel. Murdoch's company has the highest number of AWAs in the country; all their journalists are on individual contracts. Hartigan pressed hard for me to drop our policy dedicated to their abolition, but I told him there was no chance of that.

Murdoch was laidback about our plan to sell Telstra's share in Foxtel, saying that either way, it made little difference to them commercially. I tried to pump him on the state of his relationship with the Packers, the other stakeholder in Foxtel, but he didn't give much away. A neutral sort of night, like the Azuma's dinner in December, though there is something

---

Cavan Murdoch homestead and estate west of Canberra

about Hartigan I can't cop. When push comes to shove, these blokes will back the Right-wing candidate. I have nothing to offer them.

Dinner number two on Tuesday night: Paul Kelly at the outdoor Japanese café in Green Square, Kingston. Still dismissive about Murdoch and Hartigan—does he talk like this to other people? Surely he would lose his job if they knew, but maybe he's at a stage in his career where he doesn't care. No dazzling insights from the Professor. He reflects the media consensus: Howard seems rattled, I'm enjoying an extended honeymoon.

That's what Newspoll is showing, a big turnaround. When I took over, the Coalition was on 44 per cent and we were on 35, a 2PP of 53/47 the Government's way. This week they are on 41 and we are on 44, a 2PP of 45/55 our way. Crean's last approval rating was 22 per cent, with 56 disapproval. My numbers have built up since December, now at 62 per cent approval and 17 disapproval—the big undecided group has broken my way. On preferred Prime Minister, Crean trailed Howard 65/14. I've narrowed the gap to 44/39.

My line to Kelly: this thing will be an arm-wrestle. I may be on top now, but Howard will come back, I'll have to counter and so on, up and down until polling day. It's more than a line—instinctively, this is my strong feeling. Howard will find a way of shifting the agenda back onto the economy and national security. A bomb will go off, something will happen.

Kelly agreed with this assessment, curious about how I plan to handle the economic debate. The same as my plan as Shadow Treasurer: roll out a new reform agenda, emphasise our fiscal rigour versus waste and mismanagement by the Government, and point to clouds on the horizon. Realistically, we have to hope that people have put their prosperity in their pocket and go for my 'prosperity with a purpose' agenda. The only way forward I can see.

The important thing is for me to stay positive—that's why my numbers are so high: no whingeing—and stick to the various phases of my plan. I let slip to Kelly that I had a plan and he almost jumped out of his chair trying to find out what it was. I told him to watch this space, and went to fetch some more sushi.

Dinner number three: my old China plate, Bob Carr, along with Knowles, Brereton and Faulkner in Carr's office earlier tonight. Bob came at me, gushing about my success so far, especially the superannuation triumph over Howard: 'You've proven your policy credentials. You don't have to do any more, you can just sit there'. If only it were that simple. Bob's motto: if in doubt, do nothing. Mine: attack, attack, attack. That's the difference between a State conservative and a Federal radical. Anyway, it was nice of him to say it.

The purpose of our gathering was to attack the poor quality of Labor Caucus by injecting new talent, starting with Faulkner's protégé, Peter Garrett. I had lunch with the legend at his Mittagong home the day before Australia Day. My conclusion? Simply outstanding: charismatic, humane, full of ideas, dedicated to his gorgeous family, took a real interest in Ollie. I felt like giving him my seat. So much better than the union hacks and branch-stackers promoted by Sussex Street. Carr agrees: 'We must have this man in Parliament'.

Our target is Cunningham. It's close to Peter's home, and we'll out-green the Greens to win back the seat. Sharon Bird has the preselection at the moment, but after her bruising loss in the by-election she can't be too keen. A simple plan: Carr will talk to Roozendaal, Bird will get the vacancy for the NSW Upper House, Garrett will get Cunningham, and my environmental credentials will be secure.

A fine night's work, so now we can move onto Faulkner's next super-star recruit: Steve Waugh. John is sure he's interested—spoke to him about it during his trip to the West Indies last year. The seat is obvious: replace the log Hatton in Blaxland. A Bankstown boy with ability, we have always done well out of those. In fact, John regards him as a future Party Leader—a huge rap. Also some chance that Kerryn Phelps might run as our candidate in Wentworth.

And the stalker? I went for a jog at 6.15 this morning from my unit in Queanbeyan. I went round the corner and two guys pulled up in a car. Then they jumped out in the semi-darkness, looking menacing. I thought to myself, 'Bloody hell, not another taxi-driver incident. These bastards are here to roll me and I'll have to fight back. Why does this always happen to me?'

Turns out they were from the *Daily Telegraph*. Luke McIlveen and a photographer wanted to do a story on my exercise habits. The silly bastards staked out my unit—who knows how long they had been sitting out there in their car? I bolted down the road, leading the photographer on a merry chase. When I got back to the unit, they were waiting outside, so I told them to pull their heads in. Seriously, what does it say about two young men sitting in the darkness outside another guy's place? They should be out having a good time. Journalism is just a fancy name for voyeurism.

Why the interest in my exercise habits? Last Sunday I scrubbed up pretty poorly for the Labor versus Press Gallery cricket match. No spare time in this job, bad diet and I've put on some pud. Too much media

---

Peter Garrett Lead singer, Midnight Oil; head of Australian Conservation Foundation

Kerryn Phelps Former AMA head; prominent media health commentator

interest in how I looked. Matt Price wrote a man-boobs story that seems to have caught on. A real good bloke: I lose a testicle to cancer and he ends up writing about man-boobs. Lesson in life: if a journalist makes out he is your mate, he is lying to you.

Sunday, 14 March

Trying to have a quiet weekend but, in practice, there is no escape. At Jody's this morning, I read yesterday's profile in the *Age*. They have had three journalists looking into my past for months, but have come up with next to nothing. Gwyther is all over the article, inventing stuff, exaggerating things. If I was a private citizen I would sue her, but that is not an option in this job.

I give up on the Gwyther front. The Knowles family preselected her on the South Ward ticket for the Liverpool Council election, but here she is, trying to spear the Party's Leader. Nothing will ever shut her up, short of my responding in kind. It's the last thing I need, so I'll have to grin and bear it.

Lunch at Bob Hawke and Blanche's place: a multi-storey mansion on Middle Harbour with a separate unit/meeting space down below on the water. Hawke offered this to me for 'secret meetings—you can come in here on a water taxi'. He must think I'm James Bond or something. I politely declined his offer.

An amiable enough lunch and conversation, more workman-like than warm. These two are tightly focused on money, far more than Janine and me. I suppose you don't end up in a posh joint like this otherwise. I kept on thinking about Chifley's house in Bathurst and Curtin's in Cottesloe. Yes, we have changed too much as a Party. Maybe I'm the odd man out these days, but I dislike wealth on this scale.

Hawke was a legend when I first joined the Party 25 years ago. Is this why it is so hard to have a normal conversation with him? I can't stop grinning when I look at him, thinking of the great story Ralph Willis tells from the early 1970s. Ralph was a research officer at the ACTU and Hawke was President. One day an announcement came through at around lunchtime that Hawke was Australia's Father of the Year, so Bob grabbed his mates and went to the pub to celebrate.

Ten hours later it was Ralph's job to haul him out of the pub, get him into a car and take him home. Ralph dropped him, full as a boot, on the doorstep as Hazel came out the front and gave him both barrels, calling him every name under the sun. Ralph drove away thinking to himself, 'There's Australia's Father of the Year'.

Jody Latham My sister

The Party has glorified Hawke's alcoholism and womanising but, in its day, it must have been horrendous for his family. I can laugh at the Willis story because I wasn't there, but imagine being Hazel—the true hero of the Hawke years.

All up, a strangely ambivalent day, memories of my first wife and Hawke's. What can you do about it: history is fixed in concrete. Bob and Blanche, what a combination. As Janine and I left, the masseur was arriving for their afternoon session—a good time to get out of there.

Friday, 19 March

I'm pushing things too hard, trying to do too much. This is when mistakes creep in, the errors that can wreck everything. That's what happened this week. I won't survive if it happens again.

Three speeches on Monday: the MUA National Conference in the morning, the launch of our superannuation policy at lunchtime, and then a BCA dinner. Too many. The super policy was spoiled by a stuff-up on the indexation measure for aged pensions. We were confirming the existing arrangements, 25 per cent of male total average weekly earnings, so it didn't even need to be in the document or my speech. Sloppy, sloppy work by Sherry and his staffer. I also need to put a rocket up Cooney: the preparation of the material last week was policy by chaos theory.

Hit the media on Tuesday morning to sell the super policy. It was going well, but then in the afternoon, Glenn told me about the mistake. I was at Sydney Airport on the way to Tasmania. I needed to sit down to deal with the horror of it. This is the thing that worries me most: basic errors. Not too much damage on the TV news: Janine says that Oakes is the only one who ran hard. That would be right, I never get a break from Jabba the Hutt, that's a given in this job.

I saw Sherry on Tuesday night at Michelle O'Byrne's fundraiser in Launceston. He looked rooted. His wife Sally said to me, 'Please don't go mad on him, he feels bad enough as it is'. Not hard to know what she was talking about, so I tried to cheer him up, as much as that was possible. You can only feel sorry for him, I suppose.

Spent Wednesday and Thursday looking at trees. Not normally my scene, but this is what the New Politics is about: opening up issues for a public dialogue, examining the facts, trying to find points of common interest. I suspect the communitarian textbook may have met its match,

---

Michael Cooney Dir. of Policy in my office 2003–05
Glenn Byres My Press Sec. 2003–05

Michelle O'Byrne ALP member, Bass 1998–2004

however, on the preservation of the Tasmanian forests. There's a bit of bull-shit on both sides of the argument.

The industry people have got a lot of pull with the Tasmanian Government. Maybe Gunns is the new Hydro—no goodwill to the environmentalists whatsoever. The BBQ on Wednesday night was a hate session on the Greens, led by Barry Chipman. But the industry itself looks archaic. Visited the Gunns veneer plant at Boyer and it was like stepping back in time: the industrial archaeology of old machines and old workers. No future there.

Earlier in the day, they took me to the Franklin Wooden Boat Centre, where I ran into Matthew Romalis from Hurlstone days. A good guy who had the best view of anyone I spoke to. He said that value-adding is the key: supporting the timber artisans who respect the resource, producing quality products and jobs while harvesting less timber. His final message: 'Protect the trees'. This was someone the industry took me to see.

But which trees? On Thursday, Bob Brown took me on a helicopter trip over the Styx Valley, a patchwork quilt of giant old trees, logged coups, plantation and regrowth. Five out of ten: only the North Styx is worth protecting. Then we went over the neighbouring Valley of the Giants, which was truly magnificent, one of the greatest things I have ever seen. Ten out of ten. And it's already fully protected. It's not clear to me what assessments have been made of the different areas around the State and the conservation arguments. Claim versus counter-claim.

The flight with Brown followed a walk through part of the Styx, accompanied by a bevy of media, including the detestable Price. Embarrassing stuff: I had to keep my opinions to myself, otherwise the media would have been concocting headlines about our policy position. This visit was supposed to be about process, not outcomes. Great endorsement by Brown at the end of the day: 'The Prime Minister in waiting'. Green preferences looking good, not because he loves me, but because he despises Howard.

Dick Adams has to eat his words. When I announced that I was accepting Brown's invitation to look at the Styx, Dick said that I couldn't trust him, that Brown would do me in. In fact, Adams threatened to blockade my entry to the forests. The Big Tasmanian has gone crackers: too close to Gunns, driven by bile and hatred of the Greens, instead of a rational assessment of the issue.

Gunns is the new Hydro Before the Franklin Dam controversy in the early 1980s the Hydroelectricity Commission in Tas. was prominent in determining State govt policy; Gunns is the largest timber company in Tas.

Barry Chipman Tas. Coordinator of Timber Communities Australia
Matthew Romalis I went to school at Hurlstone, and Matthew was in my year
Dick Adams ALP member, Lyons 1993– ; nicknamed 'The Big Tasmanian'

Hard to get a handle on Paul Lennon, a cold and dogmatic character, reminds me of the pro-development mayors I used to see in local government. Obviously quite close to the industry, but says he can give some ground on issues like the phasing out of clear-felling. I need to get further concessions out of him to find a way through the middle of this issue.

Tuesday, 23 March

Just put the little fellas to bed, reading books, hugs and kisses. But this is a sitting day. That's right, I've had enough. Told Alison to clear the diary and drove home after Question Time to spend the evening with Janine, the boys and Mum. Time away from home is killing me inside.

I flicked through my quote book on the weekend and found one that applies to me. Barbara Tuchman in *The March of Folly*: 'Government remains the paramount area of folly because it is there that men seek power over others, only to lose it over themselves'.

That's me. I've lost the power to have a normal life with the people I love and respect. So I got up and drove home to be with them. Power and control in my hands for one night. Feels better, even if I have to go back to that place tomorrow.

Wednesday, 24 March

Away for one night and there is a new crisis to manage: a raging argument between Rudd and Cooney about placing caveats on our commitment to get the troops out of Iraq. Rudd, the king of the caveats. He gave them to Simon and now he wants to give them to me. He sounds incomprehensible in the media whenever he talks about Iraq, so I needed to firm up our rhetoric and avoid the mistakes of twelve months ago.

Initially, Rudd wanted our policy on the troops to be a review when we get into government. Imagine the pounding we would have taken on such a wishy-washy stance, so I overruled him and said yesterday that we wanted them home by Christmas. I've had a firm position on every other issue and it's worked for me; why not this one?

Now Rudd is at it again, arguing that we should keep the troops in Iraq if the UN takes over the show. But Cooney is right: 'If you use the UN as an escape clause, you will look as indecisive as Crean or, even worse, Beazley'.

Paul Lennon Tas. ALP Premier 2004–
Alison Byrnes Personal assistant
Barbara Tuchman Prominent American historian

Kevin Rudd Shadow Foreign Affairs & International Security Min. 2003–

No more caveats, no more conditions in our foreign policy, no more leaving ourselves exposed to the Greens or the Left. Or to Right-wing criticism in the media about our ability to take a stance and stick to it.

Macklin agrees. During Caucus yesterday she said, 'Oh yes, we need a firm position, we can't afford to do what Simon and Kevin did before the war'. That stinking rotten war—we should never have been there in the first place. No qualifications this time. A clear line: we need our resources back here to protect Australia. Rudd hasn't objected to the policy itself, he just wants to add caveats to it. His reaction yesterday at Question Time tactics in Gillard's office was to look at me over the table, raise an eyebrow and simply say, 'Home by Christmas, hey?'

Newspoll yesterday said that 65 per cent of Australians believe that our involvement in Iraq is more likely to make Australia a terrorist target. So the mood is with me: the defence of Australia, first and foremost. This is a 70: 30 call. Thirty per cent of the country will back Howard and US imperialism. The rest, the true patriots, will want to look after our people and let the Americans solve the problem they created. No more arselicking and hole-sucking. An independent foreign policy.

Professor Kelly is with me. Rang him this afternoon to see what he thought and he said, 'This is a good move, mate, it will keep the pressure on Howard'. Too right, it will. Kelly is an international affairs guru, so I must be doing something right. Whoever said I couldn't handle this stuff? This is what I have been looking for: a chance to snooker Howard on one of his strengths. He's in trouble over trying to nobble Mick Kelty; now let him explain his inability to get out of Iraq and protect Australia properly.

The rest of Newspoll is sensational: a primary lead of 46/41, a 2PP lead of 55/45, a record approval rating of 66 per cent, just 15 per cent disapproval. I'm uneasy in this job because of my guilt about the boys, but this is the compensation: the chance, the growing chance, that they can be proud of the way in which their dad snatched the Prime Ministership. For the first time, I'm actually starting to feel confident.

Saturday, 3 April

This Iraq thing has turned into a shitfight. I've been away for the weekend with Janine to New Zealand, ostensibly to speak at Colin James's conference at this resort near Queenstown, but in reality, to have a break. I'm clapped out. I can't keep going at this pace; every week's a campaign week.

Mick Kelty Aust. Fed. Police Commissioner. Howard's office interfered in his public comments about the impact of Iraq on the terror threat in Australia

More self-inflicted wounds for the Party. Three days after our troops-out policy, the front page of *The Australian* carried the headline, 'Labor split over Iraq troop exit', reporting the discontent of 'senior Labor figures'. The Little Americans at it again. What they don't agree with, they seek to destroy. The controversy last weekend overshadowed some good school policy announcements with Macklin. Treachery months out from an election; utterly self-defeating.

Howard attacked all week in Parliament. I pushed him back reasonably well but the fight is damaging. The Libs have worked out they need to engage me in hand-to-hand combat, end my honeymoon by turning me into another scrapping politician. I've got to be able to dance away in the future. Stay positive.

A lengthy debate on Wednesday about my statement that I had met with intelligence officers from Foreign Affairs and Defence and had lengthy discussions about Iraq. Downer kept on saying I hadn't received any briefings but this was bullshit. I told Parliament the dates of the briefings and then Howard revealed that they were from ASIS and the Defence Signals Directorate (DSD). In effect, he outed ASIS as operating inside Iraq. I can't believe he didn't cop major media flak for such a reckless, politically desperate move.

Howard was trying to fit me up as a liar, just like him. Maybe I should have told Parliament the full story. But I was caught between a rock and a hard place. I couldn't fully defend myself because that would have meant giving the full details of the security briefings, perhaps generating a bigger controversy than the one I was in. Politically, I just needed to get the debate behind us.

Let me record what happened at the two briefings. On 5 January I met with Ron Bonighton, Deputy Director, Intelligence and Security in the Department of Defence, in my Ingleburn electorate office to discuss Australia's contribution to the international spying network through the DSD. The meeting lasted more than an hour and concentrated on the situation in Iraq. Yesterday I found out that Bonighton also oversees Australia's contribution to the Iraq Survey Group looking for WMD—hence his expertise in this area.

He gave me an outline of the intelligence support for the ADF in Iraq. Then he talked about the nature of international intelligence gathering in Iraq. He said this was quite limited because the Iraqi mobile phone network was unsuitable for listening surveillance. The Western nations couldn't get a proper handle on Saddam's activities. Most of their information was from sources/spies on the ground in Iraq—'human intelligence'.

Then Bonighton gave an explanation of how the intelligence agencies got it wrong. Saddam was sending out money and directives for the development of WMD but the Iraqi scientists spent it on fast cars and fast women. The usual practice of Third World countries applied: corruption and chaos. There was never any conclusive evidence of the existence of WMD prior to the Iraq war. This was the big failing of the intelligence and Government decision-making.

I concluded from the briefing that the Government's policy on Iraq was a fiasco and Australia should get out of there asap—it was obvious from what Bonighton said. We ended the conversation with an interesting discussion about the cultural sensitivities of intelligence collection, the difference between First World and Third World societies and cultural norms. Bonighton was very cooperative and very forthcoming; he seemed to enjoy our long and detailed talk.

On 11 February in my Parliament House office, I met with David Irvine, the head of ASIS, and his deputy. They gave me an overview of ASIS's activities around the world. Naturally, I asked about their work in Iraq, and Irvine gave me a detailed description of what they do. Sure, it wasn't the big picture about WMD and the fall of Saddam but it was pretty interesting stuff. A sign of Australia's deep involvement in Iraq, much more than the ADF.

Based on what Bonighton had told me, it seemed to me that ASIS was committing a significant amount of resources for little or no gain in an extremely dangerous country. Another Howard Government stuff-up, risking the lives of Australian defence and security personnel who would be better deployed in this country dealing with the terrorist threat. Yes, valid reasons for getting our people out of that shithole.

The media were more interested in the Government's bogus attack than our two big policy announcements for the week. It marked a shift in their priorities and the end of my media honeymoon. Gartrell had a tip-off from within the bureaucracy that the Government was about to abolish ATSIC, trying to wedge us. I pre-empted them by getting in first: our plan is to replace ATSIC with a community-based model of Aboriginal governance, the Pearson model. The golden rule: repair the foundations of Left-of-Centre policy before the Tories exploit any weakness. And there are many weaknesses at ATSIC: corruption etc.

Swan has a seemingly endless flow of leaked documents out of FACS, there's a mole in the department. A good tip-off that the Government will introduce a new baby payment in the Budget, a big work and family initiative. So we got in first, announcing a Baby Care Payment, the equivalent of

---

ASIS Australian Secret Intelligence Service
ATSIC Aboriginal and Torres Strait Islander Commission

FACS Dept of Family and Community Services

paid maternity leave. No more small target; plenty of policy in the six strategic areas. Out of Parliament now until the Budget, the Government's chance to strike back.

Not a bad little conference after all, in this beautiful part of the world. Dinner tonight in Arrowtown, where David Kirk spoke, the All Blacks legend who captained their World Cup-winning team in 1987. A really nice guy. He spoke about the key elements of a winning culture: brutal honesty, ruthless pragmatism and ferocious discipline. The importance of the self-belief within, a calm unbreakable resolve. If you have a small cadre of people with these qualities, you can build a winning team, company or political party. That's the problem with the ALP: too many Chicken Littles, a lack of self-belief under pressure.

Wednesday, 14 April

I've had a suspicion for some time now that Rudd has been feeding material to Oakes. Decided to set him up, telling Kevvie about our focus groups on Iraq. No such research exists—Gartrell says he's doing some quantitative polling but not focus groups. Today, right on cue, Jabba has written in the *Bulletin*: 'The Labor Party's polling firm has been busily running focus groups to test the public mood following Latham's 'troops-out' announcement. The most significant finding, I understand, is overwhelming support for the alliance with the United States'.

Trapped him. Two weeks ago in New Zealand, I announced our intention to have a Minister for the Pacific Islands. That's the job I'll give Rudd if we win. Joel thinks I'm joking, but I'm deadly serious. Rudd is a terrible piece of work: addicted to the media and leaking. A junior minister in Government, at best.

In Perth since Saturday to spend Easter with Janine's family and then the release of our trade practices package yesterday. A huge economic reform, but the media are more interested in Iraq. The situation there is melting down; the insurgency has begun. The Americans have another Vietnam on their hands. Howard is now handcuffed to the folly of the bonehead Bush.

As Joel said today, 'Mate, things can only get worse for Howard and better for us on Iraq. You took a risk with the troops-out policy but it's the same old story—we are better off taking a stance than looking weak'. He's a good man, a good mate, and if his political judgement is right, we can march forward on this issue. It looks a bloodbath on TV, a civil war in the making.

All Blacks New Zealand rugby union team

Mixed feedback publicly. Opened Roger Price's new electorate office in Mount Druitt last Thursday, mobbed by hundreds of well-wishers, mostly migrants, cheering me on about Iraq. Over-the-top adulation.

The Tories in the media, however, have gone feral: the Murdoch American press, led by *The Australian*. Kelly has switched his line, giving me a hard time now. Another Matt Price—two-faced indeed. Just as bad, a carping interview with Alan Jones last Thursday morning. Laws was right, it had to happen. The Tory Establishment is coming after me.

Tuesday, 20 April

Ended a long day with a private fundraising dinner at the home of a businessman, Paul Binstead of Pymble. Carr was the star turn, laying into the Americans over Iraq, a scarifying fifteen-minute critique of their faulty strategy and how it will foster Islamic fundamentalism worldwide. It's a measure of how bad the Americans are going that someone like Bob, an old Cold War warrior, is up them for the rent.

I need him to come out publicly and say these things. The thug Armitage and his underlings are in the Murdoch papers all the time: the born-to-rule mentality of American imperialism, trying to interfere in our sovereign system, trying to help Howard. They see us as a colony, not an ally. Carr is the senior Labor head of government in this country—he could play a vital role, put them back in their box.

But he won't. When push comes to shove, he's like the rest of the Labor conservatives: scared of Murdoch, scared of Packer, scared of the Americans, our great and powerful friends. Bob is going to the Australian American Leadership Dialogue in June, the foreign policy club funded by the US. He won't repeat his comments from tonight publicly, they would throw him out of the club.

I'm supposed to be going to the Dialogue as well, but I need to get out of it. The US Republicans will use it as an opportunity to set me up and embarrass me politically. Howard and Downer are sweating on it. I'll give them the slip at Budget time; say it's an early election Budget (it may be for 7 August) so I need to stay at home.

I gave a well-received speech earlier in the day on national identity; engaged Howard in the culture wars, and repaired the foundations of policies like multiculturalism—all the things that I said we needed to do in my Menzies Lecture. The enemies are always at me, saying I'm inconsistent on the policy front. So far as Leader I'm proving them wrong, setting the agenda, making Howard follow. Need to keep it up, my one-man war.

Richard Armitage US Dep. Sec. of State 2001–05

Thursday, 22 April

My worst day in the job. Our fourth wedding anniversary but I forgot about it, distracted by a plagiarism allegation exploded on me by Jabba and the Government. Janine has been very understanding about it but I feel two inches tall. No job is so important that it should get in the way of such a woman.

The speech two days ago contained some rhetoric on education targets. I pulled it out of my old notes/folder on education policy and updated it for the speech. The Government must have a unit that googles every phrase in my speeches, looking for things that might embarrass me. They found some similarities to Clinton's 1997 State of the Union address (I would have read it at the time, but I can't remember taking down notes from it) and gave the stuff to Oakes, who ran it on the news last night.

The crook thing was the way in which Channel Nine tried to set me up here in Adelaide, where I'm campaigning in Hindmarsh, Makin and Adelaide. Earlier in the day, they arranged a live cross and interview with me, supposedly about 'local issues', for their 6 p.m. news from the roof of the Hilton, where I'm staying. Fortunately, with the time difference between Adelaide and Sydney, Glenn got a tip-off that Jabba had done this plagiarism thing, so we had five minutes' notice of what they were up to before the live cross.

They tried to ambush me about the speech. But Oakes had gone a bridge too far, saying that I got my reading to children policy from the Clinton speech as well—totally untrue. I batted them away by talking about the vital role of Mem Fox, who lives in Adelaide, in inspiring the reading policy.

Today was dominated by this thing, the media and Government jumping all over it—wrecked my visit to Makin. The media love this stuff: a chance to ridicule the new guy, drag me back to the pack. My line is that I did not read Clinton's speech when preparing my own. Technically true, but not as honest as I could have been. So much for the new politics. These mistakes are killing me.

Tuesday, 27 April

The centenary of the formation of the Watson Government, the first national Labor government in the world. Watson was the youngest ever Leader of the FPLP—just 34 years old, a record that will never be beaten. I'm the second youngest ever. But I let down my predecessor today.

Faulkner organised a series of anniversary events here in Melbourne but my performance was below par. I've lost enthusiasm and confidence after the plagiarism thing, stewing over it across the long weekend. Janine is right: these things affect me more than they should. It's just a blip on the political radar screen; get over it and pep up for the next fight.

Nothing to cheer me up in Melbourne town, least of all our meeting with Bracks this morning, accompanied by Faulkner, Crean and McMullan. We tried to get him to reverse his broken promise on the Scoresby Freeway. He went to the last State election promising a freeway and, as soon as he won, announced a tollway. No wonder people hate politics and politicians. Bracks has broken his promise, hoping the odium will wear off before the next State election.

But we're copping the fall-out electorally—disastrous polling right through the eastern suburbs. We can kiss goodbye to any hope of winning La Trobe, Deakin, Aston or Dunkley, and Anna Burke will be lucky to hang on in Chisholm. I might as well not bother campaigning in the marginal seat belt of Melbourne.

Bracks, however, was unmoved, even when Faulkner put it right on him: 'The stakes are high in what we are talking about. You need to know, Steve, this could be the difference between forming a Federal Labor Government and falling a few seats short. You need to think about how history will see that'. Yes, a day of deep and abiding Labor history, as Bracks refused to help, not budging an inch. Sat there like a statue, that silly grin on his face.

These State people are in it for themselves. They open a few schools and hospitals, and think they are King Shit. They couldn't give two hoots about the damage they might cause to the Federal Party. The legacy of State-based political machines—I need to win an election despite them. And then I can clean out the Augean stables: abolish the National Executive for what they did to Cookie, and abolish the primacy of the State branches. That is, nationalise the ALP.

Thursday, 13 May

A mixed week on both sides of the fence. Costello foolishly spiked his own Budget by reigniting leadership speculation. It's now clear that he and Howard detest each other. The Budget is a $52 billion giveaway, throwing money at everything; cynical vote-buying but, incredibly, restricting tax cuts to people above $52 000 per annum The media seem shocked at the Government's strategy.

Augean stables From the Greek legend.
Hercules cleaned out the Augean stables
in a day

On our side, it renders the Access Economics work redundant. It now looks like a calamity of a project. Realigning the tax rates was going to cost $15 billion per annum, but Access and Sanchez only identified tax expenditure savings of around $3 billion per annum—a huge funding hole. Even with an increase in the company tax rate to 33 per cent, Access estimated a funding shortfall of $39.5 billion over four years and concluded: 'There is still a lot of financing ground to make up. No credible estimate of any efficiency or integrity dividend, nor any credible estimate of additional savings from interactions with other policy measures, will make up anything like this financing shortfall'.

I'm all for bold policy, but not if it's going to blow our economic credibility out of the water. On top of that, the project kept on leaking—leak after leak after leak to the *Financial Review*. It was jinxed from day one—a good concept worth exploring at the time, but in practice, it went down like a lead zeppelin.

Our task is to provide relief for the low- and middle-income earners who missed out—a big political opportunity. Why did the Government go this way? The only thing I can think of is that they saw it as some kind of wedge issue. They looked at our internal divisions at the end of last year—Swan, Albanese and Tanner arguing against relief at the top end, myself in favour—and thought we would have another fight over this package by knocking off the tax cuts and redirecting the money down the income scale.

No chance of my falling for that trap. In the Budget lock-up on Tuesday night, I decided to pass through their tax relief and add our own—more Budget savings (such as the new superannuation concessions) to finance relief under $52 000. This is my trump card: our determination to cut into the Budget to clear the way for our priorities. Fiscal responsibility as an economic virtue.

I've tasked Crean with putting our package together asap. If the Government gets a boost out of the Budget (the $52 billion question), I will have to counter-punch next month. At least I will be in Australia. I got out of that nightmare US trip as planned.

An untidy effort as we tried to attack the inequity of the Government's tax cuts. Cox and Crean have stuffed around getting an accurate definition of how many taxpayers have missed out (the correct assessment is that 80 per cent of families and singles have missed out on a tax cut). I got caught

---

Access Economics work In 2004 it was clear that the realignment of the top personal and company tax rates was not feasible due to a massive funding shortfall. Some of the tax expenditure savings identified by Access Economics were used to fund Labor's tax and family policy released in the election campaign, including tax cuts under $52 000 p.a.
Alex Sanchez Councillor, Liverpool City Council 1991–99; my economics adviser 2003–05

on Perth radio yesterday morning with Howard Sattler, sounding like I didn't qualify for the high-income tax cuts. My mistake: I thought he was talking about family benefits, but no sympathy from the media. Terrible TV coverage last night.

Bounced back today with an excellent press conference with Gillard, Janine and the Brooks family. Their little girl Bella contracted pneumo-coccal on Anzac Day, so they have been campaigning to make the vaccine freely available. It was the perfect chance to unveil our policy (great TV cov-erage tonight). This is the way to attack Howard: how can he spend a motza in the Budget but still leave our children exposed to deadly diseases?

Howard talks about family policy but he has neglected the small but significant things that matter to parents: early childhood literacy, essential vaccines, childhood obesity, fair school funding, stronger community life, etc. I'm under his guard with the politics of personal connection—con-necting today with the needs of the Brooks family. This is what Dick Morris calls 'stooping to succeed'—staying out of Howard's firing line on the economy and national security (except for troops out of Iraq), and rolling out a new agenda for families in the outer suburbs.

A rollercoaster week: down one day, up the next. I feel the weight of the world on my shoulders. My only relief is to have the boys in the office. I played a game this afternoon with little Issie, spinning him around and rolling him up in the curtains—his face exploding with laughter. Inside the curtains was our little cocoon. Nervous about my Budget Reply speech, I didn't want to come out of the cocoon. I would have happily stayed there, and promised Isaac that one day we will. I'll escape and become a proper dad again. Our little secret.

The Budget Reply speech went okay, no stumbles. Good text and delivery for the TV audience; I took the messages from the community forums directly to Canberra, turning community consultation into Labor policy, avoided talking too much about dollar amounts, and tried to emphasise the human impact of our policies. The bevy of yahooing, half-pissed Government backbenchers helped calm my nerves; they made me more determined not to stuff up.

I reread the speech before going to bed tonight. We should be proud of so much policy released in advance of an election. Hats off to Crean, who started the process of defining ourselves by the things we propose; no more small targets. He's a robot, that bloke: just keeps chugging away, fighting and gouging to get us back into government. After what

---

Howard Sattler Perth radio shock-jock

the bastards did to him, he deserves to be Treasurer. Do this one for the Gipper.

The speech was like a campaign policy speech. On national security: a Department of Homeland Security, an Australian coastguard, plus better port and airport security.

On the economy: trade practices reform, BAS simplification for small business, cutting the superannuation contributions tax and implementing our Budget Pledge—guaranteed surpluses, cutting net debt and holding down interest rates, reducing the size of government (Commonwealth expenditure and taxation as a proportion of GDP). In office, we are committed to significant budget savings, abolishing seven government agencies and cutting a further thirteen government programs. Better services, fully paid for.

On the environment: ratifying the Kyoto Protocol, establishing an emissions trading system, saving the Murray–Darling, stronger beach and coastal protection. On education: a national reading program, needs-based school funding, incentives to lure the best teachers to the struggling schools, a school discipline package, and TAFE and university expansion. On health: saving bulk-billing, a national dental program and extra vaccines for children.

For social capital: a national mentoring foundation, 10 000 new mentors and more men in our schools to help troubled boys. For work and family: the Baby Care Payment, partially introduced in the Budget, and improved IR rights for working parents.

The major announcement in the speech: a Youth Guarantee, so that all young Australians are either learning or earning, with no third option of sitting around doing nothing. The abolition of TAFE fees in schools, and the introduction of new apprenticeships, TAFE places and wage and training subsidies. A new Labor emphasis on mutual responsibility: government provides the training and work opportunities, young people must have a go in return.

And finally, our work program for the future: broader and fairer tax relief, and a new family payments system (resolving the family debt crisis, increased financial incentive to work and paying the benefits fortnightly).

The people sitting at home listening to this must have thought: he's only been in the job five months, how has he put down so much policy, so many new plans for the nation? Answer: ask Isaac.

The Gipper A famous line in politics associated with Ronald Reagan, who played Notre Dame's legendary doomed half-back (American football), George Gipp, in a Hollywood football movie released in 1940

Monday, 17 May

I'm at the start of a four-day bus trip from Bundaberg to Brisbane, reinforcing my Budget reply themes. Three community forums scheduled: one in Bundaberg tonight (seat of Hinkler), then Caboolture (in Longman) on Wednesday and Ripoll's electorate, Oxley, west of Brisbane, on Thursday. It's tiring just to think of the forums: I'll be on my feet for two hours (I get a bad pain in my left hip, the result of a slipped disc in my lower back), answering 30-odd questions, with the media looking on for any slip-ups or novelty to jump on. Politics by exhaustion.

But my spirits have been buoyed by great news from Byres. A welcome phone call while I grabbed some dinner at an outdoor café in sunny Bundy. The Newspoll to be published tomorrow shows that the Budget has flopped as a vote-buyer. We have a primary lead (44/41) and a 2PP lead (54/46, up from 52/48 two weeks ago). My numbers have also jumped back up: 57 per cent approval, 24 disapproval, a net plus of 33. This confirms the good polls in the Sunday papers. Could not be happier.

This is the break we have been looking for. Sometimes nothing goes right for a long-serving Government. The public has astutely seen through Howard's vote-buying exercise and ticked off my better targeted and fiscally restrained response. No lasting damage from my ragged period last month. Our strategy now is to keep the pressure on Howard: more Liberal leadership tension, force mistakes on their side, consolidate our position. The sniff of victory still in our nostrils.

Also leaves Shaun Carney from the *Age* looking like a goose. His column on Saturday described my Budget Reply as 'an opportunity lost', while proclaiming Costello's policy's political brilliance. He said the Libs are 'Now tantalisingly close to overtaking the Labor Party in the opinion polls, right at the time the Government needs to get out in front. Momentum counts for a lot in politics during an election year. The Government has it and Labor is losing it'.

Another snake in the grass, this Mr Carney. When I was Shadow Treasurer he rang me to offer his services in 'psychoanalysing' Costello, identifying his weaknesses and exploiting them, all because he wrote a book on him a few years ago. I never took up his offer; he sounded weird and self-absorbed. Maybe that's why he's tickling me up now.

Shaun Carney *Age* associate editor and
columnist

Tuesday, 18 May

It doesn't get any better than this. Howard's mate and biographer, David Barnett, is reflecting on the thirtieth anniversary of the little man's election to Parliament in *The Australian* today:

> In 30 years he has only had three bad moments. He was shaken in 1989 when he was dumped by his party as Leader. He was shaken, soon after he became PM in 1996, when his wife became seriously ill. What has it all been for, he wondered. And he was shaken when Mark Latham became Opposition Leader after eight years of Latham's two carping predecessors and was immediately embraced by the media as the next PM, as if nothing good had come of the Coalition Government.

High praise. If nothing else, I have shaken Howard to the bone. I'm up there with his missus almost falling off the twig.

Sunday, 23 May

Back for a fortnight of Parliament, which starts tomorrow. Called the inner circle together for a planning meeting. Faulkner's worried about the imagery coming out of my FM radio interviews. A critic of Vivian, he thinks she has lost control of my media coverage. I need to monitor her performance closely; Byres is doing most of the work in the press office. Now that the honeymoon is over, the media management has to be much tougher.

We have got a fair bit out of the FM interviews, a youth audience Howard would not even attempt to relate to. But now that the TV guys have seen me for a while, they are looking for novelty/wacky images. That's the risk with letting them take footage in the FM studios. Solution: still do the interviews, but don't notify the TVs.

Gartrell is worried about the Government's drumbeat on Liverpool Council; there's been some bad reaction in our focus groups. I need to do a rebuttal speech in the Parliament and put it to bed. This is what the Tories do best: take a sliver of information and stitch up their opponents, especially through their Dancing Bears in the media, Akerman, Milne, etc.

The truth is, I couldn't have driven that Council harder for economic efficiency and savings: I got rid of the bludging staff, got massive savings from contractors, busted open the old, self-serving club. Paciullo came in

---

David Barnett Malcolm Fraser's Press Sec. 1975–82; author (with Pru Goward) of *John Howard: Prime Minister*, Viking, Ringwood, 1997

Vivian Schenker Communcations Dir. for Simon Crean; she stayed on in my office when I became ALP Leader

as Mayor in mid-1994 (big mistake, I should have backed Sanchez) and didn't understand any of the reforms. He was an old clubman, lunching proudly. The General Manager, John Walker, left in disgust. Paciullo recruited a Left-wing dill from South Australia, Brian Carr (Peter Duncan's mate) and the place fell to pieces.

Paciullo's Italian mates all say that he had an edifice complex: he wanted to match my achievements asap. The Council ended up with the worst possible combination: a new Mayor who embarked on too many projects—he bought the old post-office site and went too far with Oasis, etc.—and a new General Manager who unwound the efficiency gains. By 1996 they were getting themselves into trouble, so they played the oldest trick in the book: blame the previous Council. Carr and Lynch's mate, Wendy Waller, tried to fit me up for their problems. I called for Waller's resignation.

The irony of it: the Liberals and Independents (mostly Labor rats) on Council called me for everything under the sun when I was Mayor, but they never accused me of financial largesse. In fact, they used to complain that the cost savings went too far, that I was driving the workforce too hard. They put a private detective on me, followed me around the streets, and attacked my sister. You name it, they did it, except criticise my financial management. That was left to the Left-wing of the Labor Party (Waller) two years after I left the place.

Carr and Waller have spent eight years (1996–2004) trying to blame me, all the while getting deeper and deeper into the Oasis mess with the Bulldogs. No wonder the Council was sacked: they spent $20 million on Oasis and all they have to show for it is a concrete slab out the back of the Council building. And they have the hide to question my financial record ten years ago!

I gave up on Paciullo when he wanted to build residential towers in the CBD to bail Oasis out of its financial strife. It was a conflict of interest between Council's role as a land owner and the development consent authority. The Council solicitor, John Marsden, tells me Paciullo may end up in bigger trouble once this thing is fully investigated.

Tim's other concern about our economic credibility is Crean—he says that the Liberals are bound to attack Crean because he's so unpopular. I'm not convinced. Sure, he's seen as snarly and mean in the electorate, but nobody questions his competence. In fact, meanness can be an asset in that job. I'm more worried about the Council stitch-up.

Peter Duncan ALP member, Makin 1984–96; min. in Hawke govt
Oasis Controversial Liverpool Council development that led to the sacking of the

Council in 2004
Wendy Waller Councillor, Liverpool City Council 1995–2004

We need to start planning phase three: post-Budget through to the end of July. Phase one was close to perfect. Phase two was ragged, although we have bounced out of the Budget well enough. Maybe I'm too hard on myself: the honeymoon spoiled me, gave me a false view of what this job is really like. The workload is huge: four or five issues to master every day, a narky media to placate, internal Party crap, plus policy development, plus marginal seat campaigning, plus my fading memory of family and friends. Not everything is going to go according to plan.

Objectives for phase three: regain competence, dance away from Lib attacks in Parliament, a steady program of policy releases, keep the pressure on a long-serving Government. Communication style is to be conversational. Tell a story, realise the importance of word pictures, and stay positive. Add value to the debate. Use quiet media days to maximise coverage. Roll out policy nuggets on a weekend, a series of Sunday specials.

Good advice from Rod Cameron in the mighty Ramsey's column yesterday: 'Latham has to revisit where he was a few months ago, when he was beating Howard on values. Cynical journalists might be tired of hearing about reading to kids, but middle Australia thinks it's a pretty good idea. So all the symbols of what he stands for, that he did so well in the early days, he's got to revisit'.

Rocket Rod will be glad to see I'm launching Mem Fox's new book tomorrow week. I'm going back to my six themes, releasing new policies in each area:

- the Ladder of Opportunity: better services in childcare, public housing, Federal–State cooperation (health, education and the environment) and new forms of mutual responsibility: the Neighbours From Hell policy, tough on unruly housing tenants
- a Big Country: one that's big enough to protect the environment, starting with my Fraser Lecture this Wednesday. We have been holding back in this area, waiting for Garrett, but we can't afford to wait any more. Carr and Roozendaal duped us on the Cunningham plan— Roozendaal took the Upper House vacancy for himself. That won't stop me; I'll roll Sussex Street on this if it kills me. One day I'll put out a release saying that I want Garrett in Fowler and the Party should disendorse Irwin because of her involvement in branch-stacking with Joe

---

Rod Cameron ALP pollster during the Hawke and Keating years

Fraser Lecture Annual lecture organised by Bob McMullan in memory of Jim Fraser, after whom the electorate is named—ALP member, ACT 1951–70

Tripodi and Sam Bargshoon. No one will argue: Garrett versus Irwin, it's like Kingston Town racing a Clydesdale—no contest

- the Economy: our tax and family policy is still to come: a big statement on economic incentive, tax cuts for all, reward for work, cutting EMTRs. Other new policies: making the First Home Owners Scheme more equitable, and our strategy for banking and corporate social responsibility. Also a special package for competition in the petrol industry—relief for motorists. Plus relaunch the Budget Pledge: Labor surpluses holding down interest rates—a reminder of our economic discipline
- National Security: hold the line against the Murdoch/American attacks on me. Let the Government deal with the crisis in Iraq and the horror of Abu Ghraib, which is turning public opinion against Bush and Bonsai. We don't have to do much on the issue; the media is doing the work for us. We just have to put up with Rudd leaking Question Time tactics to the media (e.g. Ramsey last Saturday week), complaining about a lack of questions
- Community Development: roll out the next round of Tanner reforms, policies that address loneliness among the aged, the issue of work stress etc. Solving social problems: an anti-gambling package, reducing urban sprawl (will Melham deliver?) and Roxon's women's policy
- the New Politics: pick up ideas from Gillard's Parliamentary Reform Group and Carmen's agenda. More community forums, more public consultation. Badge Howard as part of the Club: 30 years in the system, ignoring public participation and community politics.

Sunday, 30 May

Dinner with the Campaign Strategy Group (State Secretaries, Kaiser, etc.) at the Water's Edge Restaurant in Canberra. Mainly a social gathering, in the poshest restaurant in Canberra—these Party officials know how to look after themselves. Tim said it was a good thing to do, to make them feel part of the scene. In reality, our inner circle/planning group will continue to run the strategy.

Joe Tripodi ALP member, Fairfield in the NSW Parl. 1995–
Sam Bargshoon Self-confessed ALP branch stacker; prominent in the Orange Grove development controversy in Liverpool in 2004
Bonsai A little Bush, nickname for John Howard

Daryl Melham Shadow Housing & Urban Development Min. 2003–04
Nicola Roxon Shadow Min. assisting me for the Status of Women
Parliamentary Reform Group A committee of Labor MPs working on policies to improve the Parliament

No leaks from those planning meetings so far—an encouraging sign, except for one shocker. Cooney gave Michelle Grattan my strategic agenda at Caucus and staff drinks last month. No need for my Policy Director to talk to the press, especially on something as sensitive as this; it's self-defeating, and tips off the Libs as to what I'm up to. I've threatened to sack anyone who did this but gave Cooney one more chance; he's a good, loyal man.

At the end of tonight's dinner, Danger wanted to see me outside. He dropped a bombshell on me: he's going to retire at the next election. My right-hand man is pulling the pin, leaving me stranded. I don't see how I can survive without him: his steady point of view, his dislike of the machine men, his sound instincts and impeccable loyalty. Terrible for me, good for him. Trish has a second chance health-wise, and he's going to spend it with her. Can't begrudge him that—in fact, it's a measure of the man that he's making this his top priority.

He said to me, 'Mate, I've done as much as I can for you anyway. You're set up to win this now. And I won't be too far away if you need a hand with anything'. Maybe. He announcing it to his FEC next Friday, so it's under wraps until then. He doesn't have a preferred successor and out of respect to the locals, he doesn't want to be associated with any push for Garrett. Fair enough.

But Garrett is the logical replacement—my dilemma solved at long last. It's a traditional Right-wing seat, full of young hopefuls (union hacks and branch-stackers) waiting for Laurie and/or Carr, the local State Member, to retire. Roozendaal will hate the idea of Garrett, but bad luck, he should have given us Cunningham. Carr will be in no position to argue. Remember: we must have this man in Parliament. Too right, he's going to be the next Member for Kingsford Smith.

The other news tonight: a research briefing from John Utting, our first look at the key seats (the 29 battleground marginals, he calls them). Excellent results: ALP 44 per cent on primaries, Coalition 39 per cent, Greens 7 and independents/others 10. A 2PP lead of 55/45, a clear election win on these numbers. Faulkner threw in a note of caution, however: the Libs normally drive us 1–2 per cent lower during a campaign because of the weight of their advertising money.

Gartrell was relieved. He was worried that I had rallied the True Believers but not anyone else. This research shows that my leadership has done more than lift the base Labor vote, it has penetrated the key marginals, the middle ground. Nationwide polls count for little at this point of

---

John Utting Head, UMP Research; ALP pollster

the electoral cycle—the marginals decide the result. A happy National Secretary.

Utting said that my numbers were the key: 'A funny thing has happened. Most people think the country is headed in the right direction but they are still willing to change the Government. Your net approval rating (plus 24, versus Howard's plus 10) has lifted the Labor vote into this good position'. His advice: run hard on public cynicism about the Budget, keep my winning formula in place and watch out for heavy Government attacks. In other words: situation normal.

We are defying gravity with this growth economy and the prominence of national security issues. But how else can we win? Without blowing my own trumpet, Howard has found me harder to handle than Beazley or Crean. Imagine if he were promising or introducing a GST right now: we would be unstoppable. But Faulkner is right: this is our high-water mark. Still, an intoxicating thought: marginals like McEwen, Richmond and Longman looking good; tough seats like Robertson, Corangamite, Kalgoorlie and Dickson (6 per cent margins) now on our radar screen.

A stunning day in every sense. I did my first Sunday special on petrol prices in McClelland's electorate. Easy TV coverage, a model for phase three policy announcements. My novelty value has worn off with the media, but they can't ignore me on a weekend. It also keeps me away from the Canberra gallery; I just have to deal with the second stringers and kids they send out on Sundays. Too easy Campese.

Friday, 4 June

Just a piece of trivia for the diary today: I was attacked by the world's most powerful man, the US President. Howard is in Washington, brown-nosing around, looking for an election endorsement from his masters. He got one from Bush at their press conference on the White House lawns. The perpetual prattler, Steve Lewis from *The Australian* (where else could the question have come from?), asked a Dorothy Dixer about my policy to get the troops out of Iraq.

The dangerous and incompetent one called my stance disastrous. Fifteen all. His policy has been a big success, has it? I haven't sent young men to an early grave in search of WMDs that do not exist. I sleep easy on that front. Glenn rang me this morning to tell me about it. Sat down at the kitchen table and wrote a statement standing my ground, saying that the

---

David Campese Australian rugby union great, 1980s and 1990s

Alliance is bigger and stronger than Bush's mistakes in Iraq. No doorstop today. That's what the Tories want: TV images of me taking the bait, slagging the dunderhead. I'll just dance away with a written statement.

What does this prove? Hopefully pride inside the Latham family. My grandparents taught me to stand up to the powerful. Just because they have money and influence doesn't make them better than us. When I said I was anti-Establishment, I meant it. It's not just a political ethos, it's in my blood, a way of life. If it's still the Australian way, I will win the election. If not, what the people are saying is that they don't mind being an American colony under Howard. That's a nation not worth leading.

Looking at it this way, I can't lose. It's like the old Groucho Marx line: I don't want to belong to any club that will accept me as a member. A good description of how I feel about the American club. A good description of my attitude to public life: the fatalism of conviction politics.

Sunday, 6 June

The Garrett cat is out of the bag. Janine and I were leaving the movies last night at Macarthur Square and Garrett was plastered across the front of the *Sun Herald*. They give Sunday's paper away at the movies on Saturday night—next week I'm going down there a few hours earlier to get the race results. It looks like Head Office is at it again, trying to spike my push for Kingsford Smith.

They're too late, I've told Gartrell and Faulkner it must happen, if not through NSW, then the National Executive. Peter's over the moon, and willing to buy a place in the electorate. It suits his wife, who works in the city. Willing and ready to serve the Labor cause. Quite a coup. The story, however, eclipsed my Sunday special at Oyster Bay this morning: phasing out plastic shopping bags. I was sceptical about this Kelvin Thomson policy, but my mother supports it—a shopping traditionalist who sees the sense in environmental protection. It must be the coming way.

No doubt about where the Murdochs are coming from. A disgraceful article in the *Sunday Telegraph* today, branding me a 'Copy Cat, where Mark Latham gets his lines from', accompanied by 36 silly photos of me. No longer lurking in the dark outside my unit, Luke McIlveen has reprinted a Coalition research job on my alleged plagiarism. The Clinton thing is long past, so they have googled all my statements to find someone, anyone in the world, who has ever said something similar to me. A hatchet job.

Check this out: in September 2003 I said, 'Quality teaching is a passport out of poverty'. McIlveen reckons I got it from Sandra Feldman of the American Federation of Teachers who, in July 2001, said, 'Education is the best passport out of poverty'. Yeah, he's right onto me: I've been stealing Feldman's ideas for years. Who the hell is Sandra Feldman?

Also cites that strange academic in Melbourne, Brian Galligan, who reckons I stole his ideas on multiculturalism from his recent book on Australian citizenship. He sent me his book, but it didn't even make it into my in-tray, that's how low in the pecking order it was. I get a thousand letters and emails every week and Galligan must think I read them all, plus a couple of dozen books. Christ, I don't have time to read to the boys any more; why would I look at his thing?

Thursday, 10 June

It's done. A joint press conference at Maroubra Beach formally announcing Garrett as our candidate for Kingsford Smith. The most significant Left-of-Centre figure in Australia not in Parliament is now joining my team. There was huge media interest: TV helicopters, live crosses, a massive scrum of journalists—the works.

Garrett's a natural, charisma-plus, and the whole event went well. The only downside is this *Daily Telegraph* campaign about his enrolment: there's confusion over how many times he has voted over the past decade. The information was fed to them by our people, out of Sussex Street. Luke McIlveen is leading the charge for the *Tele*, of course.

Fancy Johno Johnson running the local ALP campaign against Garrett. He's been part of every Head Office strategy for 30 years, denying the rights of local branches in NSW. His only contribution to Federal policy was to convince Brian Harradine to support the Government's private health insurance rebate in 1998—the decisive vote that got it through the Senate. That's the Grouper connection: Johno going against Party policy via his mate Harradine. Shanahan later wrote an article about it and then dobbed Johno in to me. A disgrace all round.

The union hacks and branch-stackers in Kingsford Smith are frustrated that their tireless work in rorting the books has not been rewarded. Why should it be? Do we really need another Steve Hutchins in Caucus? It's never good to override the rights of the rank and file, but if we had a ballot here, only 10 per cent of the voters would be genuine; the rest of them are Right-wing stacks, Johno's God squad, etc.

Met with Garrett and his offsider, Simon Balderstone, at my place last night to prepare for his transition to the Party. All the lessons of the Kernot

---

Johno Johnson Former ALP member, NSW Legislative Council and Right-wing powerbroker with close National Civic Council connections experience were placed on the table: don't rush things, try to get used to the culture, don't worry if it looks mysterious (no one fully understands it), and be honest about past political affiliations and personal issues.

Faulkner laid it right on the line: 'Peter, I've got to ask you the thing I never asked Cheryl and should have: is there anything we need to know about your past, any issue we need to pre-empt and deal with in advance?' Garrett looked sincere and relieved when he said no. He's led a quiet lifestyle by rock-and-roll standards; Peter's hidden side is his dedication to his family and Christian values. No Gareth-style skeletons lurking in his cupboard.

The only glitch is this enrolment thing. Surprising, really—Faulkner is usually more thorough than this. It'll take some of the gloss off our coup, but Peter's appeal is already well established: impeccable green credentials with the leafy middle class, impeccable Oils energy for the head-banging working class, myself included.

Out of Maroubra and flew straight to Geelong: fundraising and campaigning with Gavan O'Connor and the impressive Peter McMullin, our candidate for Corangamite. First time in Geelong, first time to the legendary Kardinia Park, where we had the fundraising lunch, first time to Barwon Heads, the setting for ABC TV's *SeaChange* series. Also, I regret to report, first time I have met Deborah Snow.

She did Danger over in a profile a few years ago; she's as negative as they come. Now she's working on a hatchet job on me. Word back from several mates that she and other *SMH* journos have rung around, sniffing for dirt. Obviously spoken to Gwyther. Word from Faulkner is that she's investigating the Ray/Gray/Beazley bullshit from 1998. It had to happen one day; the enemies can't help themselves, and it's too salacious a rumour to let rest. And too tempting for a piece of work like Snow to ignore.

She followed me around this afternoon, a haunting presence. But no interview—anything she wants to put to me she can put in writing. I did some local media shots with Gavan and young Geelong students/trainees to promote our Youth Guarantee. The look on Snow's face when I stood next to one of the girls was pretty scary. She thinks I'm some kind of pervert, some lewd, dribbling character who can't keep his hands off women. But the irony of it: she's the one who has a problem, investigating something that never happened.

I'm over all this crap. Sick and tired of talking about myself, of feeding the media's hunger for Lathamology. There is no hidden story, nothing new to say about myself. No more profiles, no more navel-gazing interviews; I've done enough. If I clam up on that front, it will force the media to focus

---

Deborah Snow *SMH* journalist

on our policies, on the huge differences between us and the Government, on a new way of running the country. The outsiders' revolution.

They can't say I haven't cooperated: there are books by Michael Duffy (my parallel life with Abbott), Craig McGregor (with his brother Adrian), Bernard Lagan (not the world's most accurate journalist but a good bloke who has promised a full biography on me) and Barry Donovan (Crean's mate from Melbourne) in the pipeline. Long, long interviews with them all, plus countless newspaper profiles. Even one on my dad, with idiots like Heyhoe bullshitting about him again.

Four is enough: all other requests declined. If I cooperated with them all, I would end up doing no other work. Annabel Crabb is doing a book. Margaret Simons is doing a *Quarterly Essay*. The *Sunday* program is doing a profile. Repetition, repetition: I did one with Helen Dalley two years ago; my life story 1961–2002 has not changed. And now, the Abominable Snow Woman. Enough. I don't get to talk to my family these days, why would I want to talk to them?

Friday, 11 June

A special meeting of the National Executive in Canberra to formally elect Garrett as the candidate in Kingsford Smith. Gartrell had things well organised in advance and provided a perfect summary of the gathering: 'The worst collection of arseholes you could fit into one room'. I like this side of Tim: honest, irreverent, even about the people who employ him. Powerful speeches by Faulkner and Albanese in support of Garrett. We won the debate easily.

The dissident voice of Bill Ludwig stayed away. When I first became Leader, Ludwig and Little Billy Shorten pledged AWU support for me, but you can't trust them as far as you can kick them. Ludwig has been in the media complaining about Garrett because he has a few timber workers in his union and, most importantly, the local fellow who missed out in Kingsford Smith is an AWU acolyte. The union machines look at these seats as if they own them, the fiefdom effect for authoritarian types like Big Bill.

The Right-wing union, anti-Garrett view at the Executive was put by Joe De Bruyn from the Shoppies—so superbly described by Gough as the only Dutchman who doesn't like dykes. I closed my eyes during Joe's speech, an amazing effect, because he sounds just like Santamaria. What is it down at the NCC? Do they give them Santa voice training or something? Eric Abetz talks exactly the same way: that methodical, elongated, unusual speaking style.

Monday, 14 June

The fourth anniversary of Pills' death. Out of desperation to spend time with the boy, I took Ollie to the Mick Young Scholarship Trust races at Randwick today, a fundraising day that honours Mick's memory. A mistake, as the cameras swarmed all over him, even during our meal. We snuck away for one race down at the rails and spent some time together near the stables, but otherwise too public a place for the little champion. In the dog-house with Janine over it.

Gough greeted Garrett as a comrade (excellent thing for people to see) and paid out severely on Beazley and Swan: 'I'm glad you're here this year, comrade. Last year they turned it into a platform for their leadership challenge, sullying the memory of Mick Young. I see Swan's here again. This year he can't use it for internal Party purposes'.

During lunch Janine leant over and said, *sotto voce*, 'Mark, who is that woman who keeps staring at us through the window over there? It's really creepy'. I replied, 'That, honey, is the lovely Deborah Snow from the *SMH*. She's here to destroy our lives'. Janine knows the rubbishy story too well; it has haunted me and bugged her for six years. And Snow never stopped staring.

A day that has galvanised the full horror of this job: no time to play with my sons, journalists spooking Janine, the worst elements of the media and the Labor Party coming together over this wretched, ancient rumour. The image in my mind: that hand coming out of the ground in *Melrose Place*. An absurdity returning to plague me.

Thursday, 17 June

Overnighting at the Marriott Hotel: the end of a sitting week, did the McKell ALP Dinner earlier tonight in the huge Le Montage Function Centre in Leichhardt. There must have been 800 people there—when I spoke, I couldn't see the back of the room. There's a meeting of the PRC in the city tomorrow morning.

A horrendous phone call from Glenn at 6.30 p.m., just before I left for the function. He has two tip-offs that Snow is dining out on the sexual harassment and other bullshit stories. Friends of hers have contacted the office to warn us of what she is up to. It's an attempt to destroy my career, and portray me as a lecher, with a pattern of sexual misbehaviour. It's crystal clear that she is collaborating with Gwyther.

Mick Young ALP member, Port Adelaide 1974–88; min. in Hawke govt; died of cancer 1996

This is how bad it is: Snow's friends are dobbing her in. She is totally obsessed, spruiking this stuff at dinner parties. Given the nature of Sydney's rumour mill, it will end up all over the city. I am going to protest to the Fairfax management about this: it is shockingly salacious and unprofessional behaviour by the media.

Stunned by the call, I batted on and went to the function. Saw Craig Knowles outside and did my nanna about Gwyther. Found out that he still employs her part-time in his electorate office. Craig is a good person, but how am I supposed to feel: a State Labor minister employs this witch who's helping Howard. Unbelievable, truth is stranger than fiction.

Somehow I managed to give a decent speech, then arranged to have a few beers with Joel back in the city to talk about things. Felt better to tell someone about Snow. We discussed my options but they are limited. Defamation action sounds good, but it's impractical for someone in my position before a Federal election. Ignoring it is not an option, since she's bound to print something. I could maybe pre-empt it, but it would look extraordinary and panic-driven. I have no choice but to sit pat and see what happens. Funk, in a deep funk.

Saturday, 19 June

Fairfax with the Abominable Snow Woman running loose. Murdoch putting the drip on me. The media enemies are lining up one by one. The front page of today's *Daily Telegraph* screams, 'The Dismissal: How Mark Latham's Temper Ended A Proud 115-Year Cricketing Tradition'. A story from 25 years ago when I gave an umpire the bird for a crook LBW decision when playing for Sydney University and copped a one-week suspension for my troubles. They reckon I was the first player in the club's history to be suspended. I doubt it, and anyway, how could they hold records for 115 years proving that? Sounds ridiculous.

I was eighteen years old. The umpire was 'Boundary' Bob Brooks, an old sparring partner in Liverpool park cricket. He speared me out, so I gave him a razz in return. Now it's big news in the *Tele*, a quarter of a century later. Published on a Saturday, of course, junior sports day.

How low will these people go? I mean, if you were standing in the bar of the uni pavilion in 1979 and said to someone, 'You know, Latho's blue with the umpire today, that will be front-page news in 25 years' time', they would have locked you up in the madhouse. That's what I'm in now: a political/media madhouse.

Monday, 21 June

I would rather not be here. Parliament is back for its last week before the winter break. Terrible news for the True Believers: Jim Bacon has died, the Spanish Dancer finished him off yesterday morning. If you wanted to be a good Labor man, you wanted to be like Zorro. A tearaway radical in his youth, kept his larrikin spirit, a rebel in spirit and style—Zorro in appearance and character. The best of the Labor Premiers by a mile.

No good for my spirits, I can tell you, a deep feeling of funk. The Snow thing has got the hook in me. I feel guilty about being away from the boys, and personal crap like this blows up the emotions on me. Freddie Funk, as Janine calls it.

The last thing I needed today was a crisis meeting of the National Executive to sort out the Western Australian State preselections. The Shoppies (Mark Bishop and Billy Johnston) formed an unholy alliance with the Miscos (Marn in the thick of it, a so-called Leftie in bed with the worst elements of the Right) to roll Gallop and his preferred slate of candidates. Laurie came to see me this morning to drag me into the Right-wing Caucus to unpick their deal at the last minute. I went in hard, and told them to pull their heads in—publicly humiliating the Premier months before the Federal and State elections was not an option.

They looked daggers at me when they worked out I was fair dinkum. Gallop's humiliation is now theirs. Commonsense has prevailed and the union ticket has been rolled. Albo and Smith played good roles, perhaps not surprisingly: their intra-factional enemies (Marn and Bishop respectively) lost out. I went out on a limb on this one—am accumulating enemies big time—and for what? Gallop didn't even have the decency to call and say thanks. Had a big whinge to Danger about it tonight.

Other trouble is brewing. On McMullan and Cox's recommendation, the PRC decided last Friday to fold our tent on opposing the Government's PBS changes. No choice but to reverse our position, pass the price increases through the Senate and strengthen our Budget bottom line by $1.1 billion. Fiscal responsibility is paramount—we cannot expose ourselves to Government attacks on this flank. Unless we prove to the electorate our seriousness in maintaining surpluses, we might as well not turn up on election day.

A lot of spending plans have had to be dropped or postponed. There is no alternative. I would like to push forward, for instance, with my asset-

---

Jim Bacon Tas. ALP Premier 1998–2004, nicknamed 'Zorro'

Billy Johnston WA ALP State Sec.
Geoff Gallop WA ALP Premier 2001–

based programs (Nest Egg Accounts, Learning Accounts, etc.) but we can't afford them at this stage. If we win, I don't want to end up like Bracks and that rotten tollway. The golden rule in politics: the best way of keeping your promises is not to make any that you can't afford.

A long Shadow Ministry debate today, resisting the policy change. Smith was the most passionate speaker against the recommendation, harking back to his PBS plan when he was Shadow Minister for Health. In practice, it was nothing more than smoke and mirrors. It's typical of our culture: these people know how to spend money but don't know how to save it. Reports tonight from Danger of a Caucus revolt in the morning. More Freddie Funk.

Two articles in this morning's papers I have snipped out for my folder. Michael Baume in the *AFR* forecasting a Liberal campaign based on fear and smear. Baume is very close to Howard: do they know about the Snow bucket, and are getting ready to run off it, resurrect Abbott's research in Liverpool, the so-called character issue? Fear and smear, the standard Howard/Baume methodology.

The second: unusually supportive comments from Tanner in Milne's column. He was addressing a lobbyists' forum (Parker & Partners) and said that the old politics of pork-barrelling and budget programs is facing its Waterloo:

> What the press gallery sees as unusual, and indeed eccentric, on the part of Mark Latham and Labor, of actually talking about the issues that matter to people and talking about them in terminology that they can relate to, rather than about $23 million over four years and all that sort of nonsense, I think is ultimately going to triumph … I am confident the history that is going to be written at this election is that that politics is dead in Australia, and that a very different political paradigm has emerged.

That's our great hope: stooping to succeed, talking the language of the outsiders, the small nuggets of policy that matter to people. I must be doing something okay if Tanner is praising me.

Tuesday, 22 June

A disgraceful Caucus meeting this morning. The geniuses were getting ready to roll Comb-over on his PBS recommendation; there was a rollcall of speakers against him. Laurie said if I didn't jump into the debate the thing could be lost. So I exerted the Leader's authority: telling them that Caucus cheers when we make spending announcements but no one gives the economic Shadows credit for finding the savings—today we need to back them to keep the budget in surplus.

When I mentioned the surplus, Sharryn Jackson threw her head back and rolled her eyes, as if it doesn't matter. Well, try holding Hasluck with Labor's finances falling into deficit. She would be slaughtered by 20 per cent. I stared them down, avoiding a show of hands. I've got these people ahead in the polls (Newspoll and A. C. Nielsen showing the same thing, 52/48 our way), but realistically, we don't deserve to be in government.

The show lacks the discipline and foresight of sound economic management. All the instincts are for spending and spending, no sense of savings and financial prudence. And no sense of political discipline. Someone leaked news of the stoush to Channel Ten—it appeared on their morning news before the meeting had even finished. The person who did it must be deranged, consumed by bitterness, determined to junk our election prospects at any cost.

Crean blames Smith, says he saw him scurrying out of the Caucus room to the phone. He also reckons all the speakers against the recommendation were Beazley supporters. I didn't notice, but I suppose Simon still looks for these things. Other recriminations: Gillard is spewing about Macklin and Faulkner's failure to participate in the debate, to back the PRC decision and hose down the Left's anger: 'They call themselves leaders in the Left but when the hard fights are on, they are always missing in action'.

In fairness to Macklin, she strongly opposed McMullan in PRC, saying it was politically crazy to increase pharmaceutical prices. As for John, he's not a policy man, and is happy to sit and watch these debates. He's seen so much of it over the years, I think he just enjoys the carnage, almost resigned to the worst. As Governor-General, he then comes in to inspect the ruins, mop up some of the damage, and counsel the victims. I need to go on his list today.

The fools have turned a good story about fiscal responsibility/economic credibility into a huge yarn about Labor division. It made terrible TV tonight. First Snow, then Bacon, and now this. Disheartened by the Caucus debate, I couldn't be bothered announcing the PRC decision to the media, so I pushed McMullan out to fly solo.

What's the point of this place? It's a waste of time, makes you a stranger to your children, makes you a tourist in your own home. Then you have to sit there listening to the Caucus economic vandals, trying to throw away an election victory.

Poor Comb-over. Gartrell saw him on TV tonight and said, 'He looked like something was wrong with him, blinking at a million miles an hour', as he tried to explain the PBS decision. I probably should have helped him out with the media; it's the first time I have refused duty in this job. I'm too homesick to care, that's the truth of it.

Prompted by Laurie, Gallop finally rang to say he was grateful for my intervention, that he was contemptuous of Bishop and the unions. He's surprisingly upbeat about our election chances, impressed by my positive policies and speeches. Told me about and then faxed through some interesting research from the US (an article by Jonathan Chait in the May *Atlantic Monthly*). In every Presidential election since 1948, except one, the most optimistic/positive candidate, measured by the content of their acceptance speeches, was victorious. 'The exception was in 1968, when the "Happy Warrior" Hubert H. Humphrey came roaring from behind, only to lose narrowly to Richard Nixon.'

Love that nickname. That's what I need to be, the happy warrior. I need to put this funk behind me, to look positive and upbeat, even if I'm not.

Friday, 25 June

They gave Zorro a beautiful send-off in Hobart yesterday, but still horribly depressing for me. I wept and wept through the service, seated next to my five-eights Howard and Schieffer. As I get older, these things seem to affect me more severely. Is it that or my empathy with the man, a rebellious Labor larrikin who got knocked off by cancer? No justice for Jimmy.

Some good news: I'm home at last, out of that place early as they finish the sittings. I've left behind a terrible mess, however: the PBS controversy is still bubbling along, there's Caucus confusion about how to vote on the FTA legislation through the House (Gillard relied on Emerson's advice for parliamentary tactics, a recipe for disaster), and the Premiers are in town for COAG, cuddling up to Howard on the FTA and national water initiative.

Saw the ABC news. By far our worst night this year. No wonder there is plenty of speculation for an election on 7 August. Hard to see it, however, given what our marginal seat polling shows. Richards is convinced Howard has decided on 7 August, but I'm convinced he's wrong. Howard likes long, grinding campaigns, he might even push it into next year if he needs to. It's political water torture.

Reached for my quote book tonight and naturally turned to Nixon: how to find peace of mind in a crisis. He spoke of political crises as 'exquisite agony', as if he couldn't live without them, the outrageous highs and lows of public life. Thomas Jefferson called his Presidency a 'splendid

Hubert H. Humphrey US Vice-Pres. 1965–69; Dem. Presidential candidate 1968

Thomas Jefferson Third US Pres. 1801–09; drafted the Declaration of Independence

misery'. It's all bullshit. The Labor leadership is a miserable piece of agony. Full stop. I wouldn't mind if it just disappeared.

A telling moment earlier today. I left Canberra to attend a much post-poned lunch at Channel Nine in Sydney with their executives and news presenters. Towards the end of the function, I felt this thing swelling up on my right elbow—Christ knows what it is, but it's the size of a tennis ball tonight. For one moment I hoped it might be something serious, something that could get me out of this job.

Not good, hey, to think that way, even for a nanosecond. Talked to Janine about it tonight—she's as strong as ever. Told me to wake up to myself and keep going, and to get down to the doctor's to get this thing seen to. She's the Nixon/Jefferson in this household, more than me.

One last thing to report. Met with Beazley in my Parliament House office first thing this morning, a discussion brokered by Faulkner. (Danger also involved but with no great enthusiasm.) The Big Man wants to come back to the frontbench. John is very keen: a symbol of unity, put last year behind us, a chance to shut up the Americans on Iraq, bound to be well received in the electorate. My mood is so blasé at the moment, I put aside all our past differences (a million of them in this diary) and agreed to meet with Kim.

He seemed genuine enough: 'If you can get onto the domestic agenda, you will beat Howard, I have no doubt about that. That's why you can't afford to have an election campaign on foreign policy, on the American Alliance'. He's very confident that he can assist on that front, with his con-tacts in Washington and so on. He also said, 'We must win this time. If we don't, then the Party will implode in the next term of Parliament. We can't afford another term of Opposition, so I want to help out if I can'.

He said that his big turning point was at the Leadership Dialogue in Washington: he decided that he wanted to pursue a lifetime career as a parliamentarian. Then he put three conditions on a comeback:

* Rudd must not be demoted in any reshuffle—he called Rudd 'the best Shadow Minister for Foreign Affairs in the history of this Parliament'. Lavish praise, indeed.
* Beazley must get one of three Shadow Ministries: Defence, Homeland Security or Foreign Affairs. Sounds like he's had a discussion with Faulkner along the lines of Rudd for Shadow Treasurer, himself for Foreign Affairs and Crean for the scrapheap.
* He also wants a few modifications to our Iraq policy: 'Your policy is actually a good one, it just needs to be improved at the edges'. He said when he was sick with his brain leakage, lying flat on his back for

weeks, he turned himself into an expert on Iraq. He wants our policy to ensure that the Australian ship in the Gulf can protect Iraq's great strategic asset, the oil pipeline. He wants us to provide non-combatant assistance to the UN protective force. And he wants us to keep the Australian troops guarding our embassy in Baghdad, as Gough apparently did when he got out of Vietnam.

I'm not too keen on the last bit—it will be seen as a back-flip on troops out by Christmas. I told him I was positive about the idea of his coming back, and asked him to give me a bit of time to see what we can work out. I don't want to commit myself to his full list. The meeting ended on a very cordial note, and a strong handshake. Is this the end of six years of animosity?

Maybe this is the circuit-breaker I'm looking for, a chance to get out of this funk. The test for Beazley is to keep it under wraps. Any leaks and it becomes so much harder to manage. If he keeps it tight, I'll bring him back. Defence looks the best option.

Saturday, 26 June

The last thing I need, Bob Carr on the front page of *The Australian* today reigniting the Iraq debate. Somehow Shanahan has got hold of an interview to be aired on ABC radio tomorrow, where Carr's warning me to exercise the 'utmost diplomacy' on getting the troops out of Iraq, saying that when he was in Washington they felt 'wounded'. Obviously the Binstead doctrine has gone out the window. They must have re-indoctrinated him at the Leadership Dialogue.

If he's done an interview with the ABC for tomorrow, how did Shanahan get hold of it for today's paper? Carr was in Canberra yesterday for COAG. Shanahan is a regular vehicle by which Carr interferes in Federal issues—they know each other from Shanahan's time in the NSW gallery, circa 1988. You do the maths. Looks like Carr has given it to him. Two bites of the cherry: headlines today, the interview tomorrow, spearing me.

A replay of the last election. This is what Carr wrote in his diary on 6 November 2001, four days before polling day:

> Published polls and the Party's polling start to show Federal Labor edging up. Can't believe it. All those stories of people slamming doors in our faces. 'Maybe they're working class Tories who were always against us anyway' says Egan. 'We'll be the only ones weeping if Labor wins.' Yes—the secret agenda: State Labor wants to run

against a rotting, hated Coalition government in Canberra. A Labor Government there only makes a third (State) term harder.

People used to get expelled from the Party for this sort of treachery. Yet when it appeared in Marilyn Dodkin's book on Carr last year, no one batted an eyelid. Has it become part of the system? Everyone now expects Carr Labor to selfishly look after itself, cheering for a Howard victory, the supremacy of the State branches over the national interests of the Party.

You get isolated in this job, the degree of difficulty rises all the time. This is what Keating keeps saying: 'Only those who have been in the job know the loneliness of the Federal Labor leadership'. Too right.

Monday, 28 June

No end to the bad news. Dick Adams has launched an attack on Garrett—spooked by an article in the *Women's Weekly*, of all places. So foolish, so unnecessary. All bets are off with these galoots on forestry policy. Last Wednesday week I met with Adams and his industry mates (Terry Edwards and Barry Chipman) in Canberra. A jaundiced account of the meeting is in Milne's column today. It is now impossible to work with them in a constructive way. Now they are leaking to the worst of the worst, the Dwarf.

Everything they do is driven by hatred of the Greens and now Garrett, a man with good Labor values who did the right thing by joining the Labor Party. I also like Brown: other than economic policy, our beliefs are quite similar. I prefer his political values to the likes of Adams and Michael O'Connor, with their close links to the timber and woodchip bosses. It's a shame that people like Bob Brown have been lost to the Party. Gough tells me he was a member in Western Sydney in the 1970s.

A busy day in the city. Two highlights. Met Bill Gates—a regular sort of guy, contrary to his geeky public image. He's very community-minded, full of ideas for social entrepreneurship and helping the disadvantaged, in contrast to the business culture in this country. We need more capitalists like this to solve the problems of the world.

Had dinner with Kerry Stokes at his home in Darling Point. The exact opposite of Gates: he spent three hours talking about himself. A long convoluted story about what he sees as a massive conspiracy between Murdoch, Packer, Telstra and the AFL to do him out of the Aussie Rules

---

Marilyn Dodkin Author of *Bob Carr: The Reluctant Leader*, UNSW Press, Sydney, 2003
Terry Edwards Chief Executive, Forest Industries Association of Tas.

Michael O'Connor Senior Official, Forestry Div. of the CFMEU

broadcast rights at Channel Seven. I couldn't follow most of what he was saying, but if only half of what he said is true, it's the corporate story of the decade. Stokes is going to run it through the courts next year. But the case might last forever: this bloke can talk the leg off a chair.

Monday, 5 July

Enough is enough. I'm not going to have the media wanking themselves into a lather about my private life. I ended their silly little game this morning, and decided to call a press conference in Parliament House to clear the air, to answer any questions they wanted to ask on any subject. Surprised the journos (plus my staff). The objective: exhaust all their rumours and smears, plus pre-empt the Snow job on me. Took some skin off myself, but that's okay, her little exercise is looking decidedly sick as a news item.

There is no new story, just a new media game. I'm no longer a novelty. Now the contest is to see who can land the big fish, produce the story that wrecks my career. They must lie awake at night thinking they are Woodward and Bernstein. Australian investigative reporting, my arse; they wouldn't get a run writing for *The Bulls Roar*.

This all started with the profile on the *Sunday* program that went to air yesterday—a non-event, an embarrassment to Channel Nine, given all the hype they put into it. All they had was the Don Nelson incident from the *Age* profile in March. They couldn't even keep their so-called exposé under wraps: I knew what they were up to last week.

The *Sunday* reporter, Ross Coulthart, dined out on his story with Paul O'Grady (the former Labor MLC), foolishly big-noting himself, saying he had uncovered a scandal, that I thumped a bloke one election night in Liverpool. O'Grady passed it onto Faulkner, who then told me. John was quite cool about it, thought it was funny. He's right: it was hilarious when it happened.

On the night of the Liverpool by-election in 1989, the Labor campaign workers were having a few beers just before closing Peter Anderson's campaign office in Macquarie Street. I was the campaign director and had the keys. Peter Fraser was there and saw his mate Nelson stumbling around out the front. The RSL across the road had just closed and he wandered over, full as a boot. Fraser invited him in, as you do.

But then Nelson spotted me (I was on Liverpool Council at the time) and started to complain about the big pot plants in Macquarie Street.

Bob Woodward and Carl Bernstein Journalists for the *Washington Post* who broke the Watergate story in 1972

Apparently he had backed his car into one of them. This guy was a real pain
in the bum, an ugly drunk. I took the mickey out of him by saying I was a
man of direct action, let's go out to the street and move the pot plants ourselves. Everyone laughed at him, so he then took a swing at me.

Nelson was so pissed he couldn't have knocked his grandmother over.
I grabbed hold of him, wrestled him to the ground and then we chucked
him out of the campaign rooms. The only time I heard about it again was
when Conway (Nelson and Fraser's mate) told a Council meeting in mid-
1989 that I had been beating up old guys.

He fancies himself, vainglorious Ross, as an investigative reporter,
striding around like Sherlock Holmes. But he investigated something that
was reported three months ago as no big deal, and then shot his mouth off
about it. First Snow, and now Coulthart. The politics of the absurd: in its
day this thing was so newsworthy it never made the local rags in Liverpool.
Now it's a national event. First I have heard of Nelson for fifteen years. I
thought he was dead.

Last Thursday and Friday, Channel Nine started hyping the program,
talking up a 'violent incident in Latham's past' in the newspapers. On
Friday morning I was driving into the city for PRC when Vivian rang me to
say that Laws wanted to give me a sympathetic run, let me put my side of
the story. I rang him and he was right onside. So I kept on driving to the
2UE studios in North Sydney—a chance to pre-empt *Sunday*. I knew I was
on safe ground; the O'Grady tip was a beauty.

It went well with Laws, we laughed it off as a joke. But in all honesty,
I've got to hand it to Conway, Nelson and Fraser. From the point of view of
wanting to cause me grief, they have turned a sow's ear into a silk purse.
They could have used this story any time in the last fifteen years, dressed it
up as the Rumble in the Jungle, and got a run in the *Liverpool Champion*,
maybe the *Tele* on a quiet day.

But the buggers have got smart: they saw the taxi-driver thing, saw
me become Leader and then they let rip. My higher profile and the media
have done the work for them. They drew a blank with the *Age*, but got
lucky with big-noting Ross. He was sniffing around Liverpool determined
to find a smoking gun, old Sherlock tracking me down with his magnifying
glass.

I should be pissed off about it but I'm not. I'm getting good at conditioning myself to trivia. The only things that wound me now are things that
upset the family, things that might embarrass the boys one day.

I got asked about the family at the press conference today and felt
upset when thinking of the *SMH* stuff. I can't help it. But I shouldn't be
ashamed of showing emotion about Janine and the boys. I've never felt this

way before—a sign of how lucky I am at home. The rest of the conference was disciplined and controlled. I'm glad I did it.

That's Coulhart out of the way. I didn't watch his thing yesterday: I walked the dog and then Ollie pricked his hand with a nail, so we ended up at the doctor's. No point doing my Sunday special, so I cancelled the press conference at the top of my street re-announcing the Budget Pledge. Janine said the profile was boring (thanks, honey) but John Walker was good and Conway/Heyhoe looked like bitter old men (funny, that).

Once I dealt with Nelson, the media moved onto its next rumour, its next chance to land the big fish: a bucks' night video. Apparently the shit-sheet *Crikey* started it on Friday. Then, Louise Dodson in the *SMH* on Saturday: 'The Labor Leader is yet to respond to other revelations, reports of a raunchy video taken at his bucks' night before his second marriage'. Louise speculating about my private life: there's an interesting concept. Then the Dwarf was onto it yesterday: 'Over the past 48 hours, there's been fevered speculation in Canberra about the existence of a raunchy bucks' night video involving Latham, and whether that was the smoking gun to be fired by *Sunday*'.

The facts: I did not have a bucks' night before my second marriage. Carl Habib, a good bloke and dedicated ALP member, organised one at his home in Austral before my first marriage in November 1991. They chained my foot to a black ball, fed me beef rolls and beers, and organised a stripper to do what strippers do. Carl asked me if I was interested in anything else and I said no. That was it. Quite frankly, I was a bit embarrassed to be there at all, but Habib offered to pay for the night, so what could I do? I can't remember any video or cameras—that sort of thing wouldn't have been allowed. Carl assures me there were none.

It's all bullshit. So where did the rumour come from? On Saturday Craig Knowles, who was at the bucks' night, rang me to say that a *Sun Herald* reporter had asked him about it at a press conference in Sydney. He also told me that last month Gwyther, out of the blue, asked him whether I ended up with a prostitute that night. I asked Craig to think about how the paper knew he was even there. He agreed with me: Gwyther. At last, he has agreed to get her out of his office. He said he would do it slowly, so that she doesn't go off at him. Better late than never.

Craig also rang Byres, who then rang the *Sun Herald*'s editor, Phil McLean, to find out what was going on. Glenn says McLean told him the paper had a tip-off that Craig had photos of me having sex with a stripper/hooker. Two and two make four. The first wife is campaigning for Howard.

There she was yesterday in the *Sunday Tele*: so-called 'friends of Gabrielle Gwyther' saying that I was intimidating to live with. She's trying to give the impression that I'm a wife-beater. Well, I'm not. I've never laid a hand on a woman in my life. Our marriage broke up because of infidelity on both sides.

For me, the tipping point was Gabrielle's behaviour at an ALP function at Campbelltown RSL in August 1997—fondling another person under the table while I was sitting next to her. Then she told me all about her nursing days. Hooley Dooley, if I had known this I wouldn't have married her in the first place. She kept me in the dark for a decade.

That's how the marriage melted down; I did the wrong thing and so did she. A bitter mess, as can happen with these things. I found her story and background hard to handle. I was terribly embarrassed to start with—I couldn't tell any of my mates—but now I'm angry that she's attacking me. But by political necessity, I can't tell my side of the story—the tabloids would have a field day.

Anyway, who does Gwyther think she is, Princess Diana? Friends of Gabrielle Gwyther, what a joke. Like Conway, she's got smart—she put her head up in December and came off second-best. Now she's acting as a research assistant for the likes of Snow and Damien Murphy from the *SMH*—in fact, any journalist who wants to do me in.

I've had enough. I blew the whole thing sky-high at the press conference today, outing Gwyther, Conway and the Liberals for feeding the gutter campaign. The pressure is now on her. The media tonight staked out Gwyther's home at Casula. Her Greek husband (they named him Con Gwyther!) was on the news defending her, saying she hasn't been involved in any of it. Wait till he sees what Snow and Murphy have been up to. I should send him the list of Gwyther-inspired questions they sent me.

At the press conference I dropped in a reference to Gwyther and how the marriage really ended: 'It was really hard, it was messy, I would've made mistakes. I mean, there were things that you just wouldn't believe'. Yes, like August 1997 and the things she told me about herself.

I also told the press gallery about the 1998 sexual harassment smear. The fourth source of these rumours: our own people, the lovely Labor Party. Just as I pre-empted Coulthart, I needed to get out there and pre-empt Snow and Murphy. If the media worked themselves into a lather about a non-existent video, imagine what it would have been like when the *SMH* started pumping up its article: leaks about Gough's involvement etc. It was good to kill it today, to expose the sexual harassment thing as a myth.

Damien Murphy *SMH* journalist, co-author of a profile on me with Deborah Snow

Sam Maiden knew exactly what I was talking about; she was screaming out stuff about it on my right. A barfly from the Holy Grail, she knows the rumour from the bottom of her beer glass. So does Milne; he was into it like a rat up a drainpipe at the time. And on the job again yesterday: 'Political insiders have always been aware of rumours about Mr Latham's attitude to women'. Not relationships or history with women, but attitude. That's why they call him the Poisoned Dwarf.

And Louise Dodson this morning: 'Labor sources close to Mr Latham said yesterday there were more claims about his love life that were not raised in Nine's *Sunday* program'. Another interesting concept: Ab Fab moralising about my love life. What next: Michelle Grattan saying I am too ugly to be Prime Minister? So I had to raise it. Pre-emption is the only way to handle the Abominable Snow Woman. The only way to cut off another round of hysterical Lathamology, Fyshwick style.

Anything else happen today? Oh yes, met with the Prime Minister of Thailand, spoke at his parliamentary lunch and received a briefing from Gartrell on our latest polling. Now 53/47 our way 2PP, Howard catching up. But Tim's pretty relaxed about it: 'The previous numbers were a bit too good to be true; we expected them to come off like this'.

Flew to Brisbane this afternoon. Spent the night making notes and talking to Janine—she hopes the press conference will be a circuit-breaker. But honestly, what sort of life is this? The world's gone crazy.

Tuesday, 6 July

I've got to get out of this job. Rang Janine this morning: she was distressed and bewildered by something she saw on Seven's *Sunrise*. They had a discussion about the video. Steve Price claimed to have a copy of it, saying that it showed me in an intimate act with a stripper. Janine said he kept on reaching down under his chair, saying 'What if I had it here, what if I had it here?' He reckons some guy who rang his radio program yesterday has a copy as well. My two sons were watching this in our living room. No wonder Janine said she feels sick in the stomach.

I rang Habib to triple-check. There is no video. Glenn rang this evening to say that Price fessed up on his program. The call was a hoax. Small consolation for Janine and the damage at home. We can't go on like this. I should have taken my own advice in that Steketee article at the end of 2002—having young children and leading the ALP do not go together.

Politics: a million judgements on you all the time, the sense of privacy violation is extreme. Attack me, yes, but why should my wife and children

---

Sam Maiden *The Australian* journalist based in Canberra | **Steve Price** 2UE radio shock-jock in Sydney

suffer for the antics of a primate like Price? If the media had any standards
they would sack him for incompetence. But no, he's a radio shock-jock: the
more sensational and inaccurate he is, the more he gets paid.

Somehow managed to drift through the rest of the day. Unloaded on
Snow and Murphy on Brisbane radio. There is no limit to their investiga-
tion: tracking down Janine's dancing school teacher; asking questions
about my sisters when they were teenagers, irrelevant nonsense. Calling
my mates from the Bulls, telling them they got their names and addresses
from Gwyther. Doorknocking up and down our street in Glen Alpine,
looking for scuttlebutt. A pair of sick puppies.

Launched our housing policy with Melham at the Kyabra Community
Housing Association in Brisbane. The idea was to roll out a social investment policy, a down payment to the social sector after our PBS fiasco. A
good document: investment in new stock, revitalisation of the CSHA, an
enhanced role for community housing, plus an innovation fund to lure in
superannuation investment, the Kelty plan. I thought the media might give
it a decent run, moving on from videos that don't exist, but television
tonight was still down at Fyshwick. More fool me for thinking it might be
different.

Wednesday, 7 July

The trauma of this Steve Price thing is going to be around for a while. I'm
worried that it has broken Janine's spirit. She has been the strong one so
far, domestically and politically. Just imagine what it was like for her with
the boys at her feet. I need to get out of this mess asap. The barbarians are
at the gates, coming inside my home, hurting the people I'm supposed to
protect.

Got through the rest of the day by conditioning my mindset, by
sending up the absurdity of what I do. Toured the Townsville Show with
Anita Phillips, our hapless candidate for Herbert. When I said troops out by
Christmas, she told the local media, 'He didn't say which Christmas'. Where
do we get them from? And how do I give them back?

Flew down to Sydney for State of Origin III, a big NSW win. Attended
the NRL pre-game function: the would-bes from the Murdoch and Packer
empires strutting around, disgracing themselves in various ways. I despise
the commercialisation of sport. Up close, these people are simply horrible.

Sat next to David Gallop, Murdoch's man running the game. He was
ticked off that Bob Carr was late, saying that 'We are never going to invite

State of Origin III Game 3 in an annual rugby
league series between NSW and Qld

him again. He does this to us every time, we can't start the function until he gets here'. I told him to relax: 'Come on, everyone knows Bob hates the footy. He'll thank you for it if you never invite him again. Just start the function without him. He couldn't care less, I can assure you'.

Just then Bob walked in, the butt of jokes for the rest of the night. He doesn't know the difference between Ronald Reagan and Reg Reagan, etc. Both sides of this charade should be honest with each other and let Bob have a night off; send him bushwalking somewhere.

David Britton tells a funny story of taking Carr to an Eels game at Parramatta Stadium in the early 1990s. Bob sat there uninterested and then disappeared at half-time. David got worried and went looking for him; he found him getting into his car out the back of the grandstand. David asked what he was doing and Bob said he was going home, the match was over. David explained it was half-time and Bob protested, 'No, I can't go back to watch more of that; they walked off the field, so it must be over'. Now the NRL delays the pre-match functions for him.

A footnote to the *Sunday* program: Vivian tells me that Coulthart rang her, saying that he wanted to resign over the way John Lyons had hyped the profile and then left him (Coulthart) looking ridiculous. Yes, that's how he looks, but the bigger question is this: why shouldn't Channel Nine sack him for being a flapper-mouth and a fool? One of your best, Sherlock.

I tried to offer some comfort for what had happened when I got home tonight. But I'm only here for twelve hours; I leave in the morning for two days' campaigning in Dobell and Paterson. There must be a better life than this.

Saturday, 10 July

A thud on the front lawn. The Abominable Snow Woman and her story have made it onto my property. It is as awful as I had imagined. So bad, in fact, that it was almost amusing. I got to the end of it and couldn't decide what it reminded me of most: a long Gwyther therapy session or a long *Penthouse Forum* letter. An amazing piece of journalism that tries to fit me up as a lecher and a pervert, but never produces hard evidence; it just skates around the issue with titbits of soft porn.

It starts with the Mick Young race day. I'm a loner because I went down to watch a race at the rails with Janine and Ollie. Maybe I like to spend time

---

Ronald Reagan US Pres. 1981–89
Reg Reagan Ocker character/rugby league supporter played by Matthew Johns on the Sydney *Footy Show*

John Lyons Executive Producer of Channel Nine's *Sunday*

with the people I love, silly weird me. Then it gets into a cacophony of Gwytherisms. Here's a sample.

Her good Christian family was upset when the *Freaks of Nature* video was screened at her thirtieth birthday party. And no, they weren't five-legged horses on the screen, it was a porno. She blames me for it. But this is what happened. It was up at Javed's Pakistani restaurant in Liverpool, September 1994. It was a good night: the Bulls on the grog, Gwyther's family drinking iced tea, Javed playing his videos on the screen in the background. He owned the video store next door.

Towards the end of the night I was joking with Javed, 'What's the story, mate, with these girls dancing under the waterfalls on the screen? How about jazzing it up a bit; come on Javed, have a go'. I never expected him to do anything about it, I was just taking the piss out of him. Then he disappeared next door and whacked the *Freaks* on. The fellas were crying with laughter as the Gwythers scurried out the door tut-tutting. The birth of a legendary story. Every time I see David Britton we still laugh about it. It still cracks up Sanchez today, the mere mention of the *Freaks*.

Gwyther also rolls out her version of how the marriage ended. No mention of her hi-jinx, of course. The story is woven into the 1998 rumour. After all this time, there it is in black and white: 'Gary Gray became concerned over the fallout from a liaison he believed Latham to be having with a young staffer in the office of a then federal Liberal Minister'. Thanks, Gary, for your concern. I'm sure Penny Fischer is also delighted with your bullshit, your concern about a fallout from a liaison that never happened.

Snow and Murphy have delved right into this thing, asking people on both sides of politics. If the Libs (Nutt in Howard's office) ever received a complaint about me they would have dropped it into the mix right now. Nothing is more certain. But there is nothing, no complaint about me whatsoever. A story as credible as the bucks' night video—the sick Canberra culture at work.

Snow and Murphy have come up with some weird stuff. There's one about a date with a woman while I was working for Gough. I've no idea who they are talking about, but apparently we had dinner in Darlinghurst and then I invited her up to the office in William Street: 'While in the library she claims he made an advance, which she rejected. He took her down in the lift without another word. Latham chose not to comment on this incident. It showed a strange mix of solicitude and insensitivity which, his former wife claims, would become a hallmark of their marriage'.

Solicitude and insensitivity because I am supposed to have propositioned someone, been rejected and then gone home. Well, that's it, 95 per cent of single men are shot to pieces. The *SMH* ought to put the spotlight on the real shockers: the blokes who get knocked back and then bat on regardless. Now, that's insensitivity.

Here's another Gwyther ripper: 'The problem was his behaviour affected my family, particularly my parents'. No mention of her behaviour, of course. And I wonder how Con Gwyther is feeling today? His statement to the media looks a bit shaky. Pardon the pun, but he's been Conned.

Something else that jumps out of this *Penthouse* letter. It quotes Les Stubbs, an old school friend whom I haven't seen since the bucks' night: 'There was a stripper, and there were a few cameras with people taking photographs but there was nothing that went on to make it a big deal'. The first source that mentions cameras or videos at Habib's place.

Is this how the rumour started: Snow feeding Stubbs's stupid comments into the Sydney grapevine? The *Sun Herald* asked Knowles about photographs, not a video. Another indication in the article: 'Carl Habib staged a roistering bucks' night for the mayor at his isolated giant truck and auto repair workshops in Fourth Avenue, Austral. An impressive amount of salacious lore has grown up around the event. Gwyther says she and Latham were still arguing about it "years later"'.

The only time Gwyther raised it 'years later' was with Craig Knowles. We never argued about it at all, it was a non-event. Plus Snow/Murphy have the address wrong: it was at Carl's house in Austral, kilometres away. The only time Gwyther ever visited Austral was to attend the Habib Bros' Christmas party, conducted—you guessed it—in the workshop at Fourth Avenue. She thought that's where the bucks' party was held, and has passed on this misinformation to the journos.

Gwyther, Snow and Murphy are in this up to their armpits. A hatchet job in the paper and on the rumour mill as well. The profile is to be continued on Monday. I can hardly wait.

Finally getting this Beazley thing sorted out. Under pressure all week from Gartrell and Faulkner to make the reshuffle more substantial. They want me to move Crean and make Rudd the Shadow Treasurer, putting Beazley into Foreign Affairs. Their great fear is that the Coalition will target Simon during the campaign, attacking our economic credibility through his unpopularity. Crean's polling numbers are still terrible.

That's Tim's hierarchy of fear: negative advertising about Simon, my inexperience and Liverpool Council. He's upbeat about bringing back the Bomber: 'I know he's weak and doesn't stand for much, but the punters like him—no doubt about that from our research. This will be a plus for us, no matter what job you give him'. We need something, a bounce from somewhere, that's for sure.

Spoke to Laurie about it this morning and he said, 'Mate, if you replaced Simon with Rudd your Caucus supporters would go into meltdown'. He's right. Instinctively, I have never liked the idea: Crean is competent, that's the main test, and I can't stomach the thought of promoting Rudd. So it's Beazley for Defence and Chris Evans into a junior defence role. I'll announce it on Monday, and follow with a speech on national security at the Australian Institute of International Affairs in Sydney.

Cooney has done a good job with Kim working on the text of the speech and fine-tuning our Iraq policy. He reckons Kim's first draft was 'incomprehensible, typical Beazley, using 50 words when a dozen will do'. I'm knocking it into shape this weekend.

Beazley's list of policy changes has been sorted. No problem in protecting the pipeline; we have said from day one we support Operation Slipper in the Gulf. A good package of assistance for Iraq: border security, health care and non-combatant personnel for the UN protective force. However, no change in our stance on security at the embassy. We will take the appropriate advice in government and act on it.

The burdens of this job. There is the *SMH* article, sitting on our dining table, a reminder of Beazley's role in the 1998 smear. Yet here I am, getting ready to announce his return to the frontbench. Anything for Party unity, anything to beat Howard. I'm treating Kim better than he ever treated me. Laurie reminded me this morning of his attempt to get me back on the frontbench in early 2000. He fronted Beazley in Sydney and put the suggestion to him. Kim leaned back, looked dismissive, crossed his legs in disdain and replied, 'Next question'.

Monday, 12 July

Got home tonight and Janine was worried about me. Said I looked white and petrified on TV while announcing Beazley's comeback. That's a good description of how I felt. He's a funny guy; he scared the shit out of me.

We were getting ready for the press conference in the CPO, running through the questions the media might raise. I asked him what he would say if they asked about the budget black hole in 1995–96. He replied, 'I'll defend it. Deficits can be appropriate, depending on the economic circumstances. I'm sure when we get back into government we will have deficits again; there's nothing wrong with that'.

Operation Slipper Australia's contribution to
the anti-terrorist campaign in the Persian Gulf

Yes, there is. That's not my intention, nor is it good economic policy. I told him to stick to the rhetoric and contents of our Budget Pledge. No wonder I was pale. In the end, the press conference was fine—no one asked the nightmare question. No leaks, so the surprise factor was full on.

And the speech went well this evening. A good policy combination: troops out of Operation Catalyst, helping rebuild Iraq through the UN, and the Bomber back to gag the Americans. I've made my point about them, I suppose. People know where I stand and they know where Howard kneels. Hopefully, this will shut them up during the campaign, and let me focus on our vote-switching issues: health, education and the good society.

This morning's *SMH* had the second half of the Snow job. No end to Gwyther's rant. Now she's an expert on how I grew up in Ashcroft, talking about Mum and me: 'They're a psychological case study. She didn't have such an intense relationship with her daughters ... Growing up, it was all to do with Mark'. I met Gwyther in August 1987, four years after we left Ashcroft. I was 26 . She didn't see any of my childhood or that of my sisters, who have always had an 'intense relationship' with Mum. The psychological case study is in Gwyther's head.

The profile peters out today. Not much media interest in Saturday's burst, just a few of the Murdoch mob sniffing around. The media are as exhausted as I am. Shows the wisdom of pre-emption. The Sunday papers would have jumped all over the *SMH*'s salacious piece if I hadn't got in first. It's now known as the emotional press conference, but it was better than facing sensational front pages and speculation day after day.

One last point: Snow and Murphy's profile is full of errors: that I played with the Bulls while at uni (untrue), Frank Heyhoe lived in the same street as us (he didn't even live in the same suburb), Heyhoe put me in contact with Gough for my uni thesis (big-noting bullshit, as usual) and the wrong location for the bucks' night. How do two journalists spend months investigating someone and still make so many basic mistakes? They were more interested in their preconceived view of me than in reporting the facts, that's how.

Friday, 16 July

A good week's campaigning through McEwen, Bendigo and Ballarat. The Beazley announcement has helped us regain some traction in the media. I followed up in Melbourne yesterday with a cooperative agreement with the Premiers, *sans* Beattie, about needs-based schools funding and health system reform, eliminating waste and duplication.

Operation Catalyst Australian contribution to the invasion of Iraq

We wanted to include Kyoto in the agreement by setting up a national carbon-trading system, but Beattie refused to cooperate, so it had to be dropped. He's super-sensitive about the coal industry, but it's crazy in terms of Queensland's long-term interests. Global warming is killing the Great Barrier Reef, the State's main economic and environmental resource, and Beattie won't support Kyoto to do something about it. He's the only person I know of who wrote his autobiography, *In the Arena*, before getting into Parliament—he must think he's Teddy Roosevelt. Now he's rough-riding over the Reef, watching it die because of coral bleaching.

Went to the AWU Annual Ball at Crown Casino tonight. Little Billy sitting on my right, Big Bill on my left—the things you do in this job. Good feedback from Peter McMullin about his doorknocking in the new housing estates in Corangamite. He reckons I'm travelling well, lots of positive comments.

Little Billy was in my ear about the FTA, telling me the Party has to support it. I said that I thought both he and his union were against it, to which he responded, 'That's just for the members. We need to say that sort of thing when they reckon their jobs are under threat. I want it to go through. The US Alliance is too important to do otherwise. Politically, you have no choice'.

Great, the two faces of Little Billy Shorten: Public Shorten against the FTA, Private Billy in favour of it. Is this why he's being groomed for one of the top slots in the corporation? Political courage is not his long suit. Not a bad night otherwise. It's a long way from the shearing sheds, but the AWU puts on a good show.

Monday, 19 July

A good event at a children's play centre in Murphy's electorate this morning to launch our women's policy. The women's policy was put out as an after-thought in the last campaign, so the sisters were keen to get it out early this time. Roxon has done a good job pulling it together.

Excellent interview with Michael Duffy on Radio National this after-noon about social capital: the quality of our society, the way in which we relate to each other, the nuggets of social policy that can help build stronger communities. This is the big Labor item: without trust in society there can be no mutualism, and without mutualism there can be no lasting

---

Kyoto agreement International agreement to limit the emission of greenhouse gases into the atmosphere

Teddy Roosevelt US President 1901–09; famous for his contribution to the Rough Rider Regiment during the Spanish–American War

redistribution of public resources, no progressive social reform. The foundation stone of good society lies in trusting, cooperative relations between people.

Duffy is a thoughtful journalist in wanting to talk about these issues. The press gallery wouldn't know what social capital means. They have a new mantra: show us your tax policy. It's still not ready; Crean is taking forever. They have lost interest in the social issues I raised earlier in the year—they have the attention span of budgies.

I'm going to check out the set of *Big Brother* on the Gold Coast tomorrow, officially to look at its economic spin-offs. But it's my chance to look at the voyeur phenomenon, to perve on the perves. I talk about mutualism but our society is built around voyeurism: the cult of instant celebrities, people mesmerised by strangers on TV. *Big Brother* has become a substitute for social capital. I need to write more about this; I touched on it in *Civilising Global Capital* but there's a lot more to be said.

A sick society and a sick political system feed off each other. I'm still thinking of the Coulthart/Snow drama. It's bloody amazing that the so-called cream of Australian journalism have looked into all corners of my life, devoting months of research, but failed to come up with anything of substance. The hysteria has been about bullshit and trivia. As I said to Glenn last week, there are a handful of things in my political career that I genuinely regret. He didn't want to know about it, so let me record them here:

- accepting Heyhoe and Conway's charity. I should never have done it. They broke their word, and it was never worth the trouble it caused. Mum was right
- the Liverpool preselection, my one flirtation with machine politics, a hopeless mess that dragged on for months, and then it took me years to recover in the local branches. I should never have run for a State seat in the first place. Just think: if I had won, I would still be trapped in Macquarie Street, wasting time in the do-nothing Carr Government
- losing contact with Don Craig in the mid-1990s. He was my mentor in local government days, and shared my dislike of the Council club. He had no phone or car, so I used to drop by his house in Maryvale Avenue, Liverpool, but then I moved to Campbelltown and lost touch. I feel sad about that; he was a superb anti-Establishment strategist

Big Brother Reality TV show where people are locked up together in a house for a certain number of weeks with live cameras on them 24/7; a worldwide phenomenon

- puffing on a joint at a corridor party in the ministerial wing in 1994. A new chum in Parliament, a journo, passed it down the line and I didn't see any harm in joining in. But pretty dumb when you think about it. Plenty of people were around at the time, so how come no one has raised it?
- calling Albrechtsen a skanky-ho. It was stupid, immature and reckless, no wonder the Tories keep raising it. I can't apologise publicly because the reason for saying it was actually worse than what I said.

More fallout from the Snow/Murphy profile: Keating is urging me to strike back at Howard. He wants me to read something Mungo MacCallum has written on the Internet about Howard's past indiscretions: his relationship with one of his secretaries and the parties he used to throw during the Fraser years. According to Paul, 'It was all laid on for the blokes with Howard in the middle of it. We've got to get the *Herald* to investigate those parties'.

I told him I'm not interested. The truth is, I'm over it—solemn and uninterested in this sort of stuff. It's like the old nuclear doctrine during the Cold War: mutually assured destruction (MAD). Anyway, imagine Howard throwing the leg over someone—it's unbelievable. The Canberra rumour mill is insane with some of the things it comes up with. For years, Howard has had to put up with rumours about Pru Goward, just like I've copped them about her daughter, Penny Fischer. Is that what they mean by generational change in Australian politics?

The Libs have stirred up shit on me but, truth be known, most of it has originated from our side of politics, people who were in the Labor Party at one stage or another. Look at the list: Heyhoe, Conway, Fraser, Harrington, Waller, Lynch, Gray, Ray and Beazley. They couldn't stop me getting the leadership, but bloody hell, they have given the Libs a bucketload of bullshit to chuck at me. And it's not just me. The worst hatchet jobs seem to come from inside our show: the job on Kernot, the rumours about Bob Carr, the Sussex Street gay mafia, etc.

You get used to hearing this stuff in politics, it's part of the culture. But I can honestly say I haven't been a player, trying to drag down colleagues this way. I've tried to handle it with a bit of humour, inventing the odd nickname or two. That's the best way of handling gossip: treat it as a joke. But I can't find anything funny in the shit they have thrown at me.

Mungo McCallum Long-time Canberra press gallery journalist and political commentator, now living on the north coast of NSW
Pru Goward Fed. Sex Discrimination Commissioner, Human Rights and Equal Opportunity Commission
Colin Harrington Councillor, Liverpool City Council 1987–2004; defected from the ALP to become an Independent in 1990

Then there is Gwyther—I married her, sure, but the Knowleses adopted her politically. After our marriage broke up, they housed her in their Leacocks Lane unit, gave her positions at branch meetings, made her part of their Liverpool South operation (the branch books and all that), employed her in Craig's electorate office and even put her on the Council ticket. They have had her on the State Labor payroll while she's been running this campaign against me.

How much do I owe these people now? Not much, really. I'm doing this job on my own terms, according to my own values and standards. It was ever thus. I started with nothing down in the old Valley and that's what I've got to lose: nothing. Year zero.

Wednesday, 21 July

A dysfunctional day's campaigning in Richmond. I rarely seem to get a clear day any more, of good events without the hiccups. A sign that the office is struggling with the pressures of continuous campaigning. That's my concern about Richards: he's not a political strategist. He just needs to run an efficient office but that's not happening. A terrible dilemma: I don't know what he does of a day but not much I can do about it—it's too close to an election to find a new Chief of Staff.

Vivian fluffed the media program today: she failed to send out the notices herself, and left them to Malinda. As a result, the local media missed my main media event at the Tweed Hospital, so they jumped all over me at the opening of Justine Elliot's campaign office. It was a shambles; the event hadn't been advanced properly and a railway protestor grabbed the lime-light. The worst possible outcome: the main focus of my visit is the Carr Government's decision to close the Murwillumbah–Casino rail line.

Another part of State Labor's secret agenda? For the sake of a few million dollars in budget savings, Carr and Costa have closed down a rail line in the most sensitive Federal marginal seat in NSW. Why not wait until the end of the year? Better still, why not make the savings in a blue ribbon Coalition seat? One option is for Federal Labor to rescue the line finan-cially. It's terrible public policy, and a precedent for rescuing every State Government stuff-up around the country.

I've resisted pressure from Faulkner to announce a rescue plan. Marn is not keen, Danger agrees with the precedent problem, but now we have no choice. Based on today's fiasco, if we don't save that wretched rail line we can't save Elliot's campaign in Richmond. It has to be done. I've been forced into a corner by the Carr/Costa wrecking ball.

Justine Elliot ALP candidate, Richmond | **Michael Costa** NSW Transport Min.

Saturday, 24 July

I spoke too soon about the hooch. Addressed an early childhood education conference in Melbourne this morning and then, from left field, faced a volley of questions from reporters at my doorstop about marijuana smoking. I should have told them to nick off because it's old news—I answered questions about this in December when I first became Leader. But foolishly, I repeated my confession about having tried it in the past.

Horrified to watch the TV news tonight; Channels Nine and Seven went off about it. Geof Parry on Seven made me look like a criminal, with an inference that this may have been a recent event. Plus he said I must have known the question was coming and didn't need to answer it. Why's that? I was down there talking about early literacy and playgroups—I was expecting questions about childcare places, not bongo juice.

Another unnecessary distraction. Asked Alison Crosweller to call around the Sunday papers to let them know this is not news, that it was first reported seven months ago. The last thing I need is a burst of tabloid sensationalism about it. The media must know about the 1994 thing, so I'm bracing myself for the worst, quite frankly. When will I ever get to stop talking about myself and all this crapola? This job is worse than being locked up in the *Big Brother* house.

Tuesday, 27 July

Spent the day in Adelaide launching our anti-gambling policy: a program of comprehensive Federal involvement in what has always been seen as a State issue. It's the sort of policy issue that should ignite a major public debate, but was overshadowed by injudicious comments by Kate Lundy about her opposition to the FTA. She rang me last night to tell me that she had said too much to an ABC radio reporter. Howard's jumping all over it today.

It was a mistake to let the FTA debate run this far. The Party doesn't have the maturity to handle these things without it spilling over into a public brawl. Klundy is a classic example: she can't control her emotions or her mouth. After the Caucus fiasco on the PBS, I have been careful not to override the Party's right to have a proper debate on the FTA. Parliament should also respect the Senate Committee process, and be guided by the evidence, the virtues of empirical politics. No marks for this in the media, however; they only report conflict in the political arena.

Alison Crosweller Press Sec. in my office 2004 | **Kate Lundy** ACT ALP Sen. 1996– ; Shadow Arts, Information Technology & Sport Min. 2003–04; nicknamed 'Klundy'

Howard is all over me, trying to brand my leadership as weak, the ALP as split in two. He has plenty of material to work with, that's for sure. The Little Americans on the Right want to tick the thing through as quickly as possible. The Left is resolutely opposed; a delegation from Faulkner and Albanese yesterday reinforcing the point. Cookie is in the middle, trying to craft a third option: to defer the FTA-enabling legislation in the Senate until a Labor Government can renegotiate a better deal with the US.

The unions are all over the shop, with ranting Doug Cameron leading the opposition. Yet Combet, supposedly on the Left, is telling me to pass it (a long conversation yesterday). He's like Shorten: he maintains a public façade of opposition but supports it behind the scenes. Is this what they mean by internal Party consultation? I could consult until the cows come home, but it wouldn't resolve the huge differences inside the show.

I appreciate Combet's candour, but his relationship with Sharan Burrow sounds poisonous. He wants me to ignore her opposition to the FTA as an irrelevance and follow the political necessity of getting it out of the way so that we can campaign on our issues. Yesterday he told me: 'Listen, Mark, Sharan and I often have different points of view. She can be a very difficult person to deal with and on this issue you need to ignore her. It's not clear the FTA will cause any real damage to the manufacturing sector. What we're more worried about is a FTA with China'.

I'm not the leader of a political party; it's actually a loose coalition of interest groups. How can I realistically deal with the union movement when the ACTU Secretary tells me to ignore the public views of its President and a decision of its Executive? I'm at a loss to know what to do, that's the truth of it. The FTA has mild economic benefits for Australia but plenty of loopholes and anomalies: the tariff triggers, possible damage to the PBS, intellectual property, etc.

The Party is fundamentally divided and I feel paralysed, unable to find a third way through. In the end, I think it may be best to back Cookie's recommendations and push them through as Party policy. He's head of the Senate Committee, he's heard all the evidence, he's a trade policy expert and he's no mug politically. Also one gutsy guy: having to deal with the Spanish Dancer while trying to help me out of this mess.

Crunch day in a week's time when Parliament comes back. At the moment I'm in Micawber mode, hoping that something turns up. That, and grinding through this job, day after day. All I do is campaign from one marginal seat to another, from one policy announcement to another,

---

Micawber Character in Charles Dickens's *David Copperfield*

trying to regain momentum while Howard gets a trouble-free run in the media. My only consolation is that some day this campaign is going to end.

Saturday, 31 July

We can't win. Tim faxed through the latest research (polling and focus group analysis) this afternoon, a lengthy report from Utting about our political situation, with a set of recommendations on how to get back into the race. It makes for bleak reading: our position has fallen away over the past month; all the trends are running Howard's way. Our lead has been cut to 51/49—not enough to win government. *(See Appendix 2 for a summary of the Utting report.)*

I read the report and then went out to the backyard to break the bad news to Mum and Janine, to get them used to the idea of defeat. Mum doesn't believe it, and Janine still sounds optimistic. True believers in my ability to defy gravity. That's what we need to do: the economy is so strong and the Government is travelling reasonably well. The national mood is upbeat and, according to Utting, 'doesn't present a strong structural case for change'. We need to rewrite the political textbook to win this thing.

After everything we have been through, this is hard to accept, but it's not going to happen. Utting is no fool; the subtext of his report is that we are now pitching at a respectable defeat. A jolt to the system, and I need to use it that way. I have nothing to lose, so I might as well fire up, take some risks and break the shackles of this flat period I have been through.

Since the Budget, Howard has lifted his game—busy all over the country with clear-air announcements. The electorate no longer sees him as running out of puff. My numbers are still okay, but they need to be in the stratosphere if we are going to win. The Government's attacks on me have had an impact: people no longer clearly associate me with the Ladder of Opportunity rhetoric and policies. The rollout of the policy nuggets has not cut through after all.

The electorate is pretty perceptive. According to Utting, 'Concerns have emerged from the most recent focus groups that Mark Latham appears distracted, tired or disinterested'. That shouldn't surprise me, I suppose—I have been distracted and disinterested, and people have picked up on it. I can't afford to let the personal stuff get me down any longer, that's clear. I can't allow the slide in our vote to continue. If the funk runs through the election campaign, we'll get smashed, reduced to the size of the State Opposition parties around the country.

The economy that we built in government is now sustaining incumbents everywhere. We need to keep repeating our economic credentials:

the scale of our Budget savings, that we can pay for our promises—in fact, we will run a bigger surplus than Howard and Costello in government. But more needs to be done to close down this Liverpool Council nonsense; Utting says it's a worry in the focus groups. Tim has been talking to Maurie Daly and apparently he's keen to help out.

Disappointing that the rollout of my social policy announcements has fallen flat. The Government/media mantra about releasing our tax policy has had an impact. Too many of the Sunday specials were overwhelmed by other stories. It's hard to break the mould of the traditional media agenda (the hip pocket nerve) and get them to focus on the breakdown of society.

Plus Howard has worked overtime to run me into the ground. He seems to be able to launch negative attacks without paying the normal political price for negativity. It's the advantages of incumbency, plus he's been around so long he must have a reservoir of goodwill in the electorate that he can draw on when he needs to. Utting has summed it up well:

> [The voters] don't directly link the Prime Minister with the blame [for their concern about problems in the health and education systems]. It's surprising when one reflects on this. Consider the facts: the Prime Minister has launched and orchestrated a ferocious personal attack on the Opposition Leader, presided over the wholesale destruction of Medicare and bulk billing; and skewed higher education policies against average Australians. Despite all this, he remains popular and respected by voters ... [Howard] has managed to triangulate himself out of the political equation, riding serenely above the tumult and combat of day-to-day politics.

The report makes a series of recommendations, Utting's plan to halt the move away from us. We must campaign hard on the vote-switching issues our way: health, education and the cost of living—people are worried about Howard's support for user pays. We need to resurrect the Ladder of Opportunity message and attack Howard's credibility, label him a blame shifter, point out how he won't tell the truth about the Liberal leadership succession and so on.

Plus steer clear of Iraq. Yes, the troops-out policy has not worked as I'd hoped it might. The electorate is polarised: 50 per cent hate Howard's policy on Iraq and 50 per cent hate mine. Not a great vote-shifter, not a

---

Professor Maurie Daly Appointed by the NSW govt in 2003 to investigate and report on the financial management of Liverpool City Council and its controversial Oasis development

frontline policy for our campaign. Gartrell keeps saying it's a 50/50 issue in our polling—we should move on to other issues.

I called Tim back to run through the document but he didn't have much to add. He's the world's most laid-back campaign director. I hope that's an asset. We agreed on Utting's analysis and recommendations—a campaign based on the Ladder of Opportunity that concentrates on health, education and the cost of living.

I'm worried about the loss of the ladder identity, the way in which it has faded from the electorate's mind. Journalists have been saying that I use this rhetoric/imagery too much, but now the public can't even remember it. Tim, however, was pretty relaxed: 'It happens to all Oppositions, but the campaign will sharpen it up, I'm sure. We are not going to have a Beazley problem'.

The small nuggets/policy announcements didn't work, so what can I do now? No choice but to go down the Utting path and follow his recommendations. I tried to keep the pressure on a long-serving government but the pressure came onto me and the FTA is keeping it there.

We have one good shot left in the locker: the user pays/cost of living agenda, praying all the time that our tax and family policies stand up to scrutiny, that there are no funding holes. Cooney is reporting good progress in that area; meetings with Anne Harding and Peter Dawkins next week to finalise the package. A chance to catch the Government by surprise.

First, I've got to sort out this FTA mess. For the first time in this job, I've got no idea what to do. I'm all over the shop, just like the colleagues and the range of options the Party keeps pushing at me. A dog's breakfast.

Thursday, 5 August

Utting is right, absolutely right: we do better when we campaign on the big issues of health and education. I think I'm off the hook on the FTA, a last-minute decision to craft an internal Party compromise: support the FTA in principle for its economic benefits—thereby pacifying the Right. But amend the enabling legislation to protect Australian cultural content and the PBS, guarding against evergreening by the big US drug companies, where they use bodgie patents to keep cheaper generic drugs off the market. This gives the Left something to fight for.

I was trying to hold the Party together but it also seems to have wrong-footed Howard. The political advantage for us is to fight for the future of the PBS: it turns the FTA into a health and cost of living issue, per the Utting doctrine. It also compensates for our PBS stuff-up in June. This may be a miracle weapon, more by accident than design.

I worked out the compromise on a RAAF plane on Monday, on my way back from one of those terrible things you do in this job: glorifying war at a military parade in Townsville. I was re-reading Cookie's report on the FTA and then it occurred to me, like I was shot by a diamond bullet. We could find a third way—triangulation beyond straight opposition or support for the FTA—by amending the enabling legislation in the Senate.

I ran the proposition past Graham Edwards on the plane, and Stumpy agreed with my strategy. The Right will be happy because the thing will get through, sooner rather than later if Howard accepts our amendments, and the Left can tell their constituencies they are fighting to save the PBS and TV content rules from the Americans. I cut the Gordian knot.

Back to Canberra, and I organised meetings on Monday night with the key players in Caucus to push it through. Conroy and Beazley looked like stunned mullets; they must have thought I was committing suicide or something. Not supportive, but in the end, willing to tolerate my crazy-brave ploy. Got it through Shadow Ministry and Caucus on Tuesday morning. Most of the colleagues were stunned, others were relieved that someone had finally worked out a position we could all live with.

Danger liked the amendments, as did Faulkner. All week John has been telling me to fire up, to show the spark that I had earlier in the year. He's spot on: I'm just another politician if I meander along with nothing to fight for. I feel much better boxing my way out of a corner.

Only one hitch: a flurry of Shadow Ministry leaks. Someone from the Left gave the Shadow Ministry submission to Ramsey, who reproduced it in his column yesterday. Not very helpful. An even bigger shocker: Conroy gave the details of our private meetings and discussions to Jennifer Hewett in the *AFR* today. I called Conroy and got into him about it and he came back with an incredible excuse: he was trying to help me by backgrounding Hewett on what happened.

Help me? The article shows that I vacillated on the issue and it talks of our amendments as 'political showmanship'. Conroy must think I came down in the last shower. He's a serial leaker, but at least this time he owned up to it. Still, the golden rule applies: Conroy didn't want us to do the amendments and that's why they are working well for us.

On another issue, Emerson is launching our IR policy tomorrow. All week he has been at me, coming into my office with that hang-dog look on his face, trying to include pattern-bargaining in the policy. He's fallen out with Ludwig and Hawke, and lost his power base in the Party—if he wasn't a Shadow Minister he would probably lose his preselection for Rankin, it's that bad. So he's trying to re-establish himself by cultivating the ACTU as his power base.

He's an errand boy trying to write their demands into our policy document. The Miscos want a return to pattern-bargaining, the same industrial agreement for every hotel in Melbourne is the example they always use. This saves their officials extra work and uncertainty, compared with the enterprise-bargaining approach, where they have to go out and negotiate agreements enterprise by enterprise.

Emmo regards himself as an economics guru, but there he was in my office, wanting to return to the IR system of the 1980s. I told him to stick his pattern-bargaining clause in his bottom drawer. He can pull it out in the future if he likes, but I won't be supporting it now, or then. We must embrace the flexibility of enterprise bargaining and the compassion of a decent industrial safety net. Anything else is a trade union pipe dream, an ambit claim as far as I'm concerned.

Saturday, 14 August

A great week, saddened only by Dominic Vitocco's funeral in Liverpool today. We routed Howard on the PBS amendments—somehow they stood up to legal scrutiny (great staff work by Banks and Conroy's office) and Howard caved in. Groundhog Day: just like with parliamentary super.

I gave a rousing speech on the FTA to end the sitting fortnight. I could feel it buoying Caucus—I am back in form. In fact, I have never felt so confident and effective in the House, electricity running through my veins. Howard didn't even come in for the debate, leaving it to Vaile. A massive turnaround, need to keep it going, now until polling day.

Gartrell and Faulkner also released Maurie Daly's letter, which was sent to us on Monday, to the media, putting the Liverpool furphies to rest. This is what Daly says about his inquiry into the Council:

> The reason Mr Latham features so little in my reports is because the Inquiry received no evidence of imprudent financial management between 1988 and 1995, nor was there any evidence that the activities of various Mayors, both Liberal and Labor, had any real relationship to the Council's rather disastrous involvement in infrastructure projects between 1997 and 2003.
>
> In 1994–95, my investigation showed that Liverpool's debt servicing ratio was 10 per cent. Of the (comparable) 12 urban fringe Councils in Sydney, eight have debt service ratios higher than

---

Dominic Vitocco Prominent builder and ALP supporter in Liverpool
Simon Banks Deputy Chief of Staff in my office

Mark Vaile Nat. Party member, Lyne 1993– ; Trade Min. 1999–

Liverpool, and one had a ratio more than two and a half times larger than Liverpool. My reports did not focus on the period between 1988 and 1995 because the financial position of the Council in those years had no real bearing on the outcomes that appeared in 2002 and 2003, and which led to the sacking of the Council ... I made 59 adverse findings concerning various governance and financial management issues related to the Liverpool City Council. None pertained to the period 1991–1994.

All the Liverpool characters were there this morning to send off Dominic at All Saints: the Knowles family, Paciullo, the Italian developers. I should feel triumphant going back to see these people; I've risen so far through the ranks. But I don't. More a feeling of sadness than satisfaction from the things I did for Liverpool. Too many haunting memories, sitting in the same church where I married Gwyther. It was good to come home and see the future instead of think about the past.

Sunday, 22 August

I had never heard of pancreatitis until it ripped out my guts last Tuesday. It's a malfunction of the pancreas that spews enzymes into your stomach with incomprehensible pain. Now the whole future of my health and longevity is up in the air, with a Federal election just around the corner. Faulkner reckons Howard will go as soon as the Olympics are over to take advantage of my illness. It could have been worse. If he had gone for 18 September, I would have spent the first week of the campaign in hospital.

Is politics killing me? I used to be so fit; triathlons in my twenties. Then I went into politics: local government gave me testicular cancer, and now Federal politics has given me pancreatitis. On top of that: weight gain, man boobs ridicule, irregular hours, too much travel, not enough exercise. Somebody save me, I want to be fit again.

I was in a meeting with Bob Hawke in the Sydney CPO last Tuesday at 5 p.m. He wanted to give me some tips about the election campaign, and actually had some practical, useful ideas on how to manage my time. He also gave me a few policy nuggets to think about, unlike Gough and Keating—Gough, with his obsessions about trains and international conventions, and Paul with his 100 per cent bile on Howard.

Hawke wants me to announce an economic roundtable–business consultation in government; a good idea. Plus he's going to organise a letter from prominent economists backing our economic credentials.

Hopefully it will have a strong impact, like the 43 Eminent Australians on national security. Maybe I've been wrong about this guy: he's putting his shoulder to the wheel when I need it.

I started to feel sick in the stomach during the meeting and thought it was food poisoning. I went to the toilet, threw up and then, like a crazy man, tried to continue as if nothing had happened. But I was rooted and told Hawke I couldn't go on. He left the office looking totally confused.

I was lying on the lounge in agony, like I was being stabbed in the stomach, and a shooting pain through my left shoulder. Glenn Byres decided to ask Andrew Refshauge, a medical doctor and NSW Deputy Premier who has an office across the road in Phillip Street, to come over and take a look at me. Refshauge told me to get up to Sydney Hospital in Macquarie Street as quickly as possible.

It must have been around 7 p.m. and straight away I had three doctors doing tests and fixing me up with painkillers. They had no doubt it was pancreatitis. And then the moment of truth. I asked the specialist what happens if your pancreas conks out—do you get a new one or something?

He replied, 'No, you die. You can't live without a functioning pancreas and there is no way of replacing it. Unfortunately, in this area, medical science is no more advanced than it was 30 years ago. The only way of recovering from an attack is rest and a controlled diet. Sometimes it comes back, sometimes it doesn't. In severe cases, it can kill you'.

In a strange sort of way, it felt worse than when I was first told about my cancer ten years ago. Back then the specialist was more precise about my condition and the treatment it required. This time, I was walking into the unknown, without a lot of medical science to help me. The next day, they transferred me to St Vincent's for further tests. There were three possible causes: alcohol, gallstones or, in a minority of cases, an unspecified problem. It wasn't alcohol—I have never drunk less in my adult life than in the last twelve months. The tests confirmed that I did not have gallstones, so I was in the unknown category.

Most likely, my pancreas was permanently damaged from the radio-therapy treatment I received on the stomach region for testicular cancer and, over the years, it has worn down (no help from a political lifestyle). Further attacks are possible, with varying degrees of severity. Basically, I'm in the hands of fate—anything can happen. Serious shit that might grab hold of me one day and kill me.

---

43 Eminent Australians Former diplomats and senior military officers who, in August 2004, released a letter critical of the Howard govt's policy on Iraq and national security

I got out of hospital yesterday and spent the night talking to Janine. How do we make sense of this? It came from nowhere and now threatens everything I love. Forget politics and the Labor movement, what about making sure I see my children go to school, play sport, graduate from university—my primary responsibility and priority in life? The doctors said a quiet life would definitely help, but they assumed it wasn't possible.

Maybe I need to make it possible. Janine and I talked through the options. Heavy stuff, but it was good to get our thoughts in order. I could resign the leadership now and take it easy on the backbench. We both agree that it's too close to the election campaign and we've worked too hard, so let's hang on and see how we go.

I could bat on regardless of this and any further attacks—just manage it within a public life. Nice try, but I would be an idiot to risk our home life and time with the boys. We are jack of all the personal stuff anyway. A few weeks ago I was promising to get out altogether. I'm not going to put up with pancreatitis as well as media hanging around the hospital every time I get crook.

The middle ground is this: let's do the election and see what happens. If I have another attack and the problem is chronic, I can give it away then. That's our thinking for now, our promise to each other: see through this long election campaign but, if push comes to shove, put my health first. Politics is not worth it.

I've given up too much of my private life, but not this time. Howard won't commit to serving a full term and let people know about his plans for the future, so why do I need to blurt out everything? The media can get stuffed. When they screen the bucks' night video, I'll tell them everything about my health. I owe them nothing. Not after the animals put in another shocker at the hospital. When I was admitted to Sydney Hospital, the head doctor said he wanted to put me under a false name but I refused. Maybe he was right—I had no idea how bad it would be. Photographers were caught in the corridors and stairwells looking for my room. We had to put staff on my door to keep them away.

On Friday morning I woke up, opened my blinds and recognised a News Limited photographer on the street below, snapping photos with a long-range lens. A Peeping Tom through the hospital window. The hide of them: no limits, no decency, no respect for privacy, whatever it takes to publish their trashy little rags. I was outraged but also determined not to give them a scoop, so I called a press conference at the front of the hospital, outlining the bare basics of my condition.

Yesterday, when we left the hospital, a crazy woman was yelling at our car, trying to sell us raffle tickets in the driveway, just as Janine was about to turn onto a busy street. Incredibly, she made it onto the evening news, claiming that I snubbed her. I rang her this morning to square off the bad publicity and buy her raffle tickets. She said that one of the TV journalists put her up to it. Another set-up, another stunt by the maggots.

Tuesday, 24 August

I'm struggling to get back on my feet. Went to the launch of Barry Donovan's new book on me, *The Circuit Breaker*, at Sydney University. Hawke did the honours and spoke really well. Unfortunately, the book is not much chop—a long series of quotes and speech extracts. It's like an Alan Ramsey article in book form.

I did a press conference straight after the launch and felt unsteady on my feet. I'm pushing this too hard, too soon, but there is no alternative—Howard will go soon. I can't see him allowing Parliament to come back next week so that we can get stuck into him about Mike Scrafton and the Kids Overboard affair. We killed him on the FTA and this is even worse for him. At last, Howard's lies are catching up with him.

The best thing about Scrafton is how it allows us to counter-attack Liberal Party crap in the campaign—a real breakthrough. Whether it is personal stuff, Liverpool Council or anything else, we have the perfect comeback: why trust Howard on this when he lies about everything else? Steve Loosley wrote an excellent article about it in the *Sunday Telegraph* two days ago. I clipped it out for future use:

> Voters are simply growing tired of denials. The practical impact of the return of Children Overboard means that any opportunity for the Coalition to run a hard national security campaign along the lines of Tampa has evaporated, and the chances of a character assault on Mark Latham have gone.
>
> On the other hand, Labor has a cudgel with which to beat its opponents. A few years back, Senator Al D'Amato, a New York Republican, tried to blackguard the Congressional record of his opponent, Chuck Schumer, during a campaign. The Democrats' response annihilated D'Amato. A television commercial stated bluntly: 'Al

Mike Scrafton Former adviser to Peter Reith who in August 2004 blew the whistle on Howard's knowledge of the Kids Overboard affair before the 2001 Fed. election

Kids Overboard An attempt by the Howard govt before the 2001 Fed. election to convince Australians that parents on an asylum-seekers' boat had thrown their kids overboard, when in fact no such thing had happened. The govt then tried to cover up the truth

D'Amato—too many lies for too many years.' An Australian variant is likely to hit our television screens in a few weeks' time.

There is nothing new in campaign strategy, you just need to use the best stuff from elsewhere. When I was in hospital, I finished Bill Clinton's autobiography, all 957 pages of it. The key part of the book is his 1992 election campaign, reinventing the Democrat cause and beating Bush Senior.

It also has some good tips for our campaign. In the first debate, President Bush said that (independent candidate) Ross Perot didn't have government experience, to which Perot replied, 'The President has a point. I don't have any experience running up a $4 trillion debt'. A nice line for batting away the Liberal Party charge that I am inexperienced. That's right, I don't have any experience attacking Medicare, making education less affordable or covering up Kids Overboard.

Clinton was also well prepared for the negative Republican campaign against him:

> Our rapid-response operation would be out in force. It had to be. The Republicans had no choice but to throw the kitchen sink at me. They were way behind, and their slash-and-burn approach had worked in every election since 1968, except for President Carter's two-point victory in the aftermath of Watergate. We were determined to use the rapid-response team to turn the Republican attacks back on them.

I spoke to Gartrell this afternoon to make sure he had seen the Loosley piece. He hadn't, so I read it down the phone. Also told him about Clinton's rapid-response team. Tim was enthusiastic: 'Yes mate, we're putting a unit together. Whatever shit the Libs put out, we'll be ready to respond to it straight away. Don't worry'. He still expects the Liberal attack on the economy to be directed at Crean: 'He's our weakest link—they would be crazy not to go for him'.

He was noncommittal, however, about our advertising strategy. He doesn't seem to have a game plan in mind, or maybe he's guarding it against too much interference by me. He's relying on an 'advertising think-tank' to do the trick—we haven't got a single agency but a team of experts pulled together for the campaign.

For what it's worth, here in my little think-tank, I told Tim the strategy should include the following:

- Early in the campaign, run positive ads about my life story—fill in the gaps in the voters' minds before the Libs go hard at the end of the campaign. We've taken plenty of footage for this over the past five months, so it should be easy to pull together.

- When they go negative, use our rapid-response team to hit back. If we do that well enough then our positive education and health ads will carry the day. The voters want to hear about the future.
- I'm not a fan of negative advertising—it turns a lot of people off, the worst of the old politics. Anyway, in the past, our attack ads on Howard haven't worked (Utting's point). We need to get smart this time: let them attack first then counter-punch with the D'Amato ads. John Howard, too many lies for too many years.

Also some progress in sorting out our campaign personnel. Tim has been at me to do something about Vivian. She's showing up in the focus groups—people watching the TV news and wanting to know who's the lady dressed in black who follows me around. This is the point in Utting's research: people think I've come under the control of minders. Yesterday I did a press conference in Hallinan Park (near the electorate office) and told Vivian to stay out of view. She argued the toss with me—she loves the lime-light—but eventually I prevailed. Tim and Faulkner are critical of her work. They don't want her involved upfront in the election campaign and I agree.

2004
Post-election

On Sunday 29 August, John Howard called the election for Saturday 9 October, a relatively long six-week campaign. This allowed him to close down the House of Representatives to avoid scrutiny on the Scrafton affair. Labor went into the election with 63 seats. The Labor seat of McMillan in Victoria had been redistributed into a notionally Liberal seat.

On the electoral pendulum, we needed thirteen seats to form government—a uniform swing of 2.2 per cent. A swing of 1.5 per cent would have given us eight seats, enough to force the Government into a hung Parliament. The Liberal and National Parties went into the election with 83 seats, the Independents with three and the Greens with one, the Illawarra seat of Cunningham, which they won at the 2002 by-election.

Throughout the campaign, the published opinion polls fluctuated significantly, with Labor leading at various stages. The widely cited Newspoll, for instance, recorded the following results:

Date	Primary vote (%)		Two-party-preferred (ALP/LNP)
	ALP	LNP	
27–29 Aug.	40	43	52/48
3–5 Sept.	40	45	50/50
10–12 Sept.	40	46	50/50
17–19 Sept.	41	43	52.5/47.5
24–26 Sept.	40	43	52/48
1–3 Oct.	39	46	49.5/50.5
6–7 Oct.	39	45	50/50

At the election, Labor received 37.6 per cent of the primary vote and the Liberal and National Parties 46.4 per cent, resulting in a two-party-preferred vote of 47.3 ALP, 52.7 LNP—a swing to the Government of 1.8 per cent. Labor finished with 60 seats, winning Cunningham, Parramatta, Richmond, Adelaide and Hindmarsh, but losing Bonner, Greenway, Bass, Braddon, Kingston, Wakefield, Stirling and Hasluck. This gave the Government 87 seats in the new Parliament and the Independents three. The Government also won control of the Senate from 1 July 2005.

As noted earlier, I did not maintain my diary entries during the campaign period because of time pressures. But as soon as the election was over and my schedule returned to normal, I recorded a detailed account of the main campaign issues, events and personalities. This then flowed into a series of entries dealing with Labor's election post-mortem.

On 22 October 2004, the Labor Caucus met and re-elected me unopposed as its Leader in the House of Representatives, with Jenny Macklin as Deputy Leader. John Faulkner decided to retire from the Senate leadership and was replaced by Chris Evans, with Stephen Conroy as his deputy. A new Labor frontbench was also elected, after a convoluted factional and sub-factional process.

Sunday, 10 October

How bad is this? Just finished a family BBQ at home, and the scale of last night's disaster is still sinking in. Everyone's okay, except for the obvious. The boys came back from Jody's; got them into the house without the media pack out the front harassing them.

Sinking: that's the word for it. All my emotions drained by the reality of defeat and despair. I suppose I saw it coming 24 hours ago. Now it's confirmed on the tally-board, that's all. Time to put my feelings aside and write down what happened, an outlet in itself.

The whole thing came down to a single, sinking moment. The roller-coaster stopped running yesterday afternoon. I was on the swing chair on the back verandah. I had thrown everything at Howard and, by most media accounts, won the campaign. But still, we were going to lose the election. Faulkner and Gartrell reported that our polling showed small gains (three to four seats), but not enough to win. My numbers spiked up on Friday night, 49 per cent approval, 37 per cent disapproval (according to John, our best hope for an upset result).

For the first time in six weeks I had a chance to stop and think, and reality sank in. We had been smashed in the advertising campaign. I worked my ringer out on the road, but didn't pay enough attention to the other half of the campaign: TV advertising. I wasn't sitting around watching TV every night, monitoring ads; I was getting ready for the next day's campaign. It was the one that got away from me.

For the last two weeks of the campaign, Janine kept saying to me, 'How come the Liberals have so many ads, sometimes two in each ad break, and you have hardly any? They are beating you with their ads'. Why didn't Tim tell me this?

Every morning Faulkner would give me a summary of the previous night's polling. In the end, he sounded like a broken record: 'There are two forces in this campaign. Their attack ads are pulling down our primary vote, and what I call the Latham factor, your fresh and attractive policy announcements, are pulling us back up'. He kept making this movement with his hands: putting his clenched fists together and then pulling them apart, like in a tug of war.

In short, the Libs were winning the paid advertising campaign and we were winning the free media campaign. That must be why the journalists called the campaign for me—they didn't see the ads either, they were too busy filing their stories or were out on the town. They couldn't understand how I was winning the battle against Howard but losing the election.

The massive Liberal advertising blitz was the missing piece in the puzzle. And in the end, it won. On Friday, Mark Arbib said to me, 'I think their interest rates campaign broke through this week'. Broke through, and made a big difference.

Based on Janine's feedback, I started asking Gartrell and Faulkner when we were going to start winning the advertising campaign, when our ads were going to have an impact. Their standard reply was: in previous campaigns we had always been outspent by the Coalition in the last week. This time, they were determined to win the all-important last week, so they back-end-loaded the advertising budget.

After our policy launch in Brisbane on 29 September, Tim showed me the package of ads to be screened the following weekend through to the electronic blackout—the only time he ever sat me down and went through our ads. But even this was for my information only; they were all in the can. The package included nothing on interest rates. I'm told a rebuttal ad finally went to air last week, but I never saw it.

This was a fixed-artillery strategy. We were only going to fire our guns in the final week, but the Liberals had started their negative attack three

---

Mark Arbib NSW ALP Gen. Sec. 2004–

Electronic blackout A ban on TV and radio ads that comes into force on the Wednesday before election day

weeks out, first with the Liverpool Council ads and then the barrage on interest rates. Our lack of rapid response allowed these negative impressions to fester unchallenged in the public's mind for two weeks.

Gartrell's assurances about rapid-response and our opportunity to use the D'Amato ad disappeared. It's the great mystery and failure of our campaign. It was set like concrete in their heads: last week only. Like the guns of Singapore during World War II, they were fixed in one direction, incapable of dealing with any other attack.

Gartrell is a nice, inoffensive guy, but he got lost in the big campaign. He went for the safety blanket of a fixed strategy. He was fighting the last campaign (outspent in the last week) instead of this one, a fatal error in politics.

My whole advantage over Howard was mobility. He was supposed to be the fixed artillery and I was air mobile. All the surprise attacks and victories over him—parliamentary super, mentoring, the social agenda, vaccinations, the FTA—were based on mobility in the field. But not in our advertising campaign.

The Liberal ads beat me into submission. It was a miracle that my numbers were still plus twelve and higher than Howard's by the end of the campaign. Utting's advice throughout the year was that our primary vote rose and fell on the back of my ratings. That's why the Liberals loaded the Liverpool Council ads so heavily, and then tried to link me to Hawke and Keating on interest rates.

It was a replay of what the Republicans did to Michael Dukakis in 1988 with the Willie Horton ads: create a scare, no matter how tenuous; fill in the gaps about the new guy; then pray that his campaign doesn't counterpunch with rebuttal ads. The tragedy of it is exactly the point Clinton makes in his book. He avoided the Dukakis folly with a rapid-response operation. I told Tim, but it must have gone in one ear and out the other.

I should have come back to it during the campaign, but never did. Always too busy, studying my documents for the next day, practising my lines, checking that the itinerary was okay, desperate not to make mistakes and look incompetent, missing the boys and aching to go home. That sinking feeling of regret and frustration, with no way back in time.

This is the reality that hit me yesterday. All the work and effort, time away from my family, body collapsed into hospital, only to go backwards.

Michael Dukakis Unsuccessful Dem. candidate for the US Presidency against George Bush in 1988; the Republicans ran a scare campaign on Dukakis's record as Governor of Massachusetts, including the early release from gaol of the convicted criminal Willie Horton

Yesterday afternoon I got off the swing chair, told Janine to get ready for defeat and said, 'Well, just goes to show, you can't do it all yourself, all your life. I've always tried to carry the whole show on my shoulders: my family, my community, my party. But now I'm stuffed. I have collapsed under the weight of those fucking ads'.

Last night went without melodrama: a solemn, flat, surprisingly calm night. At one level, I could feel relief that it was all over. As we drove up to the Mounties Club at 5.30 p.m. I saw the media pack waiting outside and felt liberated from the voyeurs. I didn't have to be nice to them any more. I brushed past them on the way in, with the dumb girl from Channel Ten yelling at me, 'Mr Latham, are you going to have a drink tonight?' Summed it up perfectly: I was marching in to swallow the bad taste of a national election defeat and her big issue was alcohol.

For some reason, that moment stayed with me throughout the night. Politics as the theatre of the absurd. How much does it really matter? Not that much for most of the people who voted, surely—a democratic chore. Not that much for the thousands of desperadoes at Mounties on the pokies or at the bar, oblivious to the election result. Not that much for Miss Channel Ten, I suppose, it's just a job, with an endless list of inane questions.

I felt sad for Faulkner. All week after the forestry decision, he had been saying to me, 'There is no way in the world we will lose Braddon'. But there we sat, looking at the first results from Tasmania. The first seat lost was Braddon. The night was effectively over at 7.30 p.m. Some encouragement in the first returns from Petrie in Queensland, but that was it.

The polling was dead wrong. We were going backwards, losing seats in most States. Poor John, his last throw of the dice, the truest of the True Believers. And now the Tories are back for another three years.

The only light relief on the night came from one of my rugby club mates. He walked up to Matt Price and started telling him how good it was to see him again after the big day on the SCG Hill. My mate wasn't there that day. Price put on an act, greeting him as a long-lost friend, even though it was the first time they had actually met, and then tried to pump him for information about me. Our mate Matt, a bullshit artist right to the end.

The Bulls then hit the piss upstairs in the boardroom, our little tally-room, pulling stumps at 4 a.m. Half their luck; they should have asked Miss Channel Ten in for a drink.

What can I do now? Three more years in this rotten job, three more years staring across the chamber at a Tory Government. Last night in the concession speech I didn't give a commitment about my future. I wanted to sleep on it and talk it through with Janine. It's tempting to pull the pin, for all the reasons we have talked about since June. My health has picked up, but our hatred of the media will never go away.

We talked about it this morning and decided to stay on—a 70:30 call. Faulkner's optimism has made a big difference. He and Janine got on really well during the campaign. She reckons we should trust his judgement. Last week he said, 'Even if we don't win on Saturday, this campaign has shown that you will be the next Labor Prime Minister, if you want it'.

That's the point: if I quit now it will make our campaign look like a complete failure. It was better than that: I have answered my critics about my temperament and ability to master detail. Barely a stumble in the six weeks. I beat Howard in the debate and on the road—they all said that. I can only improve from here in my standing as the alternative Prime Minister.

Plus I have been true to myself and I want to keep it up. At our office dinner at Aria on Friday night, I felt so proud of what we had achieved. I'm proud of my own journey in politics. That's what I said in my speech thanking the staff. Here are my speech notes, my in-house reflections on the campaign:

> I joined the Labor Party in January 1979 and as I walked up to my first meeting, I saw Labor as a party of social reform. Not a timid, conservative party, but a progressive party. And that's what we have shown in this campaign. Back then, I had four things in my mind—four establishment groups we needed to fight. And in this campaign, they have all been against us. I am still fighting them.
>
> There's the business establishment, the shysters looking for special deals and grants off government. We've put out policies for private sector competition, not preferment, and they don't like it. That's why they are against us.
>
> There's the foreign policy establishment, the ones who say you can never disagree with the United States, the ones who want to make us a client state. Well, we believe in Australian independence, an independent foreign policy, so the Tories have come after us. I mean, how many times on the lawns of the White House has an American President ever denounced an Australian political leader? Let me tell you, I wear it as a badge of honour.
>
> The third group is the media establishment, Murdoch's mob. They have been into us all year, because they support that rotten war in Iraq and they know that I will get Australia out straight away. All their papers, of course, are backing Howard.
>
> Then there's the elite school establishment, the born-to-rule set. They don't like us because we believe in fair school funding. I told

this story at the National Secretariat on Wednesday but it's worth telling again.

I was only heckled once in the campaign and that was a businessman, pissed as a parrot, who came up to me at the hotel in Melbourne and said, 'You're the bloke I wanted to see. I pay $300 000 in taxes each year and you want to take money off my son's school'. And I thought to myself: gee, I'm glad we've got that policy. If he's that rich, he can pay for his son's education as well.

So I've been true to myself and the reasons why I got into politics. I'm proud of that and I hope the Labor movement is proud of the things we stand for. This time we stood for real Labor values and principles, that's the difference.

Despite everything we have been through, an amazing journey, more pain than pleasure, I still think it's worth doing. But the main thing is the campaign is over. I'm back with my boys. During the campaign I asked Ollie if he knew why I was away so much and he answered: 'poo'. Spot on, Big Fella, poo politics.

Friday, 15 October

We lost—words that have already sunk into the history books. But right now, believe it or not, I can see a brighter side. Sure, I lost a Federal election but I have regained my family. On Wednesday we drove up to Laurie's beach house at Pittwater, a beautiful retreat with Janine and the boys.

Such a magnificent contrast to the madness of an election campaign and being trapped in the *Truman Show* with those media wallies. Against that, the simplicity and joy of Oliver and Isaac, exploring mudflats, chasing away the birds, pretending we are sailor men. I was going to be Prime Minister but ended up as Popeye, singing his silly song.

I have lost, but I have gained. That wretched election campaign—it went for ten months, leaving me just four politics-free days all year. At one stage in the campaign, I was away from my boys ten days in a row. The agony of it. Ollie still knows me and loves me, but I'm a stranger to Isaac. It just occurred to me that I have missed the second year of his life. And such a serene, beautiful little boy.

On Tuesday I did the Bali memorial function at Coogee and met some of the parents, and saw their horror. No parent should have to bury their own child. I've lost an election but that is nothing compared with those poor, tormented souls. I could hear Warwick Smith's haunting words: every day you spend away from your children is a day you never get back. Those parents will never get anything back.

I've got my boys back now, paradise in Pittwater. Just one scare: stomach cramps early yesterday morning. I thought that horrible thing was back, but then it passed.

What can I say about our election loss? So much happened, but here are my strongest memories from the past seven weeks.

Our Strategy

Election campaigns are all about agenda-setting. Sadly, swinging voters don't follow politics closely; they pick up snippets of information from here and there, mostly from television. If they hear about an issue where they trust your side of politics most, your vote goes up. If the other side have their trustworthy issues in the news, your vote goes down. Unfortunately, it is like a game of word association. Apathy rules.

Faulkner has seen our internal polling for every campaign since 1993 and this is what it shows: word association. In particular, the last days of the 2001 campaign are seared onto his brain. Labor was coming back, then Kids Overboard flared up in the news. Even though the Government looked grubby, the general issue was their strongest for the campaign: refugees. The Liberal vote spiked, and it was all over.

A similar thing happened in this campaign. In the third last week, the Government was all over the shop on Howard's pre-emption doctrine. The commentators said they looked confused and messy. Yet their vote went up in our polling. Same in the first fortnight of the campaign, when the Beslan school siege and Jakarta bombing dominated the news.

In our track poll, a rolling average of 1200 voters in key seats, we started the campaign with a two-party-preferred figure of 48.5 per cent, no swing either way compared with 2001. After the Jakarta bombing, we dropped to 47 per cent and were in deep trouble. Word association: national security = a Liberal strength.

It is possible to change these perceptions over a full parliamentary term. To try to change them during the five or six weeks of an election campaign would be suicide. Only a moron would campaign on the other side's strengths, put their issues in the news and ignore your own. That was my dilemma after winning the leadership.

It always felt like we were six or seven weeks away from election day. A snap February/March poll, an election Budget in May, rumours of 7 August

---

Beslan school siege School siege during 1–3 September 2004 in the Russian town of Beslan in North Ossetia, where, according to official figures, 344 people were killed, among them at least 172 children

Jakarta bombing A bombing outside the gates of the Australian embassy in Indonesia on 9 September 2004 that killed 9 people and wounded hundreds and then 18 September—what was I going to do, spend every day on national security and the economy and hardly talk about social issues? Don't worry about losing, there would not have been any of us left.

Consistently, throughout the year, our polling showed that 60 per cent of people thought the country was headed in the right direction, mainly due to its economic strength, with just 25 per cent saying that Australia was on the wrong track. On election day the numbers were 61 and 27 respectively. There's not much evidence in Australian history of people changing the government in those circumstances.

We had to push the economy down the news list, and smother it with Labor's social policy strengths—prosperity with a purpose. In fact, Faulkner was so worried about it throughout the year, he kept on saying that an interest rate rise would help the Government, and put economic issues back in the news. Word association: economic management = a Liberal strength.

My honeymoon period must have driven the Liberals crazy, when they were unable to get the focus on the economy in an election year. In the end they were so desperate, they dedicated 90 per cent of their campaign to it, in the free media and paid advertising. And it wasn't really a campaign against anything I said or did as Labor Leader. They ran against the past: scrawny clippings from the local rags in Liverpool eight years ago, two years after I finished as Mayor, and reminding people about the high interest rates of the early 1990s.

That's the tragedy of our dumb Party. It gave away the best parts of the Hawke/Keating economic legacy under Beazley, got lumbered with the worst bit (high interest rates) and then spent eighteen months trying to knife poor old Simon. No wonder we lost on the question of economic credibility. The irony of it is, none of them was up on stage at Mounties conceding defeat, of having to bullshit about the wonders of Australian democracy. Just me—Mark Latham, the loser.

So none of it was rocket science. I rolled out the big agenda items: tax and family, school funding, Medicare Gold and Tassie forests, taking attention away from interest rates and national security. I beat Howard the only time he was willing to debate me and won the free media campaign. Faulkner said, 'This is the best campaign I've seen since the last time we won, possibly since 1990'. But at the end of the day, they killed us with their ads.

The day before the election, Danger said to me, 'Well, mate, you couldn't have done any more. You put out the big options for people during

---

Medicare Gold ALP's policy, announced on 29 September, that an ALP govt would provide free basic hospital insurance (public and private) for Australians aged 75 and over

the campaign. Now we'll see if they are big enough to grab them'. We got our answer 24 hours later.

The Australian people are not interested in 'the big options'. Just as, during the 1996 election, they weren't interested in Keating's big picture. For the apathetic, disillusioned middle ground, politics is a nuisance, a silly game of word association. See a few ads, must be true, that'll do me. I talked about a big country, but I was fooling myself.

The First Fortnight

Howard called the election on the last day of the Olympics, trying to cash in on the feel-good factor, but also to avoid questions about Scrafton in the House. In his opening press conference, he emphasised interest rates but I thought he looked nervy and unconvincing.

At my press conference, I followed Utting's advice and tried to relaunch the Ladder of Opportunity, only to be mocked by Oakes on Channel Nine news for having said it before. As if I were the first politician in history to stick to the same theme. No, the media wanted their performing dog to jump through new hoops.

It took a while to get the travelling party working smoothly. I was also struggling with my health. The doctors advised light exercise after the pancreatitis attack, but even this was onerous. On day five of the campaign, while out walking along the banks of the Yarra, I almost collapsed, telling the security guys that I might not be able to make it back to the hotel. It wasn't until week three of the campaign that I felt back to normal.

By week two, we were relying on our tax and family policy to create some momentum. Based on Utting's research, it was time to press the living standards button, talk about families under financial pressure, which I tried to summarise as 'ease the squeeze'. I also saw it as a contribution to the economic debate: we had policies to make people better off financially, a positive reform for the future, versus the Government's emphasis on the past.

Since the May Budget, journalists had been asking when the policy would be released. In fact, it wasn't ready until two days before its launch on 7 September. It was a huge task, designing a new family payments system from Opposition; our staff did a good job, especially Sanchez and Nathan Dal Bon from my office and Matt Linden from Swan's office. If Howard had called the election for 7 August or 18 September, we would not have been ready, a major embarrassment.

It was good public policy, but too complex to sell in an election campaign. In hindsight, we would have been better off politically with a policy for mortgage tax relief: the pointy heads would have bagged it as bad policy (adding to the housing boom) but the punters would have loved it, allowing us to counter the Government's interest rates scare. I suppose there were no easy answers.

Looking back, I shouldn't have locked myself into a policy development process by committee—Swan, Crean, Macklin, McMullan and me. This deprived me of the element of surprise and mobility that had worked so well against Howard earlier in the year. It also gave weak reeds like Macklin the chance to have a bet each way. She was the driving force behind consolidating Family Tax Benefit A and B, which inevitably had an adverse impact on low-income single parents. Then she was the first to complain about it.

In truth, we couldn't get rid of the shocking disincentives against work in the system without sending some people backwards until we could get them into a job. The media, especially the Murdoch papers, had been whingeing about the disincentives for years; we actually did something about it and they still bagged us. Lesson for the future: ignore newspapers campaigning on issues. It's designed to sell papers, not to fix problems.

The night before the policy release, I asked Swan how we deal with the $600 annual payment. He replied: 'Just say that it's not real money, that it's eaten away by the family payment debts and the indexation swindle'. The media latched onto this, supposedly as a weakness in our package. They couldn't find any problems in the policy detail, our sums added up, so they honed in on a presentational issue instead, the difference between the weekly and annual tables.

We presented the figures the same way as the Government website, with the $600 in the annual amount but not the weekly. I mean, if you win $600 in Lotto each July, you don't write it into your family budget as a weekly payment, do you? It was the media playing their silly game. They thought they were onto something, that I was as dishonest as Howard. Jabba led the charge on behalf of his buddy Peter Costello. I had a long argument with him about it on 8 September and then got into him on the *Sunday* program a week and a half later.

Family Tax Benefit A and B A is a means-tested child-endowment payment to families; B is an additional non-means-tested payment for families with children with one stay-at-home parent

$600 annual payment Supplementary payment to Family Tax Benefit A of $600 per child, payable at the end of the financial year

The Great Debate

I found out about the fatalities from the Jakarta bombing while on our RAAF plane from Bundaberg to Cairns. That night, 9 September, I said to Janine, 'It's what we have always feared: a bomb in the campaign, people focusing on national security. We need to be honest about it, we can't win this. We should just go out and enjoy ourselves and the experience. It doesn't really matter, we've been pissed off with this job anyway'.

Politically, the campaign was now at risk of falling apart. I had to perform well in Sunday's debate to get us back on track. It felt like a loaded dice, however, with Howard determining the format—no interaction between the candidates—and the panel of journalists was stacked with conservatives—Oakes, Michelle Grattan, Neil Mitchell and Malcolm Farr. Still, I felt surprisingly confident: I had always beaten Howard face-to-face in Parliament, so why should this be any different?

It wasn't. Howard was very ordinary, hyperventilating at the start, a nervous wreck. I couldn't believe it when his opening statement was about Medicare, instead of the economy. I stood there listening to him heaving for breath and thought to myself: 'I'm nervous, but it's not that bad. This is my chance to get on top of him'.

I could tell he was nervous before we even started. We stood there for what seemed like ages, waiting to get going, so I tossed some banter at him, lamenting St George's loss, a team we both support, in the NRL finals. I said, 'Yeah, they started very badly, but don't let it affect you'. The humourless sod just stood there like a garden gnome. He was so edgy, he obviously didn't think the election was over. He had a lot to lose.

Earlier in the day, planning for the debate, I decided to open up with a counter-attack on national security, arguing that Howard had neglected security in the region by putting our resources into Iraq. It worked really well. In fact, the debate couldn't have gone better; there was hardly any mention of the economy.

It went so well that Howard stormed off at the end—he didn't want to stay and chat. It's a terrible thing, politics, when it can reduce a grown man, 30 years in Parliament and eight years as Prime Minister, to a trembling wreck.

When I got back to the hotel, there was elation in the Labor camp. I was on a high, until I found out the next day that more people watched *Australian Idol* than the debate. Does politics matter that much in Australia? Not really.

Education and Health

As a vote-switcher, our schools funding policy was our best initiative of the campaign. Off the back of my debate win and this policy launch, we lifted to 50 per cent in our track poll at the end of week three. Plus we had some strong seat results, such as 60 per cent 2PP in Adelaide. No wonder we weren't worried about seats like Kingston and Wakefield elsewhere in South Australia.

The mistake with the schools funding policy was the failure to follow up with TV ads. If this was our best vote-switcher, why didn't headquarters give it an even higher profile through paid advertising?

Schools funding was a persistent issue of the campaign. It kept on coming back, especially after Big George Pell denounced the policy in the second last week. He was attacking something that gave more money to all his parish schools. One of the great own goals of the church. If the parishioners were fair dinkum they would rise up and punt Big George; he has cost their children a better education. But they just cop it from this authoritarian institution. Hey, if they encouraged people to experience Christ's teachings as individuals, free from the pulpit, all the kiddie-fiddlers would be out of a job.

We also had good success with our health policies. Peter Barron gave me the idea for declaring the election to be a referendum on Medicare's future. Medicare Gold was in the same category as the tax and family policy: it wasn't ready until the campaign. It combined my plan for killing the private health insurance rebate with Duckett and Swerissen's vision for extending Federal responsibilities in hospital care. It required a lot of work to model the private insurance implications and to secure the cooperation of the States, all handled by Gillard.

It was a miracle that it never leaked. Everything else does, all the time in our show, but Medicare Gold held tight all year, right through to its announcement at the campaign launch. Gillard always referred to it as 'the policy that dare not speak its name', almost superstitiously, like if we mentioned its name it would leak out.

Faulkner was very enthusiastic about the launch and the initial polling on Medicare Gold. I expected us to lift in the track, but the tug of war continued: policies like Medicare Gold lifting us up, but those bloody ads pulling us back down. We went into the last week of the campaign staring at defeat: the track falling into the 49s.

George Pell Catholic Cardinal of Sydney
Peter Barron He and Geoff Walsh assisted the ALP campaign on an occasional basis with policy and political advice, speech-writing

ideas and preparation for the Great Debate. I saw them on half a dozen occasions; for example, they checked the Medicare Gold policy before its release

In the post-launch debate about Medicare Gold, the Libs were very effective in creating bogeys and planting seeds of doubt. There won't be enough nurses, private hospital entitlements won't be maintained, oldies will jump the queue and young people will miss out, and so forth. Some of this resonated with self-centred voters. In one of our focus groups, one young fella complained that it would be unfair if his grandmother got into hospital ahead of him. So much for honouring our senior citizens.

The Lib lackeys on talkback radio attacked Medicare Gold relentlessly, supported by the self-serving AMA—as ever, opposed to policies that put downward pressure on doctors' fees. By comparison, the strengths of the policy were under-reported: the extra money into hospital budgets, the private health insurance cost savings, the Federal coordination of hospital and aged care, and the news that Tony Abbott had previously supported the principles of Medicare Gold—as revealed by the head of the Catholic hospitals, Francis Sullivan, on 30 September. At the time I thought this was a bombshell, but it hardly registered on the media radar.

Talkback radio—a forum for downward envy, this time directed at the oldies. It makes me feel sick about the future of our society, which has so little compassion, so little desire to help anyone bar itself. I'm glad the arse-wipe who was worried about his grandmother getting a hospital bed voted Liberal and not for me.

Tasmanian Forests

I saw the last week of the campaign as the last shove in the tug of war. To win, we needed the promised miracle weapon to work—that is, our advertising blitz. We also needed to campaign on an issue where people trusted Labor (our agenda, not the Coalition's). The last thing we needed was a non-eventful week that allowed Howard to put the spotlight back on interest rates.

The protection of the Tasmanian forests was the obvious issue. It had come up throughout the campaign and there were strong media expectations that it would be the last policy announcement by both sides. Howard had been talking about it, as had I. In fact, in our Brisbane campaign launch, I flagged our intention 'to save the mighty Tasmanian forests, conserving one of our greatest natural assets for future generations'.

A conservation debate suited me fine. Environmental protection had been a part of every winning Labor campaign, State and Federal, for as long as I could remember. I subscribed to the Dick Morris dictum that successful Centre–Left campaigns relied on the three Es: education, the elderly and the environment. We had won the education debate, our campaign launch was good for the elderly, now it was time to complete the trifecta.

At the time, I had good reason to believe this was a winning issue. Mid-year Gartrell had asked Utting to poll opinion in Tasmania on the forestry debate. He reported two firm conclusions to me. First, there was overwhelming support for a strong conservation initiative that also provided for job protection. Such a policy would win us support in every Tasmanian electorate. Second, the new Premier, Paul Lennon, was not a popular figure. If he opposed Federal Labor's policy on this issue, it would not necessarily cost us support.

Naturally, Gartrell was keen for us to go green, as was Faulkner. Following our near-death experience on the FTA, I expected the Tassie forests to be Howard's next wedge issue. And I decided to fight him from a pro-environment position. I convened a meeting with Faulkner, Garrett and Don Henry on 17 August—as it turned out, two hours before my pancreatitis attack—to secure their involvement and input to the policy.

The rest of the Party was all over the shop on this issue, as divided as they had been on the FTA. The main frustration was extracting basic information from the Tasmanian Labor Government on the forestry coups and areas worthy of conservation. Our people tried and failed as follows:

- Joel Fitzgibbon (Shadow Minister for Resources) met with Lennon earlier in the year and concluded that he was unlikely to cooperate— Lennon was too close to the industry. Mid-year, Lennon said to Joel he would support the protection of 4000 hectares in the North Styx if Federal Labor paid $100 million to Tasmania. This feeble, desultory proposal was laughed out of court at the PRC.
- Martin Ferguson (Shadow Minister for Regional Development) soft-pedalled on the issue. He is very close to Michael O'Connor, relies on him as part of his factional powerbase. Marn kept on promising to produce a policy document, but delivered nothing.
- Kelvin Thomson (Shadow Minister for the Environment) wanted us to protect the forests but agreed that he was the last person who could extract any information from the Tasmanian Government. He was happy to work on other environmental issues while others tried to sort it out.
- Simon Crean had a good idea: to identify the forestry coups in Tasmania that had the same status as the North Styx—that is, high

Don Henry Exec. Dir., Australian Conservation Foundation

conservation value areas that were not due to be logged for 15–20 years. They could be protected without any impact on employment. Unfortunately, he wasn't able to get this information out of the Tasmanian Government, even though his brother David had been, until recently, the State Treasurer.

- Mid-year I asked Mike Richards to work on the issue—he told me he had close links to the Tasmanian Government—and to draft up policy recommendations. Like Ferguson, he delivered nothing, not one scrap of paper.

Throughout the year, the advice from Crean, Faulkner and Gartrell had been to delay our policy on the Tassie forests until the election campaign. They were worried that if we went early, it would give Bob Brown time to up the ante and campaign for even greater conservation. In the end, because of the lack of cooperation from the State colleagues, the policy wasn't finalised until the last fortnight of the campaign.

I worked on the assumption that, when the whips were cracking in the middle of a national election campaign, a Labor Premier would cooperate with Federal Labor. But in reality, that assumption died when Jim Bacon died. Lennon's main allegiances in public life are not to the ALP. He was only admitted to the Party after the Tasmanian factions agreed to forgive him for working on Brian Harradine's election campaigns. Lennon is an old Grouper, so conservative that he put his relationship with the forestry industry ahead of the Federal Labor Party. I have no doubt that one day we will find out the true story, what lies beneath.

From our conversations, especially three during the campaign, I concluded that Lennon thought he could fudge and delay his way out of the issue, that it would just go away, and he could go back to his municipal activities in Tasmania. It was impossible to have a normal political conversation with the guy. During the campaign period, he took a scattergun approach: telling me about his hatred of Bob Brown, complaining about Harry Quick and Duncan Kerr, anything to change the subject.

I could never pin him down on the only thing that mattered: when would he give us the information about the forestry coups, when would he assist our efforts to form a national Labor Government. At one stage, he even gave me a burst about Richard Butler, the recently dismissed Tasmanian Governor: 'You were complaining about Butler's payout. But do

---

Brian Harradine Independent Tas. Sen. 1975–2005; member, National Civic Council
Harry Quick ALP member, Franklin 1993–

Richard Butler Former adviser to Gough Whitlam; Australian diplomat and disarmament expert; Tas. Governor 2003–04; nicknamed 'The Black Prince'

you know why I had to sack him? Do you know what really happened? He got pissed at the wedding and carried on, that's why he had to go'. The Prince on the piss, hey? Sounds like it was the carry-on of the century.

As interesting as this was, it didn't help me much. In the end, I decided to bat on without Lennon. The issue wasn't going to go away. Even when I called in to see him on 4 October, the day of the policy release in Hobart, it wasn't a political meeting between Labor leaders. He marched in with a dozen Tasmanian bureaucrats and started to tell me about his legal advice. Legalism, not Laborism.

Dick Adams was just as bad. On the first Saturday of the campaign, when we launched our Tasmanian package, I had lunch with him and naturally we talked about the forests. Howard had just announced his desire to end all old-growth logging and I advised Adams: 'The issue is in motion now and we are going to make an environmental initiative sometime during the campaign. But from your point of view, Howard's statement is ideal—just attack him. Our policy won't end all old-growth logging, so if you're worried about forestry votes in your electorate, rip right into Howard'. Adams agreed with that advice, not a word of dissent.

I also rang him on the morning of the policy release to brief him on its contents—thorough examination of 240 000 hectares for protection, no blanket end to old-growth logging, a guarantee of no net job losses and an $800 million industry package—and again told him to attack Howard. Once more, not a word of dissent; he just said he wanted to look at the detail. For Dick, that means finding out from the industry what to say. The next I heard from him, he was in the media attacking me and the policy, but not Howard.

Then Adams attended the anti-Labor rally in Launceston on 6 October, 300 metres down the road from Michelle O'Byrne's electorate office in Bass. It was simply unbelievable. A Labor MP campaigning for the Liberals in another Labor MP's electorate. Billy Hughes would have been proud of this kind of treachery.

And then there was the Forestry Division of the CFMEU which organised the rally for Howard, the same CFMEU that was subjected to a Royal Commission by the Howard Government. This one was even beyond Billy

Paul Lennon and forestry protection In May 2005 at a joint press conference with John Howard in the Styx Valley, Lennon announced a new forest protection initiative—adding 150 000 hectares of forests on public land to reserves, reducing the clear-felling of old-growth forests and ensuring the protection of 53 per cent of the Styx and 87 per cent of the Tarkine in north-west Tasmania. This was very similar to the policy concept advanced by Simon Crean, for which Fed. Labor could obtain no detailed information in 2004. It also put Lennon's proposal to Joel Fitzgibbon in perspective. The Howard govt paid $160 million for the protection of 150 000 hectares of forest

Hughes. Earlier in the campaign, O'Connor sent Gartrell sample ads attacking me, to be funded by the union if we released a pro-environment policy. One thing was certain: I wasn't going to be intimidated by that sort of rubbish.

The problem with the Forestry Division is that it has formed a dependency relationship with the companies. Their officials can't fart unless the bosses say it's okay. This was the tragedy of the Launceston rally: the forestry bosses were supporting Howard and used the hapless union as a campaign tool. I have always been sceptical about union involvement in Labor politics. Now I have been burnt by it, badly.

Come the last weekend of the campaign, I didn't think it mattered too much which party went first with its forestry policy. I knew what we wanted to achieve with ours, and all the advice to me was not to wait any longer. The night before the campaign launch, the State Secretaries met Gartrell in Brisbane and said to go sooner rather than later.

This was also the unanimous view of the travelling party, led by Faulkner. Smith, in particular, was gung-ho, recalling how well Geoff Gallop's forest protection policy worked for Labor at the last WA election. He wanted me to announce what we called the 'thermo-nuclear' option: tear up the Regional Forestry Agreement and immediately protect the 240 000 hectares. The final policy, by comparison, was mild.

Faulkner and Gartrell were worried that Howard was going to pre-empt our policy and go green himself. Maybe he had the same polling as us, so it was a possibility. But my reading was that he was close to the industry and, basically, he didn't have a green bone in his body. He was talking about the issue to soften his image with the so-called doctors' wives (small 'l' liberals disillusioned with the Government) but would never deliver a serious environmental policy. I went first because I wanted to set the agenda for the last week, to finish off on one of our issues.

Now, of course, it looks foolhardy. The polling was wrong: we cut Sid Sidebottom's throat in Braddon, and Michelle, who was already in trouble on interest rates, lost Bass. History will record it as an act of folly, what Barbara Tuchman in *The March of Folly* described as 'the awful momentum that makes carrying through easier than calling off a folly'.

But I will always wonder: what would have happened if Adams and the union officials had kept their heads down, if they had been Labor loyalists? Most likely, the issue would have been split: the conservation groups would have endorsed us, the timber companies would have endorsed Howard. We wouldn't have seen TV images of trade union officials and a Labor MP campaigning for the Government. We wouldn't have lost Braddon—that's certainly Faulkner's view.

Sunday, 17 October

Eight days since we lost. All these scribbled notes, I need to get them on the record somewhere, the things that happened in our campaign.

The Media

As detestable as ever. One thing I underestimated was the capacity of the Liberals to use large parts of the commercial media as an extension of their campaign. The Murdoch tabloids, for instance, kicked off the scare campaign against the Greens, which the Government finished off in the last days of the campaign. I knew Murdoch was backing the Government, but not as a formal part of its campaign.

The Liberals work very hard at getting up their agenda in the popular media. Their phone-tree on talkback radio was relentless, much better than ours. They are also shameless in feeding material to Tory journalists. My interviews with Glenn Milne and Alan Jones during the campaign were like sitting for an exam: fifteen subjects in ten minutes, questions fed straight from Liberal Party headquarters.

I pulled up the Dwarf on one of his quotes, and he admitted he didn't know where it came from. It didn't deter him, of course: he produced a front-page beat-up on tax increases on the last Sunday of the campaign. Shameless and pathetic. Our media monitors found that on the Jones, Ray Hadley and Chris Smith programs on 2GB, the only callers who got through were those who bagged me, never those who wanted to say something positive. So much for station owner John Singleton being a Labor supporter.

Packer also came after us, but late in the scene. For months, the head of Channel Nine, David Gyngell, was saying that they would play it down the middle. But in the campaign, their news service was a shocker. And during the last week, just to rub it in, the Scientologist James Packer publicly endorsed the Government. Given my blue with them years ago about Keating, it wasn't surprising. I think they tried to string us along for a while, worried that we might win and introduce a fourth commercial TV channel, thereby breaking their deal with Howard. But then they gave us the real stuff.

Some other media favourites from the campaign:

Sam Maiden—The one time I lost my cool on the campaign was at a press conference in Darwin on 19 September. The day before, a rumour

---

Radio phone-tree Calls to radio programs organised by the political parties and their supporters during election campaigns was circulating on 2UE in Sydney that we had booked Oliver into a non-government preschool for 2005. The only preschools in our district are non-government. Maiden knew about the radio rumour; she had asked Byres about it the previous day. But when it came to asking me about it, she framed the question as if it was a national interest matter, asking if I would set a good example and send my children to government schools. No mention of 2UE or the preschool.

I believe that if you are going to ask questions about someone's children, you should at least do it honestly. A simple, basic standard in life, but one that was foreign to Ms Maiden. It reminded me of all the reasons why I despised these people. I jotted down in my campaign folder: 'The media: no real life watching others'. I resolved not to snap a second time, just put on a show and get through the rest of the campaign looking bright and upbeat. A happy warrior.

Byres took phone calls from Sid Marris and Chris Mitchell, concerned about her behaviour. He said they described her as 'the difficult beast'. The next day in Townsville, the Beast's mate, Happy Sue Dunlevy from the *Daily Telegraph*, asked me why I objected to questions about my children, given that I had invited the media into my backyard on Father's Day. Was she for real? If someone invites me into their home, it doesn't mean I have a licence to intrude into their life thereafter. I made a mistake when I introduced my children to the media. A major error of judgement, for which I hope, one day, they will forgive me. It will never happen again.

Liz Jackson—For the sake of the campaign, I lifted my seven-year ban on *Four Corners*. Another mistake. It put me through the tedium of a Liz Jackson interview, the most self-obsessed, repetitive journalist I have come across—and that's saying something. Why ask a question once when you can ask the same question 25 times. This wasn't an interview. This was her insisting she was right and I was wrong, and trying to make that point 25 times. You know the type: upper-class background, thinks she's an expert on poverty and all things Labor, thinks the interview is really about her. I didn't watch the thing when it went to air—I didn't need to; sitting through the full interview in person was bad enough.

Paul Murray—Interviewed me on 6PR in Perth on 27 September. Before we started, he said he wanted to ask me about the Jakarta text-message controversy and handed me some papers about it. Inadvertently, he also handed over his briefing notes from Liberal staffer Ian Hanke on suggested questions for me: criticism of our coastguard policy, Gillard's

---

Sid Marris *The Australian*'s Canberra bureau's Chief of Staff | **Chris Mitchell** *The Australian* Editor-in-Chief

comments about reaching our bulk-billing target, etc. He asked me some of the questions, then started fumbling around, looking for the full list. I tossed them back to him when the interview was over. Another Liberal stooge, but also indicative of how these shock-jocks operate: highly paid and opinionated, but too lazy to do their own research. Masters of downward envy who wouldn't work in an iron lung themselves.

Michael Brissenden—Whenever I had time, I tried to catch the 6 p.m. television news and the ABC's *7.30 Report.* I thought Brissenden's coverage of the campaign was appalling: every night, he tried to trivialise issues, poke fun at people and carry on like a big kid. I half-expected him to sit on a whoopee cushion before it was all over. It was wrong, not because it was anti-Labor—it wasn't—but because it was anti-politics. Anti the idea that the campaign actually mattered, and the election result might affect people's lives. I expect this kind of rubbish from the commercial networks but not the ABC. When the national broadcaster treats politics as a joke, is it so surprising that most people join in?

Paul Kelly—Keating said never to trust him, and he was right. Iraq showed that Kelly is, first and foremost, a company man. He encouraged me on troops-out but once the Murdoch line was clear, bagged me for the rest of the year. I had always wondered about Kelly's politics, and this campaign offered an answer.

In the last week, he wrote a long defence of Tony Abbott, after Abbott had been busted lying on *Lateline* about a meeting with Big George Pell. It was ridiculous; the case against Abbott was incontrovertible. Then the penny dropped: Kelly's another Grouper. When the good folk at *The Australian* say that their politics is Right-wing Labor, what they mean is DLP.

The Colleagues

Always good for a laugh, especially with Faulkner on the campaign plane. Here are the standouts:

John Faulkner—Emerged as the head of the travelling party, pulling the show together after an untidy opening week. He brought in Smith to oversee the advancing. John was my linkman back to campaign headquarters. He spoke a lot about the shortcomings of the 2001 campaign: Beazley gave up with two days to go, and failed to finish off strongly on radio, something we avoided this time. He also gave a hilarious critique of Michael Costello's role: 'He spent the whole campaign on the toilet. We were in the car one time and he kept on saying, "I'm not going to make it, I'm not going to make it". I don't know what was wrong, but in the end, we all had the shits with him'.

Michael Costello—For a bloke with a lot to say about political strategy, he didn't sound too flash in the field. Simon Banks reckons that he would often fall asleep in meetings. When Beazley visited a hospital one day, they found the Chief of Staff asleep in one of the spare beds—I kid you not. Gartrell reckons that by the end of the 2001 campaign, Costello had racked up a noticeably big bill for in-house hotel movies. Obviously his great passion in life: the one thing that keeps him awake and off the dunny.

Kim Beazley—I appreciated his public comments on election night: 'Mark Latham has pulled us back from what looked like utter disaster. We've got the survival of a contestable Labor Party'. In private, he showed a humourous side I hadn't seen before. He put things in perspective by telling me, 'Listen, don't worry about who wins the election. Keep this in your mind: on election night you get to go home with Janine, and Howard has to go home with Janette'. Fair call.

Kim's health sounds worse than mine. On the campaign plane he told Janine and me that he was 'too scared to see his doctor' about his condition—fluid leaks from the membrane around his brain. Last Monday, when we were talking about support for my leadership, Stephen Smith told me, 'Don't worry about the Bomber, I think he's quite sick and won't run again in Brand. The war is over. The only one you have to worry about is Rudd, and he'll never have our support'. Yesterday the Bomber went to the backbench (again).

Gough Whitlam—Whenever I spoke to Gough during the campaign, it wasn't about politics—Margaret was sick. I hugged him at the policy launch because it felt like the right and emotional thing to do. After all, he's 88 and might not see another one. Hawke missed the launch because he was sick—we're a Party of the walking wounded—but I spoke to him late in the campaign and he was very positive about my performance.

Paul Keating—I don't know who did the seating at our campaign launch, but I felt bad about not being able to shake Keating's hand before I left the auditorium. I got someone to bring him backstage, but he was like a cat on a hot tin roof, very edgy. I phoned him a couple of times during the campaign; his main point was to ramp up the vision thing, advice he passed on from Hugh Mackay. He also gave me some good lines about the importance of Medicare, and submitted some material for the policy speech. It was a long lecture on the 1980s, so I couldn't find room for it. It was all about the past, not the future.

Kevin Rudd—Had a poor campaign. He stuffed up his explanation of the winners and losers in our schools policy on Seven's *Sunrise*; we're lucky

---

Hugh Mackay Australian social commentator
and author

the Libs didn't make more of it. Publicly, he promised to produce a White Paper on foreign policy. Privately, he told me he had been hoping for an early election, so he wouldn't have to do it. Finally, he produced a draft document and wanted me to release it during the campaign. But the material was unusable: wads of commentary about world events but next to no policy.

As Gartrell points out from our polling, the public like Rudd, but they think he's a commentator, not a political advocate. The consensus was that I shouldn't touch his document. Such a rich irony: more than anyone else in Caucus, Rudd has worked the media, trying to convince them that my policy ideas are inconsistent. But when he had to deliver his own flagship, it was an empty vessel. He doesn't write books or policy material, and never will.

Bob McMullan—He put in another shocker during the campaign, and was busted by Gartrell and Kaiser leaking details of our policy launch to *The Australian*. Gartrell was damning: 'He's a compulsive leaker. Every day of the campaign he wanders in, hanging around Jim Chalmers, trying to get some of the polling details off him, so that he can head up to the gallery and leak them. We laugh at him doing it, annoying Jim'. Tim reckons McMullan was at him last year to leak the bad polling on Crean. He also blames him for some of the leaks out of PRC earlier in the year—a compelling case against Comb-over.

I vowed to get him off the frontbench. But I also think Tim was weak in the way he handled him. In previous campaigns, Comb-over had been the official campaign spokesperson. This time, Tim wanted Smith in the job, but didn't have the heart to tell McMullan, so he left him with the impression that he still had some sort of spokesperson role. That's why he went down to campaign headquarters each day.

I rang Comb-over mid-week and told him he was a leaker and should go to the backbench. Someone had to be honest with him. He didn't like it, and he protested his innocence, but he sounded very nervous to me. He's got no support in the Centre group, so Bobby is stuffed. This will make a lot of people happy, especially Faulkner and Crean.

Dr Ivan Molloy—The candidate from hell, every campaign has got one. Ours was running in the safe Liberal seat of Fairfax. I wanted to disendorse him on Friday 24 September, under the cover of the AFL Grand Final, but Faulkner and Smith talked me out of it. Then he bobbed up on the front page of the *Courier-Mail* four days later, holding a gun, supposedly in the company of terrorists in the Philippines. It was like something

---

Jim Chalmers Staffer/organiser in the ALP Nat. Secretariat

out of the *Life of Brian*: was Molloy with the Moro Liberation Front or the Moro People's Liberation Front? Which ones were the terrorists?

All I could tell was that he was a Left-wing nutter (how did the Queensland branch ever endorse him?) and he caused us no end of grief. He wouldn't stop talking to the media about his theories on terrorism. Earlier in the campaign, his wife blamed Liberal MPs for the Bali and Jakarta bombings and Dr Ivan defended her. At one stage I asked, only half-jokingly, if the CFMEU could kidnap him and lock him up for the rest of the campaign.

Throughout the saga, Faulkner kept on referring to him as Ivan Milat, the serial killer who used to live in my electorate before he was relocated to Goulburn Gaol. I said to John: 'If you keep on saying that, I'll end up blurting it out in public'. And then I did, at a press conference on mental health, appropriately enough. Most of the journalists saw it as a joke, except for Jabba, who ran pictures of Molloy and Milat side-by-side on the Channel Nine news. I cried with laughter.

Monday, 18 October

Lindsay Tanner came all the way from Melbourne today to see me in my electorate office—a man on a mission. He made a long, rehearsed and slightly bizarre pitch to be Shadow Treasurer, telling me about his wonderful microeconomic reform credentials and links to the economics writers. I sat there thinking: this is the bloke who argued at Shadow Cabinet that we shouldn't proceed with trade practices reform until we cleared it with the Shoppies. Now he thinks he's Roger Douglas.

Tanner is one of Comb-over's mates, so I gave him some truth serum as well: 'Listen, Lindsay, the view around Caucus is that you have been a bit lazy, always promising big things but never delivering in the Shadow portfolios you've had. I would want to see you perform on the frontbench before even thinking about you as Shadow Treasurer'.

I had in mind his lacklustre effort in developing community-building policies. I gave him that gig at the National Conference and said I wanted a big agenda; he delivered something on mentoring and that was it. Cooney said he couldn't get anything else out of him, so we had to scramble to put a few things together for the campaign, such as combating loneliness among the aged.

Roger Douglas Ultra-dry NZ Finance Min. in the 1980s

Then Tanner cut to the chase, his real agenda for the meeting. With great indignation he told me that if he didn't become Shadow Treasurer, he was off to the backbench. So that was it: he knew I would never make him Shadow Treasurer, so this was just a way of getting to the backbench while blaming me, and throwing in some blackmail for good measure.

We went through the motions of discussing a few other possible positions, but it was just play-acting, the sort of thing you get in politics when people find themselves in an awkward situation. His mind was made up: Shadow Treasurer or bust. Guess I will have to find him a nice seat down the back. The ever-reliable Lindsay Tanner.

I'm still trying to get my head around the stuff-up in our advertising campaign, so I went back and re-read Utting's report from 31 July, which Gartrell rubber-stamped as our campaign strategy. Actually, I went through it three times. The story gets worse.

It only mentioned interest rates once, and that was in the context of one of Howard's positives: 'A good track record, with major strengths in economic management, especially interest rates, and national security'. No mention at all of the dangers of a scare campaign. It identified Liverpool Council as a negative in our focus groups, a Liberal attack point, but we knew that in May.

Why didn't Gartrell advertise my life story upfront: public housing, studied hard, served the community in local government—new facilities, efficiency gains, lower debt servicing, all the facts from my speech in the House on 1 June? We knew this attack was coming, we needed to get there first to fill in the gaps in people's minds. Let them know about my experience—the best experience in the world, raising a young family.

Gartrell's only rebuttal ad on Liverpool was a tiny radio spot, asking why the Liberals were complaining about Council pool fees when they introduced a GST. But nothing to say the claims against me were wrong, based on newspaper clippings well after the event. And nothing on TV, the place where the Liberals were hurting us. This failure to respond legitimised the Liverpool Council ads.

On interest rates, it took Tim ten days to come up with a rebuttal ad. What was wrong with going in hard early? We had the perfect material: Mike Scrafton, John Valder, the 43 Eminent Australians, all saying Howard was a liar. That's how I tried to respond on the road. My two-page list of key themes that I carried with me everywhere during the campaign included

John Valder Former Pres. Lib. Party who turned on Howard and organised an independent campaign in Howard's seat of Bennelong

the following points: Government Attacks: 1. What would you expect: dishonest tactics from a dishonest government. 2. Too many Liberal lies for too long—here's another. 3. Nothing left to say about Australia's future.

We just had to run the same lines in our ads. Why stuff around for ten days when the answer was obvious, and your parliamentary Leader was carrying them around in his campaign folder? This was the worst time to run an experiment with a 'think-tank' agency and a novice campaign director. What were they doing for ten days while the other mob killed us on interest rates?

In the last week, Gartrell spent most of our money on his beloved Costello ads. When I first saw them, I was a bit sceptical, but Tim was adamant that they worked well in the focus groups. But here's what Utting actually said about this issue on 31 July: 'Use Peter Costello and the Liberal leadership transition to demonstrate Howard's refusal to come clean with Australians about what will happen if the Liberals are re-elected. It is important not to make the mistake of making Peter Costello the sole issue in this context, disliked though he is by many swingers'.

Whenever I was asked about it, I tried to stick to the deceit angle on Howard, rather than ramp up the Costello question. But Tim, contrary to the research findings, made Costello the sole issue, right through to the ALP bunting on display at polling booths, which read, 'Peter Costello, Prime Minister, Don't Risk It'.

It's incredible. Gartrell didn't follow Utting's polling for our most expensive, highest profile advertising in the campaign. Maybe I shouldn't feel so bad that he ignored my ideas as well. The bottom line is, he's not up to it. That's the crippling paradox of our show. We have become a machine party, constructed around factions and yes-men, yet our campaign machine is shallow. We are too much of a State-based Party. The top jobs are perceived to be at State level, with the National Secretariat at the bottom of the pile. We struggle to get people to nominate for these positions, and when we do, they are usually rejects from the State systems.

What should I have done? When I was being battered before the FTA debate, I almost got in contact with Dick Morris—it'd be the first time since 2001. I asked Simon Banks to get me his phone number, worried that I was going to end up like Dukakis. Then I triumphed on the FTA, crisis averted. Morris, I reckon, would have responded to the Lib ads quickly and effectively. It was Politics 101. The one that got away.

A footnote to the stitch-up on Liverpool Council. I went to the Ingleburn branch tonight and the Branch President, Adrian Bunter, who works at PriceWaterhouseCoopers (PWC), passed on a conversation with

Dennis Banicevic, the PWC auditor cited by the Liberals as being critical of my financial management as Mayor. Apparently Dennis wanted to go public to say that he had been misrepresented but PWC management wouldn't let him. Great, PWC let us down over our financial costings and then gagged someone who wanted to defend me about Liverpool Council.

Friday, 22 October

The cruelty of politics, the things people do to each other. I'm as guilty as anyone. It's the culture of public life, the creeping cynicism and fierce tribalism in what we do. The past week sorting out the new frontbench for today's Caucus meeting has been particularly bad. We call each other colleagues, but it's really a synonym for cruelty. Is there a more pathetic sight than a demoralised Labor Party turning on itself, eating its own children? I'm yet to see it.

There are different levels of cruelty. The most brutal is dished out to the most vulnerable colleagues. Caucus regards Julia Irwin and Kelly Hoare as well out of their depth, yet both were lobbying for frontbench positions. It's a wonder they are in Parliament at all, let alone their ambitions of seeing themselves as Shadow Ministers.

Instead of telling them straight, the colleagues and Party officials like Arbib ring me to laugh at Irwin and Hoare and their delusions of grandeur. One by one, I go along with the joke. But in its totality, it's a terrible commentary on the ALP, the so-called party of solidarity. Inevitably, Irwin and Hoare missed out on the frontbench, and blamed me for their misfortunes. Perhaps the real joke is having to lead this motley crew.

The rest of the process was just as cruel. Factional hacks like Alan Griffin and Kerry O'Brien have kept their positions, while genuinely talented MPs like Catherine King have missed out. It was a chance for the factional warlords to flex their muscles, and merit was the last thing on their minds. It's a funny thing to admit, but there are so many sub-factions, personal intrigues and paybacks, that even I don't know how they all work. One that I do understand: Emmo has been dumped by the Queensland

---

Dennis Banicevic External auditor for Liverpool Council who gave evidence at the Daly inquiry in Jan. 2004. His criticism of Council's financial management related to the restructure of the Liverpool Council in 1995 and 1996—that is, after I had resigned as Mayor. This criticism was misrepresented by the Libs as a criticism of me

PWC In July PWC agreed to undertake an audit of ALP's election commitments but, under pressure from the Howard govt, backed away and provided just a cursory assessment of our election policy costings

AWU faction after his falling out with Ludwig. At least now he'll have more time to feed his cat.

The worst piece of cruelty was dished out to Crean. The Victorian Right was only entitled to three positions, but had four prominent contenders: Conroy, who was guaranteed a spot as Deputy Senate Leader, Crean, Roxon and Thomson. Before their ballot yesterday, I reached an agreement with Roxon and Thomson that Crean had to be supported. Throughout its history, Labor has honoured its former leaders, unlike the Tories, and this tradition had to be preserved. Crean supported me three years ago in the NSW ballot, and it would have been piss-weak of me not to return the favour. The irony of politics: this time I was ringing around to save him.

But this meant that either Roxon or Thomson would miss out from the Victorian Right. I assured them that I would then support the person who missed out and guarantee his or her election to the frontbench in the National Right process that followed—a system worked out by the Machiavellian Robert Ray, where each State Right-wing group would elect its own people, but those that missed out could contest one remaining frontbench spot in a ballot of the National Right, like a repechage round. Simple, hey?

It was actually, until Roxon ratted on the deal. She struck a counter-deal with Conroy to do in Crean, guaranteeing her spot without having to worry about the National Right. As it turned out, she would have won that ballot in a canter. Not only did she rat on her parliamentary Leader, but she didn't even have the decency to tell me. I only found out after the Victorian ballot, when Crean was pole-axed. He was devastated and didn't want to have to put himself through the indignity of the repechage round.

This is the terminal decline in our culture. I rang Roxon and, after five minutes of swearing, asked her, 'Why did you do this? Do you understand anything about Labor history, that our Party never did this to Scullin, or Evatt, or Calwell, or Gough, or Hayden, or Hawke, or Keating? We always treat our former Leaders with dignity and respect, what the fuck is going on?' She just ummed and ahhed, someone who joined the Party five minutes before her preselection. Now she just blows in the wind, whatever it takes to please her factional masters, even if it debases Labor history.

Well, as long as I'm Leader of the Party, I'm going to defend and honour our history. So I saved Crean: I pulled together my allies in Caucus and initially tried to get him up through the Centre group. That wasn't feasible, so I created an extra frontbench spot to accommodate him. I was willing to go to the wall on this, telling our meeting last night, 'I'm not here to stuff around in this job, I'm more than happy to go and raise my kids'.

That's the sadness of all this crap: every moment I spend with a Roxon is a moment I spend away from home. Cruelty indeed.

The ballot in the South Australian Right was just as farcical. There were only three of them in the group: the newly elected Kate Ellis, the member for Adelaide, and Senators Linda Kirk and Geoff Buckland. Poor old Buckoes, he's got no idea what he's doing here. Last year, I sat next to him during a National Right meeting in the Senate Caucus Room and he asked me if I thought the chairs were more comfortable on the Government side of the building, as if that was the big issue of the day. I told him I would love to find out.

Of the three of them, only Kirk could be considered frontbench material. Ellis is young and new to the job, while Buckoes is due to retire in July, as an outgoing Senator, to be replaced by Annette Hurley. Only one catch: Kirk has fallen out with Don Farrell, the South Australian head of the Shoppies, who control all the Right-wing preselections in that State, over the employment of his wife in her electorate office. Farrell hatched a crazy plan to defeat Kirk and make Ellis a Shadow Minister. He made Ellis nominate for the position and told Buckoes to vote for her. And that was it: Ellis two votes, Kirk one.

It's a classic case study of the arrogance and hopelessness of the factional system. Farrell was operating as a feudal lord, deciding who would be a Labor Shadow Minister, on the basis of his wife's employment. This was someone whom most Labor MPs would never have met (Joel had never heard of him) dictating to us the composition of our frontbench.

At 4 p.m. yesterday, the National Right conveners, Ray and John Hogg, came to tell me the results of their ballots: Crean out and Ellis in. I said to them: 'As Party Leader, I'm not willing to front a press conference trying to justify factional decisions that left off the frontbench a former Labor Leader and Shadow Treasurer, but included a 26-year-old greenhorn who is yet to be sworn into Parliament. I'm not going to do it, so you tell the National Right to give me something that's defensible. This feudal system of sub-factions and outside control by the likes of Don Farrell is untenable'.

I think they walked away regarding my leadership as untenable— machine men who don't like hearing that their system is rooted. Ray wasn't prepared to save Crean—I had to do that myself—but at least he fixed the Ellis/Farrell problem. Notionally, the South Australian Right-wing spot will remain vacant until Hurley, a former Deputy Leader in the South Australian Parliament, joins the Senate in July, at which point she will

---

Linda Kirk SA ALP Sen. 2002–
Geoff Buckland SA ALP Sen. 2000–05

Annette Hurley Former SA ALP Dep. Leader, due to take her place in the Senate 1 July 2005
Joel Fitzgibbon Asst Shadow Treas. 2004–

become a Shadow Minister. A compromise, a minor concession to hold back the cancer steadily eating this show: the factional warlords.

We should never have let the Shoppies back into the Party in the 1980s. They practise the worst of machine politics, fanatical and authoritarian. Joel tells a great story from when he was Shadow Minister for Small Business and Beazley was Leader. He wanted to push through a policy to help the independent grocery sector but the Shoppies objected because of their sweetheart deal with Coles and Woolworths. Joel put this to Beazley, who said, 'No, you can't do that mate, the Shoppies are the biggest Right-wing union in the country', as he puffed on a big cigar. Big Kim, big unions and a big cigar: that was the end of Joel's plan, the end of retail competition policy.

The Shoppies made policy under Beazley, so then they tried to determine the frontbench under me. I stopped them on the Ellis madness but the bastards managed to save Mark Bishop, the worst of our Shadows. In the last Parliament, as Shadow Minister for Veterans' Affairs, he managed to blow up the Western Australian branch of the Party, alienate the veterans' community and, during the election campaign, get into a well-publicised stoush with a TPI veteran. Now, I've been in a few blues myself over the years, but never with an invalid veteran.

Despite my attempt to get rid of him, Bishop is still a Shadow Minister. Ray explained it this way: 'I agree he is useless on the frontbench, but the Shoppies want him and for the next National Conference, that's very important for our Right-wing numbers'. I don't care about that, but with enough problems on my plate, I tried to buy some peace with the Right-wing powerbrokers Ray, Hogg and Arbib by conceding defeat on Bishop. I can't fight them on every front.

Another slice of Caucus chaos: Kevin Rudd. On Wednesday, *The Australian*'s Lewis and Norington carried a front-page story saying that if Rudd didn't become Shadow Treasurer he would go to the backbench. My thoughts went back to December last year and his tantrum over his title. He's such a prima donna.

Rudd came around to see me yesterday morning, lobbying to be Shadow Treasurer. He went into a long explanation of why he's so wonderful. When he finished I put my cards on the table: that I regard him as disloyal and unreliable, and he only holds his frontbench position because of his media profile and public standing among people who have never actually met him. I also told him that if the newspaper report was true, he should get ready for the backbench, as there was no way I could give him the Shadow Treasury.

Brad Norington *The Australian* industrial relations journalist

He appeared surprised, protested his innocence and then broke down badly, sobbing over the recent death of his mother, just before polling day. Rudd was in a very fragile condition. I told him to leave work and go back to Brisbane to rest with his family. But he wouldn't give up. Even though he was crying, he kept on lobbying to be Shadow Treasurer. It was becoming quite sad. Then he said words that I will never forget: 'I swear on my mother's grave that *The Australian* story is wrong, totally wrong, and that I've been loyal to you and will continue to be loyal to your leadership'.

I don't mind people bullshitting to me in politics, but not like this. Last week he rang around Caucus to gauge the mood after our loss, and told Trish Crossin that my leadership was on notice: I had until the Budget Reply speech next May to prove myself. He's always bagging me to journalists and that's not going to change any time soon. I don't trust him, no matter what he says.

A final piece of Caucus cruelty. Sharon Grierson rang me yesterday to say that she should be on the frontbench because she has emotional intelligence; apparently there's a fad American book on this subject. 'Howard wins because he's got emotional intelligence. We need more people with emotional intelligence; I've got emotional intelligence, you know.' What am I here: the Leader of Australia's oldest political party or the Hare Krishna? I feel like R. P. McMurphy in *One Flew Over the Cuckoo's Nest*, the only sane man in the asylum.

Monday, 25 October

A terrible weekend, trying to sort out the Shadow portfolios and massage the tender egos and neuroses of 30 Labor frontbenchers. Laurie tells me that, in the old days, the Leader simply issued a statement, announcing the positions without consulting his colleagues. A much better system: it would have rescued my weekend at home from a thousand phone calls.

The Shadow Treasury has been a nightmare. Gillard is the best person for the job, our rising star, but her own people have vetoed her. The leaders of the Left have lined up, one by one, to blackball her: Faulkner, Evans and Combet, plus expected criticism from Macklin and Albanese. Gillard would be better off leaving those losers behind. The Left never likes to actually exercise power. Our new Senate Leader, Chris Evans, admitted to me, 'Here I am, the most senior person in the Parliamentary Left, saying that someone from the Left cannot do the job'.

Trish Crossin NT ALP Sen. 1998–

I told Julia I couldn't give it to her because I had run out of petrol after saving Crean. I didn't have the heart to tell her about the rats in her ranks. Anyway, my feeling is she will be better off as Health Shadow and Manager of Opposition Business; it gives her a chance to grease Caucus and line herself up as the next Leader. That was certainly my experience: MOB won me Caucus support, while ST cost me votes.

My other options were limited: Rudd is too unreliable, Smith is too timid and Swan is too shrill. It's a lovely Party: we haven't got anyone capable of being Shadow Treasurer who has the support of their faction. Hobson's choice. In the end, I have gone for the Queenslander. It might help us up there—he works hard and gets around the media.

Was it difficult to make a Rooster the Shadow Treasurer? Not really. It's a hard job and Costello will carve him up in the chamber. It destroyed Gary Evans and didn't do much to help Comb-over or me. The only one who came out ahead was Crean (1998–2001); he looked good in the job because he had the GST to campaign against. Otherwise, it's a shithole of a thing.

I gave Smith the consolation prize of Industry, Infrastructure and Industrial Relations, another tough job. His job will be to promote micro-reform and to argue with the unions as we water down our IR policy. Let him take the odium for that inside the Party. The other advantage is that Smith and Swan love to parade around the top end of town. They can do the meetings I don't want to. Let them sit there for hours listening to the moaning sounds of Hugh Morgan, David Murray and Heather Ridout. I would rather watch grass grow.

Another nightmare: my decision to create an inner Shadow Cabinet of seventeen. Meetings with 30 people around the table are unworkable. Beazley did it for six years, trying to please everyone—a dog's breakfast. A proper, professional Opposition needs an inner Cabinet. Just one problem: I've got 30 prima donnas for 17 positions. My first priority is to promote progressive young women such as Penny Wong and Tanya Plibersek. All the talented Labor women are in the Left, an area where we have a clear advantage over the Coalition. I've given Plibersek the new portfolio of Work, Family and Community, doing the job that Tanner neglected.

Otherwise, it has been a torturous exercise, trying to manage so many egos. You wouldn't believe the tickets these people have on themselves. Kerry O'Brien was hopeless in the last term of Parliament, yet he sees himself

---

Hugh Morgan Right-wing businessman and head, Business Council of Australia
David Murray Member, Business Council of Australia; CEO, Commonwealth Bank of Australia 1992–2005

Heather Ridout Chief Exec., Australian Industry Group
Tanya Plibersek ALP member, Sydney 1998–

as a hotshot, so I had a half-hour slanging match on the phone, trying to get him to accept reality. A similar but less acrimonious process with Kate Lundy, who expected to be in Shadow Cabinet. After her stuff-up on the FTA, she should be on the backbench. She's lucky to have any portfolio.

After the election, Gavan O'Connor told me he had lost enthusiasm and wanted to go to the backbench. He subsequently changed his mind, but now he's miffed at missing out on the Shadow Cabinet. I should have charged a therapy fee for some of these phone calls. Some other lowlights:

Mark Bishop—I tried to move him out of Veterans' Affairs to assist Smith in Infrastructure, where Bishop reckons he has some expertise. But Smith wouldn't take him and Evans said, 'Leave him where he is, he destroys every constituency he works with [the TPI incident], don't let him near the mining industry in Western Australia'. Stuff it, he can stay in Veterans' Affairs and wallow in his own juices. That's the price we pay for putting union hacks into the Senate and then onto the frontbench.

Alan Griffin—Inarticulate and unpresentable in the public arena. What could any Leader do with him? He's also been bagging me around the place. I fronted him about that and all he could do was stutter. He's one of the big men on the blower, but not so courageous in person. I tried to give him Banking and Finance, where he claims some expertise, but he has a conflict of interest with his partner's job. He's ended up with Sport and Recreation, the best I can do.

Stephen Conroy—Told me he doesn't have any strong policy interests, and maybe he would like the Communications portfolio, which I gave him. It's a frank admission; machine men aren't interested in policy, only factions and patronage. I tried to reconcile our past differences, but it's hard-going—I like people with conviction and character. He told me he's against me on the Tasmanian forests because of his affiliation with the TWU—their members carry the logs. Nothing to do with argument, reason or public policy, but rather his factional links to a union. Has he ever driven a truck? Is it just me, or is there something fundamentally wrong with our Party?

Tuesday, 26 October

A press conference in Canberra to announce the new frontbench line-up, flanked by my economic emissaries, Stephen Swan and Wayne Smith. Cock-a-doodle-do. All went according to plan. I promised to consult the business community, safe in the knowledge that I won't have to see them very often.

TPI incident During the 2004 Fed. election campaign, Mark Bishop became involved in a public dispute with a TPI veteran, which was grossly embarrassing to the ALP

Back to my office, and read a transcript of the *Lateline* panel last Friday night: Maxine McKew, Laura Tingle and Matt Price pontificating about why I saved Crean. It was so cynical, ruling out the possibility that Labor tradition could have been my motivation. I had tears in my eyes last week, sentimental about the old Party as I saved him. But now I read that it was just self-interest. The Canberra Press Gallery: too cynical for its own good. They remind me of Talleyrand's response upon hearing the news that the Russian Ambassador had died: 'I wonder what his motive could have been?'

Friday, 29 October

The end of a dispiriting week, my worst since Bacon's funeral. And tomorrow I've got to go back to Tasmania to talk to the State Labor Conference to tell them I stuffed up on forests.

A two-day meeting of the new Shadow Cabinet ended yesterday. A lacklustre discussion of the reasons for our election defeat. Interesting to watch Smith and Swan hang back during this discussion, reluctant to give me any support. They fancy themselves as clever, but everything they do is so obvious.

Only Chris Evans showed any sign of understanding reality: we have lost the support of the economic free agents, the contractors and consultants, the big winners in the new economy, who just want government to get out of the way. All our talk about community and the active role of the state is a nuisance to them.

I told the members of Shadow Cabinet they have a supremely important role in the history of the Labor movement: Australia's economic and political base has been transformed and our future is far from assured. We either pull together and modernise our economic policies, or we will collapse as a political party. And how did they respond? With an avalanche of leaks to the media.

Complaining about them does no good; our culture is shattered. Said all of this to Danger and he was very philosophical. Maybe the joys of retirement do that to you. 'You're in the box seat, mate. If they don't pull their heads in, you can walk away from the terrible bunch of bastards any time you want.' Plan B: just walk away. Call the bullshit of Labor politics for what it is, and walk away.

Dinner with the Shadows in Manuka on Wednesday night: Crean, Gillard and Carr were ropeable about the way in which frontbench itineraries were

---

Laura Tingle *AFR* political correspondent | **Talleyrand** Legendary French diplomat during the Napoleonic era handled during the campaign. It sounded like chaos theory. The Shadows were told to 'submit something to the National Secretariat and then see how it looks'. No planning, no coordination. Our Queensland campaign guru, Mike Kaiser, prepared a five-week program—it never occurred to him that Howard might call a six-week campaign. He had twelve months to get ready and yet he overlooked this basic contingency.

A footnote to the campaign. Yesterday, for the first time, I saw footage of my handshake with Howard the day before polling day. What are they going on about in the media? It's a Tory gee-up: we got close to each other, sure, but otherwise it was a regulation man's handshake. It's silly to say it cost us votes—my numbers spiked in the last night of our polling.

The full story: Howard deserved a lot more than a firm handshake. Throughout the campaign, every time I saw him, he kept on trying to give me a bone-crusher, squeezing tight and shaking with his arm, instead of his wrist, like a flapping motion. It's a small man's thing, trying to show you can match the big guy at something. I wasn't too worried about it, thought it was funny, until the last Sunday of the campaign at the St George Leagues Club lunch, when Howard did the same thing to Janine. She said to me, 'That man just tried to break my hand. It really hurt'.

Enough was enough. Next time I saw him, at the ABC Radio studio in Sydney, I put on the squeeze and got a bit closer to him, so he couldn't do the flapping thing. The weak animal looked startled, so it had the desired effect. It's ironic, however: I'm supposed to be the intimidating one in politics, but I have never tried to break a woman's hand. How does Howard get away with it?

Monday, 1 November

Lunch with Arbib at Azuma's in Sydney. It's interesting to listen to these machine guys: they live in a world of non-stop political manoeuvres and gossip, no structured thoughts about making society better. Their only points of reference in public life are polling and focus groups. And so it is with Arbib. Some snippets from him.

The focus groups showed that people like me, but they think I need another three years in Opposition, after which they will give me a go. He was very critical of Gartrell and Kaiser for not attending the focus groups: 'They left it to Jim Chalmers, but you need to go along yourself to find out what's going on'.

The focus groups also show that it's popular to bash the blacks: 'You need to find new issues, like attacking land rights, get stuck into all the politically correct Aboriginal stuff—the punters love it'. Maybe he should have had lunch with Pauline Hanson, though not at Azuma's.

His exit poll on election day (500 people in NSW marginal seats) showed that Gartrell's Costello ads failed. Arbib's research report says that 'Only 17 per cent of voters said they had been less likely to vote Liberal because of the Costello factor, a non-issue'. Health and Medicare were our best vote drivers (37 per cent of people who voted Labor did so because of that). Interest rates and the economy were the best for the Liberals (40 per cent).

Interestingly, the exit poll seems to contradict the view that the last week of our campaign was a disaster (the forestry factor). It asked people when they made up their minds about how they would vote and found that '29 per cent of Labor voters made up their minds in the last week of the campaign compared with 17 per cent of Coalition voters'. People were still coming to us in good numbers.

Arbib reckons that Oakes was consistently against us during the campaign: 'He was the worst every night, so you must have a problem with Packer. You need to go and see the big media people every now and then and kiss their arses. Carr does it all the time, it works wonders'. Yes, if you don't mind having shit on your lips.

Otherwise, he was quite critical of Carr, saying that he would lose an election right now. That's a sign of how State issues hurt us, confirming our polling in the first fortnight of the campaign that State factors, especially in NSW, were dragging us down. Arbib is convinced that Carr will stay for the next NSW election, but doesn't sound too keen about it. He's right, of course: the best way of revitalising a long-serving government is a new generation of leadership.

We also talked about the quality of Labor MPs in NSW, and he wants to get rid of Irwin in Fowler: 'We had it all lined up before the 2001 election. Irwin was going to the State Upper House and Maxine McKew was going to run for Fowler. She would have been fantastic but then she backed out, said she couldn't stand living in Cabramatta or Liverpool'. So Maxine wants to be a Labor MP, but can't stand the sight or smell of Labor voters, hey? Thankfully, Arbib also wants to punt Hatton: 'irrelevant and on the way out'.

Wednesday, 10 November

Last night I attended a meeting of the Hinchinbrook ALP branch at the northern end of my electorate. There were just six people there; they had to phone around to get a quorum. Yet the branch is supposed to have hundreds of members—paper members, Left-wing ethnic stacks, rorted onto its books for voting purposes. How depressing. Labor's Federal Leader and his rank-and-file Party. I drove home thinking to myself, that's the organisation I lead, the one that has made me a stranger to my children.

An informative meeting in Brisbane today with a group of mothers from St Stephen's Catholic School in the seat of Moreton—confirmation of the reasons why we lost the election. Their votes were heavily influenced by the Liberal advertising campaign. In the words of one mum, 'I don't get to watch the news, I'm too busy with the children. I have one hour later in the night for my TV shows, so all I saw during the election were the interest rates ads. I know they were political propaganda but there was a bit of truth too. Whitlam and Keating didn't do a very good job with the economy'.

Fear is a more powerful emotion than hope. One of them said that as she walked out of the polling booth, she asked her husband how he voted and he replied, 'Don't worry, I voted to keep our house safe'. The frustration of it: I'm the last person who would run deficit budgets, the driest in the Party except for Cox, and he would have been the Finance Minister. But they thought they were going to lose their homes under me.

With the rise of consumerism, political advertising has become more important. One woman said, 'The ads feed us, they let me know what's going on, the new products that are out'. This is the politics of the lowest common denominator, buying the bullshit ads. I see advertising and assume it's a wild exaggeration; if something is so weak it needs to be advertised, I think it's not worth buying. Maybe my mindset is not suited to the consumerism of middle Australia.

These women were not so much conservative as reflecting the politics of 'me'. The hip-pocket nerve has always been sensitive in Australian politics, but now, after ten years of prosperity and the ownership revolution, it is out of control. People live in their highly geared McMansions, on $60–$70 000 a year, couple of kids at a non-government school, and they say to the politicians, 'I'm the real battler, help me, make me secure before helping anyone else'.

It's the rise of the material/me society—no mention of others, the poor, community concerns, etc.—and these were relatively active mums from the parents and friends association. I'm used to the larrikin/rebellious/matey side of suburban culture in Australia. But it's almost dead, replaced by a timid/insular/self-centred/material culture. This is not my idea of what Australia should be.

Apathy is the greatest enemy of progressive politics. These women have contracted out management of the economy to Howard and Costello. They don't care how many lies Howard tells or how smug Costello looks; as long as the economy is strong they will vote Liberal. My campaign was just a sidelight to them. And the really scary thing? That's how most of the country sees our democracy. Cynicism is the gold standard of modern politics, the public discount all the words and go for self-interest.

Just as scary: Gartrell's speech to the National Press Club today. Apparently he looked terribly nervous, gasping for water every five minutes. In trying to rationalise our election loss, he said that 'the public logically decided to have more of Howard, a little bit of Costello and then Mark Latham'. But this was exactly the opposite of what the anti-Costello ads were supposed to achieve. They were designed to scare people away from Howard because they would end up with Costello. If the public were so logical in their thinking, why did Gartrell give them the opposite message in our advertising?

None of the journalists picked it up; they were too busy asking questions about me. It's the unspoken bombshell of our campaign: Gartrell ignored Utting's advice and flushed our advertising money down the drain, while failing to respond to the Government's scare campaign. That's another little thing Tim didn't tell them today: his failure to anticipate the interest rates scare. He thought the Lib negative attack would target: 1. Crean's unpopularity; 2. a 'Latham's not ready yet, wait for next time' sentiment; and 3. Liverpool Council. No mention of the big one.

Saturday, 13 November

A good reception from the crowd at the Australia versus New Zealand netball test in Sydney. Tried to get the Australian captain Liz Ellis to consider standing as a Labor candidate when she retires from the game. Poor form from Janette Howard, who had a shot at Janine for wearing a black outfit, the Kiwi colours. And the way she said it, a nasty piece of work. The Beazley motto has never been so true.

And the Tories want to lecture me about manners. The husband tries to break my wife's hand and now the old girl is giving her snide fashion tips. How do the Howards get away with it? The ruling class rules and looks after its own people, that's how. They can treat us like dirt, but if we give it back to them, we're the worst in the world.

It made me think: of all the people I've been associated with—Labor people, my staff, Green Valley types, Hurlstonians, the Liverpool Council mob, the first wife, even our neighbours in Glen Alpine—the only ones who haven't snitched on me are the Liverpool Bulls, my rugby club mates. The only ones who still practise working-class solidarity.

What is it about the workers? A journalist asks them a question and they feel obliged to answer? Freaked out by the power of the press, unable to resist their fifteen minutes of fame? It's a sad thing about our society: those without power never know how to handle it, and those with power never know how to share it.

Monday, 15 November

Parliament comes back tomorrow, the moment we have been dreading. Caucus has gone feral with the destabilisation of my leadership. It will be worse this week as the troublemakers gather in one place, gossiping to each other and the press gallery. The chief troublemaker is Conroy: non-stop leaking, stirring discontent, befriending the malcontents. The moment he left my office last month, after our so-called reconciliation, his promise of teamwork went out the window.

I convened a meeting with Faulkner, his former Senate Leader, and Ray, his former mentor, to see what could be done about him. Nothing, apparently. Faulkner says he's not the full quid (tell me something new) and Ray has given up on him. It's not hard to tell where Conroy got his spite. This Fat Indian is a nasty piece of work. Apropos nothing, he told the story of the night Conroy met his wife: 'We were coming out of the tally-room after our terrible defeat in 1996 and Conroy asked me, what do you do on a night like this. I told him to go find a woman and root her silly, but I didn't tell him to go and marry her'. As ever, the Fat Indian Voyeur.

Wednesday, 17 November

Unbelievable. Paul Lennon announces a pulp mill proposal in Tasmania: 1500 new jobs, using plantation timber as best practice, with no need to cut down one old tree. This is the point I made in the campaign: the industry has fallen down the value-added chain. Ten years ago, one job relied on 1.25 hectares of harvested forest; it now relies on five. Sending it back up the chain is the best way of protecting jobs and the high conservation value forests.

On the day I released our policy, I met with Terry Edwards from the timber industry and Scott McLean from the timber union. They both said, 'Your policy means that a pulp mill can't go ahead in Tasmania'. Were they lying or are they just fools?

And what about Lennon? He must have had this announcement in the pipeline for months. All he had to do was announce it with me during the campaign, Federal and State Labor cooperating to create value-adding jobs and protect the forests. Our problems solved in one hit, and Howard would have been left to play catch-up politics. Why would a Labor Premier sell us down the river so badly?

Scott McLean Sec., Tas. branch of the CFMEU Forest & Forest Products Div.; member of the ALP Nat. Exec.

Saturday, 20 November

Last night at a Fabian dinner in Melbourne, I gave a speech recasting Labor's direction, but the media barely noticed. They are too busy reporting the destabilisation of my leadership to worry about the things I actually say. What matters to them is the flood of leaks and backgrounding out of Caucus.

I pointed out that many of our policies—early childhood education, schools funding and Medicare Gold—are designed to harness the resources of the private sector for sound public purposes. The key issue is not public or private ownership, but public access and public benefit. What matters is what works.

I also flagged the death of the trade union movement as a force inside the Labor Party, saying that people have broken free from large, hierarchical organisations and become agents of their own economic future. They have less affinity with the traditional role of capital and labour, and even the notion of a traditional workplace. Australia now has more than 800 000 home-based offices, mostly occupied by the rising middle class of economic independents. The implications for the Labor movement are obvious. Workers are more discerning and self-reliant. Large, centralised institutions (that is, the unions) are less relevant.

Ho-hum. Here's something that would interest the media. After my speech today at the Victorian Labor Conference, I met with Conroy and confronted him about his treachery. Under a bit of pressure, he spewed it all out: his unhappiness in politics, his guilt about Wilton's death, his opposition to my leadership, his leaking to the media, his mischief around Caucus and his bitterness about Faulkner. Quite bizarrely, he blames Faulkner for missing out on the Senate leadership.

He raised the history with Pills, saying that Joel and I had unfairly accused him of taking Maria's side of the argument. I said, 'No, we have never said that. We blame you for the *Herald Sun* article; that's always been our beef'. He looked down into his lap, said 'Oh yeah, that', and changed the subject.

I told Conroy I wasn't going to die the death of a thousand cuts as Crean did. If there is any move against my leadership, he's coming with me. Ludwig or Forshaw would easily beat him in a ballot for the Senate Deputy Leadership. I can safely say that our little talk put some shit in his undies.

Monday, 22 November

A great reception at a crowded community forum (my twentieth for the year) in the Leichhardt Town Hall in Albanese's electorate. The machine men loathe me, the True Believers love me—I'm leading a double life as

Labor Leader. One bloke summed up the mood at the forum: we lost, but we stood for something this time, unlike 2001. True, we mobilised the Labor base, but it wasn't enough.

Martyn Evans, who has contested elections in the northern suburbs of Adelaide for 25 years, said during the campaign he was getting the best feedback he had ever received as a Labor candidate. But he lost Wakefield. Here, in Grayndler, Albo said that before the 2001 election fewer than 100 people turned up to his pre-election function for booth workers. This time more than 400 turned up.

I've bagged these inner-city types over the years, but at least they have a sense of the common good in their politics. That's the striking thing about the election post-mortem. The people who voted Labor always mention the needs of others: the community interest in health, education and the environment, and the quality of our society. The Coalition voters only ever mention themselves: my mortgage, my money, my needs—the my/me society.

When Adlai Stevenson was campaigning for the US Presidency in 1952, a woman said to him, 'Governor, every thinking American is going to vote for you', and he replied, 'It's not enough'. Every community-minded Australian supported me, but it was not enough.

Will it ever be enough for a progressive Labor Government? The electorate has broken into four groups:

- well-informed progressive people who care about community services and dislike Howard (about 15 per cent of the electorate). This group is strongly interested in political ideas, a passionate but limited audience
- well-informed conservatives: business types, social elites and religious fanatics (15 per cent). Dedicated to the status quo in society
- people who are down and out: chronically unemployed, disabled, mentally ill, etc. (20 per cent). Often hostile and bitter about the political system, with good reason
- the disengaged, self-interested middle class, who tend to delegate economic management to the Coalition in Federal elections, but trust State Labor with their health and education services (50 per cent). Apathy rules.

That's the truth of it, a blow to my optimistic view of human nature: that people want to get more involved in community life and politics but

Martyn Evans Councillor, Elizabeth City Council 1975–84; Mayor, Elizabeth 1981–84; Independent member, Elizabeth in SA Parl. 1984–94; ALP member, Bonython 1994–2004; unsuccessful ALP candidate for the redistributed seat of Wakefield, Oct. 2004

The Latham Diaries

lack the forums in which to do so. I've spent seventeen years, first in local government and now federally, talking about the need for public participation. But only a minority are interested, the social activists who come to these community forums. I put forward the possibility of a new politics in the campaign, but the media and the voters barely noticed.

Our Machinery of Government policy proposed a radical opening up of government, but the journalists weren't interested. They had seen it before in the first part of the year, now they wanted me to jump through new hoops. New wild policies or, better still, show them the bucks' night video. I did two big community forums during the campaign but got no credit for it. Everything Howard did was tightly stage-managed but no one drew the distinction. In truth, the media don't want the public directly involved, because it means someone else gets to ask the questions.

I should have done a forum every day, shoved them down the media's throat until they noticed the difference. Yeah, sure. Gartrell and Kaiser were shitting themselves about the unpredictability of two forums; they would have ditched those if they could, and were shocked when both went well. How would they have handled 42? I'm leading a Party of control freaks in a political system where everyone wants to be in control.

What an amazing dilemma. I've got the power of ALP leadership but all I want to do is give power away to the public. It's the crippling paradox of modern politics: the insiders are megalomaniacs, and the outsiders are so far outside the political system that they think none of it matters. It's hard enough for governments to help rebuild communities and solve social problems, but if the disempowered don't really care, don't want to get involved in the first place, then it's a mission impossible. What was my conclusion at UNSW in 2001? Social democracy is insoluble. Three years later and I'm still pushing shit uphill.

Hey, I can't even get the insiders of the press gallery to understand the insiders/outsiders concept. I've written books and made speeches about it, but none of it registers. That dandy, Peter Hartcher from the *SMH*, stitched me up during the campaign, claiming that the insiders/outsiders philosophy is a revival of class warfare. But it goes past the Marxist understanding of class based on material goods, and looks at society in terms of status, influence, access to information and power.

Most of the middle-class people I talk about are outsiders—they have a four-wheel drive and a tin boat in the driveway (materially well-off) but

---

Machinery of Government policy Released during the first week of the election campaign, including parliamentary reform, such as the establishment of an independent Speaker, new freedom of information provisions, community consultation provisions, etc.

have no power or influence to change the design and amenity of their local park (politically poor). And the sad thing for this pummelled, punching bag of a Labor Leader? They could hardly care less about it. They weren't at the Leichhardt Town Hall tonight, they were at home watching *Australian Idol*, praying that interest rates stay down.

Wednesday, 24 November

Why is it that every time I come to Adelaide there's a problem? The Clinton plagiarism thing, Lundy on the FTA, the stuff-up with Mark Williams's school during the campaign, and Ivan Molloy/Milat—they all hit me in the city of churches. Maybe there is a god, and he's on to me.

Today's problem: leaks from the National Executive meeting yesterday. Misleading reports that I blamed the State Labor governments for our defeat. I didn't blame them, I said that I should have handled the various State controversies differently. It was my mistake, I should have put some distance between our campaign and State issues. The Coalition ran hard on this, because they knew they were on a winner.

Anyway, I went to the meeting expecting leaks. It's a forum for factional hacks, and the factional machines are caving in on me. What they can't control, they will destroy. Little Billy Shorten from the AWU, for instance, spent the meeting head down, taking notes. Maybe he loves the things I say and needed to record them for his children. Very obvious, very funny.

Journalists are saying I haven't publicly accepted responsibility for the defeat. So wrong, I did it three days after the election at my Coogee doorstop, after the Bali memorial service. It's an inexorable part of the job: cop the crap, and then move on. Did the same thing at the National Executive. I told them about my six great mistakes this year, then some strategies for the future. Here are my speech notes for posterity, the words the papers haven't published:

> In December 2003 the Party was hopelessly divided. The Government was managing a strong economy, with 60–65 per cent of people

---

Mark Williams Coach of the Adelaide Port Power AFL team and author of a children's book on AFL. I met him and discussed his book during the election campaign on 15 Sept. at the AAMI Football Stadium in Adelaide. At the last minute the event had to be moved away from Williams's children's school because of adverse reaction at that school to the ALP's school-funding policy. Channel Seven was aware of this, but their reporter following my campaign, Geof Parry, asked the wrong questions about it at the press conference. Thereafter, this event was known among the ALP campaign travelling party as Parry-gate

saying the country was headed in the right direction. The NSW General Secretary told me we would lose Werriwa.

I had three key goals as the new Leader: unite the Party; establish my credentials in the honeymoon period; and set a new agenda to focus attention away from the Government's strengths. The honeymoon was very strong but the polls early this year had a by-election feeling: a fresh ALP Leader talking about relevant social issues, a message to Howard to lift his game.

Things were still going well by April/May. The Government was seen as out of touch on everyday family issues, the little things that matter. We had the possibility of a Steve Bracks scenario: out-of-touch Government, they leave the new guy alone, a surprise Labor victory.

The Liberals didn't make this mistake a second time. The May Budget was full of give-aways, Howard reactivated himself and they got stuck into me big time. Come July, I was being pounded over the personal stuff and the FTA.

Mid-year, our campaign was at a turning point. Do we continue with the things that had worked previously, or do we switch onto the economic agenda, the Government's strength? I thought it was best to get outside the Government's firing range. Being pounded on their issues wasn't much fun.

Our success on the trade agreement was an important lesson about agenda-shifting. We were taking water on the FTA as an economic and American issue but then managed to turn it into a health issue, revitalising our campaign.

We went into the formal election campaign behind but still reasonably competitive. There were three phases over the six weeks:
- first fortnight—we started slowly, Howard pressed the interest rates button and national security helped him—Beslan and the Jakarta bombing
- middle fortnight—with victory in the debate, plus successful schools and health policy announcements, we came back to a competitive position
- final fortnight—despite our better policy launch (Medicare Gold), the Lib ads broke through on interest rates. Tasmanian

---

Steve Bracks scenario Bracks's surprising victory in the 1999 Vic. State election when Premier Kennett campaigned as an arrogant and out-of-touch Lib. Leader. The Libs ignored Bracks, with little negative advertising against him

forestry was designed to be the last of our non-economic agenda-setters, but the union protest rally blew us away.

I made six mistakes, six areas where I could have done better as Leader of the Party. I didn't pay enough attention to the advertising campaign. It was slow and ineffective. We needed rapid rebuttal of the Lib ads but it never happened. This allowed the Coalition to fill in the gaps about me in the electorate's mind, just like Dukakis and the Willie Horton ads. I thought the positive party would win, but I was wrong.

We didn't give people enough economic reassurance—telling them, time after time, of the things we wouldn't do. We talked about the economy, of course: the Budget Pledge, trade practices reform, welfare-to-work, etc. It would have been a mistake, however, to make this the main focus of our campaign. In hindsight, what we needed was a mini-campaign on economic policy mid-year. This was the real damage of the *Sunday* program on 4 July; it derailed our plan to re-announce the Budget Pledge.

The tax and family policy was reactive, complex and delayed too long. Policy by committee rarely works in a campaign environment, it bogs you down. I should have surprised the Government with mort-gage tax relief, blunting the interest rate scare.

I wasn't hard enough on my Chief of Staff; he didn't have the office campaign-ready. All year, it felt like we were seven weeks away from election day, so I didn't have time to find someone new. He's had a fair bit to say in the newspapers since he left two days after polling day, so this is a fair point to make.

The Tassie forests policy backfired. If I had known about the protest rally and the lack of cooperation from Paul Lennon, I would have announced it earlier and taken them on in the public debate.

I was too soft on the States. I should have distanced our cam-paign from controversial issues like the Scoresby broken promise in Victoria and the Orange Grove development in NSW. The NSW Government dropped ten points in Newspoll during the campaign, so it wouldn't have hurt us to give them a whack.

So, where do we go from here? It's horseshit to say we need to shift to the Left, per the Barry Jones remedy, or to the Right, the Billy Shorten solution. Were we too far to the Right on the environment, schools funding, saving Medicare or getting out of Iraq? Were we too far to the Left on the abolition of ATSIC, redefining multiculturalism,

Barry Jones Nat. ALP Vice Pres. 2004

holding the line on refugees, on gay marriage or our welfare-to-work policy, which was denounced by ACOSS?

I don't believe in the old ideologies. We are a modern progressive party, breaking down the old Establishment and dispersing power to citizens and communities—the enabling state. We don't do things because they are Left- or Right-wing, we do them because they are right. So I reject the Jones and Shorten analyses.

Three strategies for the future:

- We gave away our economic credibility post-1996; we need to rebuild it. It's a three-year job, appealing to the new class of free agents and entrepreneurs. We need to find a way through Howard's structure: our campaign against him on truth/responsibility is not sufficient to beat his perceived economic strengths.
- We need to maintain our existing strengths, not walk away from good Labor policy on health, education and the environment.
- We need to change the way the Party operates. Are we a political party or a federation of sub-factions? We have 88 Federal MPs and 31 of them are so-called powerbrokers, with their own little group and numbers. The main factions have broken down into personal fiefdoms and tribes. This has institutionalised conflict and made the task of leading the show more difficult. How do you consult with 31 people on a given issue on a given day? What does this Party need: a Leader or a receptionist who's on the phone all day?

The discussion after my report was subdued (maybe just 15 minutes). These cowards do most of their work on the phone with journalists. The most amazing non-contribution was from Scott McLean, the timber man. He sat there like a Trappist monk, not one word. This was such a big issue for him. He helped organise a rally for Howard, but when he had his chance to talk about it at the ALP National Executive, he dogged it. I'm still shaking my head in disbelief. He exposed the true character of Australian trade unionism.

Earlier in the year, when they thought I could win, they were all up my arse, wanting me to save them from Howard's IR policies. Now they have all turned. And the biggest fickler of all: their ACTU leader, Greg Combet. Towards the end of the campaign, he said we were going so well I was 'a Labor hero'. Two weeks later he was telling the media, 'It's up to him as to whether he stays Leader'. In truth, the unions are now so broken and rorted that no Labor Leader can rely on them. The Launceston rally was the public manifestation of that reality.

Another thing out of the Executive meeting: Gartrell admitted that the media buy for our advertising was hopeless—they bought the spots on TV but they were for low-rating shows. That explains the mystery of why so many people tell me they never saw our ads, only the Coalition's. So much for a miracle weapon in the last week of the campaign. The Libs were bombarding the Rugby League Grand Final, while we were bombarding the late-night movie on Channel Ten.

Yet another problem today here in Adelaide: the poisonous Paul Daley from the *Bulletin* has an anonymous quote from one of my key Shadow Cabinet former supporters: 'There is a sense that Latham has rewarded his enemies with high-profile positions at the expense of close supporters and allies, including myself … I am now, sadly, resigned that a leadership ballot is inevitable, if not before Christmas then early next year'.

I rang Kim Il-Carr and he admitted talking to Daley off the record, 'but that is not my quote'. Never a convincing excuse. My mind went back to the Carr/Cook/Brereton meeting last year. Carr has form in this department. I tried to award the Shadow Cabinet jobs on merit, while listening to the views of senior colleagues. But I can't win.

If I give the Beazley supporters a go, my supporters complain and vice versa. I can't manage Caucus on a permanent majority of two votes; I've got to form new alliances and try to treat everyone fairly. Supporters of mine who received promotions: Penny Wong, Laurie Ferguson, Bob Sercombe and Nick Sherry. Plus I saved Crean. Beazley supporters who received demotions: Tanner, McMullan, Marn, O'Brien and Griffin. Not a bad list.

Carr is dirty that he missed out on the Senate leadership. No one wanted him. Also, Albanese, his rival in the hard Left, got the environment portfolio. I know that Albanese will eventually do to me what he did to Crean, it's a political habit of his, but I needed to buy some breathing space for the next six to twelve months. Anyway, what is Kim going on about? I gave him Faulkner's old job of Public Administration and Open Government, Indigenous Affairs, the Arts and he's in Shadow Cabinet. Most Lefties would be dancing on the street with that bundle of jobs. I can't win with these people.

Kim Il-Carr Nickname for Kim Carr, a word play on Kim Il-Sung, North Korean dictator after World War II, the father of the current Leader
Penny Wong Shadow Employment & Workplace Participation, Shadow Corporate Governance & Responsibility Min. 2004–
Laurie Ferguson Shadow Immigration Min. 2004–05
Bob Sercombe Shadow Pacific Island Min. 2004–

Nick Sherry Shadow Finance & Superannuation Min. 2004–05
Simon Crean Shadow Trade Min. 2004–05
Lindsay Tanner ALP backbencher 2004–05
Bob McMullan ALP backbencher 2004–
Martin Ferguson Shadow Resources & Tourism Min. 2004–
Kerry O'Brien Shadow Regional Services, Local Government & Territories Min. 2004–05
Alan Griffin Shadow Sport & Recreation Min. 2004–05

Saturday, 27 November

I hate the stench of lies. Since polling day, all the major print outlets have had long feature articles, up me for the rent about the failings of our campaign. Thousands and thousands of words without one attributed quotation, full of errors. All the usual suspects have been involved: McMullan, Tanner, Conroy, Rudd, Beazley, Arbib, plus the sacked staff: Richards, Schenker and Glover.

There's another one in *The Australian* today, our reliable friends at News Limited. It's the worst of the lot, a collectors' item. A lot of the poison comes from Mike Kaiser. Not a good sign for a Leader when his National Secretariat is backgrounding against him, so I rang Gartrell. He was laidback as usual, but fessed up to Kaiser's involvement: 'Mike was badly burnt from the Goss campaign in Queensland in 1995, when he copped most of the blame. His attitude is that the Party office needs to get in first with the media, to put the blame elsewhere. Sorry, mate, but that's what he's done to you'.

I told Tim to sack him, but he refused, saying that Kaiser was on holiday in Europe and was heading back to Queensland in the new year. It's all a bit too cute: Tim knew about this but did nothing to stop it. He plays the good cop with me, while the bad cop does the dirty and then shoots through. Good cop/bad cop—a routine I first heard about while working in Sussex Street in 1987. Machine politics: nothing if not predictable.

I'm in an impossible situation. I can't speak out publicly because it would damage the Party and, on principle, I won't get into backgrounding about the campaign. The leakers have got the advantage of playing hypotheticals: I lost the election, so they can say to the journalists, 'If only Latham had done this, or listened to me on that, we would have won'. It doesn't make them right, just opportunistic. In the end, we won 60 seats. If I had followed some of the nonsense I heard, we would have won 40 or 50.

I didn't run a perfect campaign over the ten months, far from it. We were always defying gravity and, by the middle of the year, I felt rooted. I was disillusioned with the rotten lifestyle and didn't give it my best, dropped my bundle.

But I know one thing for sure: I don't deserve the torrent of shit I'm copping now. Against the odds, I made us competitive in the first part of the year, avoiding the wipe-out we faced twelve months ago. In August and September, I pepped up and beat Howard in the formal campaign. Not bad for a so-called novice.

Richards, Schenker and Glover As soon as the election ended, Mike Richards, Vivian Schenker and Dennis Glover left my office

Those who know the truth—Faulkner and Gartrell—aren't saying a word in my defence publicly. John, because he has gone to the backbench and hates talking to the media. The Governor-General doesn't engage in menial tasks like setting the record straight and defending Labor's Leader—he's too regal for that. Tim's been silent because if the truth were known, he would lose his job. Gartrell has a different agenda, as I found out today.

It's amazing that the journalists take people like Kaiser at their word. Who are we talking about here? Mother Teresa or a former State Secretary who had to resign from the Queensland Parliament and the ALP in 2001 because of electoral fraud? Hardly a reliable source when it comes to truth in politics.

Kaiser's flappy mouth will bring him down one day. After the election, he told me that when he left the Queensland Parliament he struck a deal with the woman who replaced him in his seat: she would serve three terms, qualify for her super and then hand the job back to him in 2010. It's completely Nixonian: just as he was leaving Parliament for electoral fraud he was arranging a comeback in the same seat. If Beattie were serious about cleaning out the rorts and fraud in the Queensland ALP, he would break the deal.

Kaiser has sold a pup to Christine Jackman and Cameron Stewart of *The Australian*. It wouldn't have been hard with Jackman. Earlier in the year, she wrote a profile on my dad without talking to any of his mates, the men who actually knew him. Not the world's best journalist. Kaiser must be giggling at what she has written today. He was responsible for preparing my draft campaign timetable. I've got it sitting in front of me, so let's go through his bullshit.

Kirribilli House—The article reports that I cancelled a family BBQ in Parramatta on the last Saturday of the campaign and, instead, made an unscheduled announcement about my plans for Kirribilli House—turning it over to charity. Untrue. The BBQ went ahead as scheduled, I made a speech about taking the financial pressure off families, ending it with my own family's plan to live in the Lodge, not Kirribilli. This announcement dominated the TV news coverage of the campaign that night.

Just as well, as the Coalition was pumping up stories about Labor's alleged failure to comply with the Charter of Budget Honesty. If I had left a vacuum, with no new announcements, that would have been the dominant TV story. Anyway, what is Kaiser complaining about? His draft

---

Electoral fraud Mike Kaiser was found by the Qld Criminal Justice Commission to have rorted the *Electoral Act* and had to resign from Parl. and the ALP in 2001

campaign timetable reads, 'Five days from election day, location Sydney, announcement Kirribilli House'. We always planned to do Kirribilli in the last week. Next thing you know, he'll be trying to sell Jackman/Stewart the Harbour Bridge.

Childcare Policy—The article claims that campaign headquarters tried to get me to abandon our childcare policy launch in Perth on 27 September and, instead, focus on the profligacy of Howard's campaign launch the previous day. Untrue. At 3.30 p.m. on Sunday 26 September, a few hours after Howard's launch, I left Melbourne to fly to Perth. Upon arrival, I spent hours trying to fix up the policy that had been presented by the Shadow Minister's office (Jacinta Collins). At no stage did anyone say to me that the policy should be abandoned or delayed. Kaiser is engaged in an act of fantasy.

This is a stitch-up by the National Secretariat to say that they wanted to concentrate on economic policy and I refused. Just look at Kaiser's draft timetable: it barely mentioned economic issues. The only reason we campaigned on taking the financial pressure off families is because Utting recommended it and I acted on his advice. If it were left to Kaiser and his campaign plan, this issue would have gone missing in our campaign.

The only time campaign headquarters recommended something new on economic policy was when Bruce Hawker rang me towards the end of the second last week. He wanted me to announce a Federal equivalent of the NSW debt-reduction legislation, a timetable for eliminating all Commonwealth debt. It was a 'monkey see, monkey do' idea that would have backfired on us.

The Liberal promise to sell Telstra would have eliminated Commonwealth debt in one hit. Costello would have been all over me like a rash, saying, 'The quickest way to eliminate debt is to vote Liberal. Latham needs special legislation; all we need is your support on polling day'. Plus he would have given us a long lecture about the retirement of Labor debt post-1996. Hawker Britton know a lot about State election campaigns. The Federal scene is not necessarily the same.

Campaign Arrangements—The article claims that, 'Latham saw little need to attend daily teleconferences with the rest of the campaign team', making out that I was a one-man show. The truth: I was never asked or expected to attend the daily teleconferences. This reflected the division of responsibilities in the campaign. Gartrell and his gurus looked after the

Jacinta Collins Vic. ALP Sen. 1995–2005; Shadow Children & Youth Min. 2003–04

Bruce Hawker Former Chief of Staff to Bob Carr and head of the Sydney-based political consultancy Hawker Britton, which provides assistance to the ALP during Fed., State and Territory election campaigns

advertising, the Shadows and the marginal seats. I looked after the policy announcements and my own free media campaign, with Faulkner as the linkman between Tim and me.

I've seen campaigns in the past as a staffer, and the last thing you want is the Leader trying to micro-manage everything. So I went with the flow, something I now regret. I should have gone to the teleconferences and got a daily update on the advertising campaign. My goals were too limited: to prove my critics wrong in and outside the Party by running a blooper-free, disciplined, bouncy campaign. I had heard all this crap, fed into the media about me, for so many years that I was obsessed with killing it. I was minding my own business, not interfering with headquarters.

The only time I blew up behind the scenes was before the Brisbane campaign launch, when I was rehearsing my speech. Someone kept on changing my text on the autocue, so I had a spit and marched back to the hotel. Even that was more for effect, to give everyone some nervous energy for the big occasion. As I said to Janine, 'They all think I've gone crackers but it was a bit of an act to get them going. It will be okay on the day'. And it was. But ain't it funny: all the media speculation about how I behaved behind the scenes, thousands of words, all of them wrong. And they missed the one tantie I threw.

There are many more errors in this Jackman/Stewart trash, myths that the leakers have run in all the newspaper hatchet jobs. Some of them I have already dealt with in this diary, such as our non-rebuttal on interest rates. Let me now expose the others. Was it Napoleon who described history as nothing more than a shared fable? That's what the enemies are trying to turn me into, a shared fable. I must record the truth of the matter.

Economic Policy—A myth has emerged that I said nothing about the economy for ten months. Sure, I made social issues our top priority—I have been talking and writing about social problems for six or seven years and wanted to do something about them. It was a matter of conviction. Plus it was our best vote-switcher—a nice convergence of policy and politics. I'm proud of the issues I raised and determined to stick with them.

But I also talked about the economy, it was one of my six themes from the beginning of the year. I tried to convince the electorate that Labor had good plans for economic reform, so they could put their prosperity in their pocket and vote for us on social issues. For much of the year, as Utting's polling showed, this strategy worked well.

By the time of the campaign, we had assembled economic policies in the key areas of Howard Government neglect. Just look at my speech to the National Press Club on 6 October: financial relief for families, comprehensive tax relief, income splitting (for the first time in Australia), major welfare-to-work incentives, our Budget Pledge for leaner government, $27 billion in Budget savings on top of the tough PBS decision in June, skills investment, the Youth Guarantee, our mature-age workers' plan, BAS simplification and sweeping trade practices reform.

These policies didn't drop from the sky. I announced them consistently over the previous ten months. For the first time since 1996, we actually had a plan for the economic progress of the nation. And I used it as the theme of my final speech of the campaign. But it was overshadowed by the CFMEU/Adams rally in Launceston the same day.

Business Relations—Mike Richards is putting around that I didn't do enough with the business community. With some associations it was tough going: what sort of relationship could I have after the incident with my speech at National Conference? Nonetheless, I did a stack of liaison between February and August: my diary shows 30 meetings with individual businesspeople and 39 business lunches and dinners. That's 69 events over seven months, about one every three days.

It's no secret in the Labor movement that our business fundraising events are tough going for our State and Federal Leaders. They are always a bit awkward; people have paid good money but you can't tell them too much about policy or strategy because of leaks to the Libs and media, and ethically, everyone knows that the businesses are there to buy access—and, they hope, a fair bit of influence.

Plus the events tend to be quite boring. Whenever I did a joint function with Bob Carr, he would say, 'Don't you hate these? Another night with John Thorpe, another night of tedium. I suppose we have to do them, raise the money, but it's horrible'. Bob always left early and insisted on keeping chatterboxes off his table. Can't blame him.

Attending 39 business functions in seven months, how interesting would anyone find that? They are wealthy people, obviously good at what they do, but not well schooled in the ins and outs of Federal politics. Just think of it: 39 functions and, on average, I would answer fifteen questions at each—that's nearly 600 questions and answers, the equivalent of twenty community forums. Gartrell kept on saying, 'I don't know how you keep it up'. He was happy, of course; we raised heaps more money than under Crean.

I kept it up for seven grinding months and now, for my troubles, my former Chief of Staff says I didn't do enough. I tried to put on a cheery face every time, even in the middle of mind-numbing monotony. The question they *always* asked was 'When will the election be held?' I felt like saying, how would I bloody well know? Go ask Howard.

John Thorpe Pres., AHA 2003–

But I would politely respond, 'Well, Mr Howard doesn't tell me any of his secrets (chuckle, chuckle). I'll find out when you do'. To break the monotony, I used to play bingo with Simon Banks, trying to guess how far into the Q and A session the election date would come up. Bingo!

Anyway, the goal of the ALP is not to kiss the arses of businesspeople, it's to help the disadvantaged. Keating's point: we are pro-market but not necessarily pro-business. We believe in competition but not preferment. That's the problem with business fundraising: they pay the dough, trying to purchase preferment.

Citizen Murdoch—Another Richards canard, claiming that I refused to take a phone call from Rupert Murdoch on 6 April. I was flying from Queenstown (New Zealand) to Sydney via Christchurch, and a mutually convenient time could not be arranged. Richards thought that if Murdoch said jump, we had to say how high. I treated him like any other businessperson, and I don't kiss arse. Anyway, it was no big deal. Murdoch was ringing around all prominent politicians, trying to smooth the way for the transfer of his Australian company to the US. Hardly a surprise.

Business Council of Australia—I was asked to address a BCA dinner under Chatham House rules in Sydney on 15 March. I had to be up at 5.45 a.m. the next day for media interviews to promote our new superannuation policy, so I told the organisers that I would arrive right on time at 6.30 p.m. but have to leave a bit early, around 9.30 p.m., to be home by 10.30.

Fair enough. I arrived at 6.30 and then waited 45 minutes for the BCA members to finish their policy seminar on immigration. When the night finally started, I gave a pretty well-received speech on building an enterprise culture in Australia, a theme Howard subsequently picked up, and then took questions on the standard subjects, mostly IR deregulation. And then I went home at 9.30 p.m.

A straightforward night, or so I thought. A few weeks later, the *Financial Review* carried a lengthy report from BCA sources, bagging me on several fronts, a bad breach of Chatham House rules. Richards was certain he knew the identity of the leakers, and he made the obvious recommendation: we can't have a decent relationship with the BCA.

Gender Issues—Gartrell appointed Robert Ray to review the methodology and adequacy of our polling from the campaign. Typically, Ray used it as an opportunity to brief Caucus members on the *contents* of the

---

Chatham House rules A set of ethical guidelines for the conduct of meetings in which those present cannot repeat details of the meeting, including those who attended and the matters discussed

polling, trying to make trouble for me, and filter the information into the media. Among wads of material, the only negative thing he found was the so-called gender gap; by the end of the campaign my numbers were plus 24 with men and dead even with women.

I asked Faulkner about it and he said, 'When Labor leaders rise in popularity, they always do better with men than women. The good news is that overall you were plus 12. I can assure you that Simon Crean didn't have a gender gap: he was minus 40 with men and women'. Pretty good explanation. But who's Ray to talk about gender? He's spent the last six years trying to cause me a problem with women voters. He wanted this to be a self-fulfilling prophecy.

Sacked Staffers—I've seen some porkies in my time but check this out in the Jackman/Stewart article: '[In August] Latham was all but ignoring the advice of some key insiders, including his Chief of Staff, Mike Richards and Media Director, Vivian Schenker'. What advice? I didn't hear any. Richards was an office manager, not a political person. The only useful thing he told me was the megaphone analogy. At strategy meetings he never said a word, and others used to comment on it.

Schenker's standard opinion was to do nothing—if in doubt with the media, ignore them. I reached the conclusion that she was unproductive—she shoved too much of her workload onto Byres. A number of senior press gallery people and Shadow Ministerial media advisers said they had never had a conversation with her during my time as Leader. That's why she wasn't part of the travelling party during the campaign and didn't stay on my staff thereafter.

As for Richards, by the second week of the campaign it was clear he was not up to the job. On 1 September, we were running through the next day's program—he had me visiting a young suburban couple in Melbourne to do our interest rate guarantee. I asked Mike the basic question: has anyone checked the couple's political views, given that the media will bombard them with questions. The answer was no.

I asked Byres to call them asap and he reported back that, when asked, they would say Howard had done a good job on the economy and that interest rates were likely to go up under Labor (and Liberal). The visit was cancelled and I ended up signing our guarantee in a hotel function room. Richards was all over the shop.

Thereafter, Faulkner took charge of the travelling party and I asked Mike to look after Leader's liaison—all the calls to Shadows, candidates, etc. that I didn't have time to make, and report back to me daily. Unfortunately, he never reported once but just disappeared. As it turned out, he went back to Melbourne to attend to personal matters.

When the campaign was over, I sacked Richards for two reasons. First, he went AWOL during the campaign, and second, Faulkner reported to me a series of complaints from Opposition staff. I'm very cautious about these matters, but John and Gillard have convinced me of their legitimacy. Given this information, Richards is crazy to be backgrounding against me.

On the campaign plane, Faulkner said that if Richards turned on us at any stage, he (Faulkner) would fix him up in the Senate, using parliamentary privilege to itemise the staff complaints against Richards. But nothing has happened, of course. That's the GG for you: all talk, not much action. Faulkner also said that Richards told him mid-year that he wanted to leave my office. Didn't Richards have a responsibility to tell me, rather than drift along and then walk off the field in the middle of a national election campaign? Very disappointing.

As for Glover, he didn't hit the deck as a speech-writer; most of his stuff was unusable. It came to a head on the day of my Press Club speech three days before polling day. Dennis submitted a pile of pap, and in the end, I had to write the speech from scratch, assisted by Walsh and Barron—their stuff was top-notch. Dennis looked hang-dog when he saw the final version, like his world had ended. In truth, it should have ended last December when Crean was about to sack him as the Leader's speech-writer. I kept him on but it never worked out.

Thankfully, I had some good staff as well during the campaign. Byres, Banks, Cooney and Al Byrnes held the show together. They were exceptionally competent and loyal—the two qualities seem to go together.

Campaign Strategy Group—From the backgrounded articles in the press, anyone would think this committee ran the campaign. Gartrell always said that the Campaign Strategy Group (CSG), with its State Secretaries and other odd bods, was one of those formalities we had to go through to keep people happy. He would run the real campaign, in liaison with Faulkner and me. I only met with the CSG twice and one of those was a nosh-up dinner in late May. Most of the stuff they talked about was obvious: third-party endorsements, repetition of themes/lines etc.

Now someone from the committee has convinced a bunch of journalists that he saw and heard everything. It comes up in every article. Someone like Mike Kaiser, well, I wouldn't have had six conversations with him all year. It never worked that way. All my strategic planning went through our inner circle. And none of these people was part of it. In fact, one good thing about that group was, no journalist that I'm aware of has ever reported its existence. They write this stuff, page after page, but they don't know shit from clay.

The hypocrisy of these people. I can list dozens of journalists who said before polling day that I had campaigned well, but now it's a slagfest. The herd ran in one direction and then did a U-turn on 10 October.

My favourite example is from Geoffrey Barker in the *AFR*. On 9 October he wrote: 'Win or lose, Mark Latham is the future of political Labor. There is a broad political consensus that Latham has won the campaign with a nice blend of toughness, tenderness and wry humour … Latham will be a towering figure in Australian politics of the twenty-first century'.

On 22 October, he wrote that I have 'a narcissistic and domineering personality, which rejects process, administration and advice … The message for Latham is simple and Darwinian: adapt and change or resign yourself to political death'.

One week I was the Colossus of Canberra, the next a Galapagos Duck.

Sunday, 28 November

Inevitably, news of my stoush with Conroy has leaked into the media (Friday's *Age* newspaper). I stoked the fire by having a chat with Jimmy Middleton on Friday afternoon, creating an expectation in the media that something needs to be done about him. A revealing talk with Smith yesterday: he said that when he came onto the travelling party during the campaign, Conroy rang him with a gob full of abuse, wanting to know why he was helping me.

Has there ever been a lower form of treachery in the history of our Party? In the middle of a Federal election, the Deputy Senate Leader has attacked a senior colleague for helping the Labor Leader's campaign. Move aside Billy Hughes, Joe Lyons, Vince Gair, Mal Colston and all the other rats; Conroy has entered the building. I mean, if we had won, he would have been the first down to Yarralumla for the swearing-in ceremony.

I am not going to tolerate this sort of thing. I threatened to take Conroy's disloyalty to Caucus and Smith brokered a compromise. Conroy stood on the TV news tonight, shaking and disoriented, having to read out a statement, fessing up to disunity and destabilisation of the Party. Pills would have enjoyed it.

Joe Lyons Tas. ALP Premier and min. in the Scullin govt, who defected to join the UAP and became the UAP PM 1932–39
Vince Gair Former Qld ALP Premier who was expelled from the ALP in 1957; became DLP Qld Sen. 1965–74

Mal Colston Qld ALP Sen. 1975–96, who defected to become an Independent until he left the Senate in 1999

A victory today, but elsewhere, the news is not good. Lengthy talks this week with Macklin and Evans about Conroy's treachery. I expected the other two parliamentary leaders to take a glove to him, but they were very nonchalant, couldn't care less, really. The best Evans could say was, 'I know he's no good, but I'm going to try to work around him'.

Truth is, the Beazley forces have not gone away. They were dormant through my honeymoon period and the election campaign, but now they are back in the open. The machine men are on the march: Shorten, Bill Ludwig, the Shoppies, Ray, Conroy, Swan, Marn—the usual suspects. Plus the disaffected Kim Carr.

The election loss is the catalyst, of course, but the real issue is compliance. They won't rest until they get a Leader who plays the machine game, someone so weak and pliable that they can run the show by remote control. Maybe they're calling Kim. Is he really ill? He looks okay around the place. The election result is similar to 2001: same primary vote and a net loss of three seats. How did the machine men respond back then? Twelve months later they were trying to bring back Beazley. Now they want to fry me alive.

Tuesday, 30 November

8 p.m.: a little moment in Labor history. I sat down with Gillard at my dining room table in Parliament House for a frank discussion about my situation. I've still got the numbers in Caucus (on my count, 50–38) but then again, so did Crean until the leaks and treachery wore him down. That's my point to Julia: 'We need to learn from Simon's experience and make sure there is some sort of succession plan in place, especially if there's a challenge to my leadership. If worst comes to worst and the enemies can do me in, I'll dive-bomb their candidate and try to set it up for you to win'. It's not an admission of defeat, rather a recognition of reality, something Crean never did.

Gillard was reluctant. She's never seen herself as a parliamentary Leader, but I convinced her to go through her numbers (in a notional contest against Beazley, the strongest of the possible machine candidates). Close, but not enough; she would lose 39–49. Albanese is the key, and a big disappointment. On current form, he would support Beazley and do in his Left 'comrade' Gillard. That would cost her the leadership: another sign of the madness of the Left. I advised Julia to see if she could butter up Albo for the next six months. Given his track record, anything is possible.

Meanwhile, I had better keep buttering up swinging Caucus voters. On my list: Bowen, Anna Burke, Byrne, Kate Ellis, Forshaw, Georganas, Gibbons, Kerr, Marshall, McClelland, Melham, Moore, Plibersek, Sherry and Thomson.

The long hard road to the Lodge. Faulkner said to me yesterday, 'You need to use the Christmas break to decide if you really want this job. It's so bloody hard, you need to be made of iron to get there'. Yes, yes, I'm an ironman. Over Christmas I'll be re-reading my Nixon books.

True, the going is pretty tough. So many betrayals, and now I can add Crean to the list. He's enjoying my discomfort too much: it makes his leadership period look better. Someone is in his ear, probably Richards, saying that I sidelined him during the campaign. I had enough on my plate without worrying about Simon's travel plans. Gartrell and Kaiser did the Shadows' itineraries, plus they were living in fear of a Tory attack on Crean.

A meeting with Simon this afternoon to talk about the manoeuvring in Caucus, and he gave it away. He used words identical to a background briefing given to Shaun Carney from the *Age* on 6 November, bagging me for giving Swan and Smith the economic jobs. The article said that my backers found it galling that Gillard had been overlooked and Swan/Smith's bad behaviour had been rewarded. And then the quote: '"Julia was a stand-out all the way through that last term. With no frontbench experience, she managed to fashion an acceptable policy on refugees and then took on health and made that a winner too. She had earned a promotion," one Labor MP said'.

I saved Crean but now he's backgrounding against me. This is how they usually get caught: retailing the words in too many places. Simple Simon. Bitter Simon. Ungrateful Simon.

Wednesday, 1 December

The night I could avoid no longer: dinner at the American Embassy with Schieffer-brains. Byres tells me that even Rudd calls him Brains. Janine wasn't available, so I took Shadow Defence Minister McClelland as my date. Schieffer was pleasant enough as we talked about baseball and professional sport. His wife gave it away, however, staring daggers at me. One of the golden rules of politics: the wives always let you know what the husbands are really thinking.

The Ambassador dropped three clangers:

Chris Bowen ALP member, Prospect 2004–
Anthony Byrne ALP member, Holt 1999–
Kate Ellis ALP member, Adelaide 2004–

Steve Georganas ALP member, Hindmarsh 2004–
Gavin Marshall Vic. ALP Sen. 2002–
Claire Moore Qld ALP Sen. 2002–

- He reckons that Bush would have beaten Clinton in 2000 if Clinton had been allowed to run for a third term. (Were we supposed to laugh?)
- He reckons that Bush would have been okay if he had lost in 2000, and got on with things in a carefree way, whereas 'Al Gore has been destroyed by his defeat. His life is a wreck'. (How would he know?)
- He acknowledges that Bush comes across poorly on television but reckons, 'He is absolutely brilliant in small groups; his ability to master detail is amazing'. (Did someone mention a conga-line?)

This guy is a sub-branch of the United States Republican Party. He still thinks he's a politician, and Canberra is in the hill country of Texas.

I should say something publicly on this, questioning the long-term need for the American Alliance. That's the worst thing about this job, the things that need to be said, but that would turn the Party upside down (the Big Mac faction would go ballistic). The Americans have made us a bigger target in the War against Terror—Australian lives are certain to be sacrificed on the altar of the US Alliance. Look at New Zealand: they have their foreign policy right, and it's the safest country on earth.

Labor should be the anti-war party of Australian politics. Other than World War II, every war this country has fought was disconnected from our national interests. All those young Australian lives lost in faraway lands, the folly of imperialism and conservative jingoism. I detest war and the meatheads who volunteer to kill other human beings.

The US Alliance is a funnel that draws us into unnecessary wars; first Vietnam and then Iraq. With Bush and Howard, there will be more to come. They wouldn't fight themselves, of course, but they readily send other people's children to fight in their name.

The truth is, the Americans need us more than we need them. Pine Gap is vital to their international security network. Plus the Americans restrict our capacity to trade and integrate with Asia—one day their trouble with China will be our trouble. Politically, why does the Alliance survive? Because a significant number of Australians still think we need an insurance policy against invasion by Indonesia, that's why.

Poor old Indonesia. They can barely govern themselves these days, let alone invade us. The Alliance is the last manisfestation of the White Australia mentality. Sacrificing Australian pride and independence—and our national interests, properly defined—for the safety blanket of great and powerful friends. It's just another form of neocolonialism: a timid, insular nation at the bottom of the world, too frightened to embrace an independent foreign policy. And its politicians, more comfortable swanning around Washington with their Anglo masters than doing business in Asia.

Saturday, 4 December

Two days ago, as Parliament got up for the week, Joel told me about a rumour circulating on the backbench: that when I dropped into the Holy Grail for a drink after work last Tuesday night, the first time in more than a year, 'Gillard had to be sent down there to pull you off Kate Ellis'.

What a way to mark my first anniversary in this wretched job: scuttlebutt, a filthy rumour on the backbench. It's absolute rubbish. I had one drink at a table with Joel, Ellis, Sherry, Sidebottom and a few others, left to go home and bumped into Gillard on the way out. We had been doing our numbers up in Parliament House a few hours earlier. That's all that happened.

As soon as Joel said it, my mind turned to the Ray/Beazley smear and, I must admit, I felt sick in the stomach. Is this something I will have to pre-empt at an emotional press conference years from now? Another piece of smut sent to haunt me? More rumours and media speculation: perhaps another *Crikey*/Dodson/Milne/Price special? Let me guess: the Latham/ Ellis video, shot by security cameras at the Holy Grail?

A horrible memory, a horrible thought. This is why I have grown to hate this place and the people in it. Should I tell Janine, or just ignore it? Christ, I've got two little boys, I don't need these sickoes in the Labor Party. Nothing better to do with their lives than gossip and run rumours—a lifetime spent whispering behind their hands.

Joel told me the rumour had passed from Kelly Hoare to Harry Quick to Bob Sercombe and then on to him. This is the same Hoare who rang Janine when I became Leader twelve months ago and said she wanted to help with our family's adjustment to the new job. Pathetic. I rang her yesterday and she said the rumour came from Maria Vamvakinou, Kim Carr's mate.

I asked Carr to find out what was going on and he told me Vamvakinou had picked it up from an unnamed staffer. Five people in this Chinese whisper that I know of. These things spread like triffids in Parliament House; today there are probably 50 who have heard the rumour. Next month it'll be 500, and so it goes. It's the big-noters who say to someone, 'I know something that you don't'. It's everyone in the building.

My mood: complete and utter despair. I expect shit from the Tories and their Dancing Bears in the media, but why does the worst stuff, the bits that maim, always come from our side? Over the years, I've believed too much in this show, that's why the personal crap hurts and bewilders me, cuts me to the core. I talk about the cause of Labor, but quite frankly, the culture of Caucus is killing me. Faulkner told me to watch out for the Tory

---

Maria Vamvakinou ALP member, Calwell
2001–

smut and innuendo machine. But the ALP is the worst: eating its own children. The so-called party of compassion, living off the spears it puts into its own people. None of it upfront and honest—a secret society of slurs and personal attacks.

To make things worse, I came back from the city yesterday with Janine, who was admitted as a lawyer at the NSW Supreme Court, a day of family celebration, to find a photographer jumping out into our driveway, snapping away. I've been in Federal Parliament all week, am not exactly a recluse, so why do the media need to hang around our home like Peeping Toms? More sickoes in the sick world of Australian politics.

Tuesday, 7 December

Faulkner keeps telling me that political history is written in books, not newspaper articles. So today I launched Mungo MacCallum's new book on the long election campaign, a great spray at Howard and the media, my kind of book. A welcome relief from the Labor Party crap. I gave an amusing speech at the launch, but the press gallery sat there po-faced, a miserable collection of freaks and oddballs.

Tony Wright, of Nimbin fame, asked me if I would be writing a book about the campaign. I don't need to, I have this diary. Maybe I should have repeated Jim Scullin's words. Years after his defeat in 1931, he was asked if he would write the history of his government. 'It nearly killed me to live through it', Scullin replied, 'it would kill me to write about it'.

Rang Gough yesterday to collect his best Mungo anecdotes. He couldn't care less about Mungo, as he launched into a long, repetitive tirade about the Sydney–Melbourne rail line. He spoke to me not as a friend, but as a hectoring lecturer. What's his problem with me? Every Labor Leader for 25 years tried to distance himself from Gough, until me. I hugged him at the launch but the colleagues are still bagging him, saying that any association with Gough is a vote loser. Maybe best to leave the old man alone.

Same with Keating. Gartrell tells me he spent an hour on the phone with Paul on election night, with Keating trying to convince him it was a worse result than 1996. Gee, Paul, that makes me feel better; we actually won eleven more seats. All Keating wants in life is a Labor Leader who can beat Howard, his great obsession. I shared his hatred for a while, but it's not a good emotion—it ends up hurting you more than the person you hate. Paul should stop looking backwards and start enjoying his life. For Christ's sake, he had thirteen years in government—I wish I could whinge about that.

Wednesday, 8 December

Encouraging news about McMullan. He bagged me on *Meet the Press* last Sunday but it has backfired with his local ALP branch members, who are incensed by his disloyalty. At our staff dinner in Manuka tonight, Cooney, a Comb-over critic and organiser of Right-wing numbers in the ACT, says that McMullan is ripe for a preselection challenge in Fraser.

Michael is going to work on a Left–Right deal to spear him, plus wire up the *Canberra Times*. Normally I have a rule of defending all sitting Caucus members against a preselection challenge—I even helped Sciacca earlier this year. Maybe I need a subclause: all bets are off if they attack me on national TV.

More treachery on page two of *The Australian* today, with a headline 'Beazley urges backbenchers to speak out'. First sign he's going to do to me what he did to Crean; old Arthur is at it again. He says that he 'looks forward to what Lindsay Tanner and Bob McMullan have got to say'. If he keeps it up, I look forward to telling the media his views on deficit budgeting. Imagine if he had been Leader trying to sell that rubbish in the campaign. Now that would have been an interest rate scare with legs.

Leadership speculation is Beazley's legacy to the Party. His little exercise in 2002–03 has turned it into a media sport. There's no stopping it now: it's what the press gallery looks for and focuses on as part of their daily routine.

Thursday, 9 December

Bitterness and discontent across Caucus: a thousand and one complaints about a thousand and one subjects. Sod them all. Mao Zedong was once asked about his party elite and replied, 'They complain all day long and get to watch plays at night. They eat three full meals a day and fart'. That's a good summary of how I feel about my colleagues. The only good news is that Parliament ended today. I won't have to look at them again until February. Both sides of politics are exhausted and just want to get out of the place.

Hosted Christmas drinks for the press gallery in our new press office. Gritted my teeth and tried to be pleasant. Naturally, all the grubs bagging me were there to drink my grog and see if I'm still alive. I have hardly any allies left. One of them, Paul Bongiorno, told me that during the election campaign Howard rang the head of Channel Ten to complain about his reporting. That's what I should have done: rung my mate Kerry Packer to fix up Jabba. Situation hopeless.

Paul Bongiorno Chief political correspondent for Channel Ten in Canberra

Speaking of Oakes, his *Bulletin* column yesterday was at me again, this time for quoting Napoleon in an interview with Laura Tingle last Thursday (2 December, my first anniversary as Leader and the 199th anniversary of Austerlitz). Napoleon lived by the motto 'commit and see what happens'—a man of conviction and adventure. Jabba reckons I should subscribe to 'look before you leap'. A kindergarten commentator.

Look before you leap. Everywhere I look, the system is trying to narrow me down, make me as timid as the rest of them. Last weekend, Ollie said to me, 'Dad, I'm not scared of anything. If a car comes, I'll jump between its wheels'. He's a four-year-old boy, so bold and full of adventure, our little superhero, versus the narrow, nervy, conservative shithole of a place I work in. Go the lad.

My last function of the parliamentary year—dinner with colleagues at Figaro in Kingston: Crean, Carr, Gillard, Joel, Sawford, Sercombe and Laurie Ferguson. The mood was sombre, unenthusiastic. Carr arrived late. He had been on the phone for hours with his mate Eric Locke, the Victorian State Secretary, trying to help him through his marriage break-up. I would be devastated, too, if I lost my missus to Mike Richards—time to pass the hemlock. Incredibly, Crean said he knew nothing about this.

Saturday, 11 December

Such a relief to be out of that place; it's always trying to narrow me down. What's happened to our democracy that a bit of radicalism is now stamped on, like ants on a driveway? All the influences, all the messages in modern politics are conservative.

The media are just another form of commerce, so they support the status quo in society. They see stability as good for the business environment, good for commerce and their advertising revenue—institutionalised conservatism. Their journalists are simple souls, not too keen on extensive research and original analysis. They like the one-dimensional characters in politics, who are nice and easy to report. In their view, anyone who swears, has a dig and stays up past 9.30 at night looks like a dangerous radical.

The system is conservative about ideas. In the academic world, the process of responding to new evidence, revising old findings and reaching fresh conclusions is known as learning. It is celebrated as intellectual growth. In politics, it is demonised as wild and erratic. It's another weapon with which the conservatives beat the radicals. I've suffered from this: fitted up by the Tories and their Dancing Bears, but also by Rudd and the Roosters. A century ago, Australia was seen internationally as a social laboratory. Today, we live in an intellectual backwater.

The Labor machine men only preserve their hierarchy of command and control if the people below them say yes. More institutionalised conservatism, but this time within our ranks, the Labor Tories. No wonder they oppose me. I'm always questioning their views, invariably disagreeing with them, always promoting new ways of doing things and, as often as I can, turning their apple cart upside down.

These are the institutions of conservatism, but what about the process that sustains them, the underlying culture? The medium is the message. When television became the dominant political medium in the 1970s, it hollowed out the intellectual content and idealism in the system, narrowing the politicians into seven-second grabs and shallow imagery.

I've always joked with Joel about Smith and Swan popping out of the carpark for their doorstop each morning. They live for the TV grab, review it and rehearse it. It's their daily target and performance measure, a way of life. Modern politics at work: temporary, shallow and vacuous. It's had a profound impact on the culture of our democracy.

Naturally, over time, the public saw through the artificiality of this type of politics. And how did the system respond to the public's cynicism? It became even narrower: it adopted new technologies and professionalism to get the message through. Not face-to-face argument and persuasion, but direct mail, advertising and telephone polling—replaying to the public the things they said to your pollster. Even my good self, Mr Community Forum, has done it. It's part of the culture, and it can't be avoided.

And so the vicious cycle continued: people stopped participating in politics. By the 1980s and 1990s, the limited number of Australians that used to join political parties and go to meetings dried up. In the ALP, real active party membership—as opposed to the paper members and ethnic branch stacks—collapsed. We became a virtual party, ripe for takeover.

In my electorate, for instance, there would be no more than 50 active members who devote more than two hours per week to Party matters. Multiply that by 150 Federal electorates: most likely, we have 7500 real members around the country, enough to fill a small suburban soccer ground. Perhaps one-third of them are trade unionists—the rest are students, retired and out of work. Who said this is an important job? Who said we are a labour-based Party?

With this tiny base of real membership, it was relatively easy for a handful of powerbrokers to grab hold of the Party in the 1980s. They had the resources of Head Office and the trade unions to back them and met little resistance from the so-called rank-and-file membership gutted by ethnic stacking. This was a takeover hostile to democratic principles: they stripped the remaining assets, and turned Party conferences and committees into hand-picked, stage-managed jokes. We became a tight oligarchy.

A few dozen Party officials and faction bosses have the power to run the organisation: who goes into Parliament, how they vote in Caucus ballots, the outcomes at Party forums. Very few people progress without their say so: through Young Labor, into State ministerial offices, recruited for future parliamentary service. It's a dense network of influence, a political mafia full of favours, patronage and, if anyone falls out with them, payback.

In recent years, the factional system has deteriorated even further, particularly inside the FPLP. In the 1980s and 1990s, there were three consolidated groups: the National Right, the Centre–Left and the National Left. Now it has broken down into a series of State and personality-based feudal groupings. As the factions have sent more and more machine men to Canberra, especially in the Senate, they have engaged in a process of cell division.

Each machine man is determined to run something, and if they can't run a full faction, they have split the groups into their own little fiefdoms. It may involve just two or three people, but they see it as a powerbase of sorts. Look at the way the Right conducted its selection of Shadow Ministers a few months ago—two or three was enough to give you a frontbencher. In the State Parliamentary Caucuses, it is probably manageable: they have Hard and Soft Left sub-factions and a couple of Right groupings. But at a Federal level, where the State-based sub-factions come together in the one spot, the number of groups is multiplied by six, so you end up with 30 or so powerbrokers.

The trade union amalgamations have also added to the problem, entrenching union-based power blocs within the Federal Caucus. Just look at the Shoppies, Miscos and Metals, with at least one MP in each State—all of them shop stewards for their union's interests. Not the broad Party interest or even the interests of social democracy, but the policies, power and patronage of interest to their union.

This is the point I made to the National Executive. They hated hearing it, of course. A Caucus of 88 MPs has 31 powerbrokers—on average, they represent groups of fewer than three people. This has led to chaos in Caucus, and the institutionalisation of conflict: fiefdoms fighting fiefdoms about all sorts of trivial issues. In Opposition, the problem is worse because of the lack of positions and patronage to hold them together as a cohesive federation.

While the Left has had its problems over the years, it is relatively stable, with just three or four groups. The Right, however, has become a dog's breakfast. Just look at the different interests, with their own agenda of ambition and treachery:

- in Victoria: Ray, Crean and Conroy (linked to the Shoppies)
- in NSW: Price, Forshaw, Hutchins and Sussex Street
- in Queensland: Swan, Hogg, Rudd and Bevis (AWU versus Old Guard)
- in South Australia: three people and two sub-factions
- in Western Australia: Smith versus Bishop (two groups, each with two MPs).

The only way to manage them is to minimise the things they can argue about: the politics of the lowest common denominator. That's why they liked Kim; he was a pin-cushion for their complaints and claims. He's so compliant, they all thought they were running the Leader by remote control.

In my case, it's a shocker. It's not in my nature to tolerate the lowest common denominator. I face a catch-22. I need to rip in and modernise our economic policies to win the next election. But if I do that, the unions and fiefdoms will arc up and try to destroy me. Crean tried a minor change to the Party rules and got pole-axed. I don't think labour market reform and asset-based policies are their cup of tea.

Already, since the election, it's been horrible. All those who opposed me twelve months ago are out from under their rocks. For most of the year they thought we could win, so they went to ground. They saw it as a no-lose situation: if we won, they became ministers; if we lost, they could tear me apart. People forget that between January and October, the Government led in just two out of 22 Newspolls (2PP). Like Conroy, the machine men were waiting to see what happened, and when I lost, whooska!

How to break their grip on the Party? Let's be honest, it probably can't be done. When the system gets into a second and third generation—Richo to Della to Roozendaal and Arbib—it becomes an unbreakable culture. It is the Party. The young ones know of no other world—just look at Young Labor these days.

I could propose disaffiliating the trade unions from the ALP, the core of the factional system. But this would split us in two—I would end up looking like Billy Hughes, Stabber Jack Beasley or, even worse, Santamaria. I would have to set up a whole new party, start from scratch. Not feasible.

I could rip up the Party rulebook and try to democratise the thing. But how many people would turn up and get involved in our local branches? What, Hinchinbrook meetings would skyrocket from six to eight people? When I worked for him in the late 1980s, Bob Carr asked me why I was so

Stabber Jack Beasley ALP member, West Sydney 1928–46. In 1931 he left the ALP to join the Lang Labor Party and helped to bring down the Scullin ALP govt

committed to community politics when people were not interested in going to political meetings. He was right and I was wrong.

Bob's comfortable leading an oligarchy. But I'm not. He's not interested in Party reform, in grassroots democracy. I am, but I can't see how it can be achieved in practice. Do I want another ten years banging my head against the wall? Or just face the intellectual truth that not all problems in life have an answer. As an institution, the ALP is insoluble.

That's where I'm at right now. Resigning myself to this slug of an organisation. A museum relic from a time when trade unions mattered and people cared about community politics. That time has passed and so, too, has the relevance of the shitcan I sit on as Labor Leader. Gloomsville.

Saturday, 18 December

Out of Perth, thank Christ. Not a good trip: Smith and Evans stuffed around with my program, Billy Johnston played silly buggers about the forthcoming WA election, Ollie got sick and ended up in hospital, plus the media put in a shocker.

The only bright spot was Kalgoorlie. My sort of place: the last remnants of Australian mateship culture. Sad for the Labor movement, however: it used to be a stronghold but the AWAs have wiped out the unions altogether. Made them irrelevant, a sign of the times.

Highlight of the trip was in the front bar of the Exchange Hotel on Thursday night, when a busty scrubber asked me to autograph her right boob. In the early 1980s, I saw Peter Sterling do this one night, cool as a cucumber, at Parramatta Leagues after one of their Grand Final wins. It has always stuck in my mind, so I did a Sterlo: no nonsense, no fuss and then straight back to signing scraps of paper for other people. A career ambition realised. I only hope Ray and Vamvakinou don't find out.

That's the upside of being a bogus celebrity. The downside came on Fremantle Beach on Wednesday morning. It was hot, we had a few hours to spare, so Janine and I took the kids to the beach, especially good for Ollie, who was still struggling with his tummy. Just as we were packing up to leave, these two guys in office clothes came marching towards us along the beach, one carrying a camera, the other a notebook. A sickening moment, as bad as Steve Price and the bucks' night video. The repercussions are still being felt in our family.

I mean, what sort of person sees a man and his family on the beach and calls *The West Australian* newspaper? A sick puppy. It's voyeurism at its worst. A school teacher of mine used to say that dobbers are un-Australian. Dobbing was back then, but now it's become the Australian way. Snitches and media maggots. The pressure on our family life is enormous. Maybe if we had teenagers it wouldn't be so bad, but there is something sickening when the innocence of toddlers is violated.

I don't blame their mother for going off. It's our job to protect them. Janine's just following her instincts, doing her job. I'm the weakest link: my job is a magnet for these people. What a mistake to ever let the public know I had children, let alone introduce them to the media. The only ray of light? My work commitments for the year have ended and now we have the chance to recover and holiday together. Just us, just family, until Australia Day.

Monday, 20 December

The Fremantle Beach thing has got the hook in me. All year, I've been agonising about the loss of privacy and how to handle it. Since the election, it has become worse. I was on TV in their living rooms every night for six weeks, so they think they know me, they own part of me. They want and expect a slice of our lives.

Prying eyes everywhere we go, people staring for what feels like an eternity. Some even follow us up the street to stare some more. All for what? To tell people that they saw someone who's on TV, to make themselves sound important, to fill the gap in their own lives and self-esteem. Their mothers never told them it was rude to stare. That's the thing about privacy: you don't know how valuable it is until it's gone.

Joel tells me it is part of the job, to get used to it. But he doesn't have to live with it 24/7. Public life is not a natural way of life.

It is not natural to have two men in office wear marching towards your family on the beach, barking questions and taking photos.

It is not natural for your wife and two children to watch some clown on national TV reaching under his chair for a non-existent copy of a bucks' night video supposedly featuring their husband and father.

It is not natural to have journalists asking about untrue and trivial things that supposedly happened to your family twenty years ago.

It is not natural to have so-called colleagues whispering behind their hands that I had to be hauled off Kate Ellis.

It is not natural to have school colleagues from twenty years ago ringing the newspapers to tell them about things that were supposed to have happened in the classroom, as Charlie Timm (ex-Hurlstone) did during the election campaign.

It is not natural to have a journalist and a photographer lurking in the dark outside your unit at 6 a.m. waiting to see if you go jogging. Or TV cameras waiting on your front lawn as you get the paper in the morning.

It is not natural to have people you have never met stop you on the street, talk to you as if they have known you all your life, and then try to cuddle your children.

It is not natural to have someone in your street, like Mrs Have-A-Chat across the road, gossiping about your business every time a journalist knocks on her door.

It is not natural to be on the *Truman Show*.

I've been honest and open with people about my background, my childhood, etc., but they are insatiable. But this is not just about me, it's happening everywhere. It's a symptom of the breakdown in social capital. People have so little love and trust in their own lives, they try to escape by prying into others' lives. Bogus celebrities become a substitute for relationships in real life. Voyeurism becomes a way of life.

It's easy to despise the media and blame them for the intrusion. Sure, they are a bunch of sick puppies, especially those weird snappers who make money by invading other people's privacy. But the public pays good money to consume this crap. The people who buy *The West Australian* newspaper to look at my family on the beach. The people who buy those gossipy women's magazines. The media serve it up because they know it's a huge money-spinner.

In fact, it has become our dominant public culture: on television, talk-back radio, gossip magazines (more brands of them at the supermarket check-out than lollies to tempt the kids), gossip columns (even the broadsheets have them now) and online rags like *Crikey* (the most popular website in Parliament House). I used to think of the Internet as a force for liberating the information-poor, but all it has done is liberate the voyeurs and make them worse. Same with mobile phones, as we found out on the beach.

Maybe that's how my reaction to the loss of privacy is best understood, through social capital analysis. The Abominable Snow Woman wrote that she was surprised to see Janine, Oliver and me nick out of the Mick Young function at Randwick and watch a race by ourselves down on the rails. But that's how I feel all the time. Why is it?

When I was young I was lucky. I grew up in an environment full of strong and trusting relationships: the love and nurture of family, teachers like Neville Smith, a sense of community in Green Valley, a wonderfully collegiate environment at Hurlstone, followed by a supportive work environment with Gough. It's always been my preferred way of dealing with people: I'm wary of pretension, hostile to conservatism, and look for genuine relationships of trust with people.

Then the higher I climbed the political tree, the more shallow and superficial the relationships have become. Liverpool Council was a hornet's nest of intrigue and small-town gossip, but I put up with it because you expect that sort of stuff at a municipal level.

What I never expected was the same type of environment in Federal politics. Perhaps it's worse: the bad shit has come from my own side. I expected the big debates to be about Labor policy and ideological direction, plus how much we hate the Tories. Not the fantasies of the Fat Indian and his mates.

In my circumstances, it's doubly dangerous: bad for my public life but also overflowing into my private life. After the big mistake with Gwyther, I've found the real deal with Janine. Now the public is rubbing up against the private; the shallow poison of politics threatening the things I have at home.

I often think about Hawke in this context. He got his social capital messages from lots of shallow, temporary interactions with people. What did Keating call it? Tripping over TV cables in shopping centres. Hawke loved it—the mad bastard still does it—but I'm the reverse: it freaks me out. I look at people and wonder, what's so wrong with the rest of their lives that they want to gush all over me? Where are the real relationships, love and devotion to sustain them?

They don't know me, only from TV. Why do they try to touch my hem, or even think that I've got a hem to touch? It's not a real social experience. It's something else, constructed from the false world of TV and the voyeurism of our public culture. People talking to me like they are my parents or siblings. Too weird for words.

The best times in my life have been the quiet, reflective times, reading and writing books, and now, private time with Janine and the boys. This is the value of privacy: building relationships in a pure, self-contained way, unaffected by the public arena. Concentrating your time and energy on each other, rather than having to explain yourself to others, having to justify your existence to strangers.

There is something horribly unnatural about losing your privacy. It's like losing part of yourself, and the security and peace of mind that comes from knowing that these things belong to you, your loved ones and nobody else. I've spent all my adult life talking about the public sector, without ever properly understanding and valuing the things that are private. You fool.

2005

Saturday, 1 January

The things that happen and how to explain them. First, the good news: I can retire from Labor politics, get out of that rotten, debilitating culture. And the bad news: another attack of pancreatitis. We had a BBQ with friends on Thursday evening (30 December) and just before I went to bed at 10.30 p.m. it hit me.

It wasn't as bad as the August attack, so I toughed it out and got through the night, avoiding hospital and the media maggots. Janine has been terrific, my wonder woman. I feel much better today, am up and about. Much better for knowing that the Peeping Toms don't know my business.

That will do me. I'm leaving it behind. My covenant with Janine and the boys will take me to a better life. My pancreas is struggling: a lifetime of uncertainty about these attacks. Work stress is a killer, so I need a private life, not a public one. Janine wants to practise law, so I'll look after the boys. Be a resident, not a tourist—a solution to our work and family issues.

In truth, I've run out of reasons to stay. My political career has come full circle. I'm in the same situation as five years ago: Labor politics is insoluble, we live in a sick society, with rumours and innuendo weighing me down. First it was Ray/Beazley, now it's Vamvakinou/Hoare. But this is worse, I've got everything to lose on the home front.

What are these people saying? Hey, Latham, you and your family haven't had enough false rumours and smears to handle over the past twelve months, so here's one from your so-called colleagues. It's all turned to seed: pancreatitis, time away from home, loss of privacy, impact on family, so many ficklers in politics, disdain for the media and the whingeing, gossiping, sickening Caucus. That thing they call the Labor Party.

There is no reason to stay. In fact, I've missed too many chances to get out: the first pancreatitis attack, then after the election. Third time lucky. And the timing is perfect: I'm on leave until 26 January, so I can choose the day that suits me. Friday 21 January looks good. We have family holidays ahead, beautiful, well-earned time with Janine and the boys up and down the NSW coast (Terrigal and then Bermagui). *Hasta la vista*, baby.

Rang Macklin, Banks and Byres earlier in the day to let them know I'm crook. They want me to take it easy. Of course, that's what retirees do.

Saturday, 8 January

This retirement caper is pretty good. We've had the nicest six days together here at Pat Sergi's place in Terrigal. I've been resting up, feeling 90 per cent now, but also hanging out with Janine and the boys. Jody and her children joined us on Thursday, so the lads are in their element. We head home tonight.

Only one nuisance: the media have been looking for me to comment on the Asian flood. Apparently the disaster footage is getting a huge run on TV. Macklin told me last Saturday that she would look after it, but then she went on holidays, leaving Chris Evans in charge. She's an unbelievable piece of work.

Anyway, what can I do about it? For a few more weeks, I lead the despised Opposition, unable to turn back the waves, bring back the dead or even organise the Australian relief effort. It's the middle of summer and only maniacs like Rudd are interested in interviews. When it first happened, I heard Bruce Billson speaking on behalf of the Government on radio. Howard and Downer must be spewing that it's broken their holiday at the end of an election year.

Spoke to George Thompson, my new and last Chief of Staff, on Wednesday. He said the media requests into the office need an answer; the gallery was getting toey. I told him to brief out the basics: I'm resting and

Pat Sergi Businessman in south-western Sydney, head of the Italian Affair Committee, a fundraising organisation for the Spastic Centre and other worthy causes

Bruce Billson Lib. member, Dunkley 1996– ; Parl. Sec. for Foreign Affairs & Trade 2004–

recovering from a pancreatitis attack, I'm on annual leave and the Acting Leader speaks for the Party. Still, George wants me to do more, especially this telethon thing tonight, but I fobbed him off. I'm sorry I can't tell him the full story, but our show is a leakerthon.

Imagine if Sussex Street or the National Office or any of the machine men in Caucus get a sniff of my intentions. I might as well announce it right now on 2UE. Sad but true: the modern Labor culture is that people spend all day on the phone, gossiping with each other and their media mates. I just want to enjoy my time, make up for my lost time with family. That's all, and brother, I'm entitled to it.

Anyway, news of my illness hasn't exactly got the former colleagues pressing the sympathy button. The only one to call me has been Albo, who left a message on my mobile at 9 a.m. yesterday, and he only wants to find out how sick I am so he can tell his mates Smith and Swan. For the rest of them, the silence is deafening. If they don't care about my health, they obviously won't care if I bob up one day and pull the pin. Suits me.

It will be even quieter when I'm gone. I'm not going to be like Gough or Keating, agonising over daily events, ringing up for the latest goss, trying to interfere all the time, suffering from separation anxiety. Yuck. That's the point: I'm not just leaving Parliament, I'm leaving Labor politics for good. For the last three days they haven't wanted to talk to me and, hey, I'm more than happy to reciprocate.

As for our friends in the media, what a crack-up. How hard is it to find me here? It's a big place, plenty of people around, although our unit is down the back. Pat Sergi said that the NSW Liberal Leader John Brogden and some of his parliamentary mates are staying here as well.

On Tuesday, 2UE rang the reception looking for me, so the word must be out. Still, four days later, no sign of the dumb-dumbs. Not that we're complaining. We go home tonight, then off to Toni's place at Bermagui next week. *Hasta la vista*, baby.

Thursday, 13 January

Day two of our holiday in Bermagui. Privately, things are fine, a growing sense of relief and calm. Publicly, the shit hit the fan on Tuesday. Someone called Shirley Corbett, who obviously had nothing better to do with her time than engage in voyeurism, wired up the *SMH* to run a story about us at Terrigal. It made the front page. What sort of sicko sees a man by the pool, simply making sure his sons are paddling safely, and decides to call the press?

Well, they missed the boat, the story came out three days after we left the place. So the media pack descended on our house instead, joining the desperates who had been sitting in our street, off and on, for a week. They are such drama queens. Three days after my first pancreatitis attack I gave a press conference at St Vincent's and three days after that, I was back at work. Is it such a surprise that I was watching my children in the toddlers' pool at Terrigal five days after this attack?

No, what they think they have latched on to is another chance to bag me. It's not really about the Asian flood. What I've done is offend their hunger to know all my business. The media perverts hate the idea of not knowing where I am or what's going on. They think they have a God-given right to pry into every aspect of my life. And I'm keeping them in the dark, depriving the addicts of their drug.

They should get a grip on reality, on how normal people look at life. I mean, I'm on annual leave and I've been crook. They are bagging me for doing nothing. The animals have no boundaries. It's a commercial race to the bottom. Well, go for your life, you won't have Mark Latham to kick around any more. Thanks, RN.

Our main priority is to keep the maggots away from our children. No more Fremantle Beaches. That's why we took the boys to Jody's place, a wise precaution. Janine picked them up on Tuesday and drove to Bermagui, via our unit in Queanbeyan. I left home yesterday morning and got here at lunchtime.

Now the dopes are sitting in our street, frying in the Western Sydney heat, while we enjoy paradise. Toni's place is great: isolated, next to a lake and national park, five minutes from the beach and all the cousins get on well. It's even outside mobile-phone range, very handy for my purposes.

To talk to anyone, I've got to drive into town. Get this—the media would freak out if they knew—I've found a nice, quiet spot for my calls, the Bermagui cemetery. A fine metaphor for my political career, a wonderful piece of black humour.

Among the (former) colleagues, so far I've spoken to Joel and Julia, hinting at the decision to come. It's the respectful thing to do: it gives them time to develop a strategy and look at the numbers. It won't make any difference. If his health is okay, Beazley will be back. He was going to sit there, nice and comfortable on the backbench for the next two years, waiting for me to fall over, waiting to be drafted this time. Now he can go and do the work, all the things I have grown to despise.

He'll be worse than ever, of course: good for nothing, stand for nothing. It's a conservative party run by conservative machine men, so why shouldn't they have a conservative leader? A perfect match. Carr and Crean should enjoy it.

This is the right decision. I have seen that world close-up and I don't want to be part of it, now or in the future. To paraphrase Luther, I am the ripe shit, the Labor Party is full of arseholes and soon we shall part.

One pebble in my shoe: the pesky Chris Evans. I avoided his calls for a couple of days, but on Tuesday, with the *SMH* story and all that, I had to say something to him, this former union official and Western Australian State Secretary, this Beazley machine man. People say I don't talk enough to my colleagues. Maybe I don't like them. Maybe that's one of the reasons why I'm getting out.

Gave Evans the bare basics and told him to get our media people to brief the papers, letting them know I will say something publicly at the end of the week, a holding pattern until we finish our holiday. Evans showed his true form when he put out a formal press release, deliberately inflaming the situation, raising media expectations that I will resign as Leader on Friday.

So today, I flew into the holding pattern. Gave George some ambiguous words about my health for a statement to be issued in Canberra, to which he added some gushing stuff about the flood. Here's my ploy: the statement is so vague it will inflame things further. The media hate an information vacuum, they hate not knowing what I'm up to: am I picking my nose or scratching my arse? Ditto the other enemies, of whom there are many.

A shitfight: the best atmosphere in which to resign, using their energy, their hatred to my advantage, the silly season on steroids. But hey, the decision was made two weeks ago. They are wasting their breath, wasting their bile. I'll be gone soon, a private citizen. Then the caravan will move on and find some new bastard to torment. Someone new to fill the vacuum and satisfy the voyeurs.

I'm sorry my friend, the pages of this diary, but your days are numbered. My political career and your entries are coming to an end. I can hear it marching closer. But I can assure you, I'm revelling in my new life, my real life. God has given us Bermagui, so let's enjoy it.

Monday, 17 January

Janine says the time has come, and she is right. Oliver was ready to come home, so we drove back this afternoon. No journalists in Bermagui. Without their snitches from the general public, they are nothing.

Earlier today, I toyed with the idea of resigning via a statement issued in Canberra but Danger talked me out of it. He's right, I need to front up, show my face one last time. Then I can walk away. Spent the weekend telling electorate and parliamentary staff of my decision, plus told my preferred successor in Werriwa, Steven Chaytor. Time for him to get his numbers ready.

It's all squared for tomorrow. And as we know, the press are quite prepared. The point of no return. Time to organise my thoughts, draw up some lists: ten good reasons for retiring. I must have written down this list or something similar a dozen times in the last six years. This time I'm acting on it:

1 The great joy and emotions of my life lie elsewhere, with Janine and the boys.
2 Health and fitness: politics has turned my body to seed. Seventeen years of public life is enough.
3 I have always tried to fight for the things I believe in. I no longer believe in the ALP, so I no longer need to fight.
4 Six of my last eight years in Parliament have been unhappy. Is it going to get any better having to look at Irwin and Hatton?
5 As a job, politics has become boring, uninteresting, having to spend so much time away from loved ones, in the company of people I don't like.
6 I have nothing left to say or offer the electorate. I had my shot at the top job and lost. Time to get on with my life.
7 We live in a sick society, and politics and the media are the public manifestations of that sickness. It's the wrong culture for me to work in.
8 So many fickle types—too many to list.
9 I want my privacy back. I didn't know how important it was until I lost it. No more voyeurs, rumours, smears and snitches.
10 I left my socks at home (just to prove I still have a sense of humour: the old Liverpool Bulls joke/excuse for not playing). None of it matters that much.

At one level, it feels like I have wasted my time. At another level, I can look back on five positive experiences:

1 I put something back into the place where I grew up. When I was Mayor we built more facilities for young people in Liverpool in three years than the Council had in the previous 30.
2 I saw the world and met some interesting people. I satisfied my childhood ambition of becoming a Federal Labor MP, with the added bonus of the Party leadership and a shot at the Prime Ministership. If

Steven Chaytor ALP Councillor, Campbelltown City Council 1999– ; Whitlam staffer 1999–2004

you had been standing in the playground of Ashcroft Public School in 1966 and predicted those things about me, they would have given you odds of a million to one.

3   I wrote books, made speeches and had some influence on the policy debate. I achieved a number of significant reforms from Federal Opposition. Hopefully, people won't forget the critical importance of early childhood development. We need to nurture our children and fortify them against the problems of the adult world.

4   I was true to myself and the reason I got into politics in the first place. Yes, I did some terrible things, things I will always regret, but my core purpose was sound. As Labor Leader, I tried to empower the outsiders. I'm proud of that.

5   Best of all, I met Janine and we started a family. That's the life I want for the rest of my life.

Tuesday, 18 January

Freedom day. It's done. I felt calm and determined at my press conference. Organised it for Ingleburn mid-afternoon to make the animals scurry away from the front of our home. No elitism here, just a suburban park, finishing this thing the way I started it. Basic, austere, very common.

Got out of the car, walked up, read my statement, got back in the car and drove home. Too easy, dispensing with the inevitable. Enjoyed watching the media reaction: falling over themselves, rolling around on the ground, wetting themselves with excitement, little boys and girls at play.

They gave the thing a wonderful sense of the absurd, a sense of symmetry. The first person I met in an ALP branch meeting was a nutter, Frank Heyhoe. How appropriate to end my time in Labor politics with a nutty press conference. R. P. McMurphy, eat your heart out.

Earlier in the day spoke to Macklin, who's finally back from holidays, and Gartell for the first time this year; he, too, has been on holidays. I told him I was leaving Parliament and he sounded happy enough to see me go. I suppose he can't believe his luck: I have copped it in the neck for the election loss, while he's barely been mentioned in despatches. I told him I wouldn't bucket the Labor Party on the way out; they have a by-election to fight and I will remain silent.

My statement dealt with three reasons for resigning: health, family and media intrusion. The unspoken truth is just as important: disillusionment with the ALP. I'm walking away from the Party of Ray/Beazley/Vamvakinou/Hoare and it feels good. I'm becoming a full-time member of the Janine/Oliver/Isaac party, much better.

Gave the media a decent spray on the way out. Their behaviour outside our home over the past week has been disgusting, with Channel Nine the worst offender. They were harassing our ten-year-old niece from next door as she came in to feed our dog: 'Hey, little girl, where's your Uncle Mark today? Come on, little girl, talk to us'. Her parents—my sister Tracy and her husband—called the police. No one can blame them.

Eventually my brother-in-law took the dog to my mother's place, and a few of the media chased him in their cars. Insane—a dog car chase in suburban streets. One funny thing, however: my brother-in-law went out and took their photo and they ran away, yelling out, 'Don't do that'.

A normal life lies ahead, that's what I said in my statement and I meant it. The media will ignore it, of course; they think they own me. But I'll just ignore them. The only people who own me now are my family.

Dinner with Tracy's family tonight, a mini-celebration of my decision. They are truly magnificent. I am lucky to be in the same family and live in the same street as them. They weathered the media storm and kept their good humour and grace. All my sisters say the same thing. Toni puts it best: 'Mark, all the work you've put in and the things you've had to put up with— any normal person would take the superannuation and get out. Think of your health and look at those beautiful children of yours—you're doing the right thing'. The three sisters: pillars of strength for their big brother.

A time of reflection and memories. Over the last couple of days, I have been thinking a lot about Pills. He left Labor politics in a box. I'm the lucky one, I'm leaving to enjoy the love and companionship of my wife and two children, two little blood nuts. I'm leaving that sick political party and its assassins behind. I'm stepping off the television screen and leaving it all behind.

And in case I don't see you, good afternoon, good evening and good night.

Epilogue

I did not plan to add to these diaries after resigning from Parliament. But inevitably, some things have happened that, in all fairness, the reader should be aware of. The *Diaries* would not be a true and complete record of my time in politics without an understanding of these events.

In February I had dinner with Joel Fitzgibbon. He informed me of two telephone conversations he had in mid-January before my resignation. The first was with Paul Keating, whom Joel had called to talk about my pancreatitis attacks and political future. Keating cut him short, saying, 'Why would I worry about him and his health?'

The second conversation was on 13 January with Gough Whitlam. He rang Joel to tell him that I should resign from Werriwa to make way for his former staffer, Steven Chaytor. Gough said he wanted to put out a public statement to this effect but Joel talked him out of it. I had not spoken to Gough since December, so he knew very little about my situation. He just wanted me gone from Federal politics. It was, quite frankly, the cruellest cut of all.

In April I met with a well-respected businessperson to discuss this book. She wanted me to know about a conversation she had with Kim Beazley in late August 2004 when he was Shadow Minister for Defence, just before the Federal election campaign. She said that, 'He was critical of you and very bitter. At one point he said he knew a story about you, a personal matter, that if he told your biographers would destroy your career. I hardly knew him and he didn't know if I had any links to the media, yet there he was, saying these things. It made me think: if he's telling me this, he must be telling everyone'.

Even by Beazley's standards, this was an incredible thing to do. Six weeks after I brought him back onto the frontbench in 2004, he was continuing his six-year campaign of smear and innuendo against me. It confirms the nature of the man, as recorded in these diaries. Beazley has been successful in conveying an impression of public decency, but my experience with him has been very different.

These conversations further strengthened my view that the Labor Party is irreparably broken. It's an organisation based on a corrosive and dysfunctional culture—something I am happy to be no longer associated with. It is not unusual for people who try to change the system to leave public life with feelings of betrayal and disappointment. This was certainly my experience as Labor Leader. My commitment to the cause was destroyed by the bastardry of others.

In a funny sort of way, the experience was so bad it helped me move on straight away, to make a clean break from politics. I have left the public stage for a private one, the intimacy of family life. It has been good to get out of the workforce, to combine the joys of my home-dad responsibilities with reading and new writing projects. It just goes to show, within every crisis lies a new opportunity waiting to be seized.

Indeed, I have been incredibly fortunate. And I want to thank, a thousand times over, Janine, Oliver and Isaac for their love and support in everything we have been through. These days, every day is like the weekend, something to look forward to. I have packed a fair bit into my 44 years and reached the conclusion that you can't beat this as a way of life, building your time around love and commitment. And the best is yet to come, fulfilling my ambition to coach my sons' football, hockey and cricket teams. Go the lads.

May 2005

Appendix 1

Who's Who in the Factional Zoo (mid-2003)

There are three main factions within the Federal Parliamentary Labor Party: the National Right, the Centre/Independents and the National Left. Within each faction there are various subgroupings based on geography, personalities and union affiliation/sponsorship.

NATIONAL RIGHT

New South Wales Right

Brereton Group

Laurie Brereton	Mark Latham
Janice Crosio	Robert McClelland
Annette Ellis	Frank Mossfield
Joel Fitzgibbon	John Murphy

McLeay Group

Michael Forshaw	Leo McLeay
Michael Hatton	Roger Price
Stephen Hutchins	Ursula Stephens
Julia Irwin	

Victorian Right

Crean Group

Simon Crean
Nicola Roxon
Kelvin Thomson
Christian Zahra

Ray/Conroy Group

Stephen Conroy
Michael Danby
Robert Ray

The Shoppies

Anna Burke[1]
Anthony Byrne
Jacinta Collins

Queensland Right

AWU Group

Craig Emerson	Bernie Ripoll
John Hogg[2]	Con Sciacca
Joe Ludwig	Wayne Swan

Old Guard

Arch Bevis
Kevin Rudd

Western Australian Right

Smith Group

Kim Beazley
Stephen Smith

Bishop/Shoppies

Mark Bishop
Graham Edwards

South Australian Right

The Shoppies

Geoff Buckland
Linda Kirk

Others

David Cox
Martyn Evans

CENTRE/INDEPENDENTS

Cook/Sawford Group

Peter Cook	Harry Quick
Ann Corcoran	Rod Sawford
Kay Denman	Bob Sercombe[1]
Kelly Hoare	Nick Sherry
Gavan O'Connor	Sid Sidebottom

Other

Bob McMullan[3]

NATIONAL LEFT

Soft Left/Ferguson Left

Miscos

Dick Adams
Chris Evans
Martin Ferguson
Sharryn Jackson
Kerry O'Brien

Others

Nick Bolkus	Kirsten Livermore
Trish Crossin[1]	Sue Mackay
Laurie Ferguson	Jann McFarlane
Steve Gibbons[1]	Daryl Melham
Julia Gillard	Michelle O'Byrne
Sharon Grierson	Brendan O'Connor
Jill Hall	Warren Snowdon
Harry Jenkins	Penny Wong

Hard Left/Albanese Left

Metal Workers

Anthony Albanese
George Campbell
Jennie George
Jan McLucas
Claire Moore
Tanya Plibersek
Ruth Webber

Others

John Faulkner[1]
Alan Griffin
Duncan Kerr
Catherine King[1]
Carmen Lawrence
Kate Lundy
Jenny Macklin
Lindsay Tanner
Kim Wilkie[1]

Kim Carr Group

Kim Carr
Gavin Marshall
Maria Vamvakinou

---

1   Denotes someone generally associated with this group, but also known to move across factional subgroupings
2   Part of the Shoppies but also part of the Queensland AWU group in Canberra
3   The only member of the Centre/Independents to publicly support Kim Beazley in the December 2003 leadership ballot

Appendix 2

Mark Latham's Notes on Labor's Political Position,

Based on John Utting/UMR

Research Report, 'Review of Political Environment and Strategic Directions', 31 July 2004*

The report is broken into ten sections, but basically it contains two pieces of information: the key research findings and a series of recommendations for the forthcoming campaign period. The findings show that our position has deteriorated over the past three months and we are now under 'real pre-election pressure'. Our two-party-preferred vote has fallen from 55 per cent in May to 51 per cent in July—a bad trend and not enough to win government.

What have been the contributing factors? According to Utting, the main one has been the revival in Howard's position. Earlier this year the electorate thought that Howard had run out of puff and didn't have much to offer for the future, leading to a 'time for change' mood. After the Budget in May, however, his image improved. He's now seen as safe and reliable, a known quantity who stands up for what he believes in. The Budget spending spree has obviously worked for him.

Howard has clear strengths on economic management and national security. In particular, people are buoyant about the economy and the nation's direction, making it less likely they will change government. Our challenge is to knock down the PM (back to his relatively weak standing in March–April) and give the electorate confidence in our alternative approach. Utting says that this can be achieved by concentrating on Howard's 'soft underbelly': his support for user-pays policies, concerns about his buck-passing and lies, and the decline in health and education services.

Looking at my performance, it's a mixed bag. Utting gives me credit for getting us back in the race through a new approach to the Labor leadership: young and fresh, in-touch with the community concerns and

---

* These notes are the conclusions I made about Labor's position in July 2004, drawn from the findings of the John Utting/UMR Research Report, 'Review of Political Environment and Strategic Directions', 31 July 2004. The report was based on telephone polling and focus groups conducted in the 29 'battleground' marginal seats during May, June and July 2004, with particular emphasis on political trends in July.

continuing to speak my mind. In particular, he describes me as, 'a strong, energetic leader, in contrast to [my] two predecessors'.

But on the downside, the sustained Coalition attacks have had an impact, reducing my approval rating from 54 per cent in May to 47 per cent, with my disapproval increasing from 30 to 37 per cent. Voter concerns have emerged regarding my experience, temperament and what I stand for. In other words, my extended honeymoon is over. Howard has been able to attack me without paying a political price for his negativity.

Our early success in conveying the Ladder of Opportunity message, with its focus on education and social issues, has faded away. The recent round of policy announcements has not cut through, and has even created a negative perception that we are avoiding major issues about the country's future. Seems a harsh judgement to me, but that's what the focus groups are saying. The groups have also picked up on the fact that I feel distracted and flat in the job, suggesting I have been 'tamed' by my staff/advisers.

On the question of economic credibility, Utting says the main thing we need to show the electorate is our capacity to pay for our promises. That is, keep on emphasising our commitment to Budget savings and fiscal discipline. He also fed the Government's lies about Liverpool Council into the focus groups and it produced a negative reaction to me. These are the two concerns we need to look out for on the economic front: deficit budgeting and Liverpool Council.

There are two positives I should note as well. The first is that my response to the dirt campaign has effectively closed down the issue. People have dismissed the personal stuff as political muck-raking, with little if any impact on their voting intentions. That's good news—the value of pre-empting the issue. The second positive is the clear differentiation between Howard and me. Utting reckons 'the contrast between the two leaders is greater in voters' minds' than at any time since 1996.

What about his recommendations, a way of reversing the trend against us? Reading through the report, he advocates six themes/directions for future campaigning:

1. Confront Howard on the big issues—that is, health and education. The Government's Medicare advertising campaign has taken some of the sting out of the issue but there is still plenty of scope for us to champion Medicare as a universal system, in contrast to Howard's two-tier approach. Same with education: target the inequities in the Government's school funding and higher education policies—strong vote-switchers our way.

2. Attack Howard and drive down his popularity. While Utting concedes that front-on attacks on Howard have not worked in past election campaigns, he has weaknesses that we should be able to exploit—that is, his duplicity and buck-passing.

3. As an example of Howard's deceit, we should highlight his failure to come clean with Peter Costello about the future of the Liberal leadership. A note of caution, however: don't make Costello the sole issue, stick to Howard's lack of candour. Another point about Howard's future: if he won't commit to another full term as PM, it shows that he's not committed to improving the health and education systems for people.

4. Recapture my energy and passion for the issues that affect people in their daily lives, especially concerning the cost of living. This is a clear Howard weakness—people dislike his embrace of user-pays policies and its negative impact on their living standards.

5. Relaunch the Ladder of Opportunity theme, framing our policies around this message. Utting sees this as essential for reassuring voters that we have a structured approach to policy and a coherent plan for the country's future. Back to where I started.

6. And, finally, stay away from Iraq—this is not a vote-switching issue. For some people, it is seen as Howard's greatest weakness, with his lies and sucking up to Bush. For others, it raises questions about my foreign policy experience and belief in the American Alliance. We don't have enough people in this country who believe in an independent foreign policy, that's the truth of it.

References

Barnett, David, 'Happy 30th, Mr Howard', *The Australian*, 18 May 2004, p. 15.

Beazley, Kim, 'Labor's Plan for Helping Jobless', *Daily Telegraph*, 12 July 1999.

Bentley, Tom, *Learning Beyond the Classroom*, Routledge, London, 1998.

Brock, David, *Blinded by the Right*, Crown, New York, 2002.

Card, David, and Alan Krueger, *Myth and Measurement: The New Economics of the Minimum Wage*, Princeton University Press, Princeton, NJ, 1995.

Carney, Shaun, 'The Remaking of Australia', *Age*, 15 May 2004, p. 9.

——, 'The Loneliness of Mark Latham', *Age*, 6 November 2004, p. 9.

Carr, Bob, letter, December 2001.

Castles, Francis, *Australian Public Policy and Economic Vulnerability*, Allen & Unwin, Sydney, 1988.

Chait, Jonathan, 'Sunny Side Up?', *The Atlantic*, May 2004.

Childe, Vere Gordon, *How Labour Governs*, Melbourne University Press, Carlton, 1923.

Clinton, Bill, *My Life*, Hutchinson, London, 2004.

Crimmins, Peter, (Executive Officer, Australian Association of Christian Schools) and Jack Mechielsen (Chairman, AACS), letter, 18 September 1998. Reproduced with permission.

Daley, Paul, 'Latham on the Skids', *Bulletin*, 24 November 2004.

Daly, Maurice, letter, August 2004.

Day, David, *John Curtin: A Life*, HarperCollins, Sydney, 1999.

——, *Chifley*, HarperCollins, Sydney, 2001.

Dodkin, Marilyn, *Bob Carr: The Reluctant Leader*, UNSW Press, Sydney, 2003.

Dodson, Louise, 'Latham Comes Out Fighting', *SMH*, 3 July 2004, p. 1.

Donovan, Barry, *Mark Latham: The Circuit Breaker*, Five Mile Press, Melbourne, 2004.

Duffy, Michael, *Latham and Abbott*, Random House, Sydney, 2004.

Emerson, Craig, Member for Rankin, 'Second Reading Speech: Taxation Laws Amendment Bill (No. 5) 2000', House, Bills, 14 March 2000.

Etzioni, Amitai, *The New Golden Rule*, Basic Books, New York, 1996.

Forman, David, and Nicholas Way, 'Labor Buries Keating', *Business Review Weekly*, 3 March 1997, p. 40.

Fukuyama, Francis, *The End of History and the Last Man*, Hamish Hamilton, London, 1992.

——, *Trust: The Social Virtues and the Creation of Prosperity*, Penguin, London, 1995.

Gates, Jeff, *The Ownership Solution*, Penguin, London, 1998.

Gilchrist, Michelle, 'Good Time at the Holy Grail—Allegations After Bar Clash', *The Australian*, 9 February 2001, p. 2.

Hamilton, Clive, *Growth Fetish*, Allen & Unwin, Sydney, 2003.

Hazlitt, Henry, and Felix R Livingstone (eds), *Is Politics Insoluble?*, The Foundation for Economic Education, New York, 1997.

Hughes, Vern, email, 30 July 2001. Reproduced with permission.

Kelly, CR, *One More Nail*, Brolga Books, Adelaide 1978.

Kelly, Paul, *The End of Certainty*, Allen & Unwin, Sydney, 1992.

Klein, Joe, 'Learning to Run', *The New Yorker*, 8 December 1997.

Latham, Mark, *Reviving Labor's Agenda, A Program for Local Reform*, Pluto Press, Sydney, 1990.

——, *Civilising Global Capital: New Thinking for Australian Labor*, Allen & Unwin, Sydney, 1998.

——, 'Why Australia Should Not Feel Guilty Over Timor', *AFR*, 11 October 1999, p. 21.

——, 'Paying the Price for Greed and Stupidity', *Daily Telegraph*, 27 October 2000.

——, *What Did You Learn Today? Creating an Education Revolution*, Allen & Unwin, Sydney, 2001.

——, 'ABC's Exercise in Symbolism', *Daily Telegraph*, 9 July 2001.

——, *From the Suburbs: Building a Nation from Our Neighbourhoods*, Pluto Press, Sydney, 2003.

—— and Peter Botsman (eds), *The Enabling State: People Before Bureaucracy*, Pluto Press, Sydney, 2001.

Leadbeater, Charles, *The Rise of the Social Entrepreneur*, Demos, London, 1997.

MacCallum, Mungo, *Run Johnny Run: The Story of the 2004 Election*, Duffy & Snellgrove, Sydney, 2004.

McGregor, Craig, 'The Anointed One', *Good Weekend*, SMH, 12 September 1997, p. 16.

——, *Australian Son: Inside Mark Latham*, Pluto Press, Sydney, 2004.

McLuhan, Marshall, *Understanding Media: The Extensions of Man*, McGraw-Hill, New York, 1964.

Michels, Robert, *Political Parties*, Free Press, New York, 1959.

Milne, Glenn, 'How a Latham Victory Would Change Politics as We Know It—Labor Figures Believe Values Could Trump Cynical Policy in the Election', *The Australian*, 21 June 2004, p. 9.

Morris, Dick, *Behind the Oval Office*, Random House, New York, 1997.

——, *The New Prince*, Renaissance Books, Los Angeles, 1999.

——, *Vote.com*, Renaissance Books, Los Angeles, 1999.

Murphy, Katharine, 'Inside and Out', *AFR*, 8 August 2001, p. 52.

Nixon, Richard, *Six Crises*, updated edn, Touchstone, New York, 1990 (first published 1962).

Oakes, Laurie, 'World of Difference', *Bulletin*, 14 April 2004.

Porter, Michael, *The Competitive Advantage of Nations*, Macmillan Press, London, 1990.

Putnam, Robert, *Making Democracy Work: Civic Traditions in Modern Italy*, Princeton University Press, Princeton, NJ, 1993.

——, 'The Strange Disappearance of Civic America', *Policy*, autumn 1996.

Ramsey, Alan, 'Gen X Marks the Election Soft Spot', *SMH*, 22 May 2004, p. 39.

Rawls, John, *A Theory of Justice*, Harvard University Press, Cambridge, Mass., 1971.

Richardson, Graham, *Whatever It Takes*, Bantam Books, Sydney, 1994.

Robertson, John, 'ALP Must Give a Little to Gain a Lot', *SMH*, 30 May 2002, p. 13.

Scott, James, *Seeing Like a State*, Yale University Press, New Haven, Conn., 1998.

Sen, Amartya, *Inequality Reexamined*, Clarendon Press, Oxford, 1992.

Sherraden, Michael, *Assets and the Poor*, ME Sharpe, New York, 1991.

Simons, Margaret, 'Latham's World: The New Politics of the Outsiders', *Quarterly Essay*, Black Inc., Melbourne, 2004.

Snow, Deborah, and Damien Murphy, 'Mark Latham: A Leader in Profile', *SMH*, 10 July 2004, p. 27.

Symons, Emma Kate, Louise Perry, Steve Lewis and Sally Jackson, 'Carr's Roman Holiday from Bitter Pokie Row', *The Australian*, 19 September 2003, p. 4.

Thompson, Elaine, *Fair Enough: Egalitarianism in Australia*, UNSW Press, Sydney, 1994.

Tuchman, Barbara, *The March of Folly*, Abacus, London, 1985.

Utting, John, 'Review of Political Environment and Strategic Directions', UMR Research report, July 2004.

Walsh, Peter, *Confessions of a Failed Finance Minister*, Random House, Sydney, 1995.

Watson, Don, *Recollections of a Bleeding Heart*, Random House, Sydney, 2002.

Whitlam, Gough, *The Whitlam Government 1972–75*, Viking, Melbourne, 1985.

Winston, David, 'What Voters Want: The Politics of Personal Connection', *Policy Review*, no. 95, June 1999.

Winter, Ian (ed.), *Social Capital and Public Policy in Australia*, Australian Institute of Family Studies, Melbourne, 2000.

Wolfe, Alan, *Whose Keeper? Social Science and Moral Obligation*, University of California Press, Los Angeles, 1989.

Index